K H Blacker MD

May 1973

Psychiatric Case Studies: Treatment, Drugs and Outcome

Psychiatric Case Studies: Treatment, Drugs and Outcome

DONALD F. KLEIN, M.D.

Medical Director for Evaluation

Hillside Hospital

Glen Oaks, New York

With the collaboration of

ALFREDA HOWARD, M.A.

Hillside Hospital

Glen Oaks, New York

The Williams & Wilkins Company BALTIMORE

DEDICATION

To my children

Beth
Geri
Hilary
Erika
Michelle

FOREWORD

This is a unique and uniquely useful volume. In mathe-
matical terms it is the only occupant of an otherwise empty
set. Worse, it is likely to be the only occupant of its set
for a long time to come. Detailed case histories are almost
never published in psychiatry. When they are published at
all, they are found in psychoanalytic journals. In the rest
of medicine, they occur only in clinical-pathological con-
ferences which psychiatry abandoned decades ago, perhaps un-
wisely.

The present excellent book not only serves to illustrate
Dr. Klein's clear and valuable ideas about diagnosis, treatment and prognosis, but provides the only available set of
detailed well-written case histories which relate past history, present illness and on-going treatment attempts to
treatment response and eventual outcome.

As a long-term aficionado of both clinical psychopharmacology and the Klein and Davis book Diagnosis and Drug Treatment of Psychiatric Disorders, the present volume provides
for me the only text in which theories and principles of psychopharmacological therapy are illustrated by good examples
of their application to individual patients.

It is greatly to be hoped that this volume will prove
useful not only to psychiatrists struggling to use drugs more

FOREWORD

effectively but to teachers of psychiatric residents. I pray
that this volume will not only help future residents learn
how to use drugs better but will give them a healthy respect
for the value of careful diagnosis in psychiatry.

Jonathan O. Cole, M.D.
Superintendent, Boston State Hospital
Professor, Tufts Medical School

ACKNOWLEDGMENTS

The original data concerning most of the patients in this book were derived from a study conducted by Max Fink, M.D. and Max Pollack, Ph.D. at Hillside Hospital, during 1960 and 1961. Much of the follow-up data was collected during a study conducted by Sidney Levenstein, D.S.W. These studies were respectively supported by United States Public Health Service Grants MH-2715 and MH-10191. Gary Rosenberg, M.S.W., Eli Reifman, M.S.W. and Joel Galewski, M.S.W. were active in the actual collection of follow-up data by personal interview.

The manuscript had the benefit of detailed comment by Lewis L. Robbins, M.D., Rachel Gittelman-Klein, Ph.D., Gilbert Honigfeld, Ph.D. and Charles J. Rabiner, M.D.

Gloria Podrid, Executive Secretary, supervised the interminable clerical work. Irene Majcher considerably eased the production of this book with her thoughtful, critical approach to the final manuscript typing. Alfreda Howard, M.A., wrote the case histories using clinical and research records, and was an indispensable editor and collaborator.

CONTENTS

CONTENTS

CONTENTS

CONTENTS

Chapter I

THE PSYCHIATRIC CASE STUDY

INTRODUCTION

The central purpose of this volume is to elaborate the abstract descriptions of diagnosis, treatment indications, therapeutic response, and long term prognosis made in Diagnosis and Drug Treatment of Psychiatric Disorders (36). To accomplish this, representative case studies will be presented, thus amplifying the condensed exposition of our previous book.

The case study as a means of furthering our understanding of abnormal psychology and specific treatment methods has a long career in psychiatry. It has served a variety of aims with the common core of being a persuasive rhetorical devices.

Case studies may be presented to demonstrate that a specific descriptive pattern holds for a recognizable group of psychiatric patients. Freud presents particularly good examples of case history utility. For instance, in his early paper, "On the grounds for detaching a particular syndrome from neurasthenia under the description anxiety neurosis" (20), he presents a symptom pattern of general irritability, anxious expectation, etc., that he feels distinguishes a particular syndrome labeled anxiety neurosis.

Further, he defines anxious expectation by stating, "I cannot better describe the condition I have in mind than by this name and by adding a few examples. A woman, for instance, who suffers from anxious expectations will think of influenzal pneumonia every time her husband coughs when he has a cold." Freud here demonstrates a second use for the

1

brief case report; a means of definition by example, or extensive definition.

     Case studies are also used to exemplify a theory of psy-
chopathogenesis, or as counter-examples to disprove particular theories of psychiatric illness. For instance, Freud
originally postulated that the anxiety neurosis represented
an accumulation of sexual excitation, discharged in the form
of the anxiety attack. He pointed out that the accumulation
of sexual excitation could occur in a variety of settings;
for instance, intentionally abstinent men, men in a state of
unconsummated excitation as in the period of engagement before marriage, in women who practice coitus interruptus without satisfaction, etc. Therefore, Freud substantiated his
theory of anxiety neurosis by referring to several case studies congruent with his theory. A critical reviewer might
wonder if the incidence of anxiety neurosis is actually any
higher in these sexually deprived groups than in others with
nonfrustrating sexual practices. The mere fact that Freud
saw such illnesses with these associated sexual circumstances
is not conclusive although interesting and suggestive.

     Freud states, somewhat ingenuously, in a paper wherein
he replies to critics of his initial stand (19, p. 123) that,
"When I published the paper I have mentioned I was under no
illusion as to its power to carry conviction. In the first
place, I was aware that the account I had given was only a
brief and incomplete one, and even in places hard to understand - just enough, perhaps to arouse the reader's expectations. Then too, I had scarcely brought forward any examples
and given no figures. Nor had I touched on the technique of
collecting an anamnesis or done anything to prevent misunder-
standings. I had not given consideration to any but the most
obvious objections; and as regards the theory itself, I had
laid stress only on its main proposition and not on its qual-
ifications. Accordingly, each reader was in fact at liberty

to form his own opinion as to the binding force of the whole hypothesis."

With all these reservations one can only wonder why Freud did present this paper. It would seem plain that he had indeed some "illusion as to its power to carry conviction." What happened, however, was that his critics were then able to attempt refutation by means of counter-example. For instance, Lowenfeld insists that in some cases, states of anxiety appear after a psychic shock; he gives as an example (19, p. 126) "a woman of 30, with a hereditary taint, who had been married for four years and who had a first difficult confinement a year before. A few weeks after this event her husband had an attack of illness which frightened her, and in her agitation she ran about the cold room in her chemise. From that time on she was ill. First she had states of anxiety and palpitations in the evenings, then came attacks of convulsive tremblings, and after that phobias, and so on. It was a picture of fully developed anxiety neurosis." Thus Lowenfeld concluded that anxiety states were of psychic origin and, in this particular case, brought about by a single fright.

Freud agreed that his critics could produce many similar cases and indeed stated that he could produce many cases of this sort himself, and proceeded to present four such cases in capsule form. However, he went on to say that these counter-examples were only superficially credible and that one must have a deeper grasp of the entire psychic state of the individual to properly assess the precipitating circumstances. He took the stand that psychic factors, such as frightening situations, simply serve as precipitants. People who develop anxiety states following such precipitants are regularly already in a state of abnormal sexual tension.

This further vulnerable stipulation by Freud then allowed the presentation of further counter-examples, wherein

panic attacks and anxiety neurosis occurred in patients with
normal sexual lives. Under the impact of accumulated knowledge concerning anxiety hysteria, the belief that the anxiety attack was a simple conversion of sexual excitation into
anxiety was gradually discarded from the body of psychoanalytic doctrine and eventually explicitly discarded by Freud
(21).

We have discussed this series of events at some length
because it represents a certain paradigm that runs through
psychiatric theorizing. To recapitulate, a number of observations are made that apparently fall into a pattern. This
pattern leads to a public hypothesis. Other incompatible
observations are presented to disprove the hypothesis. These
observations are criticized as being incomplete, irrelevant
or immaterial, and the hypothesis is maintained. Yet other
more elaborate contradictory observations are produced and
the hypothesis is finally abandoned, especially if an alternative hypothesis has been constructed that does a more adequate job of meeting the complexities of the data.

However, such a line of scientific disputation, by example and counter-example, depends upon hypotheses being
constructed that contain an explicit statement of universal-
ity; that is Freud stated that all cases of anxiety neuroses
suffered from an abnormal sexual life. With such strong hypotheses even one counter-example is devastating. If Freud
had stated that some cases of anxiety neurosis stemmed from
an abnormal sexual life, then even many counter-examples
would be beside the point. On the other hand, the presentation of such a modest hypothesis would not be very stimulating, since the obvious next question would be: How many is
"some"? Is it 10%, 50%, 85%, etc.? Even if one presented
the percentages of cases of anxiety neurosis that fulfilled
the hypothesis, occurring in one's own practice, the question
could be raised whether this represented a generally appli-

cable percentage, since patients come to a specific doctor via a differential selection procedure. For instance, if Freud was well-known for an interest in abnormal sexuality, it would be likely that a large proportion of his cases consisted of such patients. To recapitulate, case studies provide valuable data for the testing of strongly stated hypotheses, but are not too relevant to weaker actuarial hypotheses.

The extended case report is still another persuasive use of an individual life history, wherein a bewildering mass of data is presented concerning the patient's development, life events and psychopathology. The author then develops a hypothesis that brings order to a confusing welter of apparently unrelated facts. Freud made wonderfully effective use of this method in his famous case studies of Little Hans, Wolf Man, Rat Man, etc. Many people have compared Freud's articles to works of literary art. No doubt, much of the impact of his case studies and theorizing comes from artful exposition. Freud gives the feeling of being a scientific co-worker in that he explores the case material, raising questions and counter-questions in exact tune with the reader's own critical processes, so that when the final set of hypotheses are presented the reader feels as if he had gone through a process of intellectual work that had driven him to exactly the same conclusions that Freud was forced to develop. The bewildering and intriguing mass of data suddenly falls into place, accompanied by a profound "aha" experience that combines both esthetic pleasure and a feeling of scientific illumination.

However, one should not mistake the emotional conviction derived from a persuasive case for the power of a well-validated scientific hypothesis. It cannot be too often stressed that the systematic testing of creative hypotheses distinguishes scientific progress from artistic exposition.

Still another persuasive use of the case study is the illustration of a treatment method. The post hoc fallacy, i.e., the belief that changes after treatment are necessarily due to treatment, is probably one of the most deeply ingrained popular misconceptions. Further, the belief that some intervention has caused a change, is made even stronger if the treatment employed can be embedded within a body of explanatory theory that appears to have wide ramifications and general power. For instance, in Studies on Hysteria (9) Freud and Breuer present the cathartic method of dealing with hysterical illness. They present many strikingly interesting and convincing observations of detailed case material, wherein a proper abreaction causes a marked shift in an apparently fixed and incomprehensible psychopathological state. The abreactive method was easily related to the common experience of a swift improvement in feeling tone after "getting something off one's chest." Similarly, one could easily experience within oneself the surprising associations that come to mind upon attempting free association. In other words, there was an inherent appeal to Freud's and Breuer's proposition, since it only required the extension of everyday experience to the field of the psychopathological.

Again, one should not mistake what is reasonable or emotionally convincing for what is correct. Through hard experience we have learned that scientific validation demands careful comparative study of treatments under conditions whereby biased observation, reporting and analysis of data can be brought to the minimum. Demands for proof of therapeutic effectiveness have been most prevalent within the field of somatic treatment. There are at least two reasons for this. First, somatic treatments are not "reasonable" treatments. They are empirical and still remain inexplicable. The simple fact is that we do not yet know why the convulsive and pharmacological therapies work. Also, common

experience extends only to the use of such pharmacological
agents as alcohol or sleeping pills. Therefore, since there
is no easily apprehended reasonable explanation for their
effectiveness, it is quite understandable that somatic treatments should be greeted sceptically. Second, the somatic
therapies are comparatively easy to administer, in a stand-
ardized form, under conditions of objective study, such as
the well-known double-blind, placebo-controlled method.
Since it is relatively easy to objectively study the short
term effectiveness of somatic treatment, such study has become the necessary precondition for scientific acceptance of
treatment efficacy.

The situation is much more difficult with studies in
psychotherapy. A number of excellent reviews have indicated
the massive scientific and practical problems that arise in
attempting to deal with such complex methods of treatment in
a scientifically valid and clinically meaningful evaluative
way. Nonetheless, these methods must be evaluated scientifically, and cannot be accepted as valid until proven.

With all these reservations concerning the value of
case studies, and in particular, the potential mischief that
they may do with reference to proselytizing for particular
treatment methods, one may well wonder at this presentation.
It should be emphasized that my intention is not to propa-
gandize for the worthwhileness of particular diagnostic or
treatment techniques. We have conducted a number of studies
in this area that we do hope are convincing, since they are
properly controlled, comparative group studies. Each of the
case study sections will be documented by reference to these
scientific studies.

Nonetheless, the presentation of case studies possesses
the extremely valuable feature of definition by concrete example. It is a simple fact that for every abstract descriptive phrase, such as anxiety, hallucination, thought disor-

der, etc., the reader will have a host of internal images. Further, each reader's stock of internal referents will appreciably differ from another reader's stock. Therefore, when one describes a particular class of patients in abstract terms, it is not surprising that each reader may find the exposition somewhat unclear and vague and have a difficult time translating the descriptive abstractions in terms of his own concrete life experiences. Worse, the reader may believe that he has grasped the objective concrete content of a description and be deceiving himself. Such a self-deception may only become obvious when different readers compare with each other their understanding of the content and implications of a descriptive passage. Such confrontations can often lead to considerable distress; however, their infrequency preserves professional equanimity.

In my book, co-authored with John M. Davis, <u>Diagnosis</u> <u>and</u> <u>Drug</u> <u>Treatment</u> <u>of</u> <u>Psychiatric</u> <u>Disorders</u> (36), we take the stand that psychiatric diagnosis is both possible and necessary, and that proper psychiatric diagnosis enables valid predictions concerning treatment and long term prognosis. The definitions presented were necessarily abstract. This present volume is an essay on diagnosis, treatment definition and prognosis, by example. I hope to be able to present sufficiently cogent case descriptions so that the generalized and necessarily abstract descriptions of the previous book are exemplified concretely. It should be obvious from the above discussion that these case studies are not viewed as in any way proving various positions concerning diagnosis, treatment effect and prognosis. "For instance" is not a scientifically binding argument.

I also hope that this book may bring to professional and student attention the possible clinical values and drawbacks of drug intervention in psychiatric illness via vivid clinical anecdotes. Such an understanding must be widely

fostered if we are to arrive at rational clinical procedures
that will integrate medication with other forms of treatment.

Much of the data of this book was derived from studies
conducted at Hillside Hospital, supported in part by the
United States Public Health Service, National Institute of
Mental Health. The initial drug study was conducted during
the years 1960 and 1961 with Max Fink, M.D. and Max Pollack,
Ph.D. as Principal Investigators, (supported, in part, by
Grant MH-2715). The follow-up study, upon which much of
this book was based, was conducted by its Principal Investi-
gator, Sydney Levenstein D.S.W., supported, in part, by
Grant MH-10191. (See References 1-8, 10-18, 22-60.)

It would be well to keep in mind the historical setting
under which the initial studies were carried out. At that
time (1960), drugs such as Thorazine were just beginning to
be widely used in the United States, and the exact indications for them were still a source of considerable debate.
For instance, at the time it was thought that phenothiazines
were probably contraindicated in states of severe psychotic
depression but indicated in mild neurotic anxiety states.
We now know that both these beliefs are not only false but
largely the opposite of the truth. Similarly, antidepressants had not been released for public prescription and were
widely equated with the previously familiar stimulants, such
as dextroamphetamine. Therefore, there was much worry about
giving antidepressants to patients who showed marked nervous
tension or insomnia. Again, this belief eventually proved
false and in many ways the opposite of the truth.

Much pilot clinical experience (1958-1959) with these
drugs had convinced the research workers at Hillside
Hospital that the acceptance of glib rules of thumb concerning drug treatment could only result in blindly applied ineffective treatments. Therefore, to develop a grasp of the
proper indications for medication in various psychiatric

illnesses, those patients at Hillside who had not responded
satisfactorily to the intensive program of psychotherapy and
milieu therapy were entered into a six week, placebo controlled, double-blind, fixed dosage study of Tofranil and
Thorazine.

Patients were randomly assigned to placebo or one of
two fixed increment drug schedules for six weeks. Daily
dosage of Tofranil for each week was 75 mg, 150 mg, 225 mg,
and 300 mg thereafter. Daily dosage of Thorazine for each
week was 300 mg, 600 mg, 900 mg, and 1200 mg thereafter. To
prevent akinesia, akathisia, and other extrapyramidal disorders each dose of Thorazine was combined with 1.25%
(to a maximum of 15 mg daily) Kemadrin. Each medication
was dissolved in a highly-flavored liquid placebo vehicle,
and each patient received a constant 40 cc/day from individually labeled bottles. Maximum dosage was maintained for
two weeks, and retesting was conducted during the sixth week
of medication.

The results of this study were of such interest that we
replicated the entire program (supported by NIMH Grant MH-
8004). To gain further perspective upon the long term effects of our drug interventions, the follow-up study, referred to earlier, was conducted with the participants in the
first drug study, three years after they had been discharged
from the hospital. In addition, in 1969, a small follow-up
study (60) was conducted to gain some perspective about a
particularly puzzling group of patients, the emotionally unstable character disorders; so that we have long term follow-
up data on a particular subgroup. Those patients presented
in this book were spot checked ten to eleven years after
their discharge.

Another reason for this book is the lack of adequate
teaching materials for psychopharmacology courses. Only recently have such courses been initiated within psychiatric

residency training programs.

I believe that the best teaching is clinical teaching derived from discussion of specific cases. In general medicine one of the more powerful teaching devices is the so-called clinical-pathologic conference where a complex case history is presented for discussion. The discussor must make a diagnosis from the clinical and laboratory data and predict response or lack of response to treatment as well as the pathological findings, if the patient had come to autopsy. Following group discussion the pathologist would have the last say.

We modified this concept in our training sessions so that the residents were presented with the patient's life history and symptomatology up to the point of entry into Hillside Hospital. After discussion of diagnosis and possible treatment responses, the remaining material concerning hospital course and follow-up was presented, with rediscussion. This proved stimulating both to the lecturer and to the psychiatrists, psychologists and social workers who attended these meetings.

We hope that the publication of this book of case studies will lead to an extension of psychopharmacological training to medical schools, and also to other schools within the "helping professions." At present, schools of psychology and social work have not accepted the responsibility for presenting these important clinical and theoretical materials to their students, to enable them to make appropriate treatment referrals and to participate in appropriate treatment planning and supervision.

The organization of the book will be as follows: each section will deal with a specific diagnostic subgroup; the disorders will be defined and several illustrative case studies will be presented. These case studies have been altered in many clinically inconsequential ways to preserve

the patient's anonymity. However, major developmental and
psychiatric data are preserved.

   Each case will be briefly discussed in terms of the
broader issues, and there will be brief discussions of the
common features of the developmental history, psychopathology, response to treatment and prognosis of each diagnostic
group. I will attempt to make clear both what is typical
and atypical about each case illustration. Again, proper
scientific judgment concerning these issues cannot be gather-
ed from this case material alone. The reader must refer to
the scientific papers relevant to this complex and controversial area.

REFERENCES

1. Belmont, I., Pollack, M., Willner, A., Klein, D.F. and
    Fink, M.: The effects of imipramine and chlorpromazine
    and perceptual analytic ability, perceptual responsi-
    vity and memory as revealed in Rorschach responses. J.
    Nerv. Ment. Dis. 137, 42-50, 1963.

2. Blumberg, A.G.: Effect of chlorpromazine with procycli-
    dine and imipramine on RAI uptake. J. Clin. Endocr. 23,
    881-884, 1963.

3. Blumberg, A.G. and Klein, D.F.: Methoxy-catecholamine
    excretion and the mecholyl test. J. Psychiat. Res. 3,
    239-254, 1965.

4. Blumberg, A.G. and Klein, D.F.: Psychotropic drugs,
    mecholyl test and outcome. Excerpta Medica Internat.
    Ser. 129, 1212-1216, 1966.

5. Blumberg, A.G. and Klein, D.F.: Psychiatric diagnosis,
    activation and radioactive iodine uptake. Arch. Gen.
    Psychiat. 18, 601-611, 1968.

6. Blumberg, A.G. and Klein, D.F.: Chlorpromazine-procycli-
    dine and imipramine: Effects on thyroid function in
    psychiatric patients. Clin. Pharmacol. Ther. 10, 350-
    354, 1969.

7. Blumberg, A.G., Klein, D.F. and Pollack, M.: Age related
    changes in blood pressure with chlorpromazine and imi-
    pramine. Excerpta Medica Internat. Ser. 57. Sixth In-
    ternational Congress of Gerontology, 1963.

8. Blumberg, A.G., Klein, D.F. and Pollack, M.: Effects of
    chlorpromazine and imipramine on systolic blood pres-
    sure in psychiatric patients: Relationships to age, di-
    agnosis and initial blood pressure. J. Psychiat. Res.
    2, 51-60, 1964.

9. Breuer, J. and Freud, S.: Studies on Hysteria (1893-
    1895). Standard Edition Vol. II, Hogarth Press, London,
    1955.

10. Feldman, S., Klein, D.F. and Honigfeld, G.: A compari-
    son of successive screening and discriminant function
    techniques in medical taxonomy. Biometrics 25, 725-734,
    1969.

11. Feldman, S., Klein, D.F. and Honigfeld, G.: The relia-
    bility of a decision tree psychiatric diagnostic tech-
    nique. Presented at the 128th meeting of the American
    Statistical Association, Pittsburgh, 1968.

12. Fink, M.: Quantitative electroencephalography and human
    psychopharmacology: I. Frequency spectra and drug ac-
    tion. Med. Exp. (Basel) 5, 364-369, 1961.

13. Fink, M.: The mode of action of convulsive therapy: The
    neurophysiologic-adaptive view. J. Neuropsychiat. 3,
    231-233, 1962.

14. Fink, M.: EEG and human psychopharmacology. (Abstracts
    of Proceedings of Symposium at Third World Congress of
    Psychiatry, Montreal.) Electroenceph. Clin. Neurophys-
    iol. 15, 133-137, 1963.

15. Fink, M.: Quantitative electroencephalography in human
    psychopharmacology II: Drug patterns. In Glaser, G.
    (ed.): EEG and Behavior. Basic Books, New York, 1963,
    pp. 177-197.

16. Fink, M.: A selected bibliography of electroencephalo-
    graphy in human psychopharmacology, 1951-1962. Elec-
    troenceph. Clin. Neurophysiol. Supp. 23, 1964.

17. Fink, M., Klein, D.F. and Kramer, J.C.: Clinical effi-
    cacy of chlorpromazine-procyclidine combination, imi-
    pramine and placebo in depressive disorders. Psycho-
    pharmacologia 7, 27-36, 1965.

18. Fink, M., Pollack, M., Klein, D.F., Blumberg, A.G.,
     Belmont, I., Karp, E., Kramer, J.C. and Willner, A.:
     Comparative studies of chlorpromazine and imipramine.
     I. Drug discriminating patterns. Neuropsychopharm. <u>3</u>,
     370-372, 1964.

19. Freud, S.: A reply to criticisms of my paper on anxiety
     neurosis (1895). Standard Edition Vol. III, Hogarth
     Press, London, 1962, pp. 121-139.

20. Freud, S.: On the grounds for detaching a particular
     syndrome from neurasthenia under the description anxi-
     ety neurosis (1895). Standard Edition Vol. III, Hogarth
     Press, London, 1962, pp. 90-115.

21. Freud, S.: <u>New</u> <u>Introductory</u> <u>Lectures</u> <u>on</u> <u>Psycho-Analysis</u>
     <u>and</u> <u>Other</u> <u>Works</u>. Standard Edition Vol. XXII, Hogarth
     Press, London, 1964.

22. Gittelman-Klein, R.K. and Klein, D.F.: Marital status
     as a prognostic indicator in schizophrenia. J. Nerv.
     Ment. Dis. <u>147</u>, 289-296, 1968.

23. Gittelman-Klein, R.K. and Klein, D.F.: Premorbid asocial
     adjustment and prognosis in schizophrenia. J. Psychiat.
     Res. <u>7</u>, 35-53, 1969.

24. Gittelman-Klein, R. and Klein, D.F.: Relationships of
     the mecholyl test, premorbid asocial functioning and
     long term outcome in schizophrenia. J. Nerv. Ment. Dis.
     <u>150</u>, 301-306, 1970.

25. Goldenberg, H. and Fishman, V.: Metabolism of chlorpro-
     mazine. Confirmation of position 7 as the major site
     of hydroxylation. Biochem. Biophys. Res. Communicat.
     <u>14</u>, 404, 1964.

26. Goldenberg, H. and Fishman, V.: Comments on 7-hydroxy-
     chlorpromazine in the urines of schizophrenics receiv-
     ing chlorpromazine. Biochem. Pharmacol. <u>14</u>, 365, 1965.

27. Honigfeld, G., Klein, D.F. and Feldman, S.: Prediction
     of psychopharmacologic effect in man: Development and
     validation of a computerized diagnostic decision tree.
     Comput. Biomed. Res. <u>2</u>, 350-361, 1969.

28. Karp, E. and Pollack, M.: Comparative studies of chlor-
     promazine and imipramine. III: Critical flicker fusion
     thresholds in psychiatric patients. Psychopharmacologia
     <u>4</u>, 452-458, 1963.

29. Klein, D.F.: Behavioral effects of imipramine and pheno-
     thiazines: Implications for a psychiatric pathogenetic
     theory and theory of drug action. Recent Advances Biol.
     Psychiat. 7, 273-287, 1964.

30. Klein, D.F.: Delineation of two drug-responsive anxiety
     syndromes. Psychopharmacologia 5, 397-408, 1964.

31. Klein, D.F.: Visual hallucinations with imipramine.
     Amer. J. Psychiat. 121, 911-914, 1965.

32. Klein, D.F.: Chlorpromazine-procyclidine combination,
     imipramine and placebo in depressive disorders. Canad.
     Psychiat. Assoc. J. 11, S146-S149, 1966.

33. Klein, D.F.: Diagnostic prediction of psychotropic drug
     effect: Global outcome. Excerpta Medica Internat. Ser.
     129, 736-740, 1966.

34. Klein, D.F.: Importance of psychiatric diagnosis in pre-
     diction of clinical drug effects. Arch. Gen. Psychiat.
     16, 118-126, 1967.

35. Klein, D.F.: Psychiatric diagnosis and a typology of
     clinical drug effects. Psychopharmacologia 13, 359-
     386, 1968.

36. Klein, D.F. and Davis, J.M.: Diagnosis and Drug Treat-
     ment of Psychiatric Disorders. Williams and Wilkins,
     Baltimore, 1969.

37. Klein, D.F., Feldman, S. and Honigfeld, G.: Can univar-
     iate measures of drug effect reflect clinical descrip-
     tions of change? In Wittenborn, J.R., Goldberg, S.C.
     and May, P.R.A. (eds.): Psychopharmacology and the In-
     dividual Patient, Raven Press, New York, 1970.

38. Klein, D.F. and Fink, M.: Behavioral reaction patterns
     with phenothiazines. Arch. Gen. Psychiat. 7, 449-459,
     1962.

39. Klein, D.F. and Fink, M.: Psychiatric reaction patterns
     to imipramine. Amer. J. Psychiat. 119, 432-438, 1962.

40. Klein, D.F. and Fink, M.: Multiple item factors as
     change measures in psychopharmacology. Psychopharma-
     cologia 4, 43-52, 1963.

41. Klein, D.F., Honigfeld, G. and Feldman, S.: Prediction
     of drug effect by diagnostic decision tree. Dis. Nerv.
     Syst. Supp. 29, 159-187, 1968.

42. Klein, D.F., Honigfeld, G. and Feldman, S.: Prediction of drug effect by a successive screening decision tree diagnostic technique. In May, P.R.A. and Wittenborn, J.R. (eds.): Psychotropic Drug Responses. Advances in Prediction. Charles C. Thomas, Springfield, Ill., 1969.

43. Klein, D.F., Honigfeld, G. and Feldman, S.: Prediction of drug effect in personality disorders. In Smith, W.L. (ed.): Drugs, Development and Cerebral Function. Charles C. Thomas, Springfield, Ill., 1971.

44. Kramer, J.C., Klein, D.F. and Fink, M.: Withdrawal symptoms following discontinuation of imipramine therapy. Amer. J. Psychiat. 118, 549-550, 1961.

45. Kramer, J.C., Klein, D.F. and Fink, M.: Imipramine as an adjunct to phenothiazine therapy. Compr. Psychiat. 3, 377-380, 1962.

46. Levenstein, S., Klein, D.F. and Pollack, M.: Follow-up study of formerly hospitalized voluntary psychiatric patients: The first two years. Amer. J. Psychiat. 122, 1102-1109, 1966.

47. Levenstein, S., Pollack, M. and Klein, D.F.: Follow-up study of formerly hospitalized psychiatric patients: Procedural considerations in data collection. J. Hillside Hosp. 15, 152-164, 1966.

48. Levenstein, S. and Shahinian, S.: Three year follow-up of college students hospitalized for psychiatric illness. Unpublished manuscript, 1969.

49. Pollack, M.: Physiologically-induced neuropsychological changes and aging, behavior and the nervous system. In Welford, E.T. and Birren, J.E. (eds.): Behavior, Aging and the Nervous System. Charles C. Thomas, Springfield, Ill., 1965, pp. 272-283.

50. Pollack, M., Karp, E., Belmont, I., Willner, A., Klein, D.F. and Fink, M.: Comparative studies of chlorpromazine and imipramine. II. Psychological performance profiles. Neuropsychopharmacol. 3, 374-376, 1964.

51. Pollack, M., Karp, E., Krauthamer, G., Klein, D.F. and Fink, M.: Neuropsychologic response patterns of some psychotropic drugs. Neuropsychopharmacol. 2, 381-384, 1961.

52. Pollack, M., Klein, D.F., Willner, A., Blumberg, A.G.
     and Fink, M.: Imipramine-induced behavioral disorgani-
     zation in schizophrenic patients: Physiological and
     psychological correlates. Recent Advances Biol. Psy-
     chiat. 7, 53-61, 1964.

53. Pollack, M., Levenstein, S. and Klein, D.F.: A three
     year post-hospital follow-up in adolescence vs. adult-
     hood. Int. J. Child Psychiat. 33, 224-225, 1966.

54. Pollack, M., Levenstein, S. and Klein, D.F.: A three
     year post-hospital follow-up of adolescent and adult
     schizophrenics. Amer. J. Orthopsychiat. 38, 94-109,
     1968.

55. Rosen, B., Engelhardt, D.M., Freedman, N., Margolis, R.
     and Klein, D.F.: The Hospitalization Proneness Scale
     as a predictor of response to phenothiazine treatment:
     II. Delay of psychiatric hospitalization. J. Nerv.
     Ment. Dis. 152, 405-411, 1971.

56. Rosen, B., Klein, D.F., Levenstein, S. and Shahinian,
     S.P.: Social competence and posthospital outcome. Arch.
     Gen. Psychiat. 19, 165-170, 1968.

57. Rosen, B., Klein, D.F. and Gittelman-Klein, R.: Sex dif-
     ferences in the relationship between premorbid asocial-
     ity and posthospital outcome. J. Nerv. Ment. Dis. 149,
     415-420, 1969.

58. Rosen, B. Klein, D.F. and Gittelman-Klein, R.: Predic-
     tion of rehospitalization: The relationship between
     age of first psychiatric treatment contact, marital
     status and premorbid asocial adjustment. J. Nerv. Ment.
     Dis. 152, 17-22, 1971.

59. Rosen, B., Klein, D.F., Levenstein, S. and Shahinian,
     S.: Social competence and posthospital outcome among
     schizophrenic and non-schizophrenic psychiatric pa-
     tients. J. Abnorm. Psychol. 74, 401-404, 1969.

60. Rifkin, A., Levitan, S., Galewski, J. and Klein, D.F.:
     Emotionally unstable character disorders. A follow-up
     study. I. Description of patients and outcome. II. Pre-
     diction of outcome. Biol. Psychiat., 1971, in press.

Section I

SCHIZOPHRENIA

SCHIZOPHRENIA

DIAGNOSTIC ISSUES
The Term "Psychosis"

Terms such as psychosis and neurosis belong to the historical baggage accumulated by psychiatry in its infancy. They are used loosely and cause untold waste of words but seem indispensable and therefore probably reflect some real distinction. We shall bow to tradition and run the risks of loose usage and surplus meaning, rather than the risks associated with neologisms.

Psychosis is defined here as a persistent misevaluation of perception not attributable to sensory defect or afferent abnormality. This qualification is necessary to exclude conditions such as color blindness or phantom-limb. The emphasis is on a central misevaluation of correctly registered inputs. These misevaluations are not persistently critically self-reviewed, and this failure is often misleadingly termed "lack of reality testing." In addition, actual misperceptions may occur in the form of illusions and hallucinations.

The hallmark of psychosis is the apparently inexplicable nature of the misevaluation or misperception which has the force of reality. Misperceptions such as auditory or visual hallucinations cause little difficulty among clinicians; agreement can easily be reached that a patient with such symptoms is psychotic. However, a person's evaluation of his perception depends upon a wide variety of social, psychological, developmental and educational factors. Therefore, many of the productions of psychotic patients superficially resemble productions of people of unusual backgrounds. For instance, the belief that one is in direct communication with God, or that one can magically influence another, is common in both primitive tribes and modern cults. Such beliefs are part of a patterned social institution; e.g., spirit possession. Individuals who hallucinate God under socially inappropriate circumstances are recognized as deviant or ill in their own culture. The idea that the social practices of other cultures are due to psychopathological states (e.g., the Dobu are paranoid) is pure ethnocentrism. Similarly, the "explanation" that the hallucinations of a Haitian schizophrenic are not really "illness" but only cultural eccentricity is unthinking glib cultural relativism. Therefore, one must restrict the term psychosis to a persistent misconception of reality that is not accountable on the basis of special social indoctrination or unusual life experience.

To further complicate matters, many patients express themselves in an imaginative and metaphorical fashion during emotional periods when it is difficult to question them closely or to get them to pay attention to or cooperate with the examiner. A statement intended by the patient to have an "as if" quality may easily be misinterpreted as a delusional or hallucinatory verbalization. Also, hysterical and malingering patients may mislead the examiner purposefully.

By extension, the term psychosis is often applied to potentially psychotic conditions. A psychiatrist may diagnose as schizophrenic many patients who have some features of schizophrenic disorder although manifest psychosis is not present. In this instance the diagnosis is a statement of organismal potential.

One motivation for this often questionable procedure is readily understood from game theory. Psychiatrists and psychologists endanger their self-esteem and reputation by making a diagnosis that can be proved wrong. Therefore, in an uncertain world, the safest procedure is to diagnose a potential psychosis, such as schizophrenia, even in the absence of psychotic manifestations. The reasoning is simple: a patient diagnosed as psychotic either manifests psychosis, proving the keen ability of the diagnostician, or no psychotic manifestations ever come to light. However, this is not a "real" error; it is simple testimony to the diagnostician's ability to see past the obvious and/or his superior therapeutic abilities that have prevented the development of manifest psychosis. Therefore, the diagnosis of potential or actual psychosis always has honorific results. On the other hand, a diagnosis of neurosis, character disorder, etc., is open to public contradiction and subsequent obloquy if the patient becomes psychotic. If the patient remains manifestly non-psychotic, the diagnosis is open to verbal contradiction by other clinicians who then have the self-ascribed one-up status of superior perceptual depth. Therefore, making such a diagnosis is always asking for trouble. Since we strive for security, satisfaction and self-esteem (at least), it is not surprising that the diagnosis of schizophrenia is made remarkably often.

It is open to objective research to determine if certain signs and symptoms indicate a vulnerability to manifest psychotic process. We believe that such traits do exist. For instance, severe psychomotor retardation associated with depression is frequently diagnosed as psychotic depression, even though no delusional material is manifest. The patient may simply state that he is severely depressed, which is indisputably true. This statement represents a clear perception of internal reality rather than a misconception, and the di-

agnosis should be of a potential psychosis. If the patient
stated that he was this way because of his responsibility for
the bad Broadway season of 1942, one could speak of manifest
psychosis.

All signs of psychosis may be due to unusual cerebral
states. Organic psychoses, meaning those psychoses for which
organic etiologies have been established, are frequently associated with impairments of orientation and recent memory
that are not characteristic of the so-called functional psychoses (meaning those psychoses without known etiologic determinants). However, this is not entirely true. There are
organic psychoses which are not associated with disorienta-
tion and functional psychoses which are. Again, it behooves
the practitioner to make sure that the patient has received
a thorough medical, including neurological, examination.
This examination should attempt to rule out infection, drug
or poison intoxication, trauma, convulsive disorder, neo-
plasm, cardiovascular disease, senile disease, disturbances
of metabolism, growth or nutrition, and the variety of degenerative brain diseases of unknown causes. Furthermore,
there are temporary circumstances such as sleep deprivation,
battle fatigue, sensory deprivation, hypnagogic states, hypnosis, and intoxications that may lead to perceptual abnor-
malities and misevaluations. These conditions, if one were
to be perfectly methodical in the use of language, should be
referred to as transient psychoses. The reason for the usual objection to this sort of terminology is that the term
psychosis is historically linked to enduring conditions that
require hospital care.

The term psychosis will be used as a description of a
state that may be chronic, episodic or acute. It is analogous to such indices as fever in clinical medicine. Therefore, although it is common clinical parlance to refer to
"the psychoses," this usage makes as much sense as the 17th

Century practice of referring to "the fevers." The most common "functional" psychoses are the schizophrenias and affective disorders.

Schizophrenia is defined as a severe, cryptogenic, potentially psychotic disorder with a poor prognosis, tendency
to relapse, with permanent emotional and social deficit; thus
following Kraepelin's model. It should be clear that no
claim is made that all psychotics have a poor prognosis, but
that we are attempting, perhaps quixotically, to preserve the
conceptual usefulness of "schizophrenia."

Psychiatric History

The diagnosis of schizophrenia cannot be excluded on the
basis of the patient's pre-psychotic history, which can be of
any variety. However, many schizophrenics have a history of
early childhood asocial development, learning defect, poor
peer relationships and emotional eccentricity; this constel-
lation appears infrequently with other disorders. As children, they must be distinguished from those who are simply
situationally shy, fearful or withdrawn. The shy, withdrawn,
dependent child who is overattached to his mother and suffers
marked separation anxiety can function quite normally socially in the presence of his mother or with a trusted person.
Many shy children actually wish to socialize and will approach the outskirts of a group, hoping to be included. Once
included, they are often skilled social participants. Such
histories are quite common in the neurotic states. Follow-up
studies of such children (25) show a low incidence of emotional disturbance in general and of schizophrenia in particular.

In the particular pre-schizophrenic group discussed
here, their meagre attempts at group involvement are so blun-
dering, imperceptive and undiplomatic as to lead to social
ostracism and scapegoating. It is possible that these children suffer from minimal brain damage (1).

It is not known how many personalities with an early childhood asocial development continue to live in the community without developing psychotic episodes. But such a history in a psychiatric patient is an extremely powerful predictor of poor prognosis.

<u>Examination</u>

The diagnosis of schizophrenia should be made on the basis of a fundamental disturbance in the perception or evaluation of reality that cannot be explained on the basis of toxic etiological agents (such as dextroamphetamine), or on the basis of known organic brain disease (such as general paresis), or on the basis of certain special educational or social influences (as in various cultures), or on the basis of severe depression or elation (as in manic-depressive illness).

It is defined here as a <u>cryptogenic</u> behavioral syndrome. If the etiology is known, the diagnosis should not be schizophrenia, but rather "psychosis due to_X_ with schizophreniform symptoms." In opposition to this stand, one could logically follow Bleuler, and consider schizophrenia as simply a behavioral reaction type due to multiple causes; e.g., toxins, epilepsy, organic brain disease, etc., or unknown factors. However, this would lead to a nosology based purely on behavioral reaction which would obscure our occasional etiological knowledge. We prefer "psychosis due to chronic amphetamine intoxication with behavioral syndrome identical to paranoid schizophrenia" to "paranoid schizophrenia due to amphetamine intoxication."

The manifest schizophrenic psychosis is a concatenation of certain symptoms specified below. The extra-classificatory diagnostic correlates are a high incidence of recurrent episodes with intervening deficit and/or deteriorative course. Deterioration does not refer necessarily to gross cognitive deterioration; i.e., dementia, but rather to progressive social, educational, vocational and sexual incompetence, associated with distinct perceptual, evaluational and cognitive abnormality.

Schizophrenic Diagnostic Traits
Hallucinations

Hallucinations are perceptual disorders in which the patient experiences certain sensations, of varying degree of structure, in the absence of justifying stimuli. This differentiates them from illusions which are misperceptions prompted by external stimuli and ambiguous circumstances, frequently in a framework of heightened expectation. For instance, one may, while searching for a cat at twilight, distinctly see a heap of leaves as a cat until a closer approach reveals the error.

Hallucinations may occur in any sense modality. However, hallucinations of sight, taste and odor should prompt a close organic investigation. Schizophrenic visual hallucinations usually have marked personal significance, occur under conditions of stimulus clarity, and are associated with hallucinations in other sensory modalities. Auditory hallucinations vary in content from music to conversations apparently unrelated to the patient, to remarks directed to the patient through exhortations, praise, demands and invectives.

The emotional reaction of the schizophrenic patient to these hallucinations varies extremely widely, depending in general upon his characteristic reactions to situations of incomprehensible threat. Therefore, patients may simply deny them, shrug them off, attempt to explain them away, conceal them or become anxious, frightened, querulous, depressed or even suicidal. Eliciting material about hallucinations from patients is usually best done in a calm, objective fashion, avoiding any appearance of cross examination. Patients are frequently loathe to admit hallucinations, knowing that this

will label them "crazy." They do not wish to admit this to
themselves or others. Therefore, it is wise to preface an
inquiry about hallucinations with some face-saving device
such as, "You know, people that have been under considerable
emotional stress also have some extremely unusual experiences. Have you?" This may be followed by, "Some may get to
the point where they think they can see or hear things that
are not actually there. Have you ever had anything like
this?" Taste, tactile, and olfactory hallucinations should
be inquired about specifically, since patients rarely mention
them spontaneously.

One should not accept the report of an hallucination as
pathognomonic of schizophrenia. Patients with organic brain
disease, epilepsy, toxic states and hysteria, in addition to
malingerers, may report hallucinations.

Delusions

Delusions are usually explanatory beliefs constructed by
the patient as solutions to the problem of explaining his
various psychotic perceptual distortions and misevaluations.
Delusions appear during a period of emotional turmoil associated with misperceptions and misevaluations, culminating in
experiences of keen insight and revelations. These beliefs
are firmly held and not open to simple contradiction since
these perceptual distortions have the force of reality. The
actions of others are correctly perceived initially,but the
meaning attributed to them is unreasonable, highly personal-
ized and often considered to be a "message." This type of
misperception should be distinguished from that which occurs
in normal individuals in conditions of severe emotional distress. For instance, a guilty person may misevaluate the
correct perception of a policeman's glance as being specifically directed towards him. In the normal person, such a
misevaluation is followed by checking and "reality testing."
Psychotics may also internally debate the accuracy of their

evaluations during the early stages of their illness, but their persistent forcible misevaluations lead to abandoning doubt about inferential accuracy.

With the progress of the psychosis, more and more forced interpretations may be made to corroborate the overwhelming misevaluation of the situation. For instance, a psychotic might state that his brother is a drug addict since he coughs and belches, which everyone knows are cardinal signs of drug addiction. It is unclear to what degree such statements are forced rationalizations for a prepotent conviction or whether the inferential process has gone awry.

As stated above, delusions usually occur in the context of a delusional mood; that is, a feeling of change and new-ness in the circumstances and the occurrence of perceptions acquiring sudden abnormal significance. Such a state of de-lusional mood and perception leads quite naturally to ideas of self-reference which consist of beliefs that others are paying special attention to the patient. These may range from the belief that others are looking at the patient or talking about him,to the belief that all surrounding indivi-duals are involved in a play where every action is undertaken for its effect upon the patient.

These self-referential delusional states are usually re-ferred to as paranoid. However, the term paranoid is derived from the persecutory and grandiose delusions of paranoia. Many of these self-referential states are not persecutory. In fact, patients occasionally believe that their states of being specially attended to are with benevolent intent. The distinction is of prognostic importance within the schizo-phrenias since referential states may remit quite completely, whereas paranoid delusions usually leave at least an attitu-dinal residue.

Paranoid delusions, as defined here, consist of a belief in the persecutory intent and activity of others. Frequent-

ly, such delusions are that a group has malevolent intent toward the patient; e.g., the Mafia is out to get him or the
FBI is railroading him to jail. These ideas are quite fixed
and refractory to rational discussion, although in their early development the patient may doubt them and appear open to
discussion. Delusions with considerable systematic elaboration fit the patient's emotional state. One may believe that
he is a helpless pawn among malevolent forces, or that he has
been changed sexually; here the predominant emotion is fear.
If the patient believes that he is struggling valiantly a-
gainst the attempts of others to injure him, his predominant
affect is anger. If another believes he is receiving a justified punishment, his predominant mood is of depressive
guilt. Elation may be accompanied by grandiose delusory
states and self-misidentification as a historic or mythologi-
cal figure.

Delusional mood is a peculiar affective and cognitive
state, often occurring prior to the outbreak of acute psychosis in schizophrenics. The patient feels uneasy, suspicious,
confused, perplexed and has marked inexplicable mood shifts.
Delusions commonly occur as a sudden reorganization of evaluation, similar to moments of illumination, inspiration, or
epiphany, during a period of delusional mood. However, other
delusional beliefs develop on the basis of recurrent experiences of rejection and failure in patients with poor ability
to analyze their experiences, construct complex inferences,
or to be realistically self-critical. The apparently paranoid delusion that others dislike him or wish to derogate him
may be the result of the accurate initial perceptions of the
inept, clumsy and eccentric pre-schizophrenic who has met with
social ostracism throughout his life, coupled with a flimsy
denial of his own limitations. This system is delusional insofar as it is elaborated into a purposeful cabal, and is refractory to benevolent experiences.

During the period of recovery, delusional ideas lose
emotional force although they persist as conceptual beliefs.
Eventually, on recovery, the patient cannot understand why he
ever had such notions. In a still further stage, he will refer to them as dream-like beliefs and may develop amnesia for
them.

Thought Disorder

The term "thought disorder" derives historically from
the clinical observation that delusional patients often demonstrated peculiarities in their inferential reasoning and
communicative abilities. Attempts to describe these peculiarities without regard to the content of the delusional subject matter have led to two concepts: stream of thought disorder and formal thought disorder (lack of abstraction or deviant abstraction). There is a wide-spread, poorly founded
assumption that delusions (erroneous end product) are necessarily due to formal thought disorder (erroneous process).

The belief that formal thought disorder is restricted
to schizophrenia is undocumented. Failure to abstract (concreteness, under-inclusiveness) occurs in organic conditions,
dull intelligence, poor education, as well as in the depressive states. Over-inclusiveness and looseness of association
are typical of manic states and excited states in general.
The presence of formal thought disorder is more frequent in
the presence of disturbances in the stream of thought. Another indication of the complexity of the situation is the
fact that some delusional patients do not manifest any irreg-
ularities in their communicative ability, whereas many patients with gross looseness of association do not manifest
structured delusions but rather, fragmentary misperceptions.
Actually the most florid delusions often occur in the patient
with the least manifest formal thought disorder.

Stream of thought disorders may reflect an abnormal
thinking rate, since thinking may be excessively fast or show

psychic retardation and blocking. Disorders of the goal di-
rectedness of thinking may be manifest   by constant loss of
goal orientation (flight of ideas, tangentiality, clang associations) or inability to depart from a preoccupation.
These clinical features are commonly found with affective
disorder and should be considered signs confirmatory of potential or manifest psychosis rather than specifically diagnostic of schizophrenia.

Blocking, thought disappearance, neologisms, personal
idioms, cluster thinking and inability to focus attention are
included as indicators of schizophrenic thought disturbance.

Psychological and psychiatric studies of associational
structure, inductive, and deductive abilities have rarely
controlled for the patient's age, sex, social class, education and clinical status, or defects in other aspects of psychological function such as intelligence, attention, perception, memory, cooperativeness, motivation and affective
state. Also, the existence of indicators of neurophysiological disorder such as EEG abnormality or neurological soft-
signs, as well as concurrent drug treatment, and a history of
ECT and insulin coma have been ignored. Not surprisingly the
literature is both contradictory and inconclusive. Such apparently simple issues as demonstrating that the "anti-psychotic" drugs favorably affect psychological functioning on
tests supposedly reflective of psychotic process have evaded
clear-cut proof.

The attempt by Bleuler to diagnose schizophrenia on the
basis of inferred deviant thought processes has opened a Pan-
dora's box. The exciting promise of uniquely characterizing
the schizophrenic process in terms of fundamental psychological aberrations (splitting) and secondary accessory symptoms
has resulted in diagnostic chaos and prognostic confusion.
Bleuler's hypothesis should be considered an outline for a
research program rather than a practical diagnostic tool.

Emotional Disorders

Most emotional states (e.g., fear, anger, elation, depression, etc.) found in schizophrenia also can be found in neurotic and affective disorders and therefore cannot be considered specific. However, this is not true of emotional blunting and flatness,both of which are diagnostic. In a single examination the difficulty of distinguishing these characteristics from depressive apathy is marked. However, affective blunting and flatness are largely the residual signs of a chronic process,whereas depressive apathy is phasic and reported to be a temporary pathological state by the patient.

Severe emotional inappropriateness (incongruity of thought content and affect) and silliness are diagnostic but must be differentiated from the histrionics and blandness of the hysteric. Unfortunately, novice psychiatrists are prone to designate as inappropriate any expression of an attitude that conflicts with their own values.

Motor Signs

Certain postural and gestural characteristics are classically associated with schizophrenia. Outstanding are various forms of motor retardation such as waxy flexibility, awkward, stuporous or bizarre postures. Grimacing, mutism, inappropriate smiling or repetitive motor rituals are also described. Wild incomprehensible agitations may also occur. These features may dominate the clinical picture and elicit the diagnosis of catatonia.

Interestingly, these behaviors were frequently reported during the 19th Century and now are seen infrequently except in chronic deteriorated patients. Acute and chronic retarded, perplexed, referential, mute states are still seen but are rarely associated with catatonic postures. The reason for this change of symptomatology is quite obscure.

Motor signs are not considered to be pathognomonic

of schizophrenia but rather as strongly suspicious. Affective, hysterical and organic disorders may present similar
motor peculiarities.

Psychiatric Traits Not Diagnostic of Schizophrenia

There are many other psychiatric traits often considered diagnostic of schizophrenia. However, these traits are
not prognostic and not unique to schizophrenia. They are
mentioned only to be discounted. These include depersonalization, derealization, chaotic sexuality, panics, pan-anxiety, pan-neurotic symptomatology and impulsivity.

Schizophrenic Diagnostic Subtypes

The division of schizophrenia into subtypes has been a
favorite preoccupation of systematic descriptive psychiatrists. Numerous classificatory subdivisions have been stip-
ulated. It is not clear whether these syndromes have any
claim to an independent existence on the basis of either
their being a singular concatenation of signs and symptoms,
or having some qualitative predictive utility.

Kraepelin's subdivision of schizophrenia into the catatonic, paranoid, simple and hebephrenic groups, is the most
widely known. This schema has undergone disuse atrophy
since the diagnoses of catatonia and especially simple and
hebephrenic schizophrenia have become extremely rare. In
current practice the most common subdiagnoses are undifferentiated, paranoid and schizo-affective, either acute or
chronic. A major drawback of the Kraepelinian sub-classifi-
cation is its lack of relation either to the patient's affective state or degree of chronic premorbid social defect
— two features recurrently shown to be of utmost prognostic importance. Therefore, a schema incorporating these
features and demonstrated to have clear-cut relationships
both to drug effect and post-hospital prognosis is presented.

Three groups are considered:

        1. Schizo-affective schizophrenia

           A. Cyclic

           B. Retarded, perplexed state

           C. Manic, excited state

        2. Childhood asocial schizophrenia

        3. Fearful paranoid schizophrenia

Chapter II

SCHIZO-AFFECTIVE SCHIZOPHRENIA

Definition

The illness of the schizo-affective patient strongly resembles manic-depressive disease. There is either anger, hyperactivity, flight of ideas and loss of goal orientation, or depressed, retarded, unspontaneous behavior and psychomotor inhibition. However, these patients exceed the boundaries of manic-depressive disease by having marked Kraepelinian signs of schizophrenia, such as clear-cut persecutory hallucinations and delusions with massive ideas of reference and social misinterpretations.

The onset of their illness is often abrupt and consists of two stages. Initially it closely resembles manic-depressive illness, in that only affective symptomatology is apparent. However, this is followed shortly by the appearance of gross cognitive and perceptual difficulty.

Their early development was usually unremarkable with only a few having had difficulties in socialization or impulse control. Many were considered sociable, outgoing and capable.

Among the excited patients, hospital staff diagnoses of paranoid schizophrenia or schizo-affective schizophrenia are common. Among the retarded schizophrenics, the diagnosis of undifferentiated schizophrenia, or more rarely catatonic schizophrenia, is usually applied.

Among all the schizophrenias, the schizo-affective patient benefits most from psychotropic agents and has the best long term outcome.

MARK GLUMBERG

PRESENTING PROBLEM

Mark Glumberg, age 33, unmarried and living with his parents, had returned to graduate school to become a social worker. He was thrilled by his first case. But suddenly he began to feel immense persuasive powers, comparable to those of Hitler, which he felt would help him save the world. At the same time he became agitated, excitable, argumentative and suspicious.

At home, he started berating his parents for not sharing a bedroom. One day, he impulsively stripped off his clothes and proceeded to his mother's bedroom, intending to goad his father and mother to sexual activity.   Instead his father threatened to kill him and his mother called Mark's psychiatrist whom he had been seeing intermittently for the prior three years. Mark was admitted to a city psychiatric hospital where he was diagnosed as a chronic schizophrenic and treated with Thorazine 400 mg daily. Shortly he gained control and within two weeks made application for longer term intensive treatment at Hillside.

FAMILY

Both parents were in their early 30's when Mark, the third of their four sons was born. The family lived in a large, middle-class apartment in New York, with their lives centered around their home. There were few friends and no outside interests. They were Jewish, only moderately religious, but kept a kosher home.

The father, orphaned as a young child, came to America when he was seven, traveling only with his younger sister. He had a deprived childhood and worked to support himself after elementary school. He married at 21 and was devoted to his wife, but jealous of sharing her affections with his sons. Clever, competitive, and tremendously energetic, he worked hard both at his own grocery store and as an electrician. At home he was domineering, harsh, punitive, self-righteous, suspicious and short-tempered. High blood pressure was a chronic problem complicated by several small strokes.

The mother was kind, soft-spoken, understanding, even-tempered and intelligent. She assisted in the family business until age 55, when it was sold, and then became a practical nurse. Her role was as moderator between husband and sons.

The brothers were all academically and vocationally successful, and all but Mark were married and reasonably happy. While growing up they got along well and cared for each other while their parents worked. Because of Mr. Glumberg's envy of his sons' intellectual attainments, the more they excelled and gained academic honors, the more he harassed and criticized them. All four boys expressed considerable hostility toward their father and often found it necessary to join forces defensively, which seemed to strengthen their bonds as a close-knit family.

When Mark was 23, Mrs. Glumberg contemplated divorce, because her husband had become very excitable and was constantly fighting with his sons, making life intolerable. Further, he was extremely tight-fisted, and refused to give his wife sufficient funds to manage their home. When he learned of his wife's plans he was very upset and consulted a rabbi who helped ameliorate the situation. It was after this that husband and wife maintained separate bedrooms.

DEVELOPMENTAL HISTORY

Mark was born normally, at term, at home. His mother vomited very frequently during the pregnancy. He was breast

fed for one year, walked, talked and was toilet-trained at
approximately one year and suffered severe double pneumonia
at this time. Always a poor eater, he was thin and weak and
had prolonged aggravated episodes of the usual childhood ail-
ments. Because of this he was favored and petted more than
his brothers and was often excused from responsibilities.

His earliest memory was at age five, when he fell down
a flight of stairs into a cellar, sustaining no injuries. He
entered school at age six. At age seven he was tricked into
having his tonsils removed, and he maintained a grudge
against his father for this unpleasant deception.

An average student throughout his schooling, his marks
never compared with his brothers'. He always felt intellectually inferior to them although later testing revealed his
Wechsler-Bellevue IQ to be 135. Always introverted, shy,
quiet, withdrawn and anxious to please, he rarely had friends
and spent most of his free time working in his father's
store.

Mark's psychosexual development was stultified. At 12
or 13 he discovered masturbation and masturbated about three
times a day throughout his teens and early adulthood. He received no sex education at home but obtained information from
classmates. Disgusted by sex facts, he vomited upon hearing
about them.

During his high school years, the Glumbergs made several
moves which bothered Mark, and after having to change schools
again in his junior year he complained of losing contact with
the world and had trouble making any friends. His academic
record remained only fair, but oddly, he was outstanding at
public speaking.

After graduating from high school he was drafted into
the infantry, during World War II. While in actual combat in
France and Germany, he never fired a gun; he remained a private during his two years service. During this time he had

one foreign girlfriend, although he was not sexually attracted to her. He claimed he wished to remain a virgin so that
he would be worthy of marrying a virgin. When a homosexual
soldier made a pass at him, he reported being "ready to kill"
the fellow.

On returning from the Army he lived at his parents' home
and entered college. For the first year and a half, he attended day school, and then, working days at his father's
store, he switched to night school. Father and son argued
fearfully, so that Mark finally moved to a rented room and
found another job. The father then sold his business and re-
tired, feeling that Mark was disinterested in maintaining it.
Mark, however, felt that his father had taken the business
away from him and was quite upset.

At college, he maintained a B average, once again excelling at public speaking. Finally after nine years, at age
29, he received his bachelor's degree.

The summer after graduation, he decided to take a two
week vacation at a resort where he could meet other young
people socially. At the resort he was elated, shed his shyness and immersed himself in social activities, learning to
dance, making passes at girls, falling in love and deciding
to marry. During these two weeks he was extremely active and
slept little.

While driving home from the resort with his new girlfriend, he felt that he was Jesus Christ, destined to save
the world. When he arrived home he was elated and over-talk-
ative. Frightened by his unusual behavior, his parents contacted a psychiatrist who came to the home and administered
ECT. After a second ECT treatment the next day, Mark, confused and disoriented, wandered out and went to his new girlfriend's house where he was bizarre, excited and threatening.
Her parents called the police. They took him to a city psychiatric hospital where he was diagnosed as having dementia

praecox, catatonic type, and given a series of 15 ECT.

During this first hospitalization he hallucinated a voice which directed him to put his mouth on a fellow patient's penis, and received a kick in the face for his efforts. Also at this time several male aides made homosexual advances and one performed fellatio on him. Mr. Glumberg stated that he did not enjoy this act but participated without emotion.

After one month at the city hospital he remained confused, paranoid, grandiose, lacking in insight, and was transferred to a state hospital. Here he received 60 insulin treatments; also unsuccessful. He continued to be acutely disturbed, disoriented for place, out of contact, hallucinating voices, sullen, unkempt and agitated. After he received 150 mg Thorazine intramuscularly, plus 600 mg orally, daily, he improved quickly. His delusions and hallucinations disappeared, he became pleasant, agreeable and oriented, although definite emotional flatness remained.

Within six months he was discharged and then entered individual and group psychotherapy. He lived alone in an apartment, completed a teacher certification program and took a job as an elementary school teacher. He taught successfully for two and a half years and was liked by his students, but felt he had no control of them and began worrying over his inability to understand their "psychological interactions." This thought obsessed him to such degree that he decided to quit teaching and choose another profession. At this time he took a European tour and had his first sexual intercourse with a prostitute. He was extremely proud that he had finally asserted his masculinity.

On returning from the tour he took vocational tests and enrolled in a school of social work. At school several upsetting events occurred: he became involved in a frustrating attempt at organizing fellow students for the protection of

students' rights; the pressures of academic work were greater
than expected, and he came into open conflict with his supervisor at his field work placement. He was excited and anxious concerning the supervisor's role of overseeing and control, attempted to work independently of him and flaunted his
directives. Shortly, he became excited, delusional, received
ECT and was hospitalized.

PRESENTING CHARACTERISTICS

Mr. Glumberg was well-built and healthy looking. His
speech was circumstantial, irrelevant, garrulous and ram-
bling, but at the same time with a hyper-precise, hostile and
analytic manner. Grandiose, egotistical and hypomanic, he
talked at length about his capacity to help others. He tried
to conduct psychotherapy with fellow patients, causing considerable upset and ill-feeling among them. Toward the hospital staff he was extremely irritable, hostile, sometimes
violent, repeatedly tested limits and continually pressed to
be discharged. Nevertheless, in areas which were not emotionally charged, his insight and judgment often remained
good.

COURSE AT HILLSIDE

All physical examinations were within normal limits, as
were two EEG records. On the Wechsler-Bellevue he attained
a full scale IQ of 135, with a verbal IQ of 136 and a performance IQ of 129.

At Hillside, the Thorazine 400 mg daily he had been taking at the city hospital was discontinued. But within a
week he was entered into the drug program and received Thorazine 300 mg daily, with weekly 300 mg increments until a
level of 1200 mg was reached. Kemadrin was also given, with
weekly increments of 3.75 mg, until a level of 15 mg daily
was reached. Within five days of starting on Thorazine he
was markedly calmed. A week later he looked dull, and
claimed he was existing rather than living. However, he

seemed improved and now participated in occupational and creative therapy. As the Thorazine dosage was increased he became greatly troubled by such side effects as dry mouth,
drowsiness and sluggishness; particularly, he had severe difficulty in maintaining his train of thought. Because of
this, Thorazine was reduced abruptly to 300 mg, a day later
to 150 mg and then discontinued. Two days later he complained of nausea and vomiting, probably due to the rapid withdrawal of medication. A single dose of Thorazine 50 mg and
Dramamine eliminated this problem in three days.

Now friendly, cooperative and constructive, his grandiosity and hypomania subsided. He participated in and enjoyed
group activities, accepted hospitalization and became more
active and cheerful. A month later he developed sleeping
problems with unpleasant dreams and early morning awakening.
Thorazine 25 mg, at night, was reinstated with excellent effect. He slept well and remained emotionally even, although
rather laconic and pensive, and related to others only in a
highly intellectual way.

Psychotherapy was exclusively supportive, and it was
felt that little more could be gained from prolonged hospitalization. He was discharged after five months of hospitalization, to the custody of his brother, and was to continue
taking Thorazine 25 mg, at night. His hospital diagnosis
was paranoid schizophrenia; the research psychiatrist vacillated between diagnoses of manic-depressive, cyclic,and cyclic schizo-affective illness. The first psychotic episode
with massive hallucinations, confusion and delusions seemed
to speak for the latter. However, it was unclear how much
of the peculiar delusional content was due to the organic
mental syndrome produced by prior insulin comas and ECT.

FOLLOW-UP

Mr. Glumberg remained with his brother, helping at his
ski lodge, for five months, then returned to his parents'

home and later moved to his own apartment. He supported himself by working as an office clerk and saw his private therapist regularly.

In the ensuing nine years, he suffered seven more relapses. Each time he was hospitalized for approximately one
month, treated with Thorazine (once with ECT) and improved
rapidly. At times he remained on Thorazine between hospitalizations. Available information indicated that when he discontinued medication, he relapsed.

In response to a follow-up questionnaire sent 10 years
after Hillside hospitalization, he stated that he was still
employed at a clerical job. He had returned home to live
with his mother, after his father's death. On comparing his
feelings after 10 years to those during Hillside hospitalization, he stated that he was "the same, not feeling, just existing." He took Thorazine, 50 mg at night, and lithium carbonate 300 mg daily. He asserted that he had plans for foreign travel and eventual marriage, although his only social
activities were with a group of bridge players.

COMMENT

Even after prolonged follow-up, there is considerable
diagnostic uncertainty about this case. Most of the confusion results from the onset of his illness where he was considered bizarre, confused, disoriented, with a prolonged period of being out of contact in an hallucinatory agitation.
Nonetheless, this is obscured by the fact of his previous ECT
and insulin treatments which may have produced some measure
of organic mental syndrome. His initial elation and grandiose delusions would go along with either manic-depressive
illness or a schizo-affective psychosis.

During his period at Hillside his symptomatology could
well be considered manic-depressive, except for his definite
emotional flatness during the remission of his psychosis.

Plainly, making a distinction between these conditions

is only of practical consequence if it results in a different prognosis or in a different case management. In fact,
as far as we know, these illnesses have very similar prognoses and both require prophylactic medication. However, there
is some belief (7) that the phenothiazines are better suited
to the treatment of schizo-affective disease, with lithium
preferred in the treatment of manic-depressive illness. Certainly, further detailed work is necessary to resolve this
issue.

Of pharmacotherapeutic interest is Mr. Glumberg's relative intolerance to Thorazine. In general, schizo-affectives
and manic-depressives approaching remission object to the
"deadening" effects of phenothiazines. This leads to difficulties in maintaining these patients on a long term prophylactic phenothiazine regimen. With manic-depressives the
prophylactic use of lithium is particularly promising because
manics accept lithium more easily than phenothiazines. Evidently, at some point in Mr. Glumberg's illness, he was considered to be a manic-depressive and prophylactic lithium was
prescribed. However, the dose of 300 mg daily seems low.
His complaint that he was "not feeling, just existing" might
refer to the prolonged apathy often seen following ECT and
phenothiazines. Such patients frequently respond to treatment to tricyclic antidepressants. However, it may also refer to the blunted emotionality often seen after recurrent
psychotic episodes.

CLAYTON RICHFIELD

PRESENTING PROBLEM

Clayton Richfield, age 19, entered his freshman year at a Western university feeling apathetic and unable to concentrate. He stated, "I lost my personality, I didn't know who I was. I didn't hit it off well with the fraternity men and was unable to get to know anybody." He wrote a discouraged letter to his mother who contacted the Student Health Service and then flew out to the college.

Clayton was called to the Health Service, and in an interview with the psychiatrist told how he had come to college with high hopes of being popular, a good student and track star. While pledging a fraternity, he received severe tongue lashings and humiliations as part of a hazing ritual and was very disturbed by this. He felt unable to cope with these social exigencies and his declining hopes, nor could he remove himself honorably from the unpleasant situation. Stoically, he wanted to handle the problems by himself and indicated to the psychiatrist that he would not need further consultation.

The next day, Mrs. Richfield spoke reassuringly with Clayton and then with the psychiatrist who, in turn, reassured her that her son was only moderately depressed and anxious; she returned home. One day later, Clayton appeared at the Health Service with severe forearm lacerations and severed tendons, claiming he had been attacked by some students. After surgical repair, the psychiatrist visited him and Clayton repeated his story of the attack. Because of his flattened affect he was transferred to a psychiatric ward. Four days later, on further questioning, he admitted that he cut himself impulsively, while attempting to think out his problems, not with the intent of killing himself but more as a way out of his frustrating situation. He sought help only after weakening from considerable blood loss.

The psychiatrist diagnosed him as having "a transitory psychotic episode in a background of long-standing adolescent disturbance." He treated him with Tofranil 25 mg three times daily and Sparine 75 mg four times daily, and promptly hospitalized Clayton at Hillside.

FAMILY

The Richfields were a wealthy, refined, white, Protestant family. The father, a very successful lawyer, was quiet, competent, self-assured, and genteel. Dominant and fairly strict in his family, his relationship with his children was one of concern but distance and reserve; "I never told my father anything so it didn't seem unusual that my children didn't tell me anything." He spent most of his free time playing golf. Clayton experienced a great deal of frustration trying to compete with his father's golf game and social success, and Mr. Richfield smugly admitted that his son had not succeeded in winning his attentions.

Mrs. Richfield was kind, sweet and lovely. She had many friends and social engagements, and most of her time was involved with community activities. Clayton was her youngest and favorite child and she showed utmost compassion for him.

A sister, eight years older than Clayton, was happily married. (However, as an adult she had a short hospitalization for "an apparent schizophrenic episode.") By the time Clayton was eight years old, she was virtually out of the house, first at boarding school and then at college. A brother, six years older, was also married. He had been an outstanding student at the prep school that Clayton attended, and was very well liked by his peers. The children always got along well and Clayton especially admired his brother.

DEVELOPMENTAL HISTORY

Clayton's conception was planned; he was born full term and developed normally. There were no feeding, sleeping or toilet-training problems. A most attractive child, vigorous

and active, he had considerable attention from his mother, an
immensely indulgent grandmother, a cook and a housekeeper.
As Clayton grew, the grandmother with whom they lived, an extraordinarily dependent, manipulative person, became senile,
began having temper tantrums and vied with Clayton for his
mother's attention. Grandmother would unpredictably berate
him, prohibit him from playing with friends and interfere
with his activities. However, he was often left in her care
while his parents were out. Clayton bore this unpleasantness
with amazing stoicism and tolerance for a young child. This
situation persisted until Clayton was eight, when his parents
moved from the family estate to their own home, after provi-
sions had been made to care for the grandmother.

Prior to age eight, Clayton was successful in school and
his teachers reported that he was well-adjusted. Following
the move to his new home, he began to have some minor conduct
problems and was considered to be underachieving. But, in
general, his behavior was unremarkable during elementary
school years.

At age 14, he willingly went to a private boarding
school, as had his sister and brother. He hated it for the
first year and was homesick, but after, joined with a group
of rebels and "fit in" better. During prep school years he
was active, outgoing, participated in many extracurricular
activities and had many friendships, although none were particularly close. He maintained a low B average and was not
at all studious. He dated girls and had one special girlfriend; other information about his heterosexual development
was not available. During summers he vacationed with his mother in the country and the father visited weekends; during
winter holidays, mother, father and son travelled together.

Clayton related that at prep school he "felt something
was wrong. I didn't know what I was good at." During his
last year, his grades began to slip. When he was rejected

from the Ivy League college his father and brother had attended, he was gravely dejected.

His parents sent him to Europe to finish the year at a
small private junior college where he could "have time to
grow up." At this school, he took a limited program, attended no classes and ran wild. He bought a forbidden motorcycle
which he loved passionately, and "did all sorts of crazy
things. I was running all over the place with my motorcycle,
making noise, throwing firecrackers. I wanted people to like
me but I guess I made a mess of things." He was expelled a
week prior to the end of the year, and returned to the States
where he nevertheless spent a good summer.

In September he entered his third choice university. He
made a resolution to work hard, be serious and successful.
But quickly he found he was unable to concentrate and apply
himself and began to fear that "someone would do something to
me. When my fraternity brothers didn't like me, it was too
much." It was at this point that he became acutely ill, as
discussed earlier.

PRESENTING CHARACTERISTICS

Clayton, good-looking and well-built, appeared very man-
ly, prideful and self-contained. His affect was extremely
flat and he complained of feeling "empty, blank and discouraged," and often repeated "I don't know who I am, I have no
feelings at all." His facial expression was mask-like, with
an appearance of perplexity and apathy. Generally he was depressed, self-effacing, withdrawn and quiet. His answers to
questions were delayed but coherent and relevant. He admitted to no particular fears, peculiar thoughts, nor persecutory trends at the time of the initial mental status interview.

COURSE AT HILLSIDE

The results of all physical and neurological tests, including the EEG, were within normal limits. On the Wechsler-

Bellevue, he attained a full scale IQ of 96, a verbal IQ of
110 and a performance IQ of 81.

On entering Hillside, medication was withdrawn. Within
the first few days at the hospital, Clayton deteriorated rapidly, becoming increasingly withdrawn, isolated and mute.
He actively hallucinated voices yelling "you're a liar,
you're bad, you're queer." He had no insight that these
voices were imaginary, and no longer recognized that he was
emotionally ill. He had inordinately long latencies in response to questions. Massive referentiality and paranoid behavior were prevalent; for example, he believed that because
he was a suspected thief, his doctor was seeing him at his
office, freeing his room for police search. Convinced that
everyone stared at him and wanted to harm him, he was extremely fearful that something dreadful was going to happen.

After ten days he was placed in the drug program and received Tofranil 75 mg daily with 75 mg weekly increments to
300 mg daily. He remained incoherent, bizarre, manneristic
and isolated. Hallucinating his parents crying for help, he
was deluded that they were suffering from cold and exposure,
somewhere on the hospital grounds. He was extremely self-
deprecatory, feeling hated, stupid and weak. On the other
hand, he denied the necessity of remaining in the hospital,
claiming that he was only pretending to be ill. When his
parents visited, he attempted to leave with them and hit an
aide who tried to restrain him. Transferred to a closed
ward, he complained of bugs in his food and on his face,
which he excoriated by continual picking. Then he refused
medication and food.

After a month the Tofranil was stopped as evidentally
ineffective, if not toxic, and Thorazine 100 mg intramuscular, three times daily, was started. Within four days his
agitation ceased and he was oriented to time, place and person. But he still hallucinated his parents' voices, and of-

ten muttered "I am weak, stupid and yellow. My parents are
nothing like that at all." Oral Thorazine was started at 600
mg and increased 300 mg daily until 3600 mg daily was reached. His general condition seemed to improve gradually and he
became calmer, less frightened, more active, interested in
his environment and better oriented. Psychological testing
done at this time resulted in a Wechsler-Bellevue IQ of 113
with insignificant subtest score scatter. On the Rorschach
he was able to give a total of only eight responses.

When a brief agitated episode occurred, Thorazine was
increased to 4800 mg daily with minimal side effects, and he
was no longer hallucinated, delusional, paranoid or fearful.
However, two weeks later he had another episode of agitation
and broke a window. After a month on 4800 mg he suffered a
grand mal seizure. Thorazine was reduced to 3600 mg, but
signs of agitation and disorganization increased; he rambled
apologetically about the past and repeatedly misidentified
people as his brother or an old friend. Therefore, Thorazine
was discontinued and ECT, three times a week, was instituted.
After 15 ECT he showed great improvement, felt well, participated in activities and showed no thought disorder. Although
his affect was flat, it was appropriate and he was interested
in relating to others. As the ECT was reduced, he began to
fear he would regress. Thus, Thorazine 600 mg daily was re-
introduced, along with one ECT weekly; a total of 28 ECT were
given.

Clayton was discharged after seven months, when his a-
cute symptoms abated enough for him to continue as an outpatient. He was to continue taking Thorazine 600 mg daily.
The hospital diagnosis was schizophrenic reaction, catatonic
type with paranoid features; the research diagnosis was
schizo-affective psychosis, retarded, perplexed, probably cycloid with catatonic features.

FOLLOW-UP

Clayton wrote a letter to Hillside two years after being discharged. The information in the letter was corroborated by both his father and himself, in personal interviews with a social worker.

"I began working in a photography shop and never felt poorly while working, but I used to feel quite tired in the evening. Of course, I was taking a large dose of Thorazine (600 mg daily). The dose was cut down gradually by my new doctor (cut to 200 mg daily). I did have a rather unpleasant side effect of being burned extremely easily in the sun; this even occurred while riding in the car with the windows closed. I must say, though, I rarely felt depressed or nervous while taking the drug in relatively large quantities.

"I worked at the same job until April (nine months) and then resenting my salary I quit and found another job selling encyclopedias, for about a month, before I realized it was too much and quit. I then worked another photography shop but got involved with some wild life, and drinking cost me my job. I drank like a fish and could not sleep more than a few hours at night." (Medication and psychotherapy, once every two weeks, was discontinued by the patient at this point.)

"Returning home I felt much better and I began college in September. I love school and get along with nearly everyone..."

In an interview at the end of this year Clayton was still doing well, getting good grades in school even though he had been "thrown over" by two girlfriends.

The following Spring, he started to show signs of becoming quite ill. He was deluded that he was working with the FBI to rid the city of communists and was hyperactive, impulsive and disorganized. While riding with his parents, he suddenly jumped from the car in an apparent suicide attempt; it took several policemen to bring him back to the

car. Despite his deterioration, no psychiatric help was
sought at this time. He did poorly at school and attended
few classes. By summer, he was highly disorganized and his
parents finally committed him to a psychiatric hospital, four
years after his Hillside hospitalization. Here he was diagnosed as having paranoid schizophrenia, treated with Thorazine 200 mg daily, and discharged as much improved in two and
one half weeks.

Immediately, he returned to his college town but became
very disturbed when summer riots broke out. Claiming that he
was working for the Secret Service, he stole a boat to "survey some islands." When apprehended by the police, he was
excited, overactive and delusional. They took him to a state
hospital for the criminally insane where he was circumstantial, overtalkative, usually elated but sometimes angry, and
unable to give a coherent story of the events leading to his
arrest. Diagnosed as paranoid schizophrenic, he was treated
with Thorazine 300 mg daily. He continued disturbed, restless, noisy, hitting the wall with his head, and finally severely injured an aide by kicking him in the ribs. His medication was changed to Stelazine 10 mg three times daily, and
he gradually became quieter and cooperative. After a month
on this medication he was in fair contact but with inappropriate affect and delusions that he was telepathic.

He remained at this hospital for four months and then
returned to college for a month. Then he quit, found a job
where he was happy and worked himself into a responsible position within two years. During this period he married a
bright, attractive girl.

But suddenly, the company had a financial setback and
his employment was terminated. At this point he became erratic, paranoid and drank excessively, seeing people from
outer space and feeling he had killed someone. Rehospitalized at a private institute, he was diagnosed as paranoid

schizophrenic with manic features and treated with daily doses of Stelazine 6 mg, nicotinic acid 2000 mg, and Mellaril
200 mg, psychotherapy, and ECT. He remained a month before
being released to outpatient care and continuing ECT.

A letter received from his father three years later (ten
years after his Hillside hospitalization) follows:

"Your former patient, Clayton Richfield, died in a highway collision, a little less than two years ago. Although we
had dinner with him a few days before, and he seemed pretty
good, we believe that he felt he had a depression coming on.

"The best period he had was just after his state hospital experience. He had a job with a trucking firm, took a
college course and got a good grade, was married, and so on.
This lasted for about eight or nine months when he again had
to be hospitalized. He had quite a bit of electroshock after
that, both as an inpatient and as an outpatient.

"He didn't have much social life--of course after his
marriage. I imagine he felt little need for it. There is
little more that I can add that would be of any help to anyone."

COMMENT

Mr. Richfield's development and course exemplify that of
many schizo-affectives. Although the family is apparently
well preserved, two of the three children had schizophrenic
episodes, raising the possibility of some genetic predisposition in this case. The patient's early life and development
are above average and there is certainly no manifest difficulty with socialization.

His initial psychosis was marked by such severe retardation, perplexity and massive delusional states that he could
easily have been considered catatonic. In a subsequent psychotic episode four years later, he was overtalkative, elated, angry and severely disturbed, thus resembling a manic-
excited state. The resemblance of the schizo-affective psy-

chosis to manic-depressive disease in both the bipolarity and
periodicity of attacks is insufficiently well recognized.

Of pharmacotherapeutic interest was Mr. Richfield's lack
of response to Tofranil during the depressive phase. In general, Tofranil is not the drug of choice for the management
of such patients, although we have shown that it is more effective than placebo; however, it is much less effective than
phenothiazines (13). In view of the patient's complaints a-
bout bugs in his food and on his face, it is likely that Tofranil produced a toxic effect. This combination of visual
hallucinations of insects and formication is typically a toxic, central nervous system response (10, 20).

The patient required unusually large doses of Thorazine
at this point to bring his psychosis under control. Since in
his future psychotic episodes smaller doses of phenothiazines
were effective in establishing control, one might wonder if
the antecedent Tofranil had made him more refractory to
phenothiazines. However, this is entirely speculative. The
use of ECT in psychotic patients who are refractory to phenothiazines is a clinically well-attested procedure, especially
in combination with maintenance medication. Unfortunately,
many psychiatrists maintain an irrational aversion to indicated ECT.

The patient's course is of particular interest in that
it showed marked periodicity with almost complete restoration
to normality between psychotic episodes. Of further interest
are the marked shifts in symptomatology, running the gamut of
affective and paranoid states. Some critics of psychiatric
diagnosis point out such variable courses as proving the uselessness of diagnosis. Actually, the correct implication is
that the diagnosis should predict variability, with unpreci-
pitated shifts between the two poles of excitation and retardation, as well as intervening clear periods. The diagnosis of schizo-affective psychosis, cycloid type, is not an

academic affair but a clear call for specific prophylactic action, even in the face of apparent recovery. Regrettably, maintenance prophylactic medication could never be effectuated with this patient.

The nature of his death is, of course, moot. However, the risk of suicide in such patients cannot be underestimated; in fact this patient had made a previous suicidal attempt while riding in an automobile. There is an almost complete absence of long term data concerning the course and outcome of such cases.

SAMUEL HUFF

PRESENTING PROBLEM

Samuel Huff, age 42, an orthodox Jew, was principal of a private high school and the father of two children. Suddenly, six weeks before entering Hillside, he began to believe his Board of Trustees was trying to destroy him because he had consorted with prostitutes and had sexual relations with a teacher on his staff. Also, he felt that his wife and family were trying to poison him. Progressively immersed in his delusions and increasingly agitated, he attempted to strangle his wife when she tried to reason with him. She called a doctor who rushed him to a county psychiatric hospital.

At the hospital he remained delusional, despite treatment with five ECT and Thorazine (amount unknown); there he felt that other patients were speaking against him. Slowly, his agitation and fearfulness decreased somewhat. He was diagnosed paranoid schizophrenic.

His wife and other influential members of the community complained of the terrible indignity for Mr. Huff to be in a public hospital and managed to have him quickly transferred to Hillside.

FAMILY

Mr. Huff was born and raised with his ten siblings in a middle-class, religious community in Syria. The father, in his late 60's, remained in Syria and worked as a religion teacher, salesman, and shopkeeper. His son disliked him, described him as cold, isolated, uninvolved with his family, but dutifully sent money to help support him.

The mother was described as a mild, passive, ineffectual, long-suffering martyr, much loved by her son. She died when Samuel was in his mid 30's, and he was greatly upset. He wrote her epitaph, extolling her virtues and devotion to her children.

Of the ten children, only four reached adulthood, the

others died from unknown causes. Mr. Huff maintained communication with only one sister who remained in Syria and to
whom he sent money occasionally.

His wife, dynamic, vigorous, very intelligent, and 12
years younger, was a lovely, statuesque blond. When 20, she
immigrated to America from the Latvian ghetto where she had
been raised. During her youth she spent many years in a concentration camp and actually saw a number of family members
put to death. Released at 15, she attended school where she
excelled, worked to support herself and her mother, and showed tremendous independence and strength. After coming to
America, she casually met Samuel and knew him for only a
short time before their marriage. While she was aware of
their basic cultural differences, and the problems they might
present, especially concerning the woman's role, she felt
their common Jewish background and orthodox religious values
would compensate. Their two children, a boy age six and a
girl age two (at the time of his Hillside hospitalization)
were happy, healthy and usually gave Mr. Huff considerable
pleasure. He had been warm and giving with them.

DEVELOPMENTAL HISTORY

No developmental history was available. Mr. Huff remembered little about growing up except that he enjoyed traveling and selling with his father. He studied, became a teacher, lived away from home, and had a girlfriend whom he planned to marry. At age 30, he came to America and found a job
teaching languages. He earned a college degree, taught high
school and then became principal of the school where he worked successfully for the next ten years.

Mr. Huff corresponded with his Syrian girlfriend and was
to return to marry her. However, two weeks before the trip,
he saw an extremely attractive girl in a luncheonette, and
introduced himself. In Syria, he broke his engagement, and
on returning to America courted the new girl and later mar-

ried her.

During their courtship, Mr. Huff was sweet, considerate, generous and permissive. But immediately after the marriage he became penurious, jealous, demanding, authoritarian, domineering, critical, and difficult to live with. Because, according to the traditions of his upbringing women were held as intellectual inferiors, he never included his wife in financial planning and gave her a paltry sum to run the house. She decided to work part-time to supplement the household budget. Only during her husband's illness did she learn that he had savings extensive enough to permit them a distinctly more comfortable life.

Sex posed another problem. Mrs. Huff refused to raise a large family and insisted on family planning. Toward this end she received special dispensation from her rabbi to use contraception. However, Mr. Huff wanted a large family and rejected any contraceptive methods. Thus, starting very early in their marriage, his wife acquiesced only rarely to sexual intercourse. He complained bitterly to his friends about this denial, had liaisons with prostitutes and a work acquaintance, and had nagging suspicions concerning his wife's fidelity.

Mrs. Huff further demanded that she be allowed to continue her education. Toward this end she worked in the morning for extra money, tended to house chores and two young children in the afternoon and attended college in the evening. After ten years of night school, and in the June preceeding her husband's illness, Mrs. Huff earned her bachelor's degree. She felt that her husband would have been happier had he married a simpler, less demanding and challenging wife, from his own culture. (Mr. Huff's friends corroborated that Mrs. Huff did not behave like a "proper" Syrian wife). However, she claimed that she loved and respected her husband and tried to behave as he wished. He remained very difficult to please, repeatedly criticizing and humiliating her in public.

Mr. Huff was a hard-working, perfectionistic, highly able administrator who demanded arduous work from his subordinates and himself. His very cool, reserved, formal manner alienated most of his colleagues, and he actively made enemies by firing those who did not meet his stringent standards. While his job caused him extreme tension, he was the first person to remain in it longer than several months, and he was able to successfully administer his duties in an atmosphere of factions, intrigues and backbiting. He was constantly, re-. alistically worried that his contract would not be renewed and was always in a position of jockeying with rivals.

In an attempt to provide extra proof of his adequacy, he prepared a model school program to which school board members were specially invited to observe in progress. When no board members visited, Mr. Huff became acutely upset and, for the first time in his life, began to talk about ideas of persecution which soon mushroomed into delusions that others were trying to kill him.

PRESENTING CHARACTERISTICS

Mr. Huff, swarthy and handsome, usually dressed formally in a suit and skull-cap. He was anxious and depressed but compliant, ingratiating, eager to cooperate and thankful for the hospital's "graciousness to him." Initially his speech was relevant and coherent and unless questioned specifically about areas connected with his delusions, no psychotic material was present. Once those areas were tapped, he spoke freely of active delusions involving his work, home and social relationships. He had no insight into the irrationality of his thoughts. His affect in relation to his paranoid ideas seemed flat. He believed that he was in the hospital to be killed and pleaded only that it be done painlessly.

COURSE AT HILLSIDE

The results of all physical and neurological examinations

were negative, except for a moderate systolic heart murmur.
Psychological testing revealed a low average level of intelligence, with a Wechsler-Bellevue IQ of 93, but his grossly
impaired emotional state probably interfered with his test
performance. Intelligence was estimated at the bright normal
level.

After admission to Hillside, the Thorazine dispensed at
the county hospital was withdrawn. Within two weeks he was
actively delusional, paranoid, extremely agitated and withdrawn. Unable to sleep, he also began to fast. He was certain he would be mutilated and killed and that his family
also would be punished. Thus he prayed continually, begging
forgiveness, in order to forestall the impending doom.

Six weeks of intensive support proved ineffective, and
he was placed in the drug program. At the initial evaluation
his manner was fearful and pleading. While extremely guilt-
ridden, he felt the punishment he was receiving was intolerable. Placed on placebo for the first five days he continued
deteriorating and became increasingly agitated, pleading,
praying, and pacing incessantly. The medication was quickly
changed to Thorazine, intramuscularly, 100 mg four times
daily, and within five days to 1200 mg orally and Kemadrin
15 mg daily. His agitation promptly lessened, and after two
weeks on Thorazine he was much calmer and his delusions were
less disturbing. He voluntarily participated in activities
but interacted minimally.

Slowly, he seemed more cheerful but spent most of his
time reading the Bible and praying. At six weeks his delusions and ideas of reference subsided and he joined a work
group. He claimed that he had re-examined the factual bases
for his previous delusions, found evidence lacking for them
and decided they were imaginary. He felt greatly improved
and requested discharge.

He was discharged after three and a half months of hospi-

talization,on Thorazine 900 mg and Kemadrin 15 mg daily, to
return to his family and a modified work routine. Both he
and his wife were to attend counselling at an after-care
clinic. His hospital diagnosis was paranoid schizophrenia.
The research diagnosis was schizophrenia, fearful paranoid
type, but in retrospect, this diagnosis was incorrect.
Schizophrenia, schizo-affective type, depressed,would have
been more appropriate, as will be discussed later.

FOLLOW-UP

Mr. Huff attended the after-care clinic for three months
only. He then discontinued all treatment and medication.
For the next three years he successfully continued with his
difficult job and his family, although he still had marital
problems. His wife reported that he maintained ideas about
people plotting against him, was tense, and nightly awoke repeatedly between 2 and 4 A.M. He usually went to sleep directly after dinner in the early evening. In general, he was
functioning adequately. In his own counselling of people his
standard advice was to make the best of any bad situation.

Six years after his Hillside hospitalization, Mr. Huff
again suffered severe anxiety and symptoms similar to those
of his initial episode. He contacted Hillside for treatment,
but since he needed emergency hospitalization and Hillside
had a waiting list, he entered another private hospital where
he received a course of ECT.

In an interview eleven years after his Hillside hospitalization, Mr. Huff seemed tired, apathetic, depressed, and
had learned to consider this state his "way of life." He had
undergone repeated series of ECT for his depression but had
received no psychotherapy or medication. Two months earlier,
he and his wife finally divorced. He rarely saw his two
children, remained at his same job, rarely socialized and
spent his free time studying.

COMMENT

Mr. Huff's course is typical of the schizo-affective with
a late onset,after an unremarkable, if possibly neurotic, development in young adult life (21,22,28). The psychosis has
a very heavy affective coloration and the delusions are mood
congruent, so that one might wonder if this is not basically
an affective psychosis. Nonetheless, the delusions exceed
those considered typical of a psychotic depression in that
they are flagrantly persecutory and may entail complicated
hallucinations. Like the affective disorders, the course is
periodic with remissions and exacerbations. During exacerbations the acute psychosis can be well managed with either
intensive phenothiazine treatment or ECT.

There is no systematic evidence that prophylactic phenothiazine medication is of value in this periodic psychosis.
However, the absence of such data is simply due to the absence of the complicated longitudinal studies that would be
necessary to establish scientifically the value of prophylactic drug treatment (2, 6). Nevertheless, on a priori
grounds, it seems reasonable that in a patient with relapsing
illness, a course of prophylactic medication should be essay-
ed. However, in a recent paper (26), we question whether
there may exist a subgroup of schizophrenics for whom maintenance phenothiazine medication may actually be toxic, causing quick rehospitalization. Long term after-care studies
to resolve this important issue are mandatory; however, none
are in sight.

Another typical aspect of Mr. Huff's couse is that despite repeated exacerbations and ECT series, he was able to
be economically self-supporting at a high level; again like
the affective disorders.

Mr. Huff recurrently received ECT and was left in a
chronically tired, depressed and apathetic state. Prolonged
apathy in schizo-affective patients treated with ECT has been

clinically noted. This apathy is frequently responsive to
treatment with tricyclic antidepressants. Unfortunately
Mr. Huff did not have the benefit of such a therapeutic attempt.

This case raises a fine diagnostic distinction. Massive
fearfulness and delusional ideas of reference and persecution
are often found in prognostically poor fearful paranoids.
However, Mr. Huff's persecutory thoughts were conceived of
as punishment for his guilt, and his major affect was of depression and self-reproach. He felt himself to be a complete
failure, incapable and rejected. His persecutory ideation
was congruent with his lifelong conviction that those who
sin are punished. The fearful paranoid schizophrenic typically does not attribute the persecutory contempt of others
to his own defects, but rather sees himself as the unfortunate victim of a malign conspiracy. Thus, Mr. Huff should
have been considered schizophrenic, schizo-affective, depressed type. This diagnosis concurs with the good adolescent development, late age of onset, and acute florid illness. It also implies a better prognosis and response to
medication than does the diagnosis of fearful paranoid
schizophrenia. This case is an interesting illustration of
some of the subtleties in distinguishing sub-groups of
schizophrenics. These subtleties are not mere academic ex-
ercises but, as shown, have important prognostic and treatment implications (11-13,15,18,19,21,22).

PAUL ENGEL

PRESENTING PROBLEM
Paul Engel, 22 and single, was tall, sweet-faced, gentle
and shy. Two months prior to admission to Hillside, after
several years of increasing withdrawal, anxiety and inability
to communicate with anyone, he suffered an acute psychotic
episode while buying rubber-soled shoes. Feeling that these

shoes would enable him to bounce very high, he started jump-
ing up and down and suddenly felt transported back to his
boyhood neighborhood. The streets seemed empty of people,
and he thought he could bounce as high as the amazingly tall
buildings.

The police were called and he was taken to a city hospital. Although he had no memory of the events following the
episode, nor surrounding his entering the city psychiatric
hospital, he did remember feeling that every moment at the
hospital seemed like the beginning of his stay.

During the first five days of this hospitalization he
became withdrawn almost to the point of catatonia, and a
course of 22 ECT was instituted. He improved somewhat, although he remained confused. At his psychotherapist's suggestion, he sought more intensive psychiatric treatment and
was transferred to Hillside within two months. His diagnosis
while at the city hospital was pseudoneurotic schizophrenia
with transitory catatonic episode.

FAMILY

Paul was the youngest of three children of a lower middle
class Jewish family who lived in an extremely poor ghetto
area. The father was in his mid 60's and a salesman who had
worked hard all his life, six days a week, but supported his
family only marginally. He never had job security and lived
under the threat of being fired and/or not having enough money for necessities. Extremely stubborn, sarcastic and rigid,
he was unemotional, aloof from his family and rarely participated in their lives. He accepted no responsibility for management of the home. His life, which he characterized as a
vale of tears, revolved around working, coming home to eat
dinner, reading the newspaper and going to sleep. His family
was greatly surprised at his show of emotion concerning
Paul's illness.

Mrs. Engel, an attractive woman, was devoted to all her

children, but especially to Paul. Gentle, warm-hearted and intelligent, she was confused about Paul's illness, since her other children were healthy, well-adjusted and successfully married.

Paul idolized his brother, ten years his senior, and when he married and moved two blocks away, Paul felt deserted. Paul never got along well with his sister who was five years older; however, they became closer after she married.

DEVELOPMENTAL HISTORY

No birth or early developmental history was available. Paul was the baby and pet of the family and received much attention because he was both intelligent and adorable as a child. However, his brother reported that he was very shy and "odd, since he was a little boy." Although Paul was most intellectually endowed of the children, he realized less of his potential.

Paul stated that he was always unhappy because he was "over-protected but not recognized as an individual." He felt there was never "real" warmth or communication in his family, and the only way he could please and get attention was by excelling at school. His father and brother frequently questioned, criticized and ridiculed him about school work, even though their own accomplishments were negligible.

He attended public school for two and a half years, and at age eight, his parents transferred him to a religious school, that being the neighborhood pattern. He hated this school which required excessive time (six days a week) and work, and wanted to quit, but his rabbi persuaded him to remain. Paul claimed he had his first episode of "confusion" when he first entered religious school; he couldn't remember things and didn't know what to do with himself.

Later, he adjusted and skipped a full year. The schooling was very intense. Paul felt that he had to be outstand-

ing, and he was. Because of his schoolwork, he had little
time for anything else. He had few friends and was very
lonely. However, it was compensated for somewhat by his
closeness with his brother who spent time with him at every
opportunity. Because of Paul's precocity, quick wit and de-
lightful sense of humor, he was accepted and respected by
the brother's peers.

By the time he was 12, Paul was preoccupied with religion, far more than his parents had wished, and ambivalent
and uncomfortable because his training was more orthodox than
his home environment. In fact, his parents who had initially
forced him to attend religious school now requested that he
change to public school. However, Paul felt compelled to
continue at the parochial school, in spite of his unhappiness
there. Consistently, he felt inadequate and was obsessed
with the need to be perfect in order to gain approval.

He went on to a Talmudic high school, and with his
bright, creative thinking, his performance was excellent for
the first year. During this time he had been debating manager of his class. A situation arose where, because not enough
debaters were available, his class had to forfeit a match.
Paul became very upset that something horrible would happen
because he mismanaged the debate. The tremendous anxiety
associated with this incident carried over to his sophomore
year when he became depressed and his grades fell from the
high 90's to 70%. As if sleepwalking, he would find himself
in school, not knowing how he got there. Unable to concentrate, he also had no enthusiasm for anything. When a distant relative died during this period, he became preoccupied
with death and the differences between life and death. This
depression and confusion lasted almost an entire term, but
ended suddenly when one day he walked into the street, found
the sun shining and everything suddenly seemed brighter.

During high school he had several more periods of con-

fusion, although of lesser intensity. Consistently he feared
that people would realize he was a fraud and did not deserve
the good grades he attained. Nevertheless, his academic performance in high school was successful, if somewhat erratic,
and after graduating, he enrolled in a college engineering
program. His first semester's grades were A's and B's. But
the second semester he failed English and was so upset that
he took ten aspirin in a suicidal gesture. The intent and
circumstances of this act were not clear.

    At about this time Paul felt guilty about his recently
acquired masturbation, started at age 17. Sex seemed disgusting to him, and he feared that heterosexual relations
would somehow emasculate him; homosexual activities held no
interest.

    By age 19 he felt wholly inadequate, constantly musing
over what he was doing and what the future held. At the end
of the third semester he was no longer able to concentrate
or work and felt unable to pass any courses. Before final
exams, he took some saved money and ran away to Canada, returning home within two days, very upset and ashamed that he
had quit school. He returned to a previously held cashier's
job and shortly after switched to work as a supermarket delivery boy, a job from which he was fired for being too slow.
Then he attempted general office work from which he was fired
for "being in a fog and not knowing what to do." Following
these defeats, he withdrew from all activities except loafing
at home, daydreaming in the public library and occasional 15
mile walks. He felt empty, lost, inadequate and unable to
talk with anyone.

    An aunt prevailed upon him to enter psychotherapy, which
she paid for. The woman psychologist whom he saw twice weekly for a year and a half reported that his affect was blunted
and his thinking confused and retarded. There was no evidence of delusions or hallucinations. Physically, he appear-

ed neglected and unkempt, his hygiene and grooming were poor.

As he improved, the psychotherapist arranged for vocational counselling to help him move out of his isolation and
inactivity. At the time of the interest and aptitude testing
he became extremely anxious and then suffered the psychotic
episode which brought him to the city hospital and later to
Hillside.

PRESENTING CHARACTERISTICS

Mr. Engel seemed mildly depressed and showed little affect. Outstanding was his blocking in answering anamnestic
questions; this did not occur when responding to intellectual
queries. He also had extreme difficulty in recalling earlier
periods of his illness and remembered nothing of his catatonic episode. Mild ideas of reference and anger were elicited when he felt the hospital staff was picking on him by
requesting him to do chores. No delusions or hallucinations
were apparent although he fantasied actively about mystical
matters.

COURSE AT HILLSIDE

The results of all physical and neurological examinations, including the EEG, were normal. On the Wechsler-
Bellevue he attained a verbal IQ of 140, a performance IQ of
96 and a full scale IQ of 122.

At the hospital, Mr. Engel was generally quiet and withdrawn. While superficially sociable, he remained on the
fringe of groups. Often he was angry, suspicious and passive-aggressive; for example, he often came late for appointments and activities and complained of being discriminated
against by staff and patients.

Initially, he approached psychotherapy with enthusiasm,
but within a few weeks he felt let down by his doctor. During psychotherapy he had frequent periods of blocking, where
he appeared to be in a daze for several minutes. Often he
made requests or complaints, and if they were not acted upon

immediately, would sulk and act very angry. This was the
pattern he set with any potential friend or situation. It
seemed no one, including himself, could live up to his expectations of perfection. His doctor took a warm, permissive
approach and encouraged him to talk and ventilate his feelings.

Following his doctor's month's vacation, Mr. Engel suddenly burst forth with a flood of fears about castration,
jealousy, rage, hatred and sexual fantasies concerning his
mother and sister. Immediately following this, he withdrew
and was sloppy, rebellious and anxious.

After seven months of psychotherapy, his withdrawal,
anxiety, negativism and passive-aggressiveness increased to
such degree that he was entered into the drug program. In
interview he seemed retarded, somewhat perplexed, tangential
and allusive. He said that he had trouble sleeping because
he feared this would be when death would come. Also, he
contemplated suicide. On occasion he had disturbing fantasies about attacking others and at times felt completely
blank.

In the drug program he received Thorazine 300 mg daily,
increased 300 mg weekly until 1200 mg daily was reached, and
Kemadrin increased to 15 mg daily. During the first two
weeks, he complained about drowsiness but then became euphoric, feeling happy, even if sleepy. On the unit he was more
cooperative, participated more actively in social events and
was less negativistic.

By the time the Thorazine was raised to 1200 mg daily,
he was not as drowsy as previously and stated that the medication had enabled him to stand up and talk with people, concentrate better, feel more masculine and less irritable.
However, he mentioned that he was still preoccupied with
questions about death, and with why things happened the way
they did; occasionally he felt as if he were the only person

in the world.

After eight weeks, Mr. Engel complained about his mind
being muddled, and after ten weeks his doctor described him
as being moderately isolated, a bit depressed and a little
less active. Concerned that the medication might be obtund-
ing the patient, Thorazine was decreased to 900 mg daily and
a week later to 600 mg daily. After a week on 600 mg, he
seemed more anxious, apprehensive, distant, and unable to concentrate. He became increasingly lethargic and withdrawn.
A week later, Thorazine was increased to 1200 mg daily and he
became more relaxed but still mildly apathetic and withdrawn.
After a month on 1200 mg, he claimed that at times he felt
quite well, but that his mood fluctuated. His doctor reported that he showed markedly loose associations.

After four months on Thorazine, Tofranil 75 mg daily,
increased weekly by 75 mg until 300 mg daily was reached, was
added. By three weeks on this combined regimen Mr. Engel was
much more alert, felt better and seemed bright almost to euphoria; his hands shook considerably. He stated, "I'm doing
fine. I feel just great and want to do things, meet people
and talk to people."

On the whole, Mr. Engel made only limited cognitive
gains during his year at the hospital. Although no longer
withdrawn and depressed, his thinking remained vague and un-
focused. His doctor felt that no more could be expected and
discharge plans were made. He was released on a drug schedule of daily doses of Thorazine 1200 mg, Kemadrin 15 mg, and
Tofranil 300 mg.

He was to be seen daily in an after-care facility and
weekly in private psychotherapy with his original psychotherapist. His hospital diagnosis was schizophrenic reaction, mixed catatonic-paranoid; the research diagnosis was
schizo-affective psychosis, retarded, perplexed, probably cycloid.

FOLLOW-UP

Mr. Engel returned home and lived with his parents for 18 months. They supported him financially; he functioned at a minimal level, working as a stock clerk. He saw a psychologist regularly for psychotherapy and remained on medication the entire time. (No specific information about medication type or dosage was available.) He had no relapses but went along marginally, with somatic complaints (unexplained) and occasional grandiose delusions which he verbalized freely.

A year and a half after discharge, he entered a city general hospital with intermittent fever, joint pain and swelling, of three months duration. Treatment included penicillin injections and salicylates, until, within a day or two, he developed fainting spells. A spinal tap was normal. Psychiatric consultation was held and a diagnosis of salicylate intoxication was entertained when the salicylate level in his blood was found to be 30 mg. Within a few more days, he became unresponsive, tachycardiac, hypotensive and died. Arterial blood pH was moderately acidotic.

Autopsy revealed, "widespread focal and confluent pulmonary hemorrhage with 300 cc blood in stomach, severe widespread focal necroses of the liver and severe metabolic acidosis. Also, there was focal degeneration of cartilage at the joint capsules, splenomegaly and generalized lymphadenopathy. It was considered that he died in acidosis secondary to salicylate toxicity, perhaps iatrogenically-induced." The prior suicidal gesture with salicylates did not lead to a determination of suicide.

COMMENT

In contrast to Mr. Huff, Mr. Engel showed a much earlier onset of illness. There is some question as to whether he did not have personality distortion even as a young child. From early life he was perfectionistic and self-reproachful.

He showed episodic confusion and loss of academic ability
during high school, perhaps indicating the onset of a periodic illness. He then developed a retarded depressive picture.
However his illness was not purely affective,as in psychotherapy his thinking was confused and his affect was considered blunted rather than depressed. His acute psychotic episode occurred in the context of an elated mood.

He proved refractory to psychotherapy but responded moderately well to Thorazine. There is a frequent misconception
that the aliphatic phenothiazines should not be given to retarded, perplexed schizophrenics. But,in fact, the opposite
is true; aliphatic phenothiazines are peculiarly appropriate
for such patients. However, after a period of treatment with
Thorazine, some patients evince a moderate apathy which can
in turn be handled by adjunctive Tofranil (16).

It is often not recognized that Thorazine has a markedly
activating value for retarded, perplexed schizo-affectives.
Therefore, after a period of successful treatment with Thorazine, it is frequently reduced in dosage with a consequent
exacerbation of the retardation. At this point, a common
mistake is to continue reducing the Thorazine, misunderstanding the increase in psychotic retardation as a medication effect. The medication reduction then eventuates in a loss of
control over the psychosis.

The distinguishing features of Mr. Engel's illness,
which demarcate him from Mr. Huff, are the early age of onset, demonstrated to be a poor prognostic sign within the
class of "reactive" schizophrenias (28), his marked cognitive
difficulty in the form of recurrent confusional episodes,
persistent vagueness and inability to resume a socially productive role.

His fatal outcome, as with Mr. Richfield, is obscure;
however, it should be noted that suicide is a common outcome
for the depressed schizo-affective patient. This is under-

standable in view of the high aspirations, depressed mood
and confused delusional thinking.

PEGGY PARKS

PRESENTING PROBLEM

　　Peggy Parks was 24 years old, married, with three children. Two months earlier she became immersed in pervasive
fantasies that she was having an affair with a famous movie
star whom her husband resembled. In love with this star since
age 16, she daydreamed of sexual relations with him. The
fantasies became increasingly realistic, and finally, believing the star was watching her from an adjacent roof, a "presence" on her shoulder compelled her to parade nude in front
of her window. At least daily she hallucinated his voice or
her own, coming either from outside or her shoulder. When
alone she conversed with the voice and made love with him.
In addition, severe throbbing headaches and eye pains troubled her. Extremely labile, she alternated between violent
temper outbursts and relaxed, over-permissive behavior with
her children. Socially, she was very uncomfortable, suspect-
ing people of watching and talking about her.

　　Suddenly, she began fearing that her husband would beat
her. Unable to care for her children since she was constantly screaming at and hitting them, and too panicky to remain
at home, she entered a city hospital on an emergency basis.
Here she was diagnosed as having paranoid schizophrenia and
after three weeks was admitted to Hillside, for intensive
psychiatric care.

FAMILY

　　Mrs. Parks' father, a drifter, deserted his wife and only child when she was one year old,and there was no further
contact with him. She knew nothing of her father and refused
to listen when her mother spoke of him. However, she often
fantasied that he was a brilliant brain surgeon and that she

lived with him in a huge house.

Mrs. Parks described her mother as a quiet, nice person who was warm to others but never showed her own child any affection. Her mother worked full-time as a waitress. The mother and daughter maintained occasional, superficial contact with other family members, but no close or lasting relationships were established. The mother died of cancer when Mrs. Parks was 22.

Mrs. Parks' husband, two years older than herself, worked as a clerk and attended night school. She described him as being logical, practical, understanding, intelligent, with a good sense of humor. Always shy, he was very close to his wife, the only girl he ever dated, and felt that their marriage was ideal, with an intimacy of shared thoughts and wishes. He claimed that his wife was the only woman he could ever love and found her most attractive. Over the five years of marriage they had three children, a girl and two boys, ages 4, 2 and 10 months.

DEVELOPMENTAL HISTORY

Information concerning Mrs. Parks' childhood was scarce because she remembered very little. She lived with her mother who was rarely at home,and from an early age was self-reliant but lonely. Her mother told her that she was a good baby,but that until age 10 she had frequent temper tantrums. She was enuretic until age 12.

As a child she had friends and got along well with people, although usually she was quiet and shy. Well-liked by teachers and peers, she attended Catholic school for four years and subsequently attended public school. Her school performance was good.

At age nine she initiated masturbation, associated with marked guilt feelings and later with the fantasy of sexual relations with the movie star. She eagerly awaited her menarche, at age 15, having learned about it from her girlfriends.

At about this time, she began having difficulty concentrating and felt a "presence" on her shoulder. Suddenly, at
age 16, she started disregarding her school work, playing
truant, spending her time at a friend's house, watching TV,
reading or sleeping and finally quitting high school. At 16
she also had her first delusional meeting with the movie
star, which she firmly believed took place and described in
explicit detail. After leaving school she attempted many
different office jobs lasting from one to six months, but always found herself unable to concentrate or work properly;
mounting tension caused her to quit each job. Between jobs
she spent long unemployed periods idling about the house.

Peggy refused dates claiming she was afraid of boys,
but at 18, she accepted a date with her future husband, a
shy, reticent neighborhood boy whom she had known since age
nine. They married six weeks after their first date. Prior
to marriage she had had no heterosexual experiences. Once
married, she found that she had less sexual desire than her
husband, and made a game of trying to avoid his advances.
Occasionally she enjoyed sexual relations with him.

Mrs. Parks became pregnant very soon after marriage and
was most upset about it. Her husband was overseas, in the
Army, when she gave birth. She had great difficulty caring
for her daughter alone and had violent temper outbursts with
the infant, hitting her often. When the baby was a few
months old the family was reunited in Europe. After a year,
Mrs. Parks' mother became terminally ill. She returned to
nurse her mother for several months until her death.

While her behavior with the first baby became steadily
worse, she nevertheless wanted another child, became pregnant
and readily accepted the second child. Taking care of her
new baby boy was much easier since her husband was with her

to share the responsibility. In a short while she accidentally became pregnant for a third time and tried too late to
have an abortion. Finally she resigned herself to another
child. It was late in this pregnancy that she lost all sexual interest in her husband. Her second boy, born with a
blood disorder, aroused considerable guilt in her, and became her favorite child.

During the months following the birth of her third
child, Mrs. Parks' affect became increasingly labile, until
it was no longer safe to leave the children in her care.
After an argument where her husband threatened to leave her,
she suddenly "remembered" her earlier meeting with the movie
star and began believing that she was the victim of someone
who cast a spell over her. "I have weird, disgusting, dirty
sex thoughts which I myself could never have." She began
fearing people, felt she didn't belong, and was unable to
make any decisions about even the most minor choices, such as
whether to smoke a cigarette. She had intrusive delusions
about her father having raped her as a child, leaving her
dirty and unlovable.

PRESENTING CHARACTERISTICS

Mrs. Parks, tall, slender and attractive, was apathetic,
withdrawn and isolated. She responded appropriately to questions, spoke very slowly and softly, and with logical pro-
gression in association of ideas. However, she often spoke
with unnecessarily detailed description, especially in describing her delusional sexual encounters. She seemed sad,
worried and confused and stated, "I think I have a mental
problem. I feel I'm several different people. My moods
change constantly from one extreme to another. Sometimes I
feel as if I don't belong anywhere and don't care about anything. Yet there are times when things are clear and I know
who I am. Sometimes I'm shy and other times I do shocking
things like walking naked in front of a window, hoping that

someone is watching; whereas other times I can't undress in
front of my husband." She denied hallucinations, but spoke
about a "presence" which directed her to do things she
didn't wish to do, and although she tried to fight it, she
inevitably succumbed. She was well aware that she needed
psychiatric care.

COURSE AT HILLSIDE

All physical and neurological examinations, including
her EEG, were within normal limits. Her Wechsler-Bellevue
full scale IQ was 106, with a verbal IQ of 103 and a performance IQ of 110.

Mrs. Parks made a satisfactory adjustment to the hospital routine, feeling greatly relieved that she would be
helped. Usually she remained isolated but at times participated in some organized activities and was superficially
friendly with other female patients.

An intensive supportive psychotherapy and activity program was begun and within two months she was no longer delusional. There was no evidence of psychotic thinking and
she seemed markedly improved. Slowly her relationships with
other patients improved. She became relaxed, less formal, more
cheerful and optimistic. However, her relationship with her
husband deteriorated further. Her weekly visits with him
were unpleasant and she requested that he not visit her.
She vented feelings about having to give up her autonomy and
live under his domination and had great ambivalence about
returning to her home and family.

After six months she was placed in the drug program because her doctor felt she remained apathetic, depressed, and
unable to attain pleasure from anything. Started on placebo
medication, she showed no improvement, although at times she
was alert and active. When re-evaluated after six weeks,
Mrs. Parks said she was essentially unchanged and that she
sometimes had suicidal thoughts.

To allow a precise estimate of drug effect, she was placed on Tofranil 75 mg daily without her being aware of the
change. It was raised to 150 mg daily in the second week.
Immediately she looked less tense, was friendly, relaxed,
felt well and began looking forward to leaving the hospital.
She was discharged the third week, on Tofranil 150 mg daily,
after being hospitalized for 7½ months. Her hospital diagnosis was paranoid schizophrenia; the research diagnosis was
schizo-affective psychosis, depressed type.

FOLLOW-UP

On discharge Mrs. Parks returned to live with her husband and children. After three visits to the after-care
clinic she discontinued, took no further medication and resumed her full activities as a housewife. At the end of the
second year, she suffered what seemed like a depression,
where she stopped caring for the children and just sat and
did nothing. She had no delusions. Recovery from this relapse was spontaneous and in less than a month.

At the end of the post-hospital year she was functioning at a high level, caring for a newly purchased home, children, husband and herself.

Seven years after hospitalization, her husband contacted
Hillside, hoping to gain a therapeutic abortion for his wife.
He reported that she had received short-term out-patient care
several times during the seven years and, in general, was
functioning very well; "the best that she had ever been."
This pregnancy was unwanted and both were eager to terminate
it. Because it was not possible to arrange an abortion, she
had to carry through the pregnancy. When contacted ten years
after hospitalization, Mrs. Parks was living with her husband
and four children and doing part-time factory work. She took
Stelazine 10 mg and Artane 6 mg daily, prescribed by a psychiatrist whom she saw infrequently. Her mood was happy, and
she hoped to continue as she was, in the future.

COMMENT

The diagnosis in this case is somewhat clouded since almost the entire history depended on the patient's delusionally distorted recollections. Although she was considered schizo-affective, her psychosis occurred within the framework of very marked emotional lability rather than the more typical prolonged, retarded-perplexed depression or manic excitement.

At the time that she entered the drug program, her psychosis was no longer manifest and she presented only a moderate depression. At this point in her illness, she appeared responsive to Tofranil after having shown no response to placebo. Whether Tofranil would have been an effective antipsychotic for her remains a moot point.

The follow-up also resembles that of a periodic affective disorder rather than a schizophrenia. It is not clear to what degree her maintained health was due to the prophylactic medication that she irregularly received.

SYBIL BASALT

PRESENTING PROBLEM

Sybil Basalt was 21, divorced and the mother of a two year old daughter. About one month before entering Hillside, she and her boyfriend took a weekend vacation. Suddenly, she became anxious, panicky and fearful. After a quarrel, her boyfriend returned to the city while she remained at the hotel. After he left she heard his voice and "felt his presence." She experienced an overwhelming urge to enter every hotel room, forcing the lock when a door wouldn't yield. Crying and shouting, she begged the manager to find her boyfriend. Finally a physician sedated her and called her mother who arrived the next day and took Mrs. Basalt to a community hospital.

There, she was "markedly agitated and her speech was
pressured, circumstantial, illogical but understandable.
Her affect was inappropriate and her mood neutral." She was
diagnosed as having acute undifferentiated schizophrenia and
treated with Thorazine 400 mg daily. Within a week she
showed "remarkable restitution and related in an affable,
direct manner. Her speech was logical, coherent and relevant," but she requested a continued "rest" rather than returning to her mother's home. Thus, she was referred for
hospitalization at Hillside.

FAMILY

Sybil's father, a Catholic, had had several psychiatric
hospitalizations because of alcoholism, emotional problems
and abusive rages toward his wife. The parents were divorced when Sybil was eight years old, and the father was
forbidden to see his two daughters because of his obnoxious
behavior. Sybil had not seen him for ten years. However,
she described him with warm, loving feeling. Although he
was moody, selfish and easily enraged, he had been fun to be
with and Sybil had been his favored child.

The mother was Jewish, in her early 40's, industrious,
energetic, domineering, meddling and perfectionistic. She
found her first husband intolerable, and often needed police
protection from his harassment and abuse. Divorced after
ten years of marriage and without financial support, she had
to work to support her two daughters.

Sybil was highly ambivalent concerning her mother. At
times she expressed positive, loving sentiments and at times
she was filled with rancor toward her, blaming her for her
problems. She identified extremely closely with her mother,
stating "I swallowed her image." Six years after divorcing,
the mother remarried another Catholic, 20 years her senior,
and they had two more children. Sybil was fond of the step-

father who was kind, affectionate, understanding and dominated by his wife.

Sybil's 17 year old sister, described as very intelligent, artistic and moody, was hospitalized with an unde-
scribed "nervous breakdown," received ECT and later was rehospitalized in a chronic ward at a state hospital.

Two other half sibs from the second marriage were an
11 year old boy who had attempted suicide, and a 6 year old
girl.

DEVELOPMENTAL HISTORY

Sybil was born normally, at full term, but was jaundiced. A good baby, with no problems, she walked, talked
and was toilet-trained by the end of the first year. She
remembered her mother being pregnant with her sister when she
was 3. Her father later told her that her mother had tried
to abort this sister.

At age five, she started school, and was bright, earned good grades and showed no difficulties. Sybil vividly recalled her unhappy childhood, checkered with frequent fights
between her parents, shuttled back and forth between camps,
boarding schools, living with various relatives and appearing
in court. A singular pleasant memory concerned a two month
stay with her paternal grandmother. She also remembered
stealing "pretty things, like jewelry. I always wanted what
I couldn't have. I felt like an orphan." After her parents
divorced, her father quickly remarried. Sybil liked her father's new wife but was forbidden to see them because of her
father's misbehavior. Her mother remarried when Sybil was
14.

Menarche was at age 12. She had been prepared for it
by conversations with her mother. During junior high school,
her grades, which previously had been consistently good, began to fluctuate sharply. Thus, within a brief period, in
the same course, she could vacillate between 30% and 90%.

During this period she became preoccupied with her appearance and clothes, whereas previously she had been sloppy and overweight. Through rigid, self-imposed dieting she returned to normal weight.

For several years she became deeply interested in Catholicism, took religious instruction and observed devoutly. Subsequently, her sister joined her in this pursuit. Sybil's interest waned but her sister continued with ever-increasing fervor, until her breakdown.

In the middle of her senior year, Sybil quit school to work and ease the financial burden at home, for her stepfather's business was doing poorly. She proved a good and diligent worker and progressed quickly from file clerk to secretary. During this time she dated often, and when at age 19 she became pregnant, she forced the boy to marry her, against his wishes. He was irresponsible, sadistic, beat her frequently and tried to run her down with a car. They separated and divorced after eight weeks of marriage. She returned to her mother's home to live, had a baby daughter whom the mother cared for, and returned to her secretarial job. After the birth Sybil would frequently daydream, fearing that she would trip and fall while carrying the baby, thereby killing it. These fears subsided after several months.

She dated several men and fell in love with a fellow whom she wished to marry. However, while he was kind and affectionate, he did not respond to her marriage plans, and she suspected that he dated other women. Sybil also greatly resented the attention he paid to her sister, who spent long hours talking to him while "half-clothed." Her mother felt he had no intention of marrying Sybil.

Then, the sister had a breakdown and was hospitalized. Sybil became frightened and preoccupied that she also would have a nervous breakdown. Her identification with her sister intensified so that when the sister stopped wearing shoes, so did Sybil. She adopted her sister's mannerism of staring at objects for long periods to make sure that they did not change or drip with blood. Sybil, now 21, intensified her social life, worked overtime frequently, became increasingly tense, irritable, anxious, had insomnia, and began fearing that people were following her, causing her continually to glance over her shoulder. She wore sunglasses to avoid being recognized. After a few sleepless nights she went on the weekend trip which led to her subsequent hospitalization.

PRESENTING CHARACTERISTICS

On entering Hillside, Sybil's most striking symptom was emotional lability. She vacillated between happiness and despair, with anger, irritability, fear, boastfulness, sadness and confusion, all keeping pace with her racing thoughts. In interview she was coherent but rambled on in a markedly circumstantial, tangential, inconsequential manner. Also she had facial grimacing which detracted from her notable attractiveness. While she claimed to have had auditory hallucinations of her boyfriend's, sister's and own voices, if persistently questioned for details she would deny them. During episodes of panic she complained of "German Nazi planes flying overhead and they may drop bombs, I'm worried about nuclear warfare." When questioned about this, she seemed aware of her irrationality. Frequently she play acted as an actress or dancer and then became scared that she really believed it. Often she felt unreal and would have to touch her face to feel the contours of the bones under the skin. She became obsessed with keeping her belongings neat. Grandiosely she stated, "I'm a genius. I told my mother that her children were creative geniuses." Her intelligence seemed above average, but she presented concrete interpretations of proverbs; i.e., "a rolling stone

gathers no moss" was interpreted as "if a stone is travelling it won't pick up moss."

<u>COURSE</u> <u>AT</u> <u>HILLSIDE</u>

    The results of all physical and neurological examina-
tions were within normal limits, except for the EEG which
showed some generalized slowing. Her Wechsler-Bellevue IQ
score was 106, with both verbal and performance IQs of 106.

    Sybil entered the hospital acting pleasant and sociable.
The Thorazine she had been receiving during her previous
hospitalization was withdrawn and by the next day she was
"overhearing things about Russia"; by the second evening she
was screaming and throwing things. During the first week of
hospitalization she became progressively more uncooperative,
was extremely fearful, tearful, had attacks of panic and
anxiety, was afraid to be alone, pleaded for help, and talked about Nazi bombings. Over a four day span, during a panic when she became extremely unmanageable and demanding of
attention, she was repeatedly placed in seclusion. Here she
cried, grimaced, smiled inappropriately, walked about nude
and was tormented by "whistling noises." When not having
"an attack" she remained very labile.

    Tofranil was instituted during her second week of hos-
pitalization at 75 mg daily, with weekly 75 mg increments to
a maximum of 300 mg daily. Initially she appeared much improved,with considerably tighter associations, but after two
weeks, she regressed and looked poorly. Again, her speech
was pressured and circumstantial, she had to urinate every
five minutes, was gagging, had a pain in her side and lungs
and felt as if her brain would explode. Her tongue was
burning, she constantly had to drink water and her teeth
felt like electric shocks. However, she remained on the
medication. Slowly her complaints lessened and she became
outgoing, gregarious and made many friends. She joined many
activities and was particularly happy to see her mother and

boyfriend who both showed considerable interest in her welfare. While her mood swings became less pronounced, she
still remained labile. Finally, after ten weeks on Tofranil,
she begged to be taken off medication because of her dry
mouth, occasional nausea, itching tongue and nine pound
weight gain. Tofranil was reduced and discontinued over a
two week period during which she maintained her significant
improvement and optimistic euphoria.

     She was released from Hillside after four months, with-
out medication. At the time of discharge she was elated,
exhilarated, confident and showed no evidence of hallucinations or delusions. Her plans included returning to her
same secretarial job, establishing her own apartment and
hopefully marrying her boyfriend within the year. The hospital diagnosis was acute schizophrenic reaction, schizo-affective type; the research diagnosis concurred with schizo-
affective disorder, manic, excited type, probably cycloid.
FOLLOW-UP

     After discharge from Hillside, Sybil returned to her
job and attended the after-care clinic for six months. She
appeared rather depressed and anxious, was lonely living in
her own apartment and seemed envious of her sister who had
deteriorated to the point of being in a state hospital
chronic ward. Her after-care doctor placed her on Thorazine
200 mg daily,which she discontinued after one week, complaining of side effects. After six months, when therapy at the
clinic was terminated, she became upset and took an overdose
of pills from which she recovered spontaneously.

     After working for nine months, she decided people at
work were treating her differently than before she was hospitalized, and she left the job. She took a two month vacation and then found another job at which she worked for
several months until she became pregnant from a casual relationship. Hillside referred her to a private psychiatrist

whom she saw for six weeks. He reinstituted Thorazine 100
to 300 mg daily,which she discontinued after six weeks with
no noticeable change. She had the baby, placed it for adoption and then returned to her mother's home where she lived
with her daughter and sister who had been released from the
state hospital.

In the third year post-hospitalization she attended a
city hospital outpatient service for seven months. Parnate
and Stelazine were prescribed but were not considered helpful, neither was a three week trial of Tofranil (dosages unknown). When seen in follow-up interview, Sybil felt inadequate and unable to be gainfully employed. No blatant
pathology was shown. She seemed elated but with inferred
underlying depression. No further follow-up was obtainable.

COMMENT

This patient apparently showed an unremarkable pre-ad-
olescent development, as is typical of schizo-affective patients, in spite of extraordinary family stresses. During
adolescence, cognitive, affective and achievement lability
became manifest. Illness onset was apparently precipitated
by her sister's illness and then acutely exacerbated by her
boyfriend's abandonment. Object loss and bereavement seem
to be particularly potent precipitants for these illnesses,
relating them to the affective disorders.

Of particular interest was her good response to Tofranil. Here,too,one is led to wonder whether the schizo-affective illness does not share some common pathophysiologi-
cal link with the affective disorders. We have shown, in a
double-blind study of schizo-affectives, that Tofranil is
superior to placebo, although not as effective as Thorazine (13). The similarities between the course of manic-
depressive and schizo-affective illness as well as some similarities in their medication response lead to the postula-
tion that they share a similar impairment in self-regulation

of activation and affective states (9,14).

Her long term poor social outcome seems primarily related to her marked dependent trends and secondary demoralization, rather than a cognitive or affective deterioration.
Such patients require long term after-care contacts that will
reach out to them and ensure proper counselling, support and
rehabilitation. Medication is not the central issue at this
point in the illness course. Unfortunately, such facilities
do not exist, with consequent personal tragedy as well as
increased social welfare costs and decreased social productivity: a fine example of social myopia.

Chapter III

CHILDHOOD ASOCIAL SCHIZOPHRENIA

Definition

These patients show fragmented, vague, over-concrete and/or over-abstract thinking and often deny their illness. They are evasive, guarded, perplexed and fearful, with speech so loosely structured that communication is difficult. They are frightened rather than angry or depressed, and on close questioning show vague delusions, peculiar sexual ideation, poorly defined ideas of reference and autistic preoccupations. Although these features are regularly present, they are often overshadowed by paranoid statements, bizarre or eccentric behavior, or non-compliance.

The diagnosis depends on the outstanding history of early, extreme social deviance. As children, these patients were aloof, cold, asocial and eccentric. Some had restless hyperactivity and low frustration tolerance. If they attempted to join their peers, they behaved ineptly and eccentrically so that they were frequently ostracized and made scapegoats. Scholastic difficulty was prominent.

In the usual nosology they might be referred to as paranoid, simple or hebephrenic schizophrenics, depending on the transient, salient symptomatology. This group is the most treatment refractory and has the poorest overall prognosis.

BETH SILVER

PRESENTING PROBLEM

Beth Silver, a robust appearing, fairly attractive, 17 year old, began behaving strangely in her 16th year. She abandoned her previous superficial relationships, and acquaintances remarked that her talk was odd. She became increasingly disorganized, ruminated about feelings of emptiness and inability to make decisions, was unable to concentrate in order to complete her school work, and worked at it until 2 or 3 A.M.

Her parents contacted a psychologist whom she saw three times a week (she had seen one the previous year). He felt she was suffering from "an exacerbation of a long-standing chronic schizophrenic disorder" and found that "any pressure from the environment elicited classic evidence of psychotic regression, including feelings of unreality, feelings that she had a great mission in life and that she could accomplish anything given only the time."

Although her grades were poor, she graduated from high school. When the stress of school was removed, her strange behavior began to recede. She seemed sociable and showed good insight into her behavior of the previous months, accurately analyzing her dependent, unsatisfactory relationship with her parents. The psychologist felt that it was in Beth's best interest to separate from her parents and continue therapy, and thus recommended inpatient treatment at Hillside. Beth herself made the initial contacts with the hospital.

FAMILY

The Silvers were wealthy, upper-middle class, Jewish, and lived in an expensive home, in a fashionable suburb. The father was a markedly successful, egocentric, grandiose, labile, impulsive, angry businessman who married his wife only after she became pregnant with Beth and found an abortion

difficult to obtain. He was 40 at the time. When Beth was
7, he lost much money in business, became depressed and made
repeated suicidal threats and attempts. He received a
course of ECT at this time and then went on a nine month
cruise with a male friend. When he returned he entered and
remained in psychotherapy for five years. He contemplated
entering Hillside for psychiatric treatment,but this plan was
not realized when he had to receive extensive emergency
stomach surgery.

Mr. Silver was neutral in his feelings toward his
daughter, yet demanded immediate and implicit obedience from
her, lecturing and criticizing her behavior. At times he
would encourage her to reject all intellectual pursuits and
hedonistically enjoy life by quitting school and concentrating on swimming and horseback riding. Beth often felt that
if she could live up to her father's recommendations and expectations, all her problems would disappear.

Mrs. Silver, ten years younger than her husband, was a
passive, disorganized, thin, drawn, haggard woman. She
worked as a saleslady and studied psychology at night school
until her pregnancy and marriage at age 30. Mrs. Silver was
very ambivalent concerning her daughter. At times she was
kind and concerned about her welfare, but most often she was
angry, openly rejecting, taunting and deprecating, making
demeaning puns at Beth's expense; her favorite, "You are a
Miss Fit, Miss Fortune." Often she reminded her that she
wished Beth was never born. Outwardly, Beth seemed to be
able to withstand these attacks and excused her mother, in-
tellectualizing that "the woman has problems."

A brother, 15 months younger than Beth, was born prematurely after his mother fell down a flight of stairs. He
remained in the hospital for two months. He was described
by his mother, father and sister as outstanding in school,
with many social accomplishments and conspicuously well ad-

justed. However, he was consistently and openly abusive and
sadistic toward Beth, paralleling the mother's behavior.

The Silvers' marriage was stormy from the start, punctuated by frequent fights concerning Mrs. Silver's indecisiveness, passivity and sexual inadequacy. Mrs. Silver saw a
social worker for marital counselling when Beth was 4 and
later when she was 16. Both husband and wife travelled ex-
tensively, but separately, while the two children were at
summer camp. Six months before Beth came to Hillside, the
parents moved to separate bedrooms. While both considered
legal separation, they also realized that it was unlikely
they would pursue it.

DEVELOPMENTAL HISTORY

After considerations of an abortion were dropped, Beth
was born normally, at full term. Breast fed for several
months and then weaned to a bottle, she became a "terrible
feeding problem" and refused all solid food until 18 months.
Her motor development was normal. Her brother was born prematurely, and came home to live when Beth was 17 months old.
From the beginning Beth was jealous of him and tried to hurt
him by throwing things at him or hitting him.

By the time Beth was 2½, her parents were concerned a-
bout her "unrelatedness," her resistance to change and her
dislike of going any place. However, they contradicted
themselves by also describing her as an enthusiastic child
who played energetically and adjusted well to other children
(almost certainly a falsification).

At age 5 her mother enrolled her at a progressive private school where she remained until age 12. During these
years her mother reported that her grades were all A's
(N.B.). She had many acquaintances but no "real chums." Her
mother claimed that she was usually preoccupied with fantasies (unexplained) but they did not interfere with her school
work. She spent summers at camp. Beth had the usual child-

hood illnesses between ages 5 and 7.

When Beth was 7, her father developed the severe depression described above. Beth remembered little about it,
except feeling that if her father was depressed, she also
should feel depressed. She found it difficult to believe
that as intelligent, active and strong a person as her father could possibly be ill.

Later that year she started play therapy for her
"unrelatedness," continued several times weekly for the next
three years and then intermittently for three years longer.
At age 8½, while her mother was touring and Beth was at summer camp, Beth had an emergency appendectomy. She begged
the camp officials not to inform her mother for fear of upsetting her. At age 10, she was enrolled in a doctor's
class for prepubertal girls, to learn about sexual function
and menstruation. Her menarche was at age 13.

The Silvers decided to move to a wealthy suburb when
Beth was 12. Beth was very upset at having to leave her old
neighborhood and school and enter the notoriously competitive atmosphere of this suburb. During her second semester
at the new school she received a D for the first time. Also,
she started having trouble concentrating and felt that her
friends were functioning better than she. From 10th grade
on, she received almost all D's.

Socially, Beth was a compliant hanger-on, a fringe member of the group. Her activities conformed to her friends';
if they took piano or tennis lessons, so did she; but in no
activity was she truly absorbed or excellent. Her friends
and brother uniformly surpassed her and she felt belittled
and inadequate. Her attachments became more superficial and
her behavior grew highly disorganized. She found it inordinately difficult to do her homework and would beg her
mother to complete her assignments. If mother did the work
well, Beth would feel satisfaction; if the work was poor,

she would reproach her mother. Always, she was fearful that her teachers would discover this deception.

Eventually, Beth began to complain that she had no identity, that she was merely an extension of her mother and that she was "nebulous." She dated rarely and realistically felt that boys who asked her out did so only because they were friends of the family, although she was robust and physically attractive.

At age 15, she suffered infectious mononucleosis and made a very slow recovery, remaining quite depressed and withdrawn, complaining of fatigue and lack of interest. Her parents sent her to a psychologist whom she saw in treatment for eight months, until her summer vacation. That vacation was most satisfactorily spent at a summer stock theater where she thoroughly enjoyed amateur dramatics. However, when she returned home, she behaved strangely, again entered treatment and was referred to Hillside.

PRESENTING CHARACTERISTICS

During the intake interview, Beth was cooperative, had a facade of sophistication and maintained a pleasant facial expression with a fixed smile. Her affect was shallow, her mien depressed, although she expressed optimism and denied difficulty. Her speech was often disorganized, vague and circumstantial; she had considerable difficulty maintaining a consecutive line of thought and would abandon statements in mid-sentence to launch new topics. On occasion she had thought disappearance.

While her acute symptoms had abated, Beth still obsessed over her lack of identity and feelings of depersonalization, feeling chameleon-like and nebulous, that she continually changed to suit other people, and that she herself was nothing and didn't exist. She claimed that she was merely an extension of her mother (and born to be the target of her hostility). She considered herself a psychic since she could sense other people's feelings by intuition.

COURSE AT HILLSIDE

The results of all physical examinations, including her
EEG, were negative. On the Wechsler-Bellevue, she achieved
a full scale IQ of 107, a verbal scale IQ of 110 and a performance IQ of 101, with wide subtest score scatter. Her
judgmental ability showed gross fluctuation from good clear
thinking to highly autistic logic. For example, her response
to what she would do if lost in a forest was "get direction
from the sun, but if there were no sun I might dig a hole
and follow the water." The psychological test battery offered inadequate information to draw any conclusions about the
possibility of organicity.

Beth quickly made contact with other patients at the
hospital, commenting unrealistically that she was able to
adapt to new experiences easily; in social situations she
was always the listener and follower. Because in interview
she seemed relatively intact, it was astonishing to observe
her great difficulty in caring for herself because of gross
confusion. Despite earnest attempts at cooperation she
would forget which room was hers, where she left her possessions and when her hospital appointments were scheduled.

A carefully structured program was established and attempts were made to help her adhere strictly to her schedule.
She was placed in art therapy and many physical activities
in order to supply non-verbal outlets for expression. Psychotherapy was non-exploratory and ego-supportive, with persistent efforts to help her organize herself, clarify and
find expression for her anger and strengthen her reality
testing. The therapist took a protective, directive, en-
couraging role.

After two months of hospitalization her lack of progress led to her referral to the drug program where she re-

ceived Thorazine 300 mg daily, plus Kemadrin 3.75 mg daily,
with weekly increments of Thorazine 300 mg and Kemadrin 3.75
mg to a maximum of Thorazine 1200 mg and Kemadrin 15 mg.
Within three days she stated she could concentrate better,
was more organized and less absent-minded and scatter-brain-
ed. However, she felt tired, had a stuffed nose and was
dizzy. Ten days after start of treatment she was receiving
Thorazine 600 mg daily and appeared extremely lethargic, muddled and depressed, with many somatic complaints. These
symptoms continued for two more weeks at which time she was
receiving Thorazine 1200 mg daily. She slowly felt less
tired but very weak and drained, with a vibrating sensation
in her stomach. A week later the vibration stopped and she
felt more relaxed, but two weeks later her combination of
complaints (lethargy, drowsiness, dizziness, restlessness,
shaky hands), made her beg to discontinue the medication.

However, during the six weeks on Thorazine her performance gradually improved and she was able to attend all activities and think more coherently. The staff concluded that
Thorazine helped accentuate previous adaptive mechanisms of
denial and minimization but increased her somatic complaints
to an intolerable level, making continued treatment unfeasi-
ble. She was weaned from Thorazine and a few days later
placed on Tofranil 75 mg daily.

After five days on Tofranil, she felt much better, more
alive, but still forgetful. Her somatic complaints disappeared. The Tofranil was increased weekly by 75 mg until a
total dose of 300 mg daily was reached. During this entire
period she had no somatic complaints and was pleasant, but
remained disorganized and forgetful.

Two months after starting Tofranil, Beth had a possible
grand mal seizure. An EEG taken within half an hour of the
seizure showed nonspecific changes compatible with a post
ictal state. Since there was no clear response to Tofranil,

it was reduced to 150 mg and discontinued within two weeks, with no apparent change in her chronically disorganized behavior. A repeat EEG, taken after all medication was stopped, was normal and no different from her pre-treatment EEG.

During these first seven months of hospitalization, Beth underwent a minimal, gradual improvement, seeming somewhat better organized, less anxious, and able to express resentment toward her parents with some affect. She remained emotionally isolated from other patients, although she was an active participant and willing worker at any highly structured activity that the hospital permitted her.

At the end of this first period, because of prodding from her parents, she demanded to be allowed to participate in either the newspaper or creative therapy program, insisting that she needed to meet the challenge provided by these activities so as to assure herself of her intellectual capability. Because these activities were fairly unstructured, her therapist was reluctant to let her participate, but after exerting much pressure, she finally was allowed to join. Quickly she became confused and compulsively insistent about completing her duties, although unable to perform them within a reasonable amount of time (the same problem she had suffered with her school work). Shortly, her entire activity program was disrupted, and she became remote, guarded, defensive and fearful of her doctor, turning her head in order to avoid him in the hall and missing many psychotherapy sessions. Still she insisted that she needed no assistance, meanwhile becoming more clumsy, inept and disorganized. Each weekend at home she made plans for independent activities, and each weekend required her mother's total support.

After two months more of this aimless activity, it was felt that Beth was not benefiting from the hospital program and discharge planning was started. She became more forgetful, preoccupied with ruminations about her ability to

achieve anything she chose if she only put her mind to it,
and repetitively questioned her need for psychiatric treatment. Negligent of her own well-being, she accidentally received a severe overdose of ultraviolet light from a sun
lamp. It became obvious that she was unable to care for herself and further long-term treatment was recommended. On
hearing this Beth became agitated, dejected and suicidal,
and had to be restricted to her living unit with suicidal
precautions taken until discharge.

During Beth's hospitalization both parents were seen
individually and intensively in casework. Despite strenuous
efforts by the social work staff, as well as by Beth's doctor, they continued to interact destructively with Beth,
throughout her hospitalization. They constantly communicated their desire for her to achieve intellectually, socially
and culturally, despite her limitations; they were resentful
and retaliative toward any evidence of her illness, at the
same time infantilizing her and complying with her most unrealistic dependency wishes.

Beth was released after 11 months of hospitalization,
on no medication. Her condition was unimproved, if not
worse. The hospital diagnosis was chronic, undifferentiated
schizophrenia; the research diagnosis was chronic schizophrenia with probable childhood asocial disorder.

FOLLOW-UP

After discharge from Hillside, the Silvers took Beth to
California and placed her in psychotherapy with a female
therapist whom she saw almost daily. She received no drug
treatment and seemed to be doing adequately. The therapist
arranged for Beth to live with some friends and work with
retarded children. After several weeks of the arrangement,
Beth became very disturbed and returned to live with her
parents in a trailer in an art colony, where she spent most
of her time painting or taking music lessons.

After eight months she had deteriorated considerably, talking to herself, having grandiose ideas and being physically abusive to her parents. She entered a general hospital psychiatric service, received psychotherapy twice weekly for two months and was kept in seclusion because of "restlessness and emotional instability." Later she received nine ECT from which she emerged more stabilized. The diagnosis was schizophrenic reaction, undifferentiated. She was discharged on Trilafon 8 mg, four times daily, and returned to her parents.

After this, she entered psychotherapy, first with one and then with another therapist. The second therapist prescribed Librium and Prolixin which reportedly were not helpful, and later Thorazine (dosage unknown) which did seem to help. After several more psychotherapists and another brief hospitalization, she made several suicide attempts, once by stabbing herself superficially, once by drinking turpentine and once by walking into the ocean. Her parents placed her at a state hospital where she remained for about five months and was diagnosed as a catatonic schizophrenic. Here she received 14 ECT, discontinued when she became excitable and ruminative. Eventually ECT was resumed and 20 treatments were completed. Later she had 33 insulin treatments and 10 comas which were discontinued when nursing staff became unavailable for further treatment. Finally placed on Thorazine, 300 mg daily, later reduced to 75 mg daily, she improved remarkably, and medication was discontinued prior to discharge. On returning home she was completely inactive except for periods of agitation where she became belligerent and abusive toward her parents.

Five years after her initial hospitalization, Mrs. Silver contacted Hillside seeking further placement for Beth. She had spent the summer at a therapeutic camp and was about to come home. Both parents dreaded this thought, since the

strain of living with Beth was intolerable. Mrs. Silver was
emaciated from severe colitis and Mr. Silver had had a heart
attack. However, no placement was made and she remained at
home for the next two years. She was sent to live with another family, and attended a work-treatment center where she
remained for three years. During this time Mr. Silver died
and Mrs. Silver became seriously depressed although hospitalization was not sought. She remained unable to cope with
Beth and reluctantly saw her about once a month.

Ten years after her Hillside hospitalization, Beth
transferred to another treatment center, this one intended
for "mentally handicapped and slightly retarded individuals."
She continued to have "periodic upsets where she goes off the
deep end." She was unamenable to psychotherapy or medication,
with Thorazine having been tried periodically, to no avail.

COMMENT

Beth Silver shows many of the characteristics typical
of the schizophrenic with a history of childhood asociality.
In particular there may be early, severe feeding problems,
rejection of a new sib, combination of marked inferiority
feelings with grandiose beliefs and expectations, a pathological relationship with perplexed, vacillating parents, and
a lack of response to early psychotherapeutic interventions
made in an attempt to deal with the patient's "unrelatedness."

What distinguishes these patients from other ineffective,
self-derogatory people is their manifest thought disorder,
communication problems and incredible difficulty in self-or-
ganization. They can follow an extremely tight structure but
rapidly deteriorate when expected to develop their own organizational plans.

The patient's response to drugs is also typical in that
Thorazine helped her improve her performance, attend activities and think more coherently so that she was once again

able to maintain her previously adaptive role as a fringe
group member. However, it is accompanied by such a severe
degree of somatic complaints that the medication is often
terminated (13). With further experience, we have learned
that these patients can often be maintained on phenothiazines
if medication is given all in one dose at night. Further, it
is often valuable to transfer these patients from the more
sedative phenothiazines such as Thorazine, to a less sedative
piperazine phenothiazine such as Prolixin or Stelazine.

Childhood asocial schizophrenics frequently have their
psychosis exacerbated by tricyclic antidepressants such as
Tofranil (13,17,20). Interestingly, on Tofranil, this patient
did not have a psychotic exacerbation, but did have a grand
mal seizure. Such seizures are infrequent at the dosage level she received; its occurrence leads one to speculate about
a basic organic abnormality of the central nervous system of
the childhood asocial schizophrenic. We have postulated such
an abnormality, drawing evidence from several different studies (1,8,20,23,24).

Deterioration is also typical of these patients when
they are confronted with the need to attempt a less sheltered
existence. It is regrettable that Miss Silver was not placed
back on phenothiazines when her behavior deteriorated during
the end of her hospital stay. However, Miss Silver was
treated very early during our experience with phenothiazines,
and the indications for such treatment were less clear then
than they are now.

The patient's course is also sadly typical (3, 5, 18,
21,27). She received much psychotherapy and a variety of organic therapies including ECT and insulin. However, her
course was one of irregular but progressive deterioration,
both cognitive and social. Noteworthy is the on again - off
again treatment, wherein improvements during hospitalization
and occasionally on medication were followed by discharge,

discontinuation of medication, and relapse.

ELLIOT WALDMAN

PRESENTING PROBLEM

Elliot Waldman, age 19, pleasant looking and physically healthy, was an unmarried college mathematics major. Two months before entering Hillside, he was apprehended by the police. He and a friend had decided to communicate with a third friend, hospitalized on a psychiatric ward, by throwing a rock with a message tied around it through his window. The two climbed over an adjoining roof and down the hospital fire escape to a point outside the psychiatric ward, when the police met them. Elliot was taken to jail, booked on attempted burglary charges and released on condition that he receive psychiatric hospitalization.

The next day his parents placed him in an acute psychiatric ward. He was diagnosed as having paranoid schizophrenia, and treated with daily doses of Compazine 5 mg, Artane 2.5 mg, Miltown 400 mg and psychotherapy. After two months at this hospital, little change was evident, longer term treatment seemed indicated and he was transferred to Hillside.

FAMILY

The Waldmans were an upper-middle class, professional family with two sons. The father, in his late 50's, described himself as a hard working man who always looked after the welfare of his family. He was chairman of the economics department at a large university and author of several standard, widely-used text books. Brilliant, arrogant and aggressive, he openly rejected Elliot, criticizing him for his way of life and accusing him of bringing unhappiness to the family; he showed no insight into his son's problems.

Mrs. Waldman, petite, pleasant-faced, bright, and sharp was also in her late 50's. She was characterized by the psy-

chiatric resident as somewhat hysterical and seductive. After attaining a graduate degree, she taught elementary school
for many years until Elliot was 5 years old and a brother was
born.

This brother was described as a paragon, with many interests and activities, excelling intellectually, socially
and athletically. The parents' preference for this son was
obvious. While Elliot had initially been provocative toward
his brother, as they got older their relationship improved,
although there were no strong ties between them.

Elliot described his father as a "schmuck" who allowed
no opinion but his own to be tolerated. He saw him as rejecting, overpowering, egotistic, and even attacked his father's economic theories as distorted and one-sided. Also,
he deprecated his mother, considering her stupid and lacking
in insight and understanding.

Both parents felt dismay, confusion, bewilderment and
helplessness concerning Elliot. They viewed him as a source
of aggravation since his birth and felt that he had always
been difficult, obstinate, and rejecting of them. They nagged, threatened, cajoled and ranted, alternately gave and
withheld material benefits in an effort to relate to or control him, all to no avail.

DEVELOPMENTAL HISTORY

Elliot was born normally, at full term, when both his
parents were near 40 years old. Cared for by a nurse during
the first month, he was bottle fed on schedule and allowed
to "scream it out" until feeding time. His infancy was marked by colic and temper tantrums. He was a scrawny, squirmy
baby and never elicited cuddling from anyone.

From age 10 months to 5 years Elliot was cared for by a
nursemaid who was "strict, quiet and firm," extremely rigid
and preoccupied with scheduled feeding and bowel training.
The responsibility of raising Elliot was left entirely to

her. Mrs. Waldman had no idea how the child fared during
these years other than that he walked and talked at normal
ages. She returned to teaching when Elliot was 15 months
old. Elliot had no memories of his nursemaid. However, he
always "fell in love" with girls named Susan, his nursemaid's
name.

At age 4, his tonsils were removed and after this he
was fearful of being alone. At age 5 his brother was born
and his behavior deteriorated sharply. Mrs. Waldman discontinued teaching at this time and stayed home to care for the
two boys, dismissing the nursemaid.

In kindergarten he immediately seemed "different" from
other children, and the school recommended him for psychiatric attention. He was unruly, continually disrupted the
class and refused to obey routine demands and rules. Because
he was extremely bright (IQ 138) the teacher suggested that
he attend a private school.

Elliot was placed in a psychiatrically-oriented private
school, at age 7, but continued to disobey; being disruptive,
cursing, writing obscene words and rhymes, drawing huge pe-
nises on the blackboard, shoplifting toys, and chewing up
food and spitting it out to horrify the girls. During his
five years at this school he posed both social and scholastic
problems; he made no friends and goaded his classmates into
picking on him, never fighting back and complaining only of
his fear that he might be struck in the face.

Starting at about age 7, and continuing for many years,
Elliot had an active fantasy life involving a superhuman amal-
gamation of Batman, Superman and Captain Marvel. He would
act this role for days at a time.

Also at about age 7, he started violin lessons, since
he was always musically inclined, as were his parents; his
father was an accomplished violinist. Elliot developed considerable proficiency and his interest in music lasted. Dur-

ing high school and college he attended special professional
courses in musical composition and theory and attended summer
music colonies where he excelled.

At age 9, he entered psychiatric treatment, at his
school's insistence. He was seen in psychotherapy (usually
play) between once and three times a week, until he was 15
years old. Later he evaluated the time spent in this treatment as a total waste. He stated that he felt no change or
emotional investment in the entire experience.

During the summers he attended a boys' camp where he
was also scapegoated and bullied and again would never fight
back, but only cry. After five summers he was told by the
administration not to return.

At age 11, at the end of the 7th grade, he was labelled
'incorrigible' and expelled from private school. The family
moved to the suburbs after this rejection and Elliot seemed
to improve in every respect: academically, socially, and personally. He joined and showed great interest in the community center, attended dances and gave parties at home. His
grades improved from average to excellent and in his last
year of high school he attained a B plus average.

Since early childhood Elliot experienced episodes of
micropsia. ("I would look around and things in the room would
look smaller.") In addition, he experienced a kind of droning, jagged rhythm in his head. He described it as something
like his mother's voice, but he was unable to discern words.
It was from this phenomenon that he claimed his later hallucinations developed.

Throughout his life he was obsessed by firecrackers and
dynamite and begged his parents to move to a state where
these were legal. To his parents' dismay, he became absorbed in exotic religious beliefs and rites, e.g., cannibalism,
and stated that eating another human might be enjoyable.
Also, he was preoccupied with animals and fantasied about

forming an animal protection society which would, among other
things, prohibit the saddling of horses.

Starting at age 13 Elliot was ashamed and fearful of his
solitary masturbatory transvestite practices (which persisted) of donning female apparel such as earrings or high heels.
He had vivid sexually arousing dreams of either a woman or
himself wearing huge painful earrings. In actuality he would
often wear his mother's earrings so as to cause himself erot-
ically stimulating pain. Seeing women's girdles, high heeled
shoes, jewelry or a distorted female body(arched back,craned
neck, etc.) would excite him to erection, and he would watch
women and follow them into subways in hope of seeing one in
a sexually arousing position.

When he entered college at age 17, he engaged in dangerous stunts such as climbing mountain cliffs and bell tow-
ers, scaling derricks and walking on subway tracks. On occasion he stole books from a college store, smashed glass
candy machines, and ran from restaurants after eating so that
he would not have to pay the bill. Nevertheless, as a freshman he attained the dean's list for scholastic excellence.

At college his only friends were four outré fellows with
similar unusual practices and ideas. These five boys considered themselves insane (with some justice), and all eventually were hospitalized for intensive psychiatric treatment. Their activities were openly bizarre. They spent
much time watching horror movies, while their conversations
consisted mainly of studied derogatory routines ridiculing
non-science majors or discussions of girls fantasied about
while masturbating. None of the five showed any realistic
heterosexual interest and seldom dated. On one occasion the
group mutually masturbated in a movie lavatory.

In his sophomore year he remained on dean's list during
the first semester but earned D's during the second semester.
He and his friends continued with their stunts, and toward

the end of the second semester set a fire in the middle of a
stone dormitory floor. The college expelled Elliot for this,
but stated they would reaccept him if he received psychiatric treatment.

During the next summer, a girl who attracted him invited him to have sexual relations. He tried, but was incapable
of having an erection, feeling that he was merely an observer
or that the event was not actually happening. His only re-
gret was that he would have liked to have seen the girl
writhing in passion while he remained cool and casual, a detached observer.

Also during this summer he experimented with overt homosexuality, allowing fellatio to be performed upon him by
another student. However, he did not enjoy the experience.
Later he attempted to pose for pornographic pictures in order to make money. An older man performed fellatio upon him
in an effort to stimulate an erection, but Elliot could not
respond. On other occasions he and a friend beat each
others' arms with a belt by way of mutual masturbation.

It was in September that he engaged in the episode which
involved the police and eventually brought him to Hillside.

PRESENTING CHARACTERISTICS

Elliot considered that he had been "insane" a long time
and described his behavior as bizarre and pointless. His
most recent symptoms were auditory hallucinations of the word
"girl," droning sounds he had often heard in his head, but
which he now characterized as conversation, and other odd
noises such as "shit being rubbed between two boards." Also
recently he had been terrified by horror movies, darkness and
loneliness, had feelings of unreality and nihilism and was
distracted by sexual thoughts. He felt light-headed, dizzy,
physically weak and constantly tired.

On examination Elliot seemed "peculiar," withdrawn, hes-
itant, had occasional irrelevant speech and inappropriate

smiling. He claimed that he was paranoid and felt people
watched him and wanted to seduce him. He was well aware
that his stream of thought was sometimes abruptly interrupted and explained it as feeling as if he were hitting a blank
wall. He was very distractible and alert to outside noise
and conversation. Oriented in all spheres, his remote and
recent memory were good. While his intelligence was very
superior, he demonstrated slow, low quality thinking (e.g.,
when asked what sand was used for, he replied, "they put it
on beaches.") He was verbal, cultured and preoccupied with
intellectuality and logic. He appeared eager to discuss his
problems, although at times he was argumentative and angry.

COURSE AT HILLSIDE

His physical examination was essentially negative, except that his first EEG record showed moderate diffuse slowing, and a second record showed moderate diffuse slowing
with several spike foci. He attained an overall Wechsler-
Bellevue verbal IQ score of 130, with individual test scores
ranging between 136 and 153. Only the comprehension test
score of 104 pulled down the overall score. This seemed to
indicate either an intrusion of his personal needs overriding
his judgment or possibly a defiant negativism. For example,
when queried on what should be done if he found a stamped,
addressed envelope in the street, he said he would open and
read it rather than mail it.

In general, Elliot was sloppy, unkempt, rebellious in
a silent, withdrawn manner, and uninvolved with his treatment. During his first month of hospitalization he readily
exposed and demeaned himself during psychotherapy, often approaching himself in almost a third person manner. On the
ward he provoked other patients and personnel with a distant,
sneering manner, as well as by playing his violin in the middle of the night.

Started in the drug program after ten weeks of intensive

but ineffective care, he received Tofranil 75 mg daily with
weekly 75 mg increments. Initially he turned into a model
patient, feeling happy, pleasant, less tired and not angry.
Both he and the staff were pleased and relieved. However,
after three weeks on Tofranil he suddenly developed loud,
euphoric, elated behavior with flight of ideas, marked loss
of goal directed associations and visual hallucinations at
night (a luminescent letter "t"). Shortly thereafter he developed bizarre posturing where he growled, moved his jaw
and tilted his head in an uncontrolled manner. His elated
and activated behavior continued, with talk about inspira-
tions to kill himself so as to reach Nirvana, stereotypic
hair brushing movements, open masturbation, shrieking and
yelling. He was very paranoid and fearful of being sent to
a state hospital.

After a week of this sharp exacerbation Tofranil was
withdrawn, but his excited, delusional state continued. His
doctor placed him on a course of 19 ECT treatment over 36
days. After 6 ECT, Elliot felt better and seemed less confused and more purposeful. But after the 7th treatment he
panicked, leaped from a building and fractured his ankle in
an effort to escape "attack." At this time he also attempted to cut through electric wires with scissors. Special
aides assigned solely to him found him impossible to control
and he was transferred to a closed psychiatric hospital.

He was hospitalized at Hillside for five months. The
hospital diagnosis was schizophrenia, mixed type; the research diagnosis was chronic schizophrenia with childhood
asocial and hyperkinetic development.

FOLLOW-UP

Elliot remained at the closed county hospital for five
days and then was transferred to a private psychiatric hospital where he remained for the next 22 months, with a diagnosis of catatonic schizophrenia. Early in this period his

behavior varied from autistic, apathetic and depressed to
acutely disturbed and assaultive. He received 4 ECT and
then was placed on Mellaril 300 mg daily, plus psychotherapy
with a psychologist to whom he related well. After 9 months
he began making progress and the Mellaril was reduced to 150
mg daily plus Dexedrine 10 mg each morning. He regressed at
one point and it was discovered he had not been taking his
Mellaril. Toward the end of this hospitalization he began
taking college courses, and when he was released from the
hospital he enrolled at a college and lived at a nearby residence hotel, supported by his parents.

In the third year after discharge from Hillside (directly after his 22 month hospitalization), he functioned sub-
marginally, was unable to work, was dirty and unkempt, and
took only a few college courses. He would arise at 2 P.M.
and retire at 4 A.M. When the residence hotel closed he
moved into his own apartment. He continued in psychotherapy
with his psychologist. It is unknown whether he received
any medication during this year.

The following year he was rehospitalized when found
wandering in a stupor. Placed on Sparine 50 mg four times
daily, and daily psychotherapy with his regular psychologist,
his stupor subsided in a few days, he became interested in
improving his appearance and began to make plans. He was
discharged in a month and returned to his apartment to look
for a job and take college courses.

Ten years after Elliot's Hillside hospitalization, Mrs.
Waldman was contacted. She reported that her son had been
living by himself in the East Village since his last hospitalization about six years earlier. The parents had been
supporting him financially, and he had almost completed re-
quirements for his B.A. He had been seeing a psychotherapist weekly and took no medication. She described Elliot as
"being a loner" and not having any friends, unable to work

or take more than the minimum number of courses at the university. Over these years he had been in contact consistently with his parents, at least once every two weeks. Suddenly, one year previously, he disappeared and no one, including the police and private detectives, could discover any information on his whereabouts. They suspected he was dead.

COMMENT

Certain psychiatric patients are characterized by extremely atypical early childhood development. On the one hand, they may be awkward, withdrawn, socially inept, clumsy, and generally asocial (4). Others may be hyperactive, aggressive, assaultive, impulsive and destructive. Both groups are frequently scapegoated and ostracized.

Quitkin and Klein (24) have demonstrated that psychiatric patients with such a history have many indications of chronic brain damage. They also noted that certain patients combined the characteristics of both groups. Mr. Waldman appears to be such a patient. Of interest is Mr. Waldman's EEG, which is compatible with findings of frequent EEG abnormality in this patient group. (8, 24)

Other typical features are his slight response to medication and ECT, and his eventual grim outcome. These patients are particularly sensitive to Tofranil, which often produces an agitated, acute psychotic state. This is often ushered in by a period of marked amelioration of mood and behavior, so that the patient and doctor are often extremely pleased by the Tofranil effect (13). However, the patient's mood elevation continues into a full-fledged, activated, wildly excited state accompanied by hallucinations and delusions. This state is not terminated by discontinuation of Tofranil but requires intervention, preferably by large doses of phenothiazines.

Although the phenothiazines prevent manifest psychosis, these patients respond only partially to phenothiazines;

their chronic asocial and difficult personality remain.
Their prognosis is extremely poor and they regularly lead
parasitic lives (4) either within a hospital or in a fringe
social role supported by others.

Mr. Waldman's deviant sexual ideation and tendency toward sado-masochistic sexual excitation are somewhat atypical. However, peculiar sexual beliefs and a complete inability to develop normal heterosexual relationships are uniformly present in this group. The patient's markedly sado-masochistic tendencies might conceivably be due to the interaction of a severe obsessional nursemaid and his early hyperactivity and difficulty in self-restraint.

JILL LEVY

PRESENTING PROBLEM

Eighteen months before entering Hillside, while in her
junior year, the high school authorities began pressuring
the parents of Jill Levy, then age 16, to seek psychiatric
help for their daughter. The parents contacted a psychologist who diagnosed her as having paranoid schizophrenia and
saw her in treatment several times a week for 125 sessions.

Jill was obviously highly disturbed, doing miserably in
school and badgering her parents to allow her to quit. Because she was suspicious, feeling that her schoolmates were
staring at her, talking about her and laughing behind her
back, she often started both verbal and physical fights with
them, and withdrew increasingly from any outside contact.
Often, she contemplated suicide but "didn't have the guts"
to go through with it. She refused to use public transportation, hated Negroes and Jews, and worried about who was
behind her, fearing that someone would sneak up and harm her.

Entertaining the pleasant delusion that she was one of
the world's most beautiful women, she saw the image of
Elizabeth Taylor when she looked in the mirror, which made

her feel confident and happy. At other times she saw only
a blank, featureless face. When in a group she felt that
she actually shrank in size so that she was less conspicuous.

During her junior year she had a fight with a girl who
she thought walked into her purposely. "I really ripped the
sweater off her and told her if you ever do that again I'll
kill you."

At the end of her junior year her parents allowed her
to quit school. After, she spent all her time at home, living in her own world where she fantasied that she was a
beautiful 18th Century lady surrounded by handsome men and
servants. She spent many hours sitting in front of the mirror, combing her hair and scrubbing her face. Her only social contact was with a congenial handyman with whom she had
almost daily sexual intercourse.

Her therapist continually attempted to persuade her to
accept hospitalization, finally succeeded and referred her
to Hillside.

FAMILY

The Levys were financially comfortable, Jewish, middle
class, with three daughters. Both parents were in their 50's
and had been married over 30 years. They were a handsome,
extremely well-groomed couple.

Mr. Levy was overbearing, domineering, angry, short-
tempered and sadistic. He had had a difficult life with
great dissension between himself and his own father and
blamed his irritability on having to cope with unpleasantness in the successful family business. He often was physically and verbally abusive with his wife and Jill, who loath-
ed her father.

Mrs. Levy was docile, quiet, submissive and always excused her husband's cruelty. She was anxious, over-control-
led, dominated by her husband and felt unable to provide af-

fection for any of her daughters.

Jill's two sisters were four and nine years older than she. Both were seemingly well-adjusted to life, married and living in their own homes. The middle daughter was favored by the family, had considerable social grace, and Jill was very jealous of her.

This sister rejected Jill, calling her a wild animal and predicting she would have to be "caged." While growing up there was considerable strife among the three girls. Jill's behavior also made life intolerable for her parents. The family's life was marred by chronic yelling and physical battling, and the older daughters often recommended that their parents divorce.

DEVELOPMENTAL HISTORY

Jill was a planned child, born normally, at full term. Her mother reported that she was a healthy, responsive, good infant. She was breast-fed until five months of age. At that time, Mr. Levy developed Meniere's disease and due to marked attacks of vertigo, periodically came home on a stretcher. Mrs. Levy was extremely upset, stopped nursing Jill, placed her in the care of her grandmother until she was 2½, and was completely occupied with helping her husband through his illness.

Jill's general motor development was average, although her mother felt she was difficult to toilet-train. Training was started at age 1½ and not completed until age 4. At a very young age she used foul language and cursed her parents. She was always irritable and abusive, as well as sullen, withdrawn and disobedient.

At age 5, she started school which she hated from the beginning. She could not get along with other children, and refused to have any interaction with them, feeling that she was different and that they were staring at her. Her school work was very poor, and she had to repeat 5th grade. In high school she attended a special class for slow learners.

At age 8, her mother threatened her with hospitalization
if she continued masturbating. Menarche was at age 11. Her
mother had instructed her about it but she was still frightened. She stopped masturbating at age 13, after reading that
it was an abnormal act.

Eccentric, she refused to wear new clothing until her
old clothing was worn to shreds. Eventually she wore only
old dungarees and refused to comb her hair, keeping it in
curlers most of the time. However, she was obsessed with her
appearance, feeling that there was something wrong with her
hair, nose, bosom and height. She picked at and scrubbed her
face until it was a mass of lesions. Fearing that she didn't
look right, she never went anywhere with her parents. Petri-
fied that she would get lost, she never went anywhere alone.
At ages 8 and 13, at the school's insistence, Jill had brief
psychotherapeutic contacts, details of which were not remembered by any family member.

Jill felt completely rejected until age 14 when she met
a boy with whom she went steady for a short time. Necking
was their usual activity. Following their break-up, she met
a young handyman with whom she went for three years. Their
activities consisted mainly of going to a garage and having
oral-genital sex, but no coitus, because the boy wanted to
wait until they were married.

During their relationship she was extremely jealous and
would go into rages, hitting, clawing and screaming if the
boy as much as admired a girl on TV. She saw him as someone
who would care for her as if she were an infant. As she
pushed him toward engagement and marriage, he became frightened and finally abandoned her. They broke up nine months
before her hospitalization. Shortly after this affair, she
started seeing a married handyman with whom she had daily
intercourse. Jill found she was attracted to boys who her

parents felt were socially inferior; she totally rejected
Jewish boys of whom her parents approved.

After increasing pressure from the school, Jill finally
entered intensive treatment with a psychologist but continued deteriorating until she entered Hillside.

PRESENTING CHARACTERISTICS

Jill had an attractive, though vulpine, face but was
always ill-kempt and dirty, with her head enveloped in a
garish halo of plastic curlers. Her posture was stilted,
with a conspicuous backward lean, so that her abdomen pro-
truded. She wore skin tight, off-the-shoulder blouses, revealing an unfortunate lack of mammary development. Her appearance was bizarre.

On interview, Jill was eager to relate her problems,
spoke openly, and uninhibitedly instigated discussions of
her intimate sexual activity. Her speech was voluble, relevant and coherent, and she carried on long, non-stop mono-
logues about herself. Her angry, hostile and depressed affect was appropriate to her thought content.

When upset, Jill heard a male voice saying insulting
things; she thought this was a combination of someone playing a trick and her imagination, though she wasn't sure.
Sometimes she yelled and cursed at strangers, feeling justified because she assumed they were staring at her. Often
she clawed at her face with her nails when angry. Other
than the above, and seriously impaired insight and judgment,
her mental status was unremarkable. Her general intelligence
seemed to be above average to the examining resident.

COURSE AT HILLSIDE

The results of all physical and neurological tests,
including EEG's, were within normal limits. Severe facial
lesions improved when she stopped picking them. On psychological examination she achieved a Wechsler-Bellevue IQ of
73. Her information level was low average, judgment and

conceptual thinking were very poor and simple arithmetic
skill was completely deficient. On projective testing she
was reported to function as an overt paranoid schizophrenic.

During the first two months of hospitalization, Jill,
now age 18, became increasingly disturbed, withdrawn, paranoid and hallucinatory. She refused to undress or bathe, insisting that others were staring at her; she requested to
be placed in seclusion. She believed she was Elizabeth
Taylor and actually saw her when she looked in the mirror.
One day she leaned far out over a stairwell after "voices"
told her to kill herself.

After six weeks of decline, she was given Thorazine,
brought to 900 mg daily in four days. During her first two
weeks on the drug, she looked affectively flat, a "zombie,"
although not manifesting rigidity or tremor. She was completely denying, wanted to be home, and spent almost the entire day sleeping. Kemadrin 2.5 mg three times daily was
added. Then suddenly, she appeared happy and alert, stated
she felt better than ever before in her life, literally looked into the mirror and saw herself for the first time, and
felt reborn and alive. From that point her energies were
directed outward. She entered hospital activities, improved
her appearance, took the curlers from her hair, dressed attractively and was well-groomed. She seemed relaxed, and
while she remained feeling inadequate, she expressed an eagerness to attain social skills.

Over the next 14 weeks she seemed to increase her abilities to cope with life. She attended the hospital high
school and participated in a full activities program, particularly enjoying modern dance and grooming classes. In group
therapy she expressed an eagerness to learn how to interact
with others. In individual psychotherapy she was extremely
passive, non-introspective, and constantly begged to return
home to her mother. Therapy was concrete and supportive.

After the first seven weeks her doctor complained that the medication was interfering with expressive psychotherapy, and reduced the Thorazine to 600 mg daily; seven weeks later it was reduced to 300 mg and the following week to 200 mg daily. Two days after the last reduction, Jill was upset, withdrawn, extremely preoccupied with sexual thoughts, and complained about being in the hospital. The Thorazine was immediately increased to 300 mg daily, but she remained distracted by sexual thoughts. When Thorazine was raised to 400 mg within three weeks, she remained fixated on going home but complained less about sexual tension. Her therapist related her emotional setback to his impending vacation.

Because Jill continued depressed and apathetic, she was placed on Tofranil 75 mg daily in addition. Within 48 hours she seemed markedly brighter and continued being increasingly outgoing, very enthusiastic about her activities, self-confident and less homesick. When the Tofranil was increased to 150 mg she showed a marked increase in sexual drive, and was physically provocative with patients and aides. Therefore, the Tofranil was reduced to a 75 mg daily level after three weeks. Three weeks later the Tofranil was reduced to 50 mg daily, but she became less alert, more withdrawn, homesick and lethargic. The dose was returned to the seemingly optimal level of 75 mg daily after two more weeks; Thorazine remained at 400 mg daily and Jill resumed being bright and sociable, but in two weeks began dressing as a femme fatale and using excessive eye make-up. Thorazine was increased to 600 mg daily.

On psychological testing done at this time there was no change in IQ score, but some of the projective materials, especially drawings, were interpreted to indicate some ego-organization, and greater ability for reality testing and controlling aggression and fantasies.

Miss Levy was very proud of her many new accomplishments, such as using a pay phone, riding an escalator and especially, earning her high school diploma. However, she still maintained a severe fear of travelling which was ameliorated somewhat by the Tofranil and her doctor's and social worker's dilligent efforts at getting her to make several short trips alone, away from the hospital.

Miss Levy was discharged after one year of hospitalization, on a daily drug regimen of Thorazine 600 mg, Tofranil 75 mg and Kemadrin 5 mg. Discharged in a much improved condition, she returned to her parents' home. Plans included her attending an after-care clinic, receiving vocational guidance and later living at a girls' residence. Her hospital diagnosis was schizophrenic reaction, paranoid type; the research diagnosis was schizophrenia, with childhood asociality.

FOLLOW-UP

For a year following discharge, Miss Levy attended the after-care clinic. Three months after discharge her medication was reduced to Thorazine 100 mg and Tofranil 75 mg daily. While she functioned fairly adequately, only occasionally scratching her face when she was angry, she could not attempt to look for a job, had considerable trouble with her parents who objected to the "low element" she socialized with, worried about her promiscuity and were frustrated in their attempts to control her behavior. They felt all her problems would be solved if only she married "a nice Jewish boy."

Instead, she had an affair with an unstable, exploitative married man, 12 years her senior. She lived with him and became pregnant. With the help of her psychiatrist, an abortion was arranged.

The second year after hospitalization she no longer attended the after-care clinic, and it is unknown whether she continued taking medication. She became pregnant again.

This time her parents expedited the man's divorce, the couple married and they lived in her parents' house. Her husband left her after a few months, following which she had the baby. Her parents successfully pressured her to place it for adoption and then divorce the man. Their relationship had been rife with mutual abuse from the beginning.

After her husband left, Miss Levy went with a variety of men described as "pick-ups." Sooner or later, she would call and ask her mother to come for her. Periodically, she saw a psychiatrist who recommended group therapy. She never got a job, found no real friends and was primarily concerned with getting married. This behavior continued for two years until she met a busboy at a hotel where she was vacationing with her parents.

Quickly she fell in love with this boy, six years younger than herself. They married ten months after they met and moved to a distant state to be near the husband's family. Miss Levy described her second husband as sexually inexperienced and lacking confidence. However, he soon tried to dominate her and she claimed she liked the idea of a jealous, masterful husband. However, they began to have furious physical fights which she later felt were her fault. Finally, after a year of marriage her husband became "sullen," and she had her parents bring her home. Shortly after, he was inducted into the Army.

After five months she found living with her parents intolerable. She easily became enraged and attacked her mother with fists and nails. Her father, in turn, beat her. Yet she was afraid to be far from her mother. She felt she had a hundred different personalities and again began thinking that she looked like Elizabeth Taylor, spending hours vividly imagining situations where she was her ideal. She heard people talking about her but realized that these were hallucinations. Often she screamed at people on

the street.   It was in this condition that Miss Levy entered
Hillside for the second time, seven years after her first
discharge.

On admission she looked bizarre, with inappropriate
heavy blue eye shadow and a cupid's bow of bright red lipstick.   She remained at the hospital for ten days and was impossible to manage in an open setting.   Very depressed, hostile and paranoid, she cut her wrists once and hid a knife
in her clothing several times.   Also, she threatened to kill
other patients if they continued to talk about her.   She was
extremely seductive with all males.   Thorazine,200 mg daily,
helped calm her somewhat, but she could not be cared for in
the open setting of Hillside and was sent to a state hospital.

At the state hospital she received Thorazine and Stelazine (amounts unknown) and showed considerable improvement,
becoming relevant, coherent, friendly, courteous and cooperative.   She was discharged in one month and returned home to
continue at an after-care clinic and take Thorazine 400 mg
daily, Stelazine 10 mg daily and Akineton 4 mg daily.

Four months later she voluntarily admitted herself to a
state hospital, because of constant fighting with her mother.
Her father had just suffered a heart attack which caused her
anxiety and depression.   On admission she was well oriented
and in good contact.   She was placed on Thorazine 450 mg daily and Stelazine 20 mg daily and released in two weeks to
continue in private care.

One year later her mother wrote to Hillside requesting
help.   Miss Levy vegetated at home, leaving the house only
with her mother.   The situation was unbearable and her mother
wished to place her in a permanent residence other than a
state hospital.   Unfortunately all such placements were impossibly expensive and thus, she remained at home for the
next three years.

Our social worker made a phone contact with the Levys,
11 years after Jill's initial Hillside hospitalization.
The father was interviewed. He reported that Jill
had not worked or been away from home in the past three
years. She still took Stelazine 5 mg daily, but had received no other psychiatric care during that time. Her symptoms
were the same but more tolerable, probably due to the maintenance low dose of Stelazine.

<u>COMMENT</u>

Jill Levy showed a failing school career that is actually more typical of the childhood asocial schizophrenic than
the other patients presented in this group. Not surprisingly,in view of her severe socialization defects, she learned
that sexual activity could afford a useful substitute. Although childhood asocial males rarely marry or develop sexual liaisons, childhood asocial females are frequently capable of both sexual relations and marriage (27). Other typical aspects are the appearance of higher intelligence than
she actually had, as measured by structured tests, and grandiose trends of a transparently compensatory variety. However, to view these grandiose trends as pure Adlerian psychological over-compensation misses the marked cognitive disorganization that allows for delusion formation.

Several pharmacological aspects of this case are noteworthy. First Miss Levy showed a very marked and dramatic
response to Thorazine; her high levels of sexual tension and
manifest delusional hallucinatory state were quickly replaced
by a "zombie" appearance. Although she did not develop any
manifest parkinsonism, the addition of an anti-parkinson drug
to her regimen resulted in a very marked increase in her motility, responsiveness and alertness. It is not sufficiently
recognized that inertia and akinesia are part of a drug-induced parkinsonian syndrome, and that anti-parkinson drugs
may be a required adjunct to phenothiazine treatment even

when no manifest rigidity or tremor is apparent.

It is possible that the patient's high degree of sexual tension was a good prognostic sign, indicating a type of phenothiazine responsive activation disorder and a long term ability to maintain continued attempts at heterosexual relationships.

We have pointed out that the childhood asocial schizophrenic patient shows a variety of aberrant responses to Tofranil. Quite typically, there is a biphasic response in which an early alerting, activating effect is replaced by a florid psychosis, as with Elliot Waldman. With Miss Levy the Tofranil activating effect was sustained by combining it with Thorazine. However, even this degree of sexual activation made a well-controlled social adaptation difficult.

The patient's quick Tofranil response (within 48 hours) reversing the phenothiazine-induced apathy, is characteristic of childhood asocial schizophrenics as well as schizo-affective schizophrenics, who may on occasion develop a mild apathy when maintained on phenothiazines. However, with the childhood asocial schizophrenic, supplementing with Tofranil is risky, whereas with the schizo-affective schizophrenic, it is almost without risk.

The patient's parasitic life course is also typical.

It is noteworthy that although the families of Levy, Waldman and Silver were manifestly pathological, or at the very least, extremely difficult, all of these patients had normal siblings. These patients were not simply the scapegoats of their families, but were also scapegoated by others. Their markedly deviant social interactions led to rejection and abuse on all sides.

Our society has not as yet developed the long-term longitudinal care facilities that would provide such chronically limited patients with a structure necessary for them to live at their optimum. I think that the belief that such patients

should be maintained in the community, or are receptive to
special rehabilitative training which enables them to rejoin
the community to compete socially and economically, is pur-
est wishful thinking. Chronic care facilities, that are not
simple custodial warehouses, are indicated in view of the
uniformly poor adjustment these patients display when functioning outside such settings.

Many of these patients have circumscribed skills that
can afford them both pleasure and productivity, if their
life is maintained within a structured setting. Such a setting, if it could be permissively oriented toward sexual relationships, while ensuring infertility via medication, could
make a notable advance in aiding the patients toward a fuller
humanity than they can achieve living on their own.

Chapter IV
FEARFUL PARANOID SCHIZOPHRENIA

Definition

Fearful paranoid schizophrenics show many similar characteristics to the childhood asocial group during their manifest psychosis: they are primarily suspicious and defensive.
However, their delusions are more clear-cut, and ideas of reference and auditory hallucinations are prominent. They believe others make derogatory remarks, often of a sexual nature. Delusional ideas of bodily change and sex inversion
are common, as are depression and suicidal preoccupations.
During fearful periods, persecutory delusions, thought disorder, instability in reality testing with associative looseness and illogical trains of thought are common. Transient
angry outbursts occur in relation to apparent misinterpretations of being trapped.

Historically these patients show considerably less evidence of childhood deviance than the former, although they
were sometimes considered unfriendly and withdrawn. Their
illness appears to have its onset in early adolescence and
to have a progressive insidious course that terminates with
acute psychotic decompensation during their third decade.
In the usual nomenclature these patients would be called
paranoid schizophrenics, although this would lump them with
the childhood deviant group as well as angry schizo-affective
patients.

These patients also have a poor long term prognosis, although they benefit somewhat from medication, direction and counselling.

SYLVIA BERNBAUM

PRESENTING PROBLEM

Sylvia Bernbaum, age 24, unmarried and living with her parents, was miserably unhappy, agitated, preoccupied with fears, and involved with a cult for "mental physics" and Christian Science. She was depersonalized, life events had a dream-like quality to her, she talked glibly about suicide and felt she was not meant to live. Thoughts of death were pervasive and she feared her dreams where"the dead would come and take me by the hand." She insisted that she was telepathic. She could neither travel alone nor be in crowds, and clearly felt that people on the street were looking and laughing at her. Often she cried and screamed, fearing that she couldn't swallow and would choke to death. She believed God controlled the mind or the spirit within; however, when she heard God calling her name she considered the possibility that she was talking to herself.

Miss Bernbaum was unemployed for more than six months and finally entered treatment with a psychiatrist. Psychotherapy and "tranquilizing" medication were unsuccessful, three ECT treatments deleterious, causing severe depersonalization, and her condition worsened. The psychiatrist diagnosed her as having simple schizophrenia and recommended intensive inpatient treatment at Hillside Hospital.

FAMILY

Miss Bernbaum was the only child of socially, psychologically and economically marginal parents, in their 40's, living in a low-rent housing project.

The father was a slightly built laborer who worked for the same company for 14 years but was repeatedly laid off and

rehired. He seemed of limited intelligence and tended to
deny most of his many hardships. However, he was genuinely
concerned with his daughter's welfare.

Mrs. Bernbaum was weak, nervous and hypochondriacal.
She had had a psychiatric hospitalization two years before
her daughter was born, and later suffered three depressions
severe enough to warrant ECT, prior to her daughter's hospitalization. Between depressions she was markedly anxious,
took "tranquilizers" and had some psychotherapy. Dependent
upon her daughter's well-being for her own equilibrium, she
used massive denial for most of her problems and showed limited understanding of the realities of her life.

The Bernbaums had a very difficult, unhappy life. They
were uneducated and always had to work very hard in order to
eke out a living. For the first years of their marriage and
until Sylvia was five, they worked together at their own
luncheonette, all day and part of the night. This necessitated giving their daughter's care completely to the paternal grandmother. When the business failed, Mr. Bernbaum became a laborer, but was often unemployed for prolonged periods. By this time, his wife refused to work to help improve
their financial condition.

Affection was never expressed between husband and wife.
They always had separate bedrooms and Mrs. Bernbaum always
seemed disgusted with her husband. She taught her daughter
that sexual relations were unnecessary and repulsive, and
obviously rarely, if ever, indulged in them. For the past
five years mother and daughter slept in the same bed at night
and even took daytime naps together. Sylvia was completely
dependent upon her parents and felt that they were the only
people who cared for her or who could possibly help her.
The three Bernbaums often cried together over their unhappiness.

DEVELOPMENTAL HISTORY

Sylvia was born slightly prematurely, but weighed 5 lbs. 10 oz. She was breast fed for three months and evidently developed normally. From ages 2½ to 5 she lived with her paternal grandmother whom she loved dearly. They were devoted to each other and were happy and comfortable together. Her parents rarely visited and she regarded her mother as a stranger. When she was 5, she unwillingly returned to live with her parents and was not happy with them.

At age 5 she entered school. She enjoyed it and liked playing with children, although she was aggressive and rough with them. She had the usual childhood illnesses between ages 5 and 7. Only once when she misbehaved did her mother spank her, but Sylvia thoroughly enjoyed the spanking and was disappointed that her mother did not do this more often. Instead, Mrs. Bernbaum was gentle, greatly overprotective, washing and dressing Sylvia until age 9, and fighting her battles, much to the child's embarrassment.

Sylvia studied dancing seriously from age 7, until her illness forced her to stop lessons at age 17. She danced professionally on television and was quite talented. Throughout her schooling, Sylvia worked hard and was an honor student with high grades. Well-liked by teachers, she was often their pet. Schoolmates, however, considered her a showoff and didn't care for her, leaving her an outsider except for one or two superficial friendships.

Menarche was at age 13; she was prepared for it by her mother. From about age 12 she thought about making love to girls, and at age 17, approached a girlfriend and asked her to play the male in some sexual experimentation. The girl obliged. Sylvia's only comment about this was that actually she herself wanted to assume the male role.

At age 16, her parents, especially her mother, tried to dissuade her from continuing with dancing, feeling that it

was indecent for her to become a professional dancer.   At
about this time Sylvia began feeling that school, dancing
and life itself were becoming a burden.

Suddenly, during her last semester in high school, her
grades dropped from 92 to 65.   She felt incapable, inferior
and that people were laughing at her.   Finally during her
senior year, she had to discontinue school and dancing lessons when she became too fearful to travel and could only
remain at home.   Treated by a general practitioner with unknown medication, her symptoms subsided after six months,
and she was able to return to school and graduate with a
commercial diploma.   But residual effects lingered and her
fear of travelling alone prevented her from continuing dance
lessons.

After graduating from high school she tried working at
neighborhood jobs, but was unsuccessful.   She would be late
for work, or insufficiently involved with her duties.   She
quarrelled with fellow employees, fought with her bosses,
had sexual relationships with co-workers and had such poor
general work habits that she was fired from one job after
another.

Sexually, she was extremely promiscuous, making herself
available to every interested man.   She engaged in sex with
a vengeance, stating that she wanted to be as evil as earlier
she had been good.   She saw sex as fascinating and curious,
and adventurously participated in a myriad of heterosexual
and homosexual exploits.   Remarkably, with all her sexual
activities, she refrained from having actual intercourse for
several years, "in order to remain a virgin."

At age 18 she decided to become famous.   She and her
boss, with whom she was having a sexual affair, implemented
a plan whereby he phoned the police to notify them that a
girl was going to jump in the river.   The police and newspaper reporters arrived to find Sylvia stripping herself

down to bra and panties. The photographers took pictures
and Sylvia jumped in the river. Police rescued her and took
her to a psychiatric hospital where she was released immediately after revealing her motivations. The strip photographs
made the front page of the daily tabloid and Sylvia was
thrilled. Suddenly she was very popular, receiving many
phone calls and letters for months after the episode. She
felt she would become a great movie star.

A man who had seen the pictures began calling and writing to her regularly. One day he stopped her on the street,
promised to help her become a star and said he would be her
agent. Feeling that he was "sent by God" to help her, she
became very close to him. He sent her back to dancing school
and took a nearby apartment for them. She remained with him
during the day, acting as his wife, but returned home to her
parents at night. During the year they were together they
earned an average of $35 a day in assorted shopliftings,
burglaries and car robberies. She dressed beautifully in
stolen clothes, provided her parents with stolen food and
furniture, and she and her boyfriend went to the fanciest
restaurants and nightclubs without paying. Their sexual life
was exciting and varied with homosexuality, heterosexuality
with mixed mates, prostitution, voyeurism and combinations
of the aforementioned. The emotional relationship between
the two was varied and dramatic. At times they were tender
and kind with each other, and at other times they were vicious and assaultive. Once Sylvia hit her lover with a
chair, knocking him unconscious for ten minutes and lacerat-
ing his scalp.

When she demanded more money, they decided to pass bad
checks but were apprehended. He was sentenced to five years
in prison and her sentence was ten years probation. Their
relationship ended when he was jailed. While she did not
love him, she characterized her life with him as happy and

exciting.

For the next two years, from ages 21 to 23, Sylvia a-
gain attempted different jobs unsuccessfully. Two particularly guilt provoking incidents occurred during this period.
As a nurse's aide, she ignored an old woman's cry for help
and the woman died the next morning. Also, the grandmother
with whom she had been so close suffered a heart attack, was
hospitalized and requested to see Sylvia, who refused to visit. The grandmother died the next day. Sylvia felt that
her own sinfulness was responsible for these deaths. Her
symptoms and discomfort increased and she looked for help
from any source. Through a newspaper ad she became an avid
student of "mental physics" and Christian Science. When
even religion did not help, she sought psychiatric treatment
with the psychiatrist who was treating her mother. Her
treatment failure led to referral to Hillside.

PRESENTING CHARACTERISTICS

Miss Bernbaum had an extremely pretentious manner of
speaking. For example, she would say things like, "I had a
nervous breakdown which leaves one without perseverance," or
"The accumulation of mistakes plus the reading of literature
gives the absolute interpretation of life." While her speech
was coherent, looseness of association and thought blocking
were apparent. Her affect was not mood congruent and she
laughed and smiled inappropriately. She was fully preoccupied with obsessive and sometimes delusional thoughts about
death and suicide (e.g., a man in black shoes would knock on
the door and come and get her), although she claimed she did
not wish to die. Her judgment and insight were nonexistent,
her remote and recent memory were good. She claimed she
hallucinated the voice of God calling her. Somatically, she
felt as if she were choking and had trouble swallowing. She
wore sunglasses at all times to hide her face. Personal hygiene was lacking since she found it too difficult to keep

herself and her clothes clean, or even to change her underwear.

COURSE AT HILLSIDE

Miss Bernbaum behaved childishly and inappropriately
with an obviously hysterical, demonstrative, seductive manner. She was tense, tearful, agitated and implored help
from others although she was highly skeptical of the motivations of the hospital staff.

All routine physical and neurological examinations, including the EEG, were within normal limits. Her full scale
Wechsler-Bellevue IQ was 84, verbal IQ was 95 and performance IQ was 76. She was unable to perform on the arithmetic
or picture completion subtests. Her scores did not accurately reflect her pre-morbid intellectual abilities which were
probably in the bright normal range, according to the psychologist's estimate.

She was referred to the drug program within the first
three weeks of admission and Tofranil 75 mg daily increased
75 mg weekly until a dosage of 300 mg daily was reached, was
instituted. At the beginning she improved considerably,
feeling less confused, more able to follow hospital routine
and participate with groups of people.

A month later she complained about an odor of ether and
death which lasted one day. At this point she became depressed and hopeless. However, her behavior was less inappropriate than it had been at the beginning. She thought less
about philosophy and death, felt she could think more clearly, and was neat, pleasant and cooperative. Still she persisted in her ideas that people were looking at her disap-
provingly, and that she could read minds. At times she would
laugh and cry uncontrollably. She also complained that her
moods went from extremes of sadness to happiness, with no
middle ground. Psychotherapy was exploratory, with attempts
made to force reality testing of her ideas.

During this period she became sexually involved with a male patient, performing fellatio on him.   She was ambivalent about the relationship, but could not resist it, and demanded that her doctor restrict her activities with the patient.   She found the restrictions "tortuous," was uncooperative and increasingly depressed.   Her entire hospitalization was marked by sexual acting up, including a homosexual relationship with another patient.

After two months on Tofranil, she reported visual hallucinations.   One night she awoke and saw a sickly bird and mouse which disappeared when she turned the light on.   She was not frightened and knew that it was her imagination. Another night she saw a large glowing insect, and another night she saw a monkey that took the form of a person.   Her doctor, at first, misunderstood these visual hallucinations as part of schizophrenia, but actually they were secondary to Tofranil toxicity (10).

The medical staff decided to add Thorazine 300 mg daily and Kemadrin 5 mg daily, to the Tofranil regimen, but it was stopped within two weeks when she reported intense feelings of sinking and dying, refused to be left alone, felt very dizzy and could not taste food.   These symptoms disappeared immediately following Thorazine withdrawal.   The research staff considered that she was showing marked hysterical reactions to orthostatic hypotension.

Because she persisted in feeling that fellow patients were accusing her of some stealing that actually had been taking place, her doctor insisted that she needed a phenothiazine.   Compazine 30 mg was added to the Tofranil and increased 15 mg weekly until a dosage of 90 mg daily was reached.   Initially she seemed to improve and began to participate in activities, but after a month became progressively more withdrawn, lethargic and depressed.   She continued to see spiders and monkeys at night, and Tofranil was decreased to

150 mg daily. Her extreme mood swings were still prevalent
but she was well-groomed and socializing with male patients.
Two weeks later she demonstrated the drug-induced akathisic
syndrome of restless pacing and inability to focus on any
activity. Therefore, the Compazine was slowly reduced to
30 mg daily, and she seemed once again to become more cheerful, though she remained quite referential and sensitive.

When discharge plans were discussed, Miss Bernbaum focused on returning home, attending dancing school and taking
modelling jobs; highly unsuitable, unrealistic plans. She
refused the foster home placement which the hospital encouraged. On a trial weekend at home Miss Bernbaum panicked
about swallowing, choking and dying, upsetting her mother to
such extent that she begged that the hospital retain her
daughter. After much consideration and another weekend spent
at home, this time more successfully, her doctor decided to
let her attempt an adjustment to her parents' home. If this
did not work, it was agreed that she would admit herself
voluntarily to a state hospital. Thus, she returned home
ten months after admission, not much improved. Her hospital
diagnosis was paranoid schizophrenia; the research diagnosis
was fearful paranoid schizophrenia with severe hysterical
traits. She was to take Compazine 30 mg daily and Tofranil
150 mg daily.

FOLLOW-UP

Miss Bernbaum remained with her parents and was too ill
to work. She returned to Hillside after-care clinic once a
week for six months for supportive therapy, and spent the
rest of her time at home, often with her boyfriend. By the
next year she went to the outpatient department of a city
hospital where she received supportive psychotherapy and
Benadryl, neither of which was helpful. They diagnosed her
as a paranoid schizophrenic.

In the summer of the second year post-hospital, she saw

a psychiatrist because she was upset, had no appetite and couldn't sleep. He administered 25 ECT and Mellaril, neither of which benefited her. However, sleeping pills helped to calm her when she was upset.

Her father died of leukemia a few months later, and she and her mother went to live with the grandfather who support- ed them. By the following year, at age 27, she had deteri- orated so severely that she entered a small psychiatric hos- pital, depressed, confused and paranoid. Her speech was barely relevant, she was disoriented for time and place, her recent and past memory were vague and delusional, and in- sight and judgment were lacking. Diagnosed as a paranoid schizophrenic, they treated her with ten ECT.

She requested re-admission to Hillside, ostensibly seek- ing intensive psychotherapeutic treatment. On the other hand, she saw hospitalization only as a means of separating from her mother while enabling her to continue with her chronic infantile existence. Hillside did not feel it should serve those needs and rejected her request. She was then trans- ferred to a state hospital on a court order of certification where she was diagnosed as a paranoid schizophrenic and treated with Tofranil and Mellaril. She seemed to improve and was released in nine months on 100 mg Mellaril. After, she attended an outpatient clinic for 2½ years.

After six months of staying home and not working, she became angry, hostile and began beating her mother. Again she reapplied for admission to Hillside, at age 30. During the interview she was histrionic and seductive and describ- ed an upsurge of intense sexual feelings that she found dis- tressing and difficult to control. Once again Hillside found her unsuitable and she entered another private hospi- tal for two weeks.

At age 31, she beat her mother "almost to death." Po- lice returned her to the state hospital on voluntary application where she was treated with Tofranil and Vistaril, amounts unknown. A month later her status was changed to court certification when she remained confused, lacking judgment, seclusive and guarded. Her medication was changed to Thorazine and Stelazine, and later Mellaril. After six months she was less resistive and antagonistic. She was discharged after eight months.

She returned to live with her boyfriend who by this time was her common-law husband. Within five months she fractured her mother's skull with a hammer. Returned to the state hospital, she denied she attacked her mother and was irritable, negativistic and demanding. She was treated with Stelazine 10 mg, and Mellaril 100 mg daily. Within two months she improved, was friendly, pleasant, showed insight and improved judgment and was discharged into her own custody, with welfare assistance and arrangements for after-care clinic treatment.

It is not known if she continued her medication, but the following month she was depressed, untidy, disoriented, heard voices and was recommited to the state hospital. A month later she was improved, in good contact with her surroundings, neat and clean; however, she dressed in a "provocative" manner. She was discharged into her own custody but stayed with her common-law husband who was to supervise her medication of Thorazine 200 mg three times daily, and Stelazine 5 mg twice daily, and attendance at an after-care clinic. Her age was now 34.

COMMENT

Miss Bernbaum evidenced ideas of reference, depression, depersonalization, preoccupation with death, believed God controlled her, experienced possible auditory hallucinations, exhibited pseudo-profundity, mystical preoccupations, and delusionally insisted that she could read minds. She also had looseness of association, thought blocking and inappropriate laughter and smiling. Certainly this is compatible with the diagnosis of a severely schizophrenic state.

However, what makes the patient atypical is the marked histrionic quality that pervaded all her actions, as well as her remarkable refractoriness to a variety of somatic interventions, including ECT and phenothiazines. Of particular interest is her experience of hallucinosis with Tofranil treatment, since our studies have indicated that patients marked by symptoms of depersonalization and referential states are particularly prone to this side effect. We have speculated that this may relate to an underlying temporal lobe disorder (10).

Here too, the patient's preoccupation with religion, mystical experiences, episode of olfactory hallucinations, eventual vicious assaultiveness, and the markedly fluctuating episodic quality to her psychosis, at least raise the question whether her illness was not related to psychomotor epilepsy, in spite of her normal EEG. Slater and Beard (29) have discussed this combination of symptoms associated with psychomotor epilepsy and schizophrenia.

It has been our regular experience that apparently schizophrenic patients who demonstrate very marked hysterical trends are refractory to somatic therapy. I believe certain patients are basically hysterical characters who develop a pseudoschizophrenia as part of their neurotic armamentarium. However, with patients such as Miss Bernbaum, it would appear rather that they suffer from a severe, chronic, periodically remitting and exacerbating psychosis in the context of an hysterical personality. However, this leaves obscure the relationship between their chronically hysterical personality and the development of the psychosis, since it would seem that the hysterical personality predisposes to a peculiarly refractory psychosis.

It is conceivable that an underlying cerebral disorder

predisposes both to a prepsychotic hysterical character and
to an eventual psychosis indistinguishable from schizophrenia, except in terms of its refractoriness. Conceivably,
certain hysterical phenomena are due to a loss of role distance, within the usual role playing abilities that are part
of everyone's repertoire. Their social roles lose their
"as-if" character and achieve the force of reality. Congruent with her hysterical trends are Miss Bernbaum's exploitative and antisocial predilections, as well as her desire to
be exhibitionistically famous.

Nonetheless, we cannot consider Miss Bernbaum as simply
a chronic hysterical character disorder, in view of her
sharp deterioration in adjustment during her senior year of
high school and her unremitting maladaptation thereafter.

Interestingly, as with the next patient presented,
Lottie Biener, Miss Bernbaum was at her best on combined
antidepressant and phenothiazine. She also suffered from
fragmented after-care that depended on her faulty cooperation, and erratic self care. Her prognosis with the best of
after-care remains doubtful.

LOTTIE BIENER

PRESENTING PROBLEM

Three months before 21 year old Lottie Biener was admitted to Hillside Hospital, she took 99 aspirin-antihista-
mine cold remedy tablets because, "I wanted to die. I did
not live up to expectations. I am intolerably insecure,
lonely and inadequate." Her parents reported that while she
always had been shy and introverted, ever since her graduation from college the previous June, she had become markedly
withdrawn. She was unable to hold a job, her social relationships became confused by fears that people were accusing
her of Lesbianism, and she felt that pains in her hands were
symptoms of cancer or arthritis. Finally, she made a suicide

attempt and was hospitalized for the following three months
at a city psychiatric hospital before being transferred to
Hillside.

FAMILY

The Bieners were a middle-class family with two children. The father, age 56, married at 35, was a very quiet,
passive, white collar worker who never seemed to belong in
the family. He rarely, if ever, spoke to Lottie, who claimed, "I think he helped me with something once in my life."
He daily visited his Mongoloid brother and unmarried sister,
who both lived in the neighborhood. Lottie always hated and
belittled him, but was ashamed of it.

Mrs. Biener, age 46, worked regularly as a clerk, and
described herself as a nervous, highly emotional person who
had severe protracted crying spells. Lottie described her
mother as a tense, controlling, overbearing, demanding and
forceful person who usually was shrieking and hitting her.

A brother, three years younger than Lottie, was the favored child and always catered to. Lottie was jealous of
him and often hit and taunted him. However, as they grew,
they became close, with Lottie feeling that perhaps part of
the reason for her present illness was that her brother had
recently left to attend an out-of-town college. Often she
wished that she had been a boy like her brother.

DEVELOPMENTAL HISTORY

Lottie's birth and developmental history were reported
as normal, except that her mother remembered her as being
more troublesome and demanding than her brother. The mother
attributed Lottie's problems to the fact that she herself was
very nervous. When Lottie was about one year old, her parents found life with each other increasingly intolerable,
and the father asked his wife to return to her family. At
about this time, the father's family also told Mrs. Biener
that she was "an unfit mother." Consequently, Mrs. Biener

felt compelled to "hold onto Lottie, because she was all that
I had. It seems that I have been holding on to her all her
life."

The parents reconciled shortly thereafter, and when
Lottie was three, the brother was born. She then began hav-
ing frequent temper tantrums and would cry for hours. Mrs.
Biener often lost her temper and treated Lottie harshly.

Lottie remembered having had a close friend when she
was four years old, and being very frightened when starting
school at age six. However, she did well academically, and
was promoted to special progress classes. Also at age six,
she began music lessons and was quite talented. Throughout
her grade school years, Lottie had a number of friends; at
age seven she became particularly close with one girl. Generally, however, she was shy, introverted and passive.

She began menstruating at age 11. Her mother never
mentioned anything about it, but after noting stained under-
clothing, simply bought her sanitary supplies. Previously,
at age nine, she had asked her mother about sex and was told,
"Go away, I'm busy." She never again questioned her mother
on sexual matters.

When she was 13, she had her first date, and then for
six months,a steady boyfriend with whom she played music.
Usually she would date one boy steadily for several months
and then, getting bored, would start a new relationship. On
her dates, she rarely kissed or petted, and never had sexual
intercourse. She had no really close relationships.

When she was 14, her mother returned to work. Lottie
became depressed, feeling lonely, and frequently staying out
of school. Often she took long walks alone or went to the
movies. Her school grades dropped and she made a pseudo-
suicidal attempt by ingesting some pills; there were no physiological sequelae.

Because of her musical talent, she attended a special

high school for music and art where she did well in her music courses but graduated with only a 75% average. During
high school, she frequently socialized with a group of
friends, went to parties, and was particularly friendly with
one girl whom she nevertheless considered beneath her, socially and intellectually.

After graduating from high school, Lottie had hoped to
go away to college. However, because her grades were poor,
her parents would only provide for a teachers college. Not
wanting to become a teacher, she took special examinations
and was able to enter a city college where she achieved A's
in her music major, but C's in other courses, "not living up
to expectations." Later she thought she'd like to become a
music teacher, but didn't think she was good enough. "To
work with children, I would need to be more responsible,
more stable." Thus, she took no education courses.

Lottie held her first job at age 17, when she was a
camp counsellor. She thoroughly enjoyed this summer away
from her parents, playing with young children and successfully producing a musical extravaganza. The next summer,
she returned to the camp where she was in charge of older
children. She worked with a woman, age 28, with whom she
became very close. However, she was concerned about her relationship with this woman, describing her as very masculine
and fearing perhaps that there was a sexual attraction between them.

During college, she continued socializing with a group
of friends but was not particularly close with anyone. She
always preferred to be alone, with solitary pursuits.

Her relationship with her mother remained one of constant bickering. "I used to come home from school and spend
the afternoon dusting and cleaning for her. Then she'd come
home and say that she's too busy to talk to me, that she'd
have to do it all over again. My job wasn't good enough;

but I never answered her. Then I stopped helping her completely and she would just yell and complain. She never
talked to me about anything else, so I just didn't talk to
her."

   It was after graduating from college, at age 20, that
she became increasingly withdrawn, rarely dated and participated minimally in social activities. Since she was not
qualified to work at any special job, she found general office work and took a secretarial course at night in order to
learn stenography. She seemed burdened, fatigued, and felt
insecure that she wasn't living up to expectations at work,
even though there were no complaints about her job performance.

   After five months at the office, she became involved in
a fantasied "triangle affair" with a girlfriend's boyfriend.
When the girlfriend and her boyfriend broke up, Lottie
was convinced that the other workers were talking about her,
criticizing the role she had played in the friend's unhappy
romance. Also, she was certain that they were gossiping that
she was a Lesbian, since she had always obviously relied on
the girl whom she "looked upon as my mother."

   That month, another girlfriend whom she saw infrequently, invited her to accompany her for a weekend to a resort.
Lottie unwillingly consented to go, responding to her parents' pressure to socialize more. At the hotel, she drank
a lot because she wasn't having a good time, and after two
days wanted to lie in bed all day. Her friend came to her
room to take souvenir pictures and this distressed Lottie
considerably. She was obsessed with the highly unlikely idea
that someone from the office might see her at the hotel with
this girlfriend and would know she was a Lesbian (she claimed no homosexual activities took place).

   On returning to her job the next day, she immediately
quit and went home. Several weeks later, she found another

secretarial job, but felt that her new boss was also critical of her. She became increasingly concerned about others'
opinions of her and was certain that her fellow employees
knew she was homosexual. Confronting her boss, she told him
that there was no point in continuing working, that "the in-
evitable would happen," and she quit. Subsequently, she
stayed home, increasingly despondent that everyone in the
street knew about her sexual deviation. Finally, after a
month she took the overdose of cold remedy.

When she arrived at the city hospital, sent by the family doctor, the day after she ingested the pills, she was
mute but cried intermittently and responded only by nodding.
She denied hallucinations and her grossly referential persecutory ideas were not completely fixed. She thought she
was being controlled by machines. For two weeks she was
treated with Thorazine, which made her sleepy but less anxious, and later for six weeks with Tofranil 150 mg daily,
and she "stopped laughing and began to feel more depressed."
Within a month she reconstituted fairly well and seemed to
be relating comfortably with her therapist, although later
admitted he was very difficult to talk with. She was diagnosed as having an acute schizophrenic reaction, undifferentiated with catatonic and paranoid features. Repeatedly,
she stated she did not want to return to live with her parents, felt unable to work and incapable; she remained depressed. Her doctor had her transferred to Hillside after
three months.

PRESENTING CHARACTERISTICS

On admission to Hillside, Miss Biener was tall, slim,
neat and attractive, but dull, apathetic and indifferent.
Her voice was monotonous, barely audible and her responses
were monosyllabic. She sat picking at her nails and cuti-
cles, and would not look directly at any one. However, she
presented no evidence to suggest persecutory trends at this

time.

When questioned about her father, her eyes welled up and she immediately talked about how "I miss my doctor (at the city hospital) so terribly." When discussing her mother, she returned to her apathetic tone. In answering the question--What is your problem?, she stated, "I have to get back on my feet. I have to be able to love and handle anything that bothers me, by myself. I could never get what I needed from my parents. They think that food, clothing and shelter are enough. They didn't make me feel as if I was anyone. I think I am. I'd like my own apartment, job and marriage." Later, she reported that her mother stated on a hospital visit, "If you get well, then I'll drop dead." She asserted that her mother required that she remain ill.

COURSE AT HILLSIDE

On the Wechsler-Bellevue, Miss Biener attained a full scale IQ of 119, a verbal IQ of 112, and a performance IQ of 124, with a very close cluster of scores in all subtests except Comprehension which was considerably lower. Two EEG's were normal.

Miss Biener appeared withdrawn and reluctant to talk. She told one nurse how terrible she felt because of her inability to relate to her therapist with whom she was negativistic, hostile and aggressive. On the ward, however, she was cooperative, but seclusive. Slowly she made some positive contact with a new therapist. For a short time she was able to verbalize more freely in therapy, but then quickly resorted to negativism, hostility, staring, smiling, sitting mutely or answering questions in monosyllables. Later she indicated that she was unable to cope with her feelings during therapy, and in order to maintain the status quo, behaved the way she did.

After about ten weeks at the hospital, Miss Biener became more visibly upset, lying face down on her bed, crying

uncontrollably. When approached by staff, she was negativistic and told everyone to leave her alone. She made a point
of insisting that she did not wish to talk to her psychotherapist and finally, therapy was cancelled until she would
decide that she wished to resume it. Her negativistic, seclusive behavior continued, with crying and refusal to see
her family.

Within the next several weeks, she became increasingly
irritable, aggressive and violent, refusing to attend activities, often crying, skipping meals, throwing things at people and burning a patient on the neck with a cigarette. On
several occasions, she had to be calmed with paraldehyde.
Then, she returned to her solemn, withdrawn state, but now
she spoke of feelings of persecution by other members of the
unit. She also giggled and smiled inappropriately.

Finally, after four months, she was referred to the drug
program and reported to the research psychiatrist, "I
know that people are being very nasty to me. People say
things and then look at me and I know that they mean me."
She would not say what she thought they were saying, except
that it was about her entire life. In spite of all her ideas
of reference, she stated she was pleased with herself and
"better than a lot of people." Tofranil, 75 mg daily, increased 75 mg weekly until a total dosage of 300 mg daily was
reached, was begun and psychotherapy was resumed, although
she remained mute during her sessions. However, she made
more attempts to discuss her feelings with other hospital
staff when her doctor was not around.

After a week on Tofranil 75 mg, she became quite verbal
during her sessions, talking about her paranoid delusional
ideation; namely, that another patient to whom she had expressed her fears, was now telling staff and patients about
Miss Biener's masturbation and Lesbianism. She felt that the
entire hospital was aware of this and she could not leave her

room even for her psychotherapy sessions, because of people
staring at her. In fact, she conceived of a hierarchy
of how information about her was passed from person to person. When she finally emerged from her room, she was
mute.

After a month on Tofranil, she was silly and bizarre
with marked self-satisfaction, optimism and grandiosity,
strikingly at variance with her appearance. By six weeks,
she felt that people had stopped persecuting her, although
they might start again at any time, and she seemed somewhat
less angry and tense, but wanted to discontinue medication.
After eight weeks her doctor decided to discontinue Tofranil
since he felt it wasn't helping much, although she was in
better control, less depressed, less aggressive and generally
feeling better.

Tofranil was reduced 75 mg daily until discontinued, and
she complained of some nausea, seemed duller and more uncom-
municative. Then, three weeks after Tofranil discontinuation,
her paranoid delusions mushroomed, so that she thought the
entire hospital staff, city, and newspapers were concerned
with her reported Lesbianism. She hallucinated that radio
and TV programs advertised her name and address, so people
could send in and receive her case history, believing her
masturbation was known countrywide. She had somatic delusions that she might be changing into a man, smiled inappropriately, retreated to her room, refused to engage in any
activities and was reluctant to emerge even for meals.

During her sixth month at Hillside, Thorazine, 300 mg
daily was started and increased over three weeks to 1600 mg
daily. Her grossly fearful, paranoid behavior continued and
now included auditory hallucinations of someone saying, "Open
the door, close the door, it is hot, it is cold." After a
week on 1600 mg, with no amelioration of pathology, Thorazine
was discontinued, and she was started on a course of ECT,

three times weekly, for 25 treatments. Shortly after the
start of ECT, she responded in a striking manner, becoming
much less withdrawn, much less suspicious and able to socialize with other patients, even going to the dining room for
her meals.

During the first weeks after beginning ECT, she had a
short period of hypomanic behavior with a great deal of giddiness; she giggled inappropriately and had outbursts of
laughter for seemingly slight provocation. She referred to
her delusional ideas as "those funny ideas I used to have,"
and soon had great difficulty in remembering anything at all
about her previous paranoid state. However, after a month
of ECT, she once more became withdrawn, did not get along
with others, and some of her paranoid delusional ideation returned, albeit with doubt as to whether people were actually
accusing her of Lesbianism. In general, she was calmer,
more manageable and cooperative with hospital routine. In
psychotherapy, she remained unproductive. Three days after
the last of the 25 ECT had been administered, she returned
to her hallucinatory and delusional thinking, refusing to
leave the unit, even though she showed some slight lessening
of tension in socializing with other patients.

After ten months of hospitalization, she showed no improvement, remaining suspicious, seclusive and paranoid. She
believed that the various groups in the hospital had been
segregated according to diagnosis, such as Lesbian or homosexual, was fearful that people could influence and control
her actions and mind, and that they continually talked about
her.

By one year, it was recommended to the parents that Miss
Biener continue at another institution, since Hillside felt
it had nothing more to offer her, and thus, she was released
to another private hospital. The hospital diagnosis was
chronic, severe, paranoid schizophrenia; the research diagno-

sis was fearful paranoid schizophrenia.

FOLLOW-UP

At the next hospital, she presented the same picture, was diagnosed as a catatonic schizophrenic, and was started on a course of ICT and ECT. Once again, there was an immediate change in that she became more accessible, pleasant and sociable. ECT was stopped and within several days she developed the delusion that the charge nurse was causing her to masturbate and telling people about it. ECT was reinstituted.

After five weeks, she had received 40 ICT and 15 ECT. She was placed on Stelazine and immediately deteriorated to her previous delusional state. After two and a half months, she received six more ECT and showed almost immediate improvement. Then she resumed taking Stelazine, 10 mg, and Parnate, 30 mg, and became free from delusions, although her affect was flat and empty. She was inaccessible to psychotherapy. After six months at this private hospital, she returned home.

Once at home, she was able to find a temporary secretarial job, but in three months when the job became permanent, she again developed a full-blown paranoid psychosis with all the previous symptomatology. The psychiatrist referred her to a third private hospital where she was placed on Thorazine, 150 mg daily, raised in a week to 300 mg daily. There was no change in her condition and her parents removed her to a state hospital after five weeks.

On admission to the state hospital, less than a year after discharge from Hillside, she was grossly delusional, perseveratively fearing everyone in New York was talking about her Lesbianism and her masturbation. There, she improved slightly on daily doses of Thorazine 300 mg, Stelazine 15 mg, and Tofranil 75 mg. By five months, she was "doing very well, free of secondary symptoms and socialized considerably

at the hospital." Thus she was released on convalescent status, taking Thorazine 75 mg, and Tofranil 75 mg daily, to
live in a women's residence, look for a job and attend an
after-care clinic.

She obtained another job as a secretary and saw her doctor privately. He recommended within a few months that she
be rehospitalized when she claimed people were entering her
room and giving her injections. Then her father had a coro-
nary from which he recuperated. Two months later, almost
two years after leaving Hillside, Miss Biener, age 24, jumped
in front of a subway train and was killed.

COMMENT

The outstanding aspect of Miss Biener's course was her
comparatively unremarkable developmental history, considering
her schizoid and difficult family. Always shy, she developed
a markedly schizoid adjustment at the point where she was expected to become self-supporting. Noteworthy also was her
preoccupation with her sexual identity and her inability to
relate heterosexually. Typical of the fearful paranoid, is
the massively referential state complicated by delusions of
external control and sexual inversion.

It is not clear how typical is the fact that at various
points in her illness, she responded positively to combined
phenothiazine-antidepressant therapy and became delusion
free, although with impaired social ability. The fact that
Tofranil alone did not exacerbate her psychosis but did raise
her mood, illustrates that the effects of Tofranil on
schizophrenic patients is extremely variable. In this case
Tofranil appeared to make her grandiose, somewhat hypomanic
and more communicative, but less paranoid. With the discontinuation of Tofranil, her delusional referential state mushroomed, probably secondary to the recurrent depression. The
development of somatic delusions that she might be changing
into a man is of particularly grim prognostic import.

Her response to ECT was at best very temporary, and this is typical of the fearful paranoid schizophrenic. Relapse always followed her improvements. However, this was partially due to medication discontinuation or reduction to ineffective maintenance levels. One of the most severe problems in the treatment of the chronic schizophrenic is that many doctors fail to prescribe adequate maintenance doses. For instance, during her last hospitalization, she did well on a combination of Thorazine 300 mg, Stelazine 30 mg and Tofranil 75 mg daily. But on convalescent status this was lowered to Thorazine 75 mg and Tofranil 75 mg daily. Recrudescence of her psychosis and eventual suicide followed.

The suicide risk in fearful paranoid patients is marked since they suffer intense psychic pain, and feel helpless, hopeless and unable to forge any therapeutic alliances. It is possible that such patients may, in the future, be amenable to ultra-high dosage phenothiazine therapy. Also the use of combined antidepressant and phenothiazine therapy is worth exploring.

1. Belmont, I., Birch, H.G., Klein, D.F. and Pollack, M.:
    Perceptual evidence of CNS dysfunction in schizophre-
    nia. Arch. Gen. Psychiat. 10, 395-408, 1964.

2. Gittelman-Klein, R.K. and Klein, D.F.: Long-term effects
    of anti-psychotic agents: A review. Psychopharmacology.
    A Review of Progress. Proceedings of 6th Annual Meeting
    of the American College of Neuropsychopharmacology,
    1967. Public Health Service Publ. 1836, 1968, pp. 1119-
    1154.

3. Gittelman-Klein, R.K. and Klein, D.F.: Marital status as
    a prognostic indicator in schizophrenia. J. Nerv. Ment.
    Dis. 147, 289-296, 1968.

4. Gittelman-Klein, R.K. and Klein, D.F.: Premorbid asocial
    adjustment and prognosis in schizophrenia. J. Psychiat.
    Res. 7, 35-53, 1969.

5. Gittelman-Klein, R. and Klein, D.F.: Relationships of
    the mecholyl test, premorbid asocial functioning and
    long term outcome in schizophrenia. J. Nerv. Ment. Dis.
    150, 301-306, 1970.

6. Gittelman, R.K., Klein, D.F. and Pollack, M.: Effects of
    psychotropic drugs on long-term adjustment. A review.
    Psychopharmacologia 5, 317-338, 1964.

7. Johnson, G. and Gershon, S.: Controlled study of lithium
    vs. chlorpromazine in acute schizophrenics. Brit. J.
    Psychiat. October, 1971.

8. Kennard, M.A., Pollack, M. and Klein, D.F.: The EEG
    qualities in a group of young adult hospitalized psy-
    chiatric patients. Recent Advances Biol. Psychiat. 8,
    277-282, 1966.

9. Klein, D.F.: Behavioral effects of imipramine and pheno-
    thiazines: Implications for a psychiatric pathogenetic
    theory and theory of drug action. Recent Advances Biol.
    Psychiat. 7, 273-287, 1964.

10. Klein, D.F.: Visual hallucinations with imipramine.
    Amer. J. Psychiat. 121, 911-914, 1965.

11. Klein, D.F.: Diagnostic prediction of psychotropic drug
    effect: Global outcome. Excerpta Medica Internat. Ser.
    129, 736-740, 1966.

12.   Klein, D.F.: Importance of psychiatric diagnosis in pre-
      diction of clinical drug effects. Arch. Gen. Psychiat.
      16, 118-126, 1967.

13.   Klein, D.F.: Psychiatric diagnosis and a typology of
      clinical drug effects. Psychopharmacologia 13, 359-386,
      1968.

14.   Klein, D.F.: Psychotropic drugs and the regulation of
      behavioral activation in psychiatric illness. In Smith,
      W.L. (ed.): Drugs and Cerebral Function, Charles C.
      Thomas, Springfield, Ill., 1970.

15.   Klein, D.F., Honigfeld, G. and Feldman, S.: Prediction
      of drug effect by a successive screening decision tree
      diagnostic technique. In May, P.R.A. and Wittenborn,
      J.R. (eds.): Psychotropic Drug Responses. Advances in
      Prediction. Charles C. Thomas, Springfield, Ill., 1969.

16.   Kramer, J.C., Klein, D.F. and Fink, M.: Withdrawal symp-
      toms following discontinuation of imipramine therapy.
      Amer. J. Psychiat. 118, 549-550, 1961.

17.   Kramer, J.C., Klein, D.F. and Fink, M.: Imipramine as an
      adjunct to phenothiazine therapy. Compr. Psychiat. 3,
      377-380, 1962.

18.   Levenstein, S., Klein, D.F. and Pollack, M.: Follow-up
      study of formerly hospitalized voluntary psychiatric
      patients: The first two years. Amer. J. Psychiat. 122,
      1102-1109, 1966.

19.   Levenstein, S., Pollack, M. and Klein, D.F.: Follow-up
      study of formerly hospitalized psychiatric patients:
      Procedural considerations in data collection. J. Hill-
      side Hosp. 15, 152-164, 1966.

20.   Pollack, M., Klein, D.F., Willner, A., Blumberg, A.G.
      and Fink, M.: Imipramine-induced behavioral disorgani-
      zation in schizophrenic patients: Physiological and
      psychological correlates. Recent Advances Biol. Psychi-
      at. 7, 53-61, 1964.

21.   Pollack, M., Levenstein, S. and Klein, D.F.: A three
      year post-hospital follow-up of psychiatric patients:
      First hospitalization in adolescence vs. adulthood.
      Int. J. Child Psychiat. 33, 224-225, 1966.

22. Pollack, M., Levenstein, S. and Klein, D.F.: A three year post-hospital follow-up of adolescent and adult schizophrenics. Amer. J. Orthopsychiat. _38_, 94-109, 1968.

23. Pollack, M., Woerner, M. and Klein, D.F.: IQ differences between hospitalized schizophrenic and personality dis-order patients and their normal siblings. Proceed. Amer. Psychol. Assoc. 76th Annual Convention, San Fran-cisco, 1968.

24. Quitkin, F.M. and Klein, D.F.: Two behavioral syndromes in young adults related to possible minimal brain dys-function. J. Psychiat. Res. _7_, 131-142, 1969.

25. Robins, L.N.: Deviant Children Grown Up. Williams & Wilkins, Baltimore, 1966.

26. Rosen, B., Engelhardt, D.M., Freedman, N., Margolis, R. and Klein, D.F.: The hospitalization proneness scale as a predictor of response to phenothiazine treatment: II. Delay of psychiatric hospitalization. J. Nerv. Ment. Dis. _152_, 405-411, 1971.

27. Rosen, B., Klein, D.F. and Gittelman-Klein, R.: Sex dif-ferences in the relationship between premorbid asocial-ity and post-hospital outcome. J. Nerv. Ment. Dis. _149_, 415-420, 1969.

28. Rosen, B., Klein, D.F. and Gittelman-Klein, R.: Predic-tion of rehospitalization: The relationship between age of first psychiatric treatment contact, marital status and premorbid asocial adjustment. J. Nerv. Ment. Dis. _152_, 17-22, 1971.

29. Slater, E., Beard, A.W. and Glithero, E.: The schizo-phrenia-like psychoses of epilepsy. Brit. J. Psychiat. _109_, 95-150, 1963.

Section II

AFFECTIVE DISORDERS

RECURRENT AFFECTIVE DISORDERS, UNIPOLAR TYPE

DIAGNOSTIC ISSUES

Depression is an exceptionally difficult concept to define since it may refer to a symptom, mood, affect, state or disorder. Popularly it refers to a temporary mood of unhappiness, dejection, sadness and hopelessness, usually consequent to a loss or disappointment. Here it shall be maintained that in psychiatric illness, all these features are the inconstant secondary accompaniments of a primary pathological core disorder.

At first glance it would seem that the distinguishing feature of "pathological" depressions is that they are quantitatively out of proportion to usual experience. Either they are too intense for the provoking cause (if any is apparent), or too prolonged. Therefore, the case may be made that "pathological" depressions are simply the extreme of a continuum; within that framework the terms depressive "state" or "disorder" are misleading since they imply a qualitative division.

In contrast, the qualitative diagnostic approach is the usual nosological one. Various qualifying phrases such as psychotic or neurotic, reactive or endogenous, agitated or retarded, etc., have been promulgated in an attempt to subdivide the field of depressions. These attempts have led to anti-categorical reactions that consider these divisions as

157

either arbitrary or of no consequence, and that issues such
as suicidal risk over-ride pettifogging diagnostic decisions.

These reactions seem clinically unjustified. Several
systematic descriptive studies have statistically demonstrated discrete depressive syndromes, with clear-cut constellations of qualitative distinctions both from each other and
from normal dysphoric moods. These syndromes have distinct
prognostic and treatment consequences.

There seem to be several discrete psychiatric illnesses
that share a common core pathological phenomenon - the dep-
pressive mood. It is the distinctive traits of these disorders that have definite prognostic and treatment implications.

Since depressive states are complexes of a large number
of psychological, affective, behavioral and physiological
characteristics, one may easily pick out one or the other
trait; e.g., guilt, sadness, helplessness, low self-esteem,
etc., and insist that it is the primary, necessary, regularly occurring core disorder, and that all other traits are
inconstant accompaniments. We have found it most fruitful
to consider the sine qua non of the depressive mood to be a
phasic, temporary, severe, lack of present or anticipated
satisfaction associated with the conviction that one cannot
perform adequately.

The patient recognizes that he feels different than usual. However, he may have any of a variety of opinions as to
the nature of this subjective difference. The examiner
should not expect patients to make a clear-cut statement that
they are depressed, since depressive patients are usually not
particularly introspective. Instead, patients may complain
about physical symptoms, boredom, apathy, difficult family
or working conditions or low self-esteem. Guilty ruminations
occur, although not as frequently as stated in textbooks.
Other inconstant accompaniments of the depressive state are

a profoundly painful dejection, abrogation of interest in the outside world, loss of capacity to love, lowering of self-regard, helplessness, depersonalization, phobic and obsessive-compulsive behavior, nihilistic delusions and suicidal rumination or attempts.

Such findings should lead to specific questioning about what the patient does to enjoy himself or what he can look forward to in hope of enjoying himself. A depressed patient states, quite specifically, that he is at present not enjoying himself, and that he cannot, except abstractly and without conviction, conceive that he will ever be able to enjoy himself again. Furthermore, if he recalls that he has had similar episodes in the past from which he has recovered, he will insist that the present episode is by far the worst. This core experience of lack of pleasure and competence will be taken as the common distinguishing trait of depressive syndromes. This trait, however, may be embedded within several psychopathological constellations, and it is the nature of the associated findings that in large measure determines both the prognosis and treatment course.

Psychiatric History

As with schizophrenia, there is no specific, uniform type of childhood development associated with affective disorders. In general, the level of manifest childhood psychopathology is quite unremarkable. If anything, these patients were good, obedient children, with some degree of infant separation anxiety and early development of conscience. This conscience was only occasionally overly strict with obsessional or perfectionistic trends. They were affiliative, socially responsible and concerned with approbation and the good opinion of others. If neurotic symptoms occurred, they were usually of a phobic, dependent or perfectionistic variety.

Chapter V

RETARDED DEPRESSION

Definition

The outstanding feature of the patient with retarded depression is psychomotor deceleration. The patient is unable to respond quickly or spontaneously, either in thought or in action. Features closely related to this defect are slowed speech, fixed expression, reluctance to answer questions, difficulty in establishing contact, slowed, deliberate, labored movements, apathy, indifference, unresponsiveness, low, weak or whispered voice, dragging gait or stupor. Not every patient presents all these features, and to some extent the number of such features defines the depth of the depression.

Frequent physiological indicators of retarded depression are: early morning awakening and inability to return to sleep again, feeling worse in the early part of the day and better as the day progresses, loss of appetite and weight, loss of sexual desire, secondary impotence or frigidity, constipation, pallor, poor emotional expression, inability to cry, dry mouth, coldness of the extremities, dryness of the skin, or a general appearance of aging. All of these features should be considered confirmatory signs of a retarded depression.

Retarded depressions have been said to occur often in middle-aged females with a familial history of depression,

pyknic habitus, middle or upper class socioeconomic status
and obsessional personality traits. Although these features
are interesting as provocative of etiological speculation,
they are of no diagnostic consequence since one would neither
make or rule out a diagnosis on the basis of their occurence.

Inconstant precipitants are: psychological losses, disappointments, bereavement, prolonged exhaustion, virus and
bacterial infection, debilitation, weight loss, major surgical operations, brain pathology, endocrine disorder, electro-
lyte disorder, toxic agents such as reserpine and possibly
other psychotropic drugs.

Onset of Illness

There is nothing diagnostic about the onset of retarded
depression which varies from insidious to abrupt. Patients
often state that they went to bed feeling fine and awoke
feeling terrible. Others find it difficult to point to any
clear-cut mood transition.

Course

Retarded depressions may occur repeatedly, but it is
usually quite impossible to predict their periodicity. Some
specific cases have predictable cycles, yearly, seasonal or
even daily. A history of repeated episodes of retarded depression with intervening clear periods of social and psychological competence is one of the most distinguishing diagnostic constellations within all of psychiatry. It is
usually referred to as Manic-Depressive Psychosis, Depressed.
The term "psychotic depressive" applies to patients with a
single, severe, retarded depression. The utility of these
terms seems dubious since the first asserts a necessary uni-
ty with manic disorders, even if no manic episode has ever
occurred, and the second erects a distinction of no demonstrated prognostic or therapeutic value. Also, the use of
the term psychosis can only lead to confusion when one is

describing a patient with mild depressive retardation and no
other symptoms. One might better simply refer to these illnesses as retarded depressive states, single or repeated,
that are either potentially or manifestly psychotic. If
manic episodes have occurred also, the diagnosis of manic-
depressive state, with degree of psychosis specified, seems
reasonable.

Differential Diagnosis

The severe retarded depression may be confused with a
stuporous schizophrenic state, especially if depressive ideas
of reference or somatic preoccupations that achieve delusional significance are present. If the patient is almost mute,
it may render interview impossible. Under these circumstances, amytal interview or carbon dioxide inhalation are
valuable diagnostic devices. Both temporarily alleviate
massive retardation. Under these conditions the schizophrenic patient will then regularly display massive magical delusional states, whereas the depressive will simply demonstrate affect-congruent ideation.

Toxic states may mimic stupor, but other signs of intoxication, e.g., respiratory depression, ataxia, nystagmus,
dysmetria, etc., are usually present.

MARCIA DORN

PRESENTING PROBLEM

Mrs. Marcia Dorn was 49 when she applied for her sixth
psychiatric hospitalization. She had suffered many episodes
of depression over a 16 year period and now appeared haggard,
pale and grossly depressed. For the previous two months she
had become increasingly unable to go to work or to do household chores. Although she had some appetite, she was losing
weight, had insomnia alternating with periods of prolonged
sleep, felt "empty," had suicidal ruminations, worried about
the future and had considerable self reproach.

FAMILY

Mrs. Dorn came from a middle-class family. Her mother committed suicide at age 36. Marcia was six at the time and remembered little about her mother.

Her father, born in Europe, came to America as a young man. His education was limited, but he was hardworking and moderately successful as a life insurance salesman. Marcia had deep affection for her father who was a good provider and very fond of his children. He loved his first wife but remarried shortly after her death in order to provide care for his children. When Marcia was 20, he died of diabetes, at age 49.

The stepmother, a childless widow, was cruel and shrewish. After Marcia's father's death she remarried and had no further contact with her stepchildren.

Of her four siblings, Marcia was closest to her brother, five years her senior. He was always jovial, good-natured, extraverted and popular. Her sister, four years her senior, died accidentally in a fire, at age ten. A brother,two years younger,was "intense" with plenty of drive, affability and good looks. She was not close with him. She was very fond of a sister,six years younger, a happy, well-adjusted, outgoing person, and the two shared many confidences. Her half-brother, eight years younger, was also happy-go-lucky and outgoing.

Mrs. Dorn's husband was a year older than herself. Although an attorney, he never practiced law, but instead ran a successful business. They met when Marcia was in her early 30's and married when she was 34. Married to his first wife for 15 years, but childless, he divorced to marry Marcia. He proved to be inconsiderate, irritable, dogmatic, precise, rigid and dependent, a strict observer of Jewish laws when it benefited him. There were many arguments from the beginning of their marriage.

They had a teenage son, good-looking and sensitive, but often disobedient and lazy. He had a few friends and performed adequately in school, although he was often lost in daydreams.

DEVELOPMENTAL HISTORY

Mrs. Dorn knew nothing of her mother's condition during pregnancy, details of labor, nor conditions at birth. No developmental history was available. She recalled no particular problems as a child, at least as far as her father had told her. Despite many years of psychological exploration, memories of her early years were extremely vague.

A brother was born when she was two. Her only memory involving her mother was being given a beautifully dressed doll which pleased her very much. When Marcia was six her older sister died, her mother became pregnant to alleviate her depression, but shortly after giving birth committed suicide.

Six months after her mother's death, her father remarried a cruel childless widow, as a matter of convenience. The four children became very close, joining together to oppose her. When Marcia was eight, the stepmother bore a son who received markedly preferential treatment. There were many bitter arguments between father and stepmother, and after two years they attempted a separation. Mrs. Dorn, then age ten, recalled this period of keeping house for her father as very pleasant. When father and wife reunited, the children lived with an aunt or a grandmother for periods of time, never really returning to the father's home for a prolonged stay.

Mrs. Dorn had been a better than average student, and learned easily and rapidly. While quiet and reserved, she always had close friends.

Menarche was at 12½; she was prepared for it by her aunt and her girlfriends. She was concerned about her breast de-

velopment and wore a tight chest band to allay her embarrassment. In adolescence she became outgoing and popular. She
dated, engaged in necking and petting, but was never promiscuous.

     Because she could only afford a city college, after
graduating from high school at 17,she decided to attend business school for a year, and did very good work there. At
this time she was living with her grandmother with whom she
was close.

     At 18, she went to work at a large department store,
and over 13 years held many different jobs there, working up
to the position of executive secretary and finally assistant
buyer. Her job presented many pressures, and she worked
very successfully.

     At the death of her father, when she was 20, she and
her siblings took an apartment together; one by one, as they
married, they left this home.

     As an adult, Mrs. Dorn was quiet, reserved and undemon-
strative of affection. Her mood, while even, was not particularly cheerful. She was compulsively neat, worried excessively about inconsequentials, was dissatisfied with herself
and had strong inferiority feelings.

     Mrs. Dorn worked and socialized through her 20's. At
age 31,she met her future husband, while vacationing. It
was "love at first sight." Shortly after they met he entered the army. She travelled many hours to spend weekends with
him. Her first sexual relations which took place at this
time were pleasant and enjoyable. Because Mr. Dorn was married, their courtship was prolonged until his divorce was
final.

     At age 33, shortly before marriage, she suffered her
first severe emotional upset. She suddenly became unable to
work, jittery, sleepless,had headaches, ruminated about getting married and was generally incapacitated. Treated with

psychotherapy and six ECT, she improved after two months.

A year later she married, quit her job, moved to the army base where her husband was stationed and found work as a legal secretary. The marriage was very difficult from the beginning. Mr. Dorn behaved indifferently toward his wife, spent none of his leisure with her, instead played golf or attended to private matters. They had numerous quarrels and would not speak to each other for days at a time. Nevertheless, he demanded frequent sexual intercourse.

She became pregnant within the year and her husband behaved even more coolly. The birth was uneventful. Whereas before her pregnancy she had been passionate and sexually interested, she lost all interest in sex after the delivery. However, she complied with her husband's frequent demands for intercourse.

She seriously considered leaving her husband, once when the baby was four months old and again when he was one year. She was continually torn by her husband's lack of interest in herself and the child, his rejection, inconsiderateness, coldness, preoccupation with golf and his own affairs. However, each time he persuaded her to stay.

Mrs. Dorn's second severe depression occurred when she was 40. She was hospitalized at a private clinic, diagnosed as having a psychoneurotic depression, and treated with psychotherapy. The depression lifted; she was released after three months and claimed she felt better than she had in four years.

When she was 42, she underwent a hysterectomy for a uterine tumor. There were no emotional changes consequent to this. Five years later, at age 47, in the Spring, she had a third severe episode of depression for which she was hospitalized for five months at a private psychiatric hospital. The following Spring she was again depressed and rehospitalized for five months. Each time she received psychotherapy and ECT (unknown amount) and improved.

The next Spring she was hospitalized at a city hospital where she remained for two weeks. Because she received little attention at the city hospital, she applied for admission to Hillside for her sixth psychiatric hospitalization, at age 49.

Having long experience with her depressions, she knew when they were about to descend, what stage she was in and when they were about to resolve. At the beginning of an episode she was irritable, suffered headaches, dizziness, low back pain and was unable to concentrate on conversations, reading or television. Usually active, she would lose her desire to work. In the morning she was particularly jittery and depressed, and during the day had difficulty in doing household chores. The condition always improved within a few months, and she would resume normal life.

During the eight years that she was periodically hospitalized, she worked as a part-time stenographer. When her illness exacerbated, she would take to bed. Her husband was impatient, greatly angered by her behavior and felt that the illness was a manifestation of lack of will power. The marriage was poor, however Mrs. Dorn blamed this on her illness.

PRESENTING CHARACTERISTICS

Mrs. Dorn appeared thin, pale, dry skinned, sluggish, and grossly depressed; nevertheless, she described herself as being halfway out of her current depression. Her conversation was spontaneous, but speech and motor activity were somewhat retarded. There was no hand wringing, pacing, or motor restlessness.

She spoke of always wanting to take an overdose of sleeping pills when depressed, but never acted on this. No psychotic delusional ideation was present. Her intellectual abilities were intact and her insight and judgment were good.

COURSE AT HILLSIDE

The results of all physical tests were normal, as was her EEG. On the Wechsler-Bellevue, her full scale IQ was 132, her verbal IQ was 135, and her performance IQ was 125.

Mrs. Dorn was treated with exploratory and supportive psychotherapy, but remained considerably depressed. After four months of no improvement, she was placed in the drug program. During the first six week placebo treatment period, Mrs. Dorn continued absolutely helpless, hopeless and verging on stupor, responding slowly and laconically to questioning and demonstrating no spontaneity whatsoever. Her doctor considered that she was possibly becoming catatonic.

Preceding the course on placebo, she received 10 mg of Tofranil, intravenously, as part of an EEG research project. Twenty minutes after the injection, she felt perfectly well and normal, "as if a veil had lifted." This feeling disappeared within six hours. Following the placebo regimen, she received a course of Tofranil and after the first dose of 25 mg orally, she felt better, "as if my head just opened up." In the first few days of Tofranil treatment, she was able to plan for a weekend at home without dread. She no longer felt tense and anxious; in fact, she felt extremely good. Within two weeks she was receiving 225 mg Tofranil daily; she was excited, perhaps a bit too peppy and beginning to get "high." She was never sleepy and her appetite had decreased. However, she denied feeling giddy or euphoric.

Because of the hypomanic reaction to Tofranil, it was reduced to 100 mg, then 50 mg, then discontinued within a few days. A week after the Tofranil was stopped, she continued to feel "hopped up" and unable to waste a minute. She was hostile, angry and outspoken, although she claimed everything was wonderful. However, she was bothered by

sleeping poorly. A week later she continued to be very aggressive and domineering and was sleeping only four hours a
night. With the addition of chloral hydrate sedation at night
on an irregular basis, she felt alert, chipper, wonderfully
well, wishing others could feel the way she did.

She began to express extreme hostility toward her husband, who had been forcing her to have sexual relations
through all of her illness, not only at home on weekend passes, but on the hospital grounds behind bushes or in the
parking lot. Also, he was frequently physically assaultive,
and refused to give her money for expenses. She firmly decided to divorce him and contacted a lawyer to start proceedings.

When her doctor disagreed with her wish to be discharged, wanting her to examine her reactions more carefully, she
became very angry and vociferously refused to cooperate with
him or hospital rules. Thus, eight months after admission
she was discharged, much improved, on no medication. The
hospital diagnosis was manic-depressive psychosis, depressed;
the research diagnosis was recurrent retarded depression,
with Tofranil-induced hypomania.

FOLLOW-UP

Upon discharge, Mrs. Dorn and her son went to live with
an aunt with whom they remained for nine months, while the
divorce was pending. She saw a psychiatrist in after-care,
eight times over the first six months, but terminated because
she felt treatment unnecessary. When she obtained her divorce, she returned to her own apartment after her husband
vacated it.

In the second year post-Hillside, she suffered a "minor
relapse" after being fired from a job for the first time in
her life. She returned to her psychiatrist who placed her
on Tofranil and Compazine (amounts unknown) for five months.
Within a month she recovered and started a new job. The next

year she continued working as a legal secretary, increased
her social contacts, had an unhappy love affair, yet suffered
no depressive relapse.

Ten years after her Hillside hospitalization, Mrs. Dorn
was contacted. She reported that she was now living alone
since her son had recently married a girl of whom she was
particularly fond. She was looking forward to a close, warm
relationship with the two young people.

She had been working full-time as an executive secretary, holding her present job for six years. Socially, she
had a group of close, active friends. She took no medication
and received no psychotherapy for the previous eight years.

An excerpt from her response read: "I give a great deal
of credit for my present well-being to Hillside where I was
able to gain the insight to realize what was causing my depressions. Through therapy I gained the courage to sever a
bad marriage and to have the self confidence to support myself and my teenage son. It has turned out well. In addition to great peace of mind, I have been fairly happy, accepting things in life as they come along.

"I am more stable than most of my many friends and enjoy greater peace of mind. All of this I attribute, to a
great extent, to my eight months at Hillside. I am grate-
ful."

COMMENT

Noteworthy is Mrs. Dorn's familial history, as demonstrated by her mother's suicide. That severe recurrent depressions have an extremely strong familial trend has been
amply documented. One should distinguish between recurrent
unipolar depressions with a course marked by depressions
only, and recurrent bipolar affective illness with a course
marked by both depressions and manic states. Evidence has
been presented that both of these illnesses are familial,

and that recurrent unipolar depressions tend to be associated with a familial history of unipolar depression; in paral-
lel fashion, recurrent bipolar affective disorder is associated with bipolar familial disorder. It is likely that the
familial genetic approach will help us subdivide the depressions into more homogeneous subgroups.

Although Mrs. Dorn had apparently a recurrent unipolar
depression, in that she never spontaneously developed a manic episode, upon exposure to Tofranil she developed a manic
episode, thus leading to conjecture whether the sharp familial distinction between unipolar and bipolar affective disorder might require redefinition in terms of drug reactivity.

It is of marked interest that once the patient entered
into a hypomanic or manic stage, Tofranil withdrawal did
not lead to a normalization. This shows that such agents
are not simple stimulants but work to reset deranged control
mechanisms (4,7). Mrs. Dorn's extremely quick responses
to Tofranil were strikingly atypical: both her responses to
her initial injection and the later response to the first
oral dose of medication. It is this rare response to Tofranil which leads one to wonder whether the Tofranil antidepressant effect depends upon slow changes in the enzymatic
handling of catecholamines, as current theory indicates, or
whether some more specific neurophysiological impact may be
the case.

Another interesting, typical feature of her recurrent
depressions is their seasonal link. Several surveys have
indicated a marked tendency for recurrent depressions to develop in the Spring and Fall. The meaning of this is entirely obscure.

It is also well-known that manic-depressive patients
frequently divorce during their manic periods. Their behavior is usually intolerably egocentric, and at the same time

they don't look "ill" because they appear to be having a
good time. Therefore their spouses are alienated and punitive, rather than "understanding," as they usually are during
depressive phases. The manic patient loses both separation
anxiety and depressive expectations of failure and misery,
so that he eagerly looks forward to a free, happy, single
life and rejects the confines of marriage. This socio-psy-
chological impasse often results in divorce.

This process is one of the hazards of drug-induced mania, and permanent family disruption can occur unless adequate
family counseling is pursued. However, in this case, family
disruption seemed very much in the patient's interests.
Whether her prolonged remission should be attributed to her
divorce or Tofranil is unresolvable.

This patient is typical of a large group, where antidepressants have substituted for recurrent ECT.

WILLIAM RALL

PRESENTING PROBLEM

William Rall came to Hillside for the first time when
he was 25, shortly after he had earned a Ph.D. in biology.
While preparing for final exams several months earlier, he
became anxious and self-derogatory, accusing himself of becoming slipshod, and passing "under false pretenses." He
claimed he had falsified some of his experimental data. This
was unusual, if not unbelievable behavior, for he had always
been obsessive and perfectionistic in his work. Depressed
and irritable, he could not enjoy anything, was increasingly
self-denigrating, and withdrew from his usual social activities. However, after receiving his Ph.D., he forced himself
to function and found a good job in New York.

He found the city a crowded, noisy, ugly jungle.   The
night before starting his new job he couldn't sleep, had
shivers and buzzing feelings in his arms and legs, chills and

hot flashes. However, he went to work and managed there
for five days before his anxiety reached unbearable propor-
tions. He became severely anorexic, completely insomniac and
constipated. He had crying spells, felt hopeless in the
morning but somewhat better toward evening. Considering suicide by cyanide or carbon monoxide, he decided against it,
not wanting to "drag his family's name in the dirt." He developed headaches, backaches, felt that his hearing, vision
and memory were impaired, and that he might have cancer or a
brain tumor. His family doctor examined him, reassured him,
prescribed tranquilizers and referred him to a psychiatrist.
The psychiatrist wanted to treat him as an outpatient, but
Dr. Rall insisted that he needed emergency hospitalization
immediately and contacted Hillside.

FAMILY & DEVELOPMENTAL HISTORY

William was born normally at full term. He was bottle
fed, and a healthy, happy, chubby baby for his first two
years. By 18 months he walked, talked and was toilet-trained. From two on, his mother described him as a sickly, weak
child, mainly because he had all the childhood illnesses, including pertussis, during his first few years. After age
two, he became skinny and didn't want to eat, "only potatoes
and hamburgers." His mother spoon fed him completely until
he was eight years old, and occasionally until he was 13.
He would often vomit after eating. Always very close to his
mother, Dr. Rall described her as a wonderful woman; he found
it impossible to feel negatively toward her.

The mother had no education and was illiterate, but was
loving, tender, sympathetic, a good homemaker and deeply attached to her son.

The father, approximately the same age as the mother,
was quiet, shy, stubborn, penurious, and lacking in ambition.
Aside from working as a janitor, his only activity was listening to the radio or watching TV. His main interaction

with his son consisted of hitting him if he didn't eat.

A brother was five years older. While growing up the
two boys were not close. They fought often, usually about
possessions. The brother, a non-conforming, unconventional
go-getter, started work early in order to help support the
family. He took much pleasure in Dr. Rall's achievements.

Both parents argued often about money, the mother criticizing her husband's lack of ambition. There was no trust
and little affection between them. They often spoke about
divorce but did not pursue the matter, supposedly to provide
a stable family for their children.

As a child William made friends easily. He was not shy,
though he spent most of his time alone, reading or daydreaming. His early summers were spent at a settlement camp. Always extremely well-behaved, he resented most being scolded
by his parents or humiliated or teased in any way. He never
displayed or discussed his emotions and always tried very
hard to get along with people, in order to avoid any eruption
of ill feeling on their part. His mother confided her unhappiness with her husband to him. He disliked his father,
and from a very young age planned to set up an apartment for
himself and his mother, as soon as his schooling was completed.

In high school he had a close friend with whom he shared
many interests. The two remained inseparable until they went
to different colleges. During summers he worked at odd jobs.
Dr. Rall was quite successful both academically and socially
during his school years and remembered them as essentially
happy. Because it was obvious that he should pursue high
educational attainments, Mrs. Rall took a factory job in order to help pay for his future education.

At 16 he began masturbating, after discussing it with
his close friend. He enjoyed heterosexual fantasies and often looked at pin-up pictures.

During his four years of college he lived at home and
spent most of his time studying. On rare occasions he dated
or participated in group social activities. He attributed
the paucity of his social activities to the fact that he had
to study hard. He did extremely well in college and decided
to work for an advanced degree, helping to support himself
by working as an undergraduate instructor. Because of his
outstanding work, his Masters degree requirement was waived
and he was able to complete his Ph.D. within four years.

While at graduate school, he met a bubbly, happy, bright
girl with whom he went steady. She was interested in frivo-
lous things like parties and football games, much more than
he had the interest, time or money for. They argued continually about her wanting to do things that he did not enjoy,
and finally after a year and a half he terminated the relationship, explaining that they were incompatible. Their sexual relationship consisted of petting only. He did not feel
too bad about the breakup and immersed himself in work. A
year later, he attempted to rekindle the romance, but their
one date went poorly. Shortly thereafter, while preparing
for his Ph.D. exams, his illness, described earlier, began.

PRESENTING CHARACTERISTICS

On admission to Hillside, Dr. Rall related warmly to the
examiner. He walked and moved slowly. His speech was slow,
pedantic and obsessively ruminative, with mild blocking, ir-
relevancy and circumstantiality. His memory, retention and
recent recall were impaired; his ability to think abstractly
was definitely lower than his academic achievements would indicate. He had the somatic delusion that he had cancer, and
expressed considerable concern over what he felt were bodily
changes; for example, he felt there was an unnatural flat
place on his scrotum, indicating there was something wrong
with his genitals. Also he was alarmed about a slight normal
bilateral depression over his sacrum that he had never notic-

ed before. No persecutory trends, ideas of reference, nihilism, grandiosity or significance, delusions of influence or
hallucinations were apparent.

COURSE AT HILLSIDE

The results of all physical and neurological examinations, including the EEG, were within normal limits. His
Wechsler-Bellevue full scale IQ was 115, with a verbal IQ of
117. His performance IQ of 110 reflected the slowness with
which he performed test tasks. He also showed considerable
blocking; for example, he was unable to formulate the simi-
larity between wood and alcohol, or to answer some extremely
simple items. His IQ test performance belied his true superior abilities.

During his first two weeks at the hospital, Dr. Rall had
a full continuation of all his symptoms. Thus, he was placed
on Tofranil 75 mg daily. While he complained of increased
sweating, within four days his depression decreased somewhat.

Then, he and his mother decided that his problems were
physical and could best be treated medically, elsewhere. After persuasion and explanation by his doctor, he gave himself
ten days to get better. Tofranil was increased to 150 mg
daily and within two weeks he had a diminution of anxiety and
depression. During the following week he was smiling,
bright, alert, relaxed and friendly.

His approach to psychotherapy remained intellectual, and
he attained only superficial insights. When the depression
abated, he lacked pressure to explore his feelings. After
one month on Tofranil, he announced, "I have come to myself
both physically and mentally. It was ridiculous to think
something was happening to my brain. I drew wrong conclusions from the terrible feelings I was having."

He was released in a much improved condition after three
months of hospitalization and planned to return to his job

and set up his own apartment. His hospital diagnosis was psychotic depressive reaction, chronic type; the research diagnosis was acute retarded depression of psychotic degree.

FOLLOW-UP

Dr. Rall returned to his job and functioned well. He dated a girl who had been a patient at Hillside, and they married three years later. They were compatible and happy until suddenly, eight years after his hospitalization, he again became depressed when the head of his department, his close friend, was fired and he was chosen to replace him. His earlier symptoms including gastric disturbances, dizziness and inability to concentrate,returned. He entered treatment with a doctor who placed him on Tofranil 25 mg twice daily, for several weeks, which was not effective.

Then, Dr. Rall decided to leave his job and teach at a university instead. Through a friend he found a professorship, but after several days of teaching, he felt lost, uncomfortable and much the way he had after starting his first job nine years earlier. For several weeks he stayed at home, in a retarded state, ruminating about his inability to teach. Eventually he attempted suicide by drinking dilute cyanide. His wife found him in time and his stomach was pumped. Immediately he pointed out that this was not a true suicide attempt, for if he seriously wanted to die, he would have drunk a concentrated solution. His motive, he claimed, was to get attention and help from his family.

Five days later he repeated the attempt, and this time was found by the police. After emergency treatment, he was persuaded to accept voluntary commitment at a state hospital. There he was diagnosed as having a depressive neurosis and treated with Mellaril 75 mg daily, and Noludar 300 mg for sleep. After a week at the hospital he submitted a request to be released in order to seek longer term hospitalization at Hillside.

On readmission to Hillside, nine years after his initial hospitalization, he seemed moderately depressed, with slightly retarded motor activity, as shown by slow walk and gestures. His affect was flat and constricted. Other than this, his mental status was unremarkable. He specifically denied suicidal ideation or delusions.

At the hospital he participated in activities and was cooperative but demanding of his doctor's time. Insomnia prompted him to persistently request sleeping pills. He intellectualized and denied his illness. During this period his doctor was unable to come to a definite diagnosis and treatment plan, because of Dr. Rall's bland minimization, and the family's persistent pressure for discharge. After two weeks the patient stated that he did not think the hospital was for him and signed out, against medical advice, in the company of his wife and brother. Five days later Dr. Rall committed suicide by drinking a concentrated cyanide solution.

<h3 style="text-align:center">COMMENT</h3>

Dr. Rall was typical of most recurrent retarded depressives as his developmental history and early socialization were quite normal, although he was extremely involved with his mother, who considered him sickly.

Unfortunately typical is the fact Dr. Rall received only 50 mg daily of Tofranil while being treated as an outpatient; such homeopathy is all too frequent. Also typically, he attempted a job change as a solution to his depressive state, a common reaction in depressives who attribute their internal distress to external circumstances.

It is often felt that so called "endogenous" depressions do not have precipitating circumstances; actually this is incorrect. A higher proportion of neurotic depressions do demonstrate precipitating circumstances, however "endogenous" depressions may also have environmental precipitants.

Also supposedly atypical, although I believe quite typical, is the concreteness and abstraction deficit occurring while acutely depressed, which may progress to delusional psychosis. Such thought disorder is not restricted to schizophrenia. Finally, unfortunately typical is the eventual suicide which occurs, it has been estimated, in 15-25% of severe recurrent depressives.

This sort of patient demonstrates a defect in our procedures for the management of the probably suicidal patient who is nonetheless able to deny and minimize his suicidal preoccupation and who refuses further treatment. Many doctors are loathe to commit such patients to state institutions, which is the only practical device available, because they know that the patient will be promptly discharged from the chronically understaffed state facility.

Perhaps other social interventions could be developed for patients in this ambiguous status. For instance, it is conceivable that such patients could be provided a mandatory para-professional companion trained to deal with potentially suicidal patients and to elicit their suicidal concerns. Such a companion could conceivably be assigned for a definite short period of time; i.e., several weeks. Probably one would require several shifts of such personnel in the initial phases of the patients' supervision. I believe that the presence of a continually sympathetic person, interested in helping the patient, would frequently result in communication of the suicidal preoccupations of such cases and institution of appropriate treatment.

Chapter VI

AGITATED DEPRESSION

Definition

The premorbid personality of agitated depressives is often over-conscientious, authoritarian, obsessional and cliché-minded. These patients have little flexibility or adventuresomeness and are primarily engrossed in a stereotyped and repetitive way of life. Actual obsessive or compulsive symptoms are rare, although the entire character structure may be considered obsessional.

As with the retarded depression, the history of repeated agitated depressions with good psychosocial functioning between episodes is a striking diagnostic entity. There is no specific diagnostic feature of the course of illness.

Agitated depressions occur either as repetitions, interspersed irregularly throughout the adult life of the patient, or may occur for the first time within the involutional period. The onset is often abrupt. Even more frequently than with retarded depression, it is apparently precipitated by a loss or bereavement. However, any occurrence that derails the patient from his accustomed stereotyped routines, such as moving his home or changing jobs, may be sufficient to precipitate an agitated depression. Recovery may either be abrupt or gradual and is often associated with a denial of any residual problems. These patients are most frequently diagnosed as Manic-Depressive-Depressed, Involutional Melancholia, or Psychotic Depressive Reaction.

Diagnostic Traits

The agitated depressions share the common core depressive mood reflected in loss of present and anticipated pleasure, and often exceed the retarded depressions in the conviction of loss of competence. However, the motor inhibition shown in the retarded depressions is not apparent. Rather, the patient exhibits an excess of undirected and unproductive activity; e.g., purposeless attempts at motor discharge of tension via hand wringing, pacing, shouting and going through agonizing contortions. Somatic preoccupations and concern with physical illness are frequently associated with this syndrome. The patient is in severe manifest psychic pain so that the appearance of a doctor or nurse calls forth a burst of suppliant complaints in the hope that this will somehow coerce quick relief. This demanding feature has misled some into believing that depression is primarily a covert, coercive maneuver.

Other inconstant psychopathological aspects of the agitated depression are unrestrained feelings and emotions, overtalkativeness, hurried speech, loud, boisterous or intense behavior, anxious uneasy and apprehensive attitudes, overactivity, restless and accelerated behavior, attitudes of self-depreciation and inadequacy, difficulty in concentration and inability to prevent rumination about unpleasant things.

To sum up, the agitated depressions share with the retarded depressive disorders a derangement of the central regulatory pleasure-reward system; the associated motor response facilitory system is not inhibited, but rather is activated.

The differential diagnosis of agitated depression is more difficult than with retarded depression. The retarded depression is practically unmistakable. However, the agitated depression evinces many similarities to states often considered as depressions of a neurotic or reactive nature.

NAOMI STURM

PRESENTING PROBLEM

Naomi Sturm, an advertising agency executive, was 41, married, and the mother of a 17 year old daughter. Three months prior to admission at Hillside, severely depressed, she took an overdose of Thorazine and 50 sleeping pills. Emergency treatment was given at a local hospital from where she was transferred to a state institution. Here she was treated with Thorazine 300 mg daily and Compazine 30 mg daily. After a month on this regimen she remained anxious and depressed. The treatment was therefore changed to Compazine and Tofranil (amounts unknown). Her depression seemed to abate rapidly and her doctor at the state hospital felt she was sufficiently improved to be released. However, her husband felt strongly that she was incapable of caring for herself and had her transferred to Hillside.

This suicidal attempt was preceeded by a 15 year period of depression and anxiety for which she had received episodic psychiatric treatment. Her main symptoms were severe depression, withdrawal from all activities and contacts, and episodes of overwhelming anxiety.

FAMILY

Mrs. Sturm came from a middle-class family. Her parents both had been married and widowed previously; the father had three children by his first marriage. Naomi was the only child of this second marriage, born after both parents were over 35 years.

Her mother was very giving, loving and responded to Naomi's birth as if "Jesus had been born." She persisted in gratifying the child's needs immediately, which appeared to make the growing little girl feel helpless, incompetent and dependent. A grandmother lived with the family, and mother

and grandmother competed with each other in taking care of
Naomi and giving her gifts. Mrs. Sturm's mother later took
complete charge of raising Naomi's own daughter.

There was little information about the father, except
that he seemed to favor the three children from his previous
marriage. Naomi always appealed to him for love but ration-
alized that he couldn't give it because of his obligation to
the other children. The man worked hard and was successful
in his trade, although the family suffered economically during The Depression. When he died, Naomi, then age 37, suffered a period of intense mourning and claimed she never felt
right thereafter. The mother moved in with her daughter at
this time.

Mr. Sturm, the husband, was of a lower socioeconomic
class, had not attended college, and worked as an airplane
mechanic. He was intelligent, giving, gentle, kind, accepting and protective, but had a tic which bothered Naomi enor-
mously, even before they were married. In the first ten
years of their marriage, she made him feel constantly inadequate and unable to satisfy her in any way. She was frigid,
ridiculed his tic, his lack of social activity and his inability to express political and social views. However, he
managed to attain better, more prestigious jobs, provided
well and took a progressively stronger position in the family.

DEVELOPMENTAL HISTORY

Naomi was born 2½ months prematurely, but her early developmental history was normal. Her environment was extremely protective, with mother, grandmother and step-siblings
vying to take care of her. She was a frail child and ate
poorly. Although she was high-strung, shy, nervous, awkward
and afraid of other children, she still had friends and was
well-liked by them. She was an outstanding student and advanced rapidly. However, she never could sleep before exam-

inations and felt she was always "only next to best."

As a young child she had an intense preoccupation with
sex; with her boy cousins she would have sexual exploration
and play in a dark closet. From age nine on, she masturbated at least several times weekly. Menarche was at age 12,
and she had been prepared for it by her stepsister. She dated infrequently before she was married in her early 20's,
and had no sexual relationships other than her childhood experiences. Relating in a competitive, intellectual manner,
she always felt resentful, uncomfortable and bested by men.

At age 20, she graduated from college, missing Phi Beta
Kappa by half a point. She claimed she was relieved because
if she had won the key she feared people would expect too
much from her. However, this fear had not prevented her diligent efforts. After graduation she took a government job
and on a Summer vacation met her future husband. He was the
first man who made her feel warm and accepted, but she was
very ambivalent about marrying him because of his lower socioeconomic status, and mild facial tic. Her parents objected to the marriage, feeling that their daughter was too
good, bright and creative to marry someone of such lowly
position. Naomi stated that she wanted to stop the relationship but was afraid to admit making a mistake to her mother.
Instead, she continued going with him, trying to overlook
his tic, but relating to him in a condescending manner.

During their year of courtship, Naomi tried to seduce
him several times,but he would not respond. After his repeated proposals she finally consented, terrified that if
she refused to marry him, there would be no one else.

The marriage was full of strife but held together. Mrs.
Sturm did many things to annoy her husband. She neglected
her duties, was a poor housekeeper, entertained male "soul
mates" late into the night, and had boisterous card parties
when her husband was trying to sleep. Sexually, her husband

was active and adequate, but she was frigid and unable to
attain orgasm except by masturbation.

She remained markedly dependent upon her mother, constantly asking for advice and help in performing simple jobs;
e.g., boiling an egg or making a bed.

After a year of marriage their daughter was conceived
after a bitter argument in which Mr. Sturm threatened to
leave. This caused Naomi tremendous anxiety and she decided
to become pregnant in order to keep him. She was miserable
throughout her pregnancy. The delivery was long and arduous,
and she returned home to mother immediately after her confinement. Mrs. Sturm's mother and aunt took complete charge
of the new baby, since she felt inadequate to care for her
infant. After three months she and the baby returned to the
husband. They lived in a factory town where Mrs. Sturm was
lonely, miserable and felt she didn't belong. She gave her
husband an ultimatum that they either return to New York or
she would divorce him. They returned to New York and her
mother came to care for the baby. Finally, the three Sturms
moved into the mother's apartment.

The little girl was adorable and bright and spoke at
nine months. But suddenly, at 14 months, the child began to
have a tic and "the world caved in" for Mrs. Sturm. She was
terrified that her daughter would be a ticqueur and a failure,
and began a long correspondence with prominent professionals
who reassured her fruitlessly that it would pass.

She became obsessed, although not deluded, with the idea
that some terrible catastrophe (polio, blindness, etc.) might
befall the child, and in an effort to manage this fear, she
blocked any thoughts of her daughter. Soon Mrs. Sturm, now
age 26, began sleeping poorly, having disturbing dreams and
fearing she would be violent if she thought of the child.
She wanted to die and attempted suicide by cutting her
wrists.

Unsuccessful in her first attempt, she begged the family to obtain shock treatment for her, but the psychiatrist
they took her to recommended hospitalization, where she remained one week and then left against medical advice. At
home, despite the close surveillance of her father, she managed to slit her throat and wrists with a razor, having just
read about that method of suicide in a magazine. Once she
cut herself, the strong panic subsided and she came out of
the bathroom and calmly showed her father what she had done.
The family returned her to the city hospital where she remained three weeks and received hydrotherapy. Her main
thought during that hospitalization was "How will I commit
suicide?" She decided to set herself on fire but never implemented that plan.

From the city hospital she was sent to a state hospital
where she was diagnosed as a psychoneurotic, mixed type.
Here she received some psychotherapy, and felt fine while
talking to her doctor, but was otherwise depressed. Once
again she begged for shock treatment and was relieved by a
series of 17 ECT, claiming she felt better immediately.
However, she quickly became depressed again and another series of seven ECT was given. Suddenly,after five months,she
felt happy and well enough to go home.

Once at home, Mrs. Sturm adjusted marginally, keeping
mainly to herself and feeling nervous. (The daughter's tic
continued.) After two years, in a passing conversation, a
neighbor mentioned the name of a lay therapist whom Mrs.
Sturm contacted, liked, and saw three times a week for two
years, until she was 29. She related very well to this female therapist and felt better. The therapist encouraged her
to have affairs with other men, and she set off on a round
of sexual encounters, usually stemming from casual meetings.
Her husband knew nothing of these activities. She found no
enjoyment, always feeling dirty and guilty, and the affairs

were uniformly unsatisfactory. The only man who attracted
her strongly enough for her to consider leaving her husband
proved to be impotent.

During this time she started working at an advertising
agency. Later she saw her therapist sporadically, usually
when an affair was going poorly. Mrs. Sturm found her inability to respond sexually as a great frustration and continued to be dissatisfied with herself. However, life went
along for 11 years before she was unbearably miserable again.

It was at this point that her father died and she went
through a period of intense mourning, feeling nervous, edgy,
anxious, depressed, and in need of further psychiatric care.
In order to pay for this care it was necessary to stop her
daughter's serious music studies.

Once she began therapy again with her lay therapist,
Mrs. Sturm improved quickly. She continued seeing the therapist twice weekly, but after a year seemed to get worse.
Concerned about Mrs. Sturm's suicidal potential, the therapist referred her to a psychiatrist who diagnosed her as
having a neurotic character disorder with severe reactive
depression, and treated her with psychotherapy, Marsilid and
Thorazine. She showed improvement for a month until she developed hepatitis and the medication was discontinued.

While convalescing from the hepatitis, she became very
depressed and attempted suicide by inhaling gas from her
oven. She remained comatose for four days,requiring trache-
otomy and subsequently developing pneumonia. When her physical condition improved, she returned to outpatient treatment with her psychiatrist, requesting psychiatric hospitalization or at least shock treatment, but the doctor refused
"because it was obvious she had great guilt about her self-
aggression and regarded hospitalization or ECT as appropriate and deserved punishments."

However, she became increasingly withdrawn and he final-

ly "felt it necessary to resort to a short series of electroshock which gave moderate improvement." Following this,
she returned to her job, but with great difficulty, and her
condition deteriorated with increasing episodes of depression and overwhelming anxiety.

After several months the psychiatrist again resorted to
ECT which this time was "only moderately effective." Shortly after this course of ECT, the psychiatrist went on vacation. During this time Mrs. Sturm took the overdose of pills
which led to state hospitalization and eventually to Hillside.

PRESENTING CHARACTERISTICS

When she arrived at Hillside from the state hospital,
Mrs. Sturm's mood was only mildly anxious, under a brave façade of pleasantness and ingratiation. Her depression was
indicated by a frequent breakthrough of weeping, without any
warning, and she seemed distractible. Other than this she
maintained a rather set, pleasant facial expression. There
was no motor retardation. She showed no thought disorder
and her speech productivity was normal. In general, her mental status was unremarkable.

COURSE AT HILLSIDE

All physical examinations were within normal limits.
Her Wechsler-Bellevue IQ score was 128, but it was felt that
she was distracted and anxious during the testing and that
her true abilities were greater.

Within a few days after admission to Hillside, the
Compazine and Tofranil medication that Mrs. Sturm had been
receiving at the state hospital was withdrawn to allow proper diagnostic assessment under close supervision. A few
days later she became very depressed, spent her time alone
in her room, and would go for full days without eating. The
staff was very concerned that she would commit suicide. Several months later she stated that during this initial period

she had attempted suicide several times: by swallowing nail
polish remover, by putting one hand in water and sticking
her finger in an electric outlet, by placing a plastic bag
over her head and tying a rope around her neck, and by trying to drown herself in the bathtub.

After two months of hospitalization, she was in a state
of chronic agitation, pleading for help. While the Compazine and Tofranil she had received at the state hospital had
helped quiet her tensions, she felt medication was not sufficient and requested more psychotherapy, although she was
receiving three therapeutic hours weekly and was involved in
an active milieu program. She felt hopeless, confused, extremely jumpy, irritable and self-absorbed, with ideas of
reference that people would talk about her when she walked
down the street. She was convinced that these feelings
would plague her for the rest of her life.

Her doctor finally decided that psychotherapy was unrewarding and referred her to the drug program where she received placebo for three days, during which she was in a
state of constant terror, often wanting to scream for help.
Verbally, she was very blocked and claimed her words seemed
jumbled. This had started several weeks earlier and worsened on the "medication." She would look at people and say,
"I feel I am going to hurt that person," and her hands would
tremble. Demanding sedation and restraint, she begged to be
returned to the state hospital where she felt she would receive better control.

Interestingly, when observed by herself, she would just
sit quietly, but when a staff member approached she would
make threatening gestures or break windows. Because of her
deteriorating condition, she was removed from the drug study
after three days and placed on Thorazine 100 mg, intramuscularly, every six hours. Immediately she became less threatening, less pleading, sleepier, and talked about the diminu-

tion of the internal physical force impelling her to wild
action.

A week later Thorazine was increased to 1200 mg daily,
orally; she was quieter and more cooperative. The Thorazine
was then increased to 1800 mg daily and although she felt
dizzy, she seemed distinctly improved, less agitated and
slept better. In discussing her desire to hurt people she
stated that it was actually against her will and perhaps only
in her imagination.

Two weeks later the Thorazine was increased to 2100 mg
daily. She claimed she felt well except for the period between six P.M. and bedtime when rage and anxiety seemed to
well up overwhelmingly. Her improvement consisted primarily
of increased impulse control. Mood was only moderately
ameliorated. Tofranil 75 mg daily was added and increased 75
mg weekly until a total dosage of 300 mg daily was reached.
She began to look yet better, less depressed, more self-contained, composed, confident, well-groomed and could smile.
She remained somewhat blocked verbally and tongue-tied. Her
mood improved greatly, she related better with her husband
and spent weekends at home.

However, when her hand movements became jerky and tre-
morous, Tofranil was decreased to 150 mg daily. A week later
she panicked and became agitated. Her doctor was concerned
that the Tofranil was acting as an excitant and decreased it
to 75 mg daily. A week after that, the agitation started
again, usually after psychotherapy sessions, and she received
Thorazine 100 mg intramuscularly. In another week oral
Thorazine was increased to 2400 mg and then to 3200 mg daily
because of the noted marked agitated episodes, especially
after her psychotherapy sessions.

Her psychiatrist attributed her deterioration to his interpretation that she was "an orally dependent individual
who reacted to her father's rejection by attempting to com-

pete for his affection, and that she was competitive with all
males." He noted that when this topic was discussed, Mrs.
Sturm became very upset but quieted down when neutral subjects were presented. This was viewed by him as evidence of
the correctness of his interpretation. The research staff
believed that the patient was very dependent on her doctor
and viewed his interpretations as reproaches and criticisms
to which she was particularly sensitive.

Kemadrin 15 mg daily was added, fruitlessly, in the hope
that her agitation represented an extrapyramidal disorder.
Previously she had shown no parkinsonian effects from Thorazine, and her doctor had felt that antiparkinson drugs were
therefore not indicated.

A few weeks later, on the high Thorazine dose, Mrs.
Sturm began to twitch, jerk, stutter, was unable to read and
became photosensitive. She asked to have her medication decreased but her doctor did not think this was indicated in
view of her continued anxiety in interview.

Two months later her doctor was changed. She interacted
better with her new therapist. He took the approach that
Mrs. Sturm was fearful of rejection and criticism and focused
on that problem, which allowed her to accept her therapy sessions. Her improvement continued and two months later Thorazine was decreased slowly, over a several month period, from
3200 mg to 600 mg daily. Tofranil remained at 75 mg daily.

She was discharged after 13 months of hospitalization,
greatly improved, no longer displaying evidence of depression
or anxiety, although she still felt apprehensive and tense
in social situations. However, she was able to be more
forceful and confident in important relationships. The hospital diagnosis was chronic undifferentiated schizophrenia;
the research diagnosis was recurrent agitated depression.
After discharge she was to take Thorazine 600 mg daily, Kemadrin 15 mg daily and Tofranil 75 mg daily.

FOLLOW-UP

Mrs. Sturm returned to live with her husband and daughter. She received psychotherapy twice weekly at the Hillside after-care clinic,and her medication was changed to Tofranil 100 mg, and Thorazine 300 mg daily. She tried several part-time office jobs but none suited her, so she gave art lessons to neighborhood children. Toward the end of her first post-Hillside year she returned to her former job. Initially she had some fears that she would be mugged in a hall, but her fellow workers were supportive and these fears abated. She was also able to make a home wedding for her daughter, although she did not approve of her daughter's choice of husband. Her Thorazine was cut to 200 mg daily,while Tofranil remained at 100 mg daily.

From the second post-Hillside year she continued working full-time at her advertising job, cared for her home, gave art lessons on Saturday and saw her therapist twice a week. Six months later Thorazine was cut to 100 mg daily. Occasionally, she experienced severe depressions lasting only a few days, apparently unrelated to external events. She was able to continue her activities through these periods.

In the third post-hospitalization year she discontinued her weekly psychotherapy appointments, seeing her psychiatrist only when some untoward life event occurred (e.g., a friend committed suicide) about once every six months. For the next eight years, to the time of this writing, she continued working at her job and generally functioning at a high level. Her medication regimen consisted of Mellaril 25 to 50 mg daily, and Tofranil 25 to 100 mg daily, depending on her mildly fluctuating mood. When she suddenly developed hypothyroidism ten years after her Hillside hospitalization, it was successfully treated with thyroid replacement therapy.

COMMENT

Mrs. Sturm is typical in a variety of ways. She shows
a marked obsessional, perfectionistic character with strong
dependent trends, rejects medication as a useful treatment
and is fixated on psychotherapy as the necessary cure. Although ECT was demonstrably effective, her doctor at one
point procrastinated concerning its use, utilizing irrelevant
psychodynamic speculations. Several times she responded to
Tofranil, far better than to phenothiazines. However, because she was misdiagnosed as a schizophrenic, and Tofranil
was considered an excitant, her treatment heavily relied upon
phenothiazines and underused Tofranil. Also unfortunately
typical was the fact that emotional exacerbations produced
by interpretations made in psychotherapy were seen as verifi-
cations of interpretive accuracy.

It is of some interest that she developed thyroid disease in later life, in view of the work of Prange (13), indicating that thyroid medication is often of adjunctive value
in the treatment of female depressives with tricyclic antidepressants. The relationship of endocrine, and more particularly thyroid dysfunction to psychiatric illness remains
unclear. We have studied the relationship of thyroid function to psychiatric diagnosis and activation status without
any clear-cut results (2). Further, studies of the effects
of psychotropic agents on thyroid functions have largely been
negative. What findings exist are probably secondary to the
effects of the drug on other physiological systems such as
the kidney (3). However, certain anxiety syndromes markedly helped by Tofranil are particularly prone to occur in
a setting of endocrine disturbance (5). It is conceivable
that Mrs. Sturm's Tofranil-responsive agitated depression
may have reflected a covert endocrine disorder.

This patient had a long-term markedly unsatisfactory
marriage but was able to improve her emotional stability and

maintain her marriage when properly medicated. Such patients seem torn between a profound dependent need and their
lack of marital satisfaction. Although in principle it
might be more desirable for these patients to progress to
the point where their dependent needs are not overwhelming,
which would then allow them to be more self-determining,
this goal is often unattainable.

AGITATED DEPRESSION WITH PSYCHOPHYSIOLOGICAL DISORDER

The group of "psychophysiologic autonomic and visceral disorders" is separated from the neuroses, in the Diagnostic Manual (1), as being due "to the visceral expression of affect which may be thereby largely prevented from being conscious. The symptoms are due to a chronic and exaggerated state of a normal physiological expression of emotion, with the feeling, or subjective part, repressed."

The theoretical basis for this distinction from the psychoneurotic reactions or conversion reactions is "(1) involvement of organ and viscera innervated by the autonomic nervous system, hence not under full voluntary control or perception; (2) failure to alleviate anxiety; (3) physiological rather than symbolic origin of symptoms; (4) frequent production of structural changes... Differentiation is made from anxiety reactions primarily by predominant, persistent involvement of a single organ system" (p. 29). Again, the diagnosis is made on the basis of a mixture of presumed etiologic distinctions and descriptive traits.

It has proved difficult to isolate syndromes clearly, due to the chronic physiologic reverberations of affective disturbances. This difficulty is implicitly attested to by the Diagnostic Manual,since it does not define psychophysiological disorders in terms of specific syndromes, but rather in terms of the broad headings of a review of systems; i.e., skin reactions, musculo-skeletal reactions, respiratory reactions, cardiovascular reactions, etc. Under each of these systematic reaction types a number of well-known medical syndromes, such as neurodermatoses, backache, migraine, etc., are mentioned as psychophysiological reaction candidates. However, no clear-cut criteria are evinced to distinguish those migraines that are psychophysiological reactions from those that are not, etc. These matters are essentially left

to the individual predilections of the physician. Much work
remains to be done before it can be established which syndromes actually do represent psychophysiological reactions,
though much experimental and anecdotal evidence does support
this point of view.

SARA PAYNE

PRESENTING PROBLEM
     Sara Payne, age 39, entered Hillside because she felt
unable to care for herself, barren, without reason to live.
A month before, she had been hospitalized for an acute exacerbation of facial pain from which she had suffered severely three years earlier. Extensive neurological tests were
negative, and psychotherapy was recommended. On discharge
from the neurological service, she began to feel jittery,
nervous, obsessed with suicidal thoughts. She contacted a
psychiatrist who recommended hospitalization at Hillside.
FAMILY
     Mrs. Payne was the third of four siblings of a poor Jew-
ish family. Her birth was unplanned and her parents considered her presence an added burden on their already impover-
ished lives. Both parents came to New York from Europe, as
teenagers. The father was an orphan, physically weak, and
often unable to work because of his frequent attacks of incapacitating illness. However, he was too proud a man to
accept welfare, and strove to work hard, when he could, to
provide for his family. When he was ill, they managed on
very little money. As a child, Mrs. Payne was never close
to her father, since he was either working or ill. He died
when she was 36.
     The mother was unaffectionate, and mother and daughter
were not close until after Mrs. Payne married. Then the

mother became very ill, and Mrs. Payne, in her late 20's, nursed her intensively for several years until the mother's death.

Mrs. Payne was never close to her sister, who was six years older. Although the two shared a bed, they often fought furiously. The sister had always been emotionally disturbed; she suffered a malignancy, and later committed suicide. A brother, three years older, was sickly and married to a mentally deranged woman. Mrs. Payne was extremely close with a brother five years her junior, a quiet, tense person.

The mother and youngest brother shared another bed in the same room as the sisters; the father and older brother shared another bedroom. These were the sleeping arrangements until Sara was 14, and her older sister moved away from home. She claimed that these arrangements never bothered her since she did not know of any other way to live.

Her husband, a "gentle, warm person who would give you the shirt off his back" (though he barely had a shirt to give), suffered from ulcers, was eccentric, and unsuccessful in earning a living. Nevertheless, Mrs. Payne characterized their marriage as compatible and loving. He did not find steady employment for the first ten years of their marriage and later worked as a civil servant. It was because of the financial insecurity of their lives that they never wanted children, feeling that "children would be an overwhelming responsibility and a luxury that only richer people could afford."

DEVELOPMENTAL HISTORY

Birth was normal and little developmental history was available, except that her older brother described her as a "happy, jolly, roly-poly baby." She had convulsions during a high fever as an infant. Mrs. Payne remembered being a happy, singing, gay child.

In school she was a good student, frequently at the head
of her class. Her teachers liked her; she had many friends
and interests, particularly enjoying music lessons.

Menarche was at age 12, and she learned about sex from
her sister and girlfriends. During high school she was popular and dated frequently, but considered sexual activity with
fright.

Because her family did not have enough money to send
her to college, she took a general high school course. After
graduating at 16, she began to seriously study piano and
voice. Previously she had "naturally drifted into singing,"
and even won an amateur radio singing contest. On weekends
she sang with a band and did some classical concert work.
For five years she held an office job. Her brother characterized her as the most self-sufficent, reliable, well-
functioning person he ever knew.

She dated frequently and met her husband-to-be at age
19. He appeared eccentric, but she admired his handsomeness,
warmth and kindness, joy of living and interest in art and
music. They were married when she was 21 and he 26, and she
immediately quit her job. He held a variety of menial jobs
until he was drafted after nine months of marriage, and remained in the army for three years. Mrs. Payne moved back
with her mother, sometimes sang professionally, and when her
husband was stationed in the States, followed him to different posts. A year after her marriage, her mother became
severely ill, and Mrs. Payne nursed her for about a year.
During this period Mrs. Payne suffered from a facial tic, in-
voluntary eye blinking, nose wrinkling, and mild depression,
all of which remitted when her mother improved.

Upon discharge from the army, her husband returned to
New York, and they found a "temporary," low-rent apartment
in which they lived for the next seven years. Mrs. Payne
was unhappy with their living arrangement and finally, when

the situation became intolerable because of decay, rats and
roaches, returned to her mother's apartment. Her husband
then found a considerably more adequate apartment, although
the neighborhood was still terrible. He held numerous low-
paying jobs and failed at art school, although he considered
himself a free-lance artist. Sexually, she considered their
relationship compatible and found their sexual relations
pleasurable, although anorgasmic.

When Mrs. Payne was 28, her mother again became seriously ill and she nursed her intensively, since the mother would
not permit professional nurses near her. Mrs. Payne described this period as the most difficult time of her life. Two
years later the mother died, and while Mrs. Payne was grief-
stricken, she was able to continue functioning. One week
after her mother's death, her sister's husband, with whom
she had been very close, died suddenly; within the next
three years, another brother-in-law, her father-in-law and
mother-in-law, all with whom she had been close, died.

At approximately the time of the fourth death, Mrs.
Payne had some dental cavities filled, and following the
drilling, developed a constant dull burning in her right
cheek which spread to her eye, finally causing her to wear
an eye patch. The pain was refractory to all medical and
dental treatment, including root canal work and then extrac-
tion of the tooth, and was characterized by intermittent attacks of especially severe pain "like a hot spike in the
gum," with a varying degree of pain always present for a year
and a half. She became obsessed by the pain, the state of
her teeth and the fear of losing them.

The pain subsided after alcohol injection of the tri-
geminal nerve. At about the same time, when she was 37, her
husband became severely ill and died after a month of hospitalization. The entire experience was emotionally disastrous. She had a repetitive dream in which she went from

corridor to corridor and room to room in the hospital
searching for her sick husband, reliving many of the unpleasant events of his last few days, when she was often
forbidden to see him. Finally successful, she found him
alive, only to awake to her loss.

After her husband's death, she felt stuporous, withdrawn and floundering, unable to organize her life. She
stayed home most of the time, practiced the piano, lived on
her husband's insurance and pension, and found consolation
from her younger brother and sister-in-law who lived nearby, were very supportive of her, and with whom she spent
much time.

Six months after her husband's death, her father died
and her sister developed a malignancy; by this time, Mrs.
Payne was "numb." Nevertheless, the shocks passed and she
eventually started going out socially, learned to drive and
took adult education courses for diversion. Also, she spent
considerable time thinking about and looking for a better
apartment.

A year later, at age 38, she met a man whom she liked
and dated frequently. He wanted to marry her. However, he
was neurotic, ambivalent, insecure, and there was little
hope that he would ever earn a living. During her relationship with this man, Mrs. Payne began feeling "listless," and
her younger brother thought it might help if she took a job.
He helped her get placement in his office where she remained
for about a year,but then decided to stop, lacking interest
in the work. Also, she had finally decided to accept her
friend's marriage proposal in a "desperate, hopeless sort of
way," which she communicated and he rejected. Shortly following this rejection, her brother decided to move with his
wife and children to the suburbs. Mrs. Payne was very concerned about the separation, but brushed it aside, even helping her brother look for a house.

These were the events leading to the sudden acute exacerbation of facial pain after undergoing more dental work;
the pain had been quiescent for a year and a half. She visited several psychiatrists for one or two visits when physical treatment produced no relief, then entered a neurological hospital for further workup. All tests were normal, but
she appeared depressed and agitated, with suicidal thoughts,
and she was referred for further psychiatric consultation.
During her stay in the hospital, her brother moved to the
suburbs, leaving Mrs. Payne alone in the city. She became
increasingly anxious, insomniac, suicidally preoccupied,
agitated and depressed. When hypnosis, Ritalin, Compazine,
Miltown and Tofranil (amounts unknown) did not help (Stelazine "put me into a terrible daze" and Dilantin gave her a
rash), her psychiatrist recommended that she contact Hillside.

PRESENTING CHARACTERISTICS

Mrs. Payne was attractive, mild-mannered, soft-spoken
and appeared about ten years younger than her 39 years.
Knowledgeable about medical terms, intelligent and introspective, she attributed her inability to function and depression to her severe, constant facial pain and obsessive
concern over losing her teeth. She was somewhat overtalkative, and freely spoke of her very close feelings and attachment toward her younger brother, stating that his move affected her considerably. Living alone, she was shaky,
frightened, disinterested, and unable to care for her belongings or herself. Fearful of traveling alone, she was afraid
of continuing living and had a reeling sense of confusion.
Aside from the pain in her face, she had no other somatic
complaints. Her mental status was otherwise unremarkable.

COURSE AT HILLSIDE

The results of all physical and neurological tests, including the EEG, were negative, and no physical factors were

found accountable for her facial pain. On the Wechsler-
Bellevue, she attained a full scale IQ of 130, a verbal IQ
of 126 and a performance IQ of 130.

During the first month of hospitalization, her mood remained depressed, she spent a great deal of time alone and
complained of facial pain. In psychotherapy she showed introspective ability and insight. When her brother visited,
she requested that he provide her with sleeping pills so
that she could commit suicide. During the second and third
months, she seemed a bit more cheerful, attended activities
and dressed carefully. In therapy she spoke of her attempts
to combat her depression, explored her feelings about being
ill, and the reactions of her family to her illness.

In the fourth month of hospitalization, her sister committed suicide. Mrs. Payne appeared grief-stricken, tearful
and tense, visited with her family but did not attend the
funeral. Over the next month she was quite depressed, feeling hopeless and alone and was reluctant to attend psychotherapy for fear of losing her composure and becoming too upset. When she did attend sessions, she made demands for attention from her doctor and then obsessively ruminated about
whether having her teeth pulled would ease her facial pain.

Because of her continuing depression and lack of improvement, she was referred to the drug program and placed
on Tofranil 75 mg daily, raised 75 mg weekly until a dosage
of 300 mg daily was reached. Within the first two weeks,
she felt more lively, was very pleasant, readily engaged in
activities, but was jittery, with a hand tremor, constipation
and a feeling of having to gasp for breath. Her improvement
continued, and the Tofranil was reduced to 150 mg daily because of continuing side effects. In psychotherapy she was
quite obsessional, rehashing each statement, trying to ex-
tract all conceivable possibilities.

After a month on Tofranil, she stated, "My whole mood

is different and the pain in my face is much better. I feel
much more ambitious and enthusiastic about doing things. I
feel like maybe I was half alive and this has bolstered me
so much, I'm more like my gay old self. I'm more sociable
and can speak." Also her appetite increased, she gained
weight and the facial pain was increasingly better.

She began leaving the hospital on passes more frequently and socialized with her family and friends. Her improvement continued to such a degree that she was discharged after nine months of hospitalization with plans to continue in
psychotherapy at an after-care clinic and return to living
in her apartment alone. She refused to make job plans. She
was to continue taking Tofranil 150 mg daily. Her hospital
diagnosis was neurotic depressive reaction;   the research
diagnosis was recurrent agitated depression with atypical
facial pain.

FOLLOW-UP

After leaving Hillside, Mrs. Payne returned to her a-
partment. One week later her older brother died, but she
was able to continue without a relapse. She visited the after-care clinic weekly for ten months and remained on Tofranil 100 mg daily for seven months, and then discontinued the
drug. Severe facial pains returned and she resumed Tofranil
for another three months and then stopped both psychotherapy
and medication. She found part-time office work because she
did not feel energetic enough to pursue a full-time job. A
very close relationship existed with her long-term male
friend. At a two year follow-up interview, Mrs. Payne spoke
of her continued periodic mild depression and mild facial
pain, but felt treatment was unnecessary.

A year later, she gave up her part-time job, moved into
a new house with her boyfriend and appeared to be doing well,
with no signs of depression, but continuing mild facial pain.
She and her boyfriend did not marry in order to avoid losing

their pensions.

After a year and a half of this living arrangement, her boyfriend, who seemed manic-depressive, became increasingly manic and began looking for high prestige jobs for which he was totally unqualified. Previously, he had been unemployed and lived on an army pension awarded to him because of "anxiety neurosis." When her boyfriend threatened to leave her, Mrs. Payne decided to move to her brother's home because of an inability to cope with her friend and increasing depression. But after a month of separation, she returned to live with him. Her mild depression increased until she was suicidal and barely able to function. Her general practitioner placed her on Tofranil 100 mg daily for a short period, but since it didn't help immediately, she entered treatment with a psychiatrist who withdrew the Tofranil, believing that Mrs. Payne, by relying on it, was not assuming responsibility for her behavior. She returned to live with her brother. Her symptoms of depression, anxiety and panic increased. There was strife with her sister-in-law who described Mrs. Payne as "an impossibly demanding person who didn't contribute to her part of the work." Finally, Mrs. Payne applied for re-admission to Hillside.

On re-admission at age 45, Mrs. Payne's mental status was similar to her early admission. She was placed on Tofranil 75 mg daily, raised 25 mg weekly to 250 mg daily, and then decreased to 150 mg daily because of blurred vision. Within three weeks she showed remarkable improvement. Her depression lifted, she functioned at a very high level, working as a patient bookkeeper, assuming full responsibility and doing an excellent job. She remained at Hillside for six months.

Encouraged not to return to her boyfriend, to find a new apartment and job, she followed through with these plans, and also continued psychotherapy with her pre-hospitalization psychiatrist.   She took Tofranil 150 mg daily for six months.

Four years later, our social worker contacted Mrs. Payne, now age 50.   Since her second hospitalization, she worked at two part-time jobs and lived alone in her own small apartment.   A year after she stopped the Tofranil and psychotherapy, she experienced some "confusion," had trouble concentrating, and on two or three occasions was very fearful that her facial pain would return.   On her own, she asked her general practitioner to provide her with Tofranil, and since that time took 50 mg each evening, well satisfied with the salubrious, calming effect it afforded her.   Her psychiatrist consistently refused to prescribe Tofranil, considering it an unnecessary crutch.

Mrs. Payne claimed that sometimes she was mildly depressed, but it never interfered with her functioning.   She referred to herself as "possibly being unreasonably content," in that she enjoyed being a loner, preferring not to socialize much, even though she spent a small amount of time with a group of friends who were always available to her.   Occasionally she saw her male friend who had moved to another city.   Periodically he requested that she marry him; she regularly rejected his offer.

Her facial pain returned on rare occasions, usually in relation to her menses or anxiety-provoking situations.   It was never severe, and although she became fearful when it occurred, she felt that the pain was greatly ameliorated by Tofranil.   Both the beginning and end of her recital of the four years' events were marked by her exclamation, "I was really made for Tofranil."

COMMENT

Mrs. Payne never appeared psychotic, and in view of her numerous object losses and bereavements, her various depressions could be considered psychologically understandable and

therefore "neurotic." Further, her facial pain might lead
to a facile diagnosis of conversion hysteria. However, her
pervasive anhedonia, agitation and insomnia, as well as the
absence of other-blaming, blame-avoiding, dependent characteristics, leads to a diagnosis of recurrent agitated depression, therefore, suitable for psychotropic medication. Of
particular interest is her atypical facial pain which evidently responded well to Tofranil. Another medication, Te-
gretol (carbamazepine), an anticonvulsant structurally very
similar to Tofranil, is specifically effective in the management of tic douloureux, thus raising the question of some
specific relation between the psychophysiology of depression
and her atypical facial pain, rather than a non-specific
amelioration in her overall condition.

It is noteworthy that while on Tofranil, Mrs. Payne was
able to withstand the death of her older brother, but that
following the discontinuation of Tofranil, her facial pain
returned. At several points in her history, she was evidently undertreated with Tofranil, since she received this medication, prior to coming to Hillside, supposedly without effect, and again received it for a short period prior to her
second Hillside hospitalization, in doses of only 100 mg
daily. To compound the error of inadequate dosage, there is
the error of not realizing that for the majority of depressed patients, substantial clinical gains require at least
two to three weeks of antidepressant medication. The treatment of depressed patients with essentially homeopathic, ineffective, brief courses of medication is all too common and
results in much needless hospitalization. In this case also,
the patient suffered from not being able to maintain a continuous long-term treatment relationship with a doctor who
was not committed to an anti-medication ideology.

AGITATED DEPRESSION IN A PATIENT WITH
OBSESSIVE-COMPULSIVE REACTION

This obsessive-compulsive reaction is one of the clear-
est behavioral syndromes in psychiatry. It is characterized
by the episodic repetition and persistence of intrusive unwanted ideas and ego-alien repetitive impulses to perform
acts that are regarded by the patient as unreasonable.
Nonetheless, these patients feel compelled to carry out
these rituals and become very anxious if prevented from doing so. Because of the extent to which these people's lives
may be constricted by obsessions and compulsions, they are
often erroneously labeled psychotic, following the common
practice of equating neurosis with mild and psychosis with
severe behavioral disorder. However, inquiry shows that although the patients have obeyed their obsessions and compulsions, they have no belief in their veracity. For instance,
a patient may get the obsessional thought that he has not
turned off the gas and feel compelled to check it through a
series of doubting and checking cycles. The patient may be
perfectly sure that the gas was turned off and yet feel compelled to check again. There is no delusional elaboration
such as "immediately after I turn off the gas somebody turns
it on again."

Severe obsessive-compulsive reactions are frequently
associated with agitated depressions. The joint appearance
of agitated depression and severe obsessive-compulsive disorder may strike the examiner as bizarre enough to warrant
the diagnosis of psychosis. During an agitated depression
the ritualistic behavior of the obsessive-compulsive person
can increase to such an extreme as to seem to pass the
bounds of rationality. Patients may spend literally all
their waking time washing their hands. A patient may wash
his hands with one piece of soap and then reason that if the

dirt got off the hands onto the soap, perhaps some of it got back onto his hands from the now dirty soap. Therefore, he will then follow this washing, with washing with a new, clean piece of soap, but since the same logic applies here, this will require washing with still another piece of soap, ad infinitum. However, when asked at any time during this procedure, whether he believes that his hands are clean, he will state that they are actually clean, but the possibility remains that they are not and that is what he must guard against. Actual delusional formation can rarely, if ever, be demonstrated.

To make matters more difficult, with the onset of schizophrenia, patients not infrequently develop repetitive ritualistic behavior that is delusionally motivated. Such behavior is often referred to as obsessive-compulsive, although the cardinal ego-dystonic or ego-alien feature of true obsessive-compulsive behavior is absent.

The behavior of the severe obsessive-compulsive seems to hinge upon deranged decision-making processes, rather than in the perception and evaluation of reality. That is, the decision to perform an action is not made on the basis of the preponderance of the evidence but rather on the slight possibility that an undesired state of affairs may occur. In this way, the obsessive-compulsive acts as a normal person might when attempting to avoid an extremely dangerous situation where even the slight possibility of its occurrence is to be prevented at all costs. Since such compulsive states frequently have associated phobic features, many psychoanalysts believe that the feared occurrence is actually not an external one but symbolizes the avoidance of an eruption of unconscious disavowed impulses, frequently of a sexual, anal or aggressive nature.

RICHARD EWELL

PRESENTING PROBLEM

Four years before Richard Ewell, age 42, entered Hillside, he had removed a speck from his eye while looking in a mirror. Since that incident, he felt a compulsive, irrational need to look into a mirror and stare into his eyes, feeling that they were "stiff." He managed to go on with his usual activities for two more years, but while studying to become a lieutenant on the police force, his compulsion became extreme. Striving to cease staring at his eyes, he painted over all the mirrors in his house. But then he began to look for dirt in the indentations of his hands. When he no longer could tolerate this, he wore gloves, but became obsessed with the thought of the dirt that might be in the glove stitching. Then he had to stare at his trousers and shoes, check his socks and shoelaces, count the holes in his belt, straighten his underwear, and determine if his eyebrows were straight. The time spent performing these rituals increased from minutes to hours a day. He constantly thought about committing suicide. Finally, he confessed his affliction to his wife who helped him find a psychiatric consultation center. There, he was diagnosed as having an "obsessive-compulsive reaction of a borderline nature." They placed him on Thorazine 100 mg daily and referred him for intensive treatment at Hillside. When he arrived at Hillside, his entire day was occupied by rituals.

FAMILY

Mr. Ewell was the fourth of seven children of a lower-class Jewish family. The father was described as stubborn, domineering, temperamental and crude. Born in Europe, he came to the United States as a youngster and started work as a junk peddler,which later became profitable enough to allow him to buy several junkyards. He remained illiterate, beat his wife and children, spent no time with his family and caroused

with women. Two days after his wife died, when Richard was
20, he brought a new woman into the house and demanded that
the children address her as "mama." He remarried two years
later, and gave his minor children to the Domestic Relations
Court for housing and support.

Richard hated his father and after he left home at age
22, he refused to talk with or see him again, even though
eight years later, it was his father's deathbed request for
Richard to come to him.

The mother also immigrated to this country in her
20's. She worked in a sweatshop until her marriage, and after, was almost continually pregnant and sickly until her
death, following a stroke, in her mid 50's. Self-educated,
she was a homely, quiet, timid person, frightened by her
husband's wrath. However, she was somewhat warm and affectionate with her children. Mr. Ewell pitied her because no
one, including himself, showed her any respect or affection.

DEVELOPMENTAL HISTORY

Richard was born at term, of a normal, though unwanted
pregnancy. Early developmental history was not available.
He remembered playing in the streets until about ten o'clock
at night, from a very young age. Belonging to a "gang"
since the age of six, he was sometimes a leader or sometimes
a follower, but always well-known as one of the best fighters
in the neighborhood.

Of the six other siblings, Richard was closest with a
brother, two years older, the favored child; they shared the
same room while growing up. A sister, two years younger, was
described as nervous and talkative; another brother, four
years younger, was hypochondriacal. A sister, five years
younger, was mentally retarded, emotionally disturbed and hospitalized at a state institution, although married to an older man and the mother of a child. There had been little
closeness among the children except for Richard and his older

brother. As adults, no relationship existed between any of
the siblings.

Richard started school at age six and never liked it,
but by the time he was in seventh or eighth grade he was advanced into the special rapid class. He attributed this to
liking the teacher.

Starting at about age eight, Richard had most of the
childhood illnesses, including three very frightening, bloody
tonsil and adenoid operations. He was generally a nervous
and restless child.   At about age nine or ten, he started a
sniffing movement with his nose. Then he imitated another
boy who had an eye blink. These tics lasted for several
years. At home he was usually on good terms with his mother,
but argued frequently with his father and siblings.

His father had a peddler's horse and wagon and occasionally would take him and other children riding, a very special, happy, neighborhood event. Richard always liked
horses, and as a young boy he found his way to a park which
housed a horse stable. Here he spent considerable time after
school.

Because of his interest in horses, at age 11 he found a
job at a riding academy, working weekends. On weekdays after
school he had to attend Hebrew classes, until he was 13. At
about age 13, he began to help his brother, a milkman, on his
rounds. He remembered being very fearful walking down the
long, dark hallways,delivering bottles to each door. Finally, at age 14, he decided he wanted to earn a living, and
quit school.

During his early adolescence, Richard developed a talent
for mimicry and perfected many dialects. People found him
entertaining and would often hire him to perform at social
gatherings. This periodic employment lasted until his late
teens. To supplement this income, he ran a pony track for a
very unpleasant man who paid him little. From time to time,

when business was particularly bad, Richard took money from
his own pocket to supplement what was in the till, in order
to demonstrate that he was doing a good job.

When he was 19, his father opened a junkyard and placed
him in charge, then expanding to three junkyards, all of
which Richard managed.

During this period, his mother suffered a stroke, was
paralyzed, spent a year in the hospital and then died from
a second stroke. Richard, very affected by his mother's
death, was appalled that his father immediately started
bringing women into the house, and had bitter arguments with
him. When Richard asked for a raise from his $10 weekly sal-
ary, his father refused. Shortly thereafter, Richard and
his older brother, with whom he was very close, moved out,
and rented a room together. Richard attended a trade school
for three months, held a variety of jobs, including "dirty"
jobs such as machinist, stable boy and riding academy instructor on weekends. At age 23, he was drafted into the army where he also worked with horses for two years. During
this time he had an unexplained episode of depression.

Richard started getting interested in girls at about
age eight, and had sex play with neighborhood girls. At
home he mutually masturbated with his brother and had anal
relations with him when he was 12. After begging his brother, he finally was allowed to visit a prostitute with him at
age 14, and continued sex relations with prostitutes until
age 23, when he met a girl whom he married, at age 25.

His wife, two years younger than himself, was a moderately attractive, confident, sociable, agreeable person, who
seemed mature, caring of her husband and strong enough to
cope with many of the exigencies her marriage presented.

After his army discharge, they moved in with his
mother-in-law. He worked at several different jobs over the

next four years, all usually involving exacting work which
he often repeated because of his own needs for precision.
Sometimes he was fired because his perfectionism forced him
to work too slowly. Finally, when he was 29, he decided to
enter the police force, hoping to become an instructor in
the police riding academy. However, he was forced to work
as a patrolman for six years and then was given radio car detail. He worked well in this capacity with different part-
ners for three years.

One day, investigating a car accident, he failed to complete information on the police forms,and the driver's information proved false. Mr. Ewell was placed on trial by
the police department. He had no lawyer, pleaded not guilty,
was fined ten days salary and demoted to foot patrolman.
About this time he developed the compulsion to look at his
eyes, and the feeling that they were "stiff."

The demotion to patrolman presented a hardship, since
he now had two children to support, so he studied to become
a sergeant. After about a year of study he took the exam
but was distracted by a noisy radiator during the examination and did poorly. Nine months later, he retook the exam,
made good marks and received his promotion to sergeant when
40 years old.

Until this time Mrs. Ewell perceived her husband as
"stable as a rock." He was faithful, their sexual relations
were compatible, and while he was unaffectionate to her and
the children, he claimed he loved and took great pride in
them. But after studying for the sergeant's exam his compulsions increased, forcing him to spend more and more time
staring into the mirror, praying frequently, and worrying
about inconsequentials. Nevertheless, he strove to better his
position and decided to study for the lieutenant's examination, with the consequent ritualization of his life.

PRESENTING CHARACTERISTICS

Mr. Ewell was healthy but very anxious and fearful. His extreme meticulousness was not reflected in his appearance. Severely agitated and histrionic, he was very restless, anxious and depressed, but moderately sociable and garrulous. He paced back and forth, jabbing his fists in the air, beseeching help, "Doctor, you must do something to get me out of my misery."

In interview, he found it necessary to flick away the dust from his shoes and clothes. During the physical examination, he stood on the chair in order to undress and dress, so that no dust would get on his clothes from the floor. He was constantly distracted by his obsessive thoughts and it was difficult for him to maintain spontaneous conversation without introducing complaints about his compulsions. He showed no evidence of delusions.

When asked to state his problem, he began to talk continuously: "I am a police sergeant. I take four Thorazine a day. I'm supposed to take an examination (for promotion) next Saturday. If you say no, I won't go. I have never known how to relax. Four years ago when I got something in my eye, I looked into the mirror and took it out, and that is how it started. My eyes became stiff. I began to stare at my eyes in the mirror, five minutes, 20 minutes, two hours, five hours. I was afraid my eyelashes would get into my eyes. I wash my eyes over and over. I know there's nothing wrong with my eyes. I can't stand dirt. I'm a perfectionist. I always washed my hands and lips after eating. My compulsions went from my eyes to my hands, then to my clothes. I feel I must go through with this silly self-inflicted routine. I am going from neurotic to psychotic and I'm afraid my wishes might come true."

He was greatly frightened that he had two guns available to him, and feared the danger that this presented to himself

and others. In the weeks before hospitalization, he kept his
guns in a locker at the precinct while he remained at home.
Also, he was somatically preoccupied with skin eruptions,
dizziness, bowel movements, blurring vision, and complained
of "a loss of sensation around my anus." He took prunes and
lemon juice daily to treat his lifelong constipation.

COURSE AT HILLSIDE

Results of all physical and neurological examinations,
including the EEG, were unremarkable. On the Wechsler-
Bellevue, he attained a full scale IQ score of 122, a verbal
IQ of 128 and a performance IQ of 112.

After admission to Hillside, Mr. Ewell was quite agitated, spoke fast and loud, could not sit still, paced during
his sessions and jabbed his fist in the air in order to express how angry he felt toward himself. In psychotherapy he
would get up and go to a wall, staring, in order to imitate
his position in front of the mirror. His only social interaction consisted of requiring reassurance from personnel or
patients that he did not really have dirt on his hands and
clothes, and that his eyebrows were straight. It took him an
hour and a half to dress in the morning. He was wholly involved in his compulsions, taking every opportunity to talk
about his compulsions with his therapist, even when passing
her in the hallway. Frequently he spoke of his fears of
committing suicide. He was cooperative and extremely obedient in following hospital regulations.

After two weeks, he was referred to the drug program and
placed on Thorazine 300 mg daily, raised 300 mg weekly, until
1200 mg daily was reached, with Kemadrin 15 mg daily. Immediately, he showed a good response, feeling calmer, less
agitated and was able to sit during psychotherapy instead of
constantly pacing.

But he complained, "I still have these idiosyncracies
and keep staring." His stability increased and he was soon

able to talk about topics other than his rituals. He requested a full activities program and began to work with
clay in occupational therapy, even though it dirtied his
hands; however, he then had to wash for half an hour.

After two weeks on medication, he had severe somatic
complaints of constipation (a lack of feeling in his bowels),
dizziness, and increasing skin eruptions (questioning whether his skin was dying), dry mouth, parched tongue, blurred
vision (stiff eyes), and a numb forehead. He related these
effects to the medication and claimed that it was no longer
helping his compulsions, except that he felt more relaxed.
Instead of constantly checking the mirror to ascertain
whether his eyebrows were straight, he repeatedly asked other patients to reassure him. In the morning, he awoke very
early in order to carry out interminable pre-breakfast dressing rituals.

One month after starting Thorazine he continued with
somatizing, complaining about the above symptoms, but
not mentioning his compulsions until asked about them. In
therapy, when speaking of his wife and children, he grew
tearful, expressing tremendous guilt about the unhappy life
he had given them and spoke about hanging himself. He demanded that he receive shock treatments in order to forget
completely about his rituals.

After two months on Thorazine, Mr. Ewell was considerably calmer, although still somewhat depressed, at times with
suicidal thoughts. His obsessive-compulsive talk and activity decreased. He was very upset that his wife challenged him
to get better,since she did not want a sick husband, admitting that she no longer felt affection nor attraction to him.
Thus, he demanded that his medication be changed.

During the third month on Thorazine, Tofranil 75 mg daily, increased 75 mg weekly to 300 mg daily was added. He
seemed more enthusiastic about occupying himself with exter-

nal events and enjoyed working on a maintenance crew. He
stated he felt less "stiffening of his eyes" and stopped
staring and straightening his eyebrows. He continued his
complaint of "no feeling in his bowels," constipation and
blurred vision. At about this time he had his first four
hour pass from the hospital. He felt frightened and was
forced to stare at his hands, but in general was more relaxed and less occupied with rituals.

By the next month, he was socializing more, made jokes
with other patients, acting the amateur comedian. He spoke
about his experiences as a police officer and horseman, and
seemed considerably improved with a fairly stable, but
slightly depressed mood.

After two months on Thorazine and Tofranil, his course
fluctuated; at times he was able to control his obsessive-
compulsive acts, but at times, usually when home on a pass,
he had to stare at his hands and clothes.

At his maintenance job he would sometimes put his hands
in grease in order to prove that he could tolerate dirt. He
reacted with most anxiety to periods spent away from the hospital and feared his approaching discharge. He found he
could "hold off to the end of the day and then reward myself
by a big stare at my shoes. Now I can fight it." His doctor repeatedly discussed the possibility of the guilt allay-
ing significance of his compulsions, a la Lady Macbeth, but
there was no confirmatory evidence for this.

When he discussed with his wife that he would probably
still have some rituals when discharged, but that these would
not prevent him from doing his job, she responded positively
and he felt considerably relieved. At the hospital he was
still mildly compulsive, but able to socialize in a calmer,
more confident manner.

Mr. Ewell was discharged after almost eight months of
hospitalization, in an improved condition, taking Thorazine

1200 mg, Tofranil 300 mg, and Kemadrin 15 mg daily. He was
to continue psychotherapy at an after-care clinic. The hospital diagnosis was paranoid schizophrenia; the research diagnosis was chronic obsessive-compulsive neurosis with a
severe episode of agitated depression.

FOLLOW-UP

   Mr. Ewell returned home to his family, continued in psychotherapy at an after-care clinic and took his medications.
Because visual accommodation seemed disturbed, Thorazine was
lowered first to 900 mg daily, and when he still complained,
to 600 mg daily and then 400 mg daily. Tofranil was lowered
to 150 mg daily. He was very anxious to return to a police
desk job, and after five months, the department ruled that
he could return to work. For the next three years he never
missed a day's work.

   After a few months he discontinued at the after-care
clinic because he was dissatisfied with his doctor. Then he
attended another clinic for six months. His new doctor told
him that no one could help him, and Mr. Ewell wholly agreed
that he would have to help himself. Upon discontinuing at
this clinic, he received no more psychotherapy. He continued
taking decreasing amounts of Thorazine and Tofranil for several more months and then stopped all medication about a year
after discharge from Hillside.

   In interview after three years, he looked very well,
spoke slowly in a deliberate, measured manner. For the most
part, he was to the point, but sometimes spoke in an involved, tangential manner. He seemed to relate well to his family and friends, enjoyed his work, and his wife considered
their marriage adequate, as he did. He continued to perform
some compulsive rituals, such as hand washing and looking in
the mirror, but to a greatly reduced degree.

   Eleven years after hospitalization, Mr. Ewell was contacted by our social worker. He reported that he was still

with the police department, in a position of considerable responsibility, with its attendant job pressures. His hand
washing compulsion had improved "about 90%." Using carbon
paper didn't bother him much, although he would wash "a little cleaner, but not nearly as much as ten years ago." In
his spare time, he especially enjoyed working on automobile
repairs.

Except for Librium 10 mg, taken several times a year in
tense situations, he had taken no medication for eight years.
His health was excellent, he was happy with his family and
job, socialized comfortably and got along well with friends
and peers.

COMMENT

Mr. Ewell resembles Mrs. Sturm, as both had an agitated
depression occurring in an obsessive-compulsive personality
with perfectionistic goals.

Mr. Ewell developed ego-alien obsessive-compulsive rituals prior to the development of clinically obvious depression,
but in the context of loss of self-esteem. The obsessive-
compulsive symptomatology occupied the foreground of Mr.
Ewell's complaints, whereas the severe depression exacerbating the illness was not as immediately obvious. Characteristically, the patient responded to Thorazine by a marked
decrease in agitation, depression and ritualistic behavior,
associated with a marked increase in somatic complaints (6,
9, 10). Often such patients will have complete remissions on
phenothiazines alone, but on occasion the supplementary use
of imipramine is distinctly helpful (11). Although the affective symptomatology will remit completely, the obsessive-
compulsive symptomatology is usually only markedly decreased
but remains to some degree; the obsessional perfectionism of
the patient is not touched at all. The fact that Mr. Ewell
had a depression at an earlier age, illustrates the remissions and exacerbations of such patients' affective states.

Unfortunately, the diagnosis of schizophrenia is often applied to these patients because of the extreme nature of their symptomatology, and the peculiarity of their preoccupations which may paralyze them as totally as a major psychosis. Their hypercleanliness is often viewed as a reaction formation to pressing anal preoccupations, and thus, as a malignant sign of flooding with "primary process."

The diagnosis of schizophrenia is particularly unfortunate in such patients since it often leads to a gloomy prognosis and the misguided recommendation that the patient give up his work responsibilities and attempt to find a life niche at a lower level of competence. In fact, such patients are usually able to maintain their social functioning once their depression is under control, as was true of Mr. Ewell   (12).

Mr. Ewell's preoccupation with horses, cleanliness and self-grooming, in association with his marked constipation, could well lead one to speculate about some maldevelopment during his period of anal training. However, in psychotherapy, interpretations to this effect, as well as discussions of a presumed unconscious guilt, were to no avail.

This lack of response cannot be considered as relevant to testing this etiological speculation. It is pointed out only to contradict the still popular belief that "insightful" interpretation is a panacea. Modern psychotherapeutic theory has progressed beyond this, leaving such wishful thinking to those who "confront" indiscriminately.

It is generally agreed that obsessive-compulsive neurosis is extremely difficult to treat by any psychotherapeutic method, and since no controlled study has been performed on this periodically remitting and exacerbating disorder, it is difficult to know whether any form of psychotherapy is specifically indicated. There can be no question that these patients often require some sort of therapeutic ally and appropriate pharmacotherapy, when depressed.

Chapter VII

DYSPHORIC STATES

PSYCHONEUROTIC DEPRESSION
Definition

The terms depressive reaction and psychoneurotic depression have been applied to the residual heterogenous collection of patients who manifest an apparently depressive mood that is not secondary to other diagnosable conditions, such as schizophrenia, organic brain disease, etc. However, they are not typically mood cyclic and therefore cannot be considered either manic-depressive or cyclothymic. Also they do not display psychotic symptomatology or severe agitated states, so _faute_ de _mieux_, have been considered neurotic.

We do not consider these conditions to be continuous with the agitated or retarded depressive state. They are different in course, symptomatology, and most strikingly in response to treatment. The core pathological mood is not present, and ECT and the tricyclic antidepressants are regularly ineffective. To continue to label these conditions as depressions only compounds the confusion. In this case I will take the risk associated with neologism and refer to these as "dysphoric-complaint states," since their outstanding common characteristic is the complaint of severe subjective distress and unhappiness. There are subgroups within the dysphoric states; quotation marks about the word "depression" will be used to indicate that these states are qualitatively different from the retarded and agitated depressions.

In the American Psychiatric Association nosology, reactive and neurotic "depression" are equated, although these terms would appear to have somewhat different implications.

A reactive "depression" is unhappiness following severe disappointment in an apparently normal personality. It is often associated with anxiety, resentment, anger and a tendency to blame others. Furthermore, it is generally agreed that reactive "depressions" remit within a two month period. Winokur and Pitts (15) have shown that in almost all of a carefully studied series of hospitalized patients initially diagnosed as Reactive Depressive, other more specific diagnoses were possible. They suggest that the term is superfluous. We agree and would hypothesize that the remaining patients with Reactive Depression (self-limiting unhappiness upon severe disappointment in a normal personality) were having normal emotional reactions that received discrete disease labels from psychiatrists habituated to considering all emotional distress as reflective of pathological states. We wish to emphasize that this sort of error is the exception rather than the rule. We believe that most emotional states considered pathological by psychiatrists are due to pathological derangements, and the fact that an occasional normal, although extreme emotional experience may lead to a psychiatric diagnosis of pathology, does not mean that all psychiatric diagnosis is based on a mechanistic misperception of the richness of life experience. Each syndrome requires specific study to determine if it should be considered pathological. Transient emotional states that remit promptly, do not require therapeutic intervention, are psychologically comprehensible, and occur in normal personalities, should not be labeled pathological.

An episodic neurotic "depression" is similar clinically to a reactive "depression" but occurs in an individual who has manifested chronic difficulties in adjustment throughout

life. Neurotic "depressions" include both a) normally severe
disappointment reactions in deviant personalities who then
adapt unusually to their distress (i.e., tantrums, sulking,
suicide threats),and b) chronic passive-dependent patients
with dysphoric complaints. Neurotic "depressions" are sharply distinguishable from retarded depressions, but not so
clearly from agitated depressions.

The differential diagnosis between depression and "depression" can often be made by psychiatric examination. The
key question is whether the "depressive" reactions can be
distinguished by means of pathological depressive mood, i.e.,
an inability to experience pleasure, the core trait of retarded and agitated depressions. The prognostic importance
is that the retarded and agitated depressions are potentially
psychotic, whereas uncomplicated dysphoric states are not.
Dysphoric patients suffer from angry unhappiness and low
self-esteem, but they can enjoy themselves, and much of their
activity is aimed at producing situations in which they feel
relatively comfortable, although they often cannot admit it.

One valuable diagnostic clue is temporary fluctuations
in the manifest affective picture and attitude towards the
future. Patients with reactive or neurotic "depressions"
will demonstrate, under some circumstances, a hopeful affect
and periods of enjoyment that are not linked to a diurnal
cycle. Neurotic "depressives" often maintain a façade of
chronic unhappiness when confronted with interested or sympathetic observers. However, under some social circumstances
they participate in an active, outgoing, friendly and pleasurable manner. A particularly favorable environment for this
affective shift is the company of the similarly afflicted or
admiring, subservient friends. Here, sad tales of lifelong
distress may be zestfully related.

Chronically inadequate individuals with low self-esteem
may profess hopelessness and depression as a coercive method

for manipulating their environment. Their actual emotional
status can best be inferred from their behavior when apparently not under observation. Again, this group of "depressives" has misled some into raising the coercive aspect of
depression into a universal core phenomenon.

Other syndromes frequently referred to as neurotic depression are hypochondriasis, without dismal and hopeless affect, but with somatic preoccupation, and addiction to stimulants or sedatives.

CAROLE SEID

PRESENTING PROBLEM

Carole Seid was 26 when she came to Hillside, after having made five suicide attempts in the preceding year.

FAMILY AND DEVELOPMENTAL HISTORY

Carole was the second child of three, of an affluent,
middle-class family, living in a private home in a wealthy
suburb. Her father was a successful real estate broker, a
hard worker who devoted much of his energy to his business.
Cold and removed from his family, he spent little time with
them, never talked with his children or got involved in their
lives. His philosophy of life stressed the importance of an
individual being strong, self-sufficient and economically
successful.

The mother, also unloving and remote, obviously was the
dominant, controlling member of the family. Strong-willed,
she ruled the family (and everyone else with whom she came in
contact) with an iron fist, and demanded independence and
strength from her children. The care of her three children
was turned over to a nursemaid, a kind, understanding woman,
who provided them with considerable warmth, love and nurture.

The oldest brother, two years older than Carole, was always the favorite child of the family. Strong, self-reliant,

bright and alert, he became a successful professional.

Carole had been planned for and was born normally and spontaneously. She was raised by the nursemaid until she was 12 years old, and a warm relationship developed between the two. Her growth and development were uneventful. She rarely had anything to do with her parents; any involvement consisted of their giving her gifts.

When she was five, a younger brother was born. At this time, Carole was taken from her bedroom and placed in her older brother's room. She felt considerable resentment toward both brothers and repeatedly requested that her new brother be sent back to the hospital; no closeness ever developed with either brother. Throughout her school years, Carole presented little problem, either in school or at home. Once however, when she was eight years old, she was found playing in a closet, nude, with a boy. Her father beat her severely, and both parents did not speak to her for days afterward.

Carole always tended to be chubby and was self-conscious about her weight. However, she never shared any of her problems or feelings with her parents. Her mother reported that she had a "host" of girlfriends, and that their home was a "hang-out." Carole concurred that she had a large circle of friends with whom she did things, but that she never felt particularly close with anyone.

Menarche was at 13, and she was prepared for it by her girlfriends from whom she had gained all her sexual knowledge. In high school she dated occasionally but was shy and related best with girls.

Throughout her adolescent years, she had transient episodes of depression with suicidal ideation. At 15, her depressions led her parents to seek the help of an endocrinologist who spent time talking with her. She continued feeling distant from her family, but kept her unhappiness, increasing resentment and anger to herself.

At 17, she entered college, but shortly her father suffered a financial setback, and Carole was forced to leave school in order for there to be enough money to pay her brother's tuition. Carole harbored considerable resentment toward her family for this new slight.

Unable to continue college, she went to secretarial school for two years, where she did very well. She found a job as a secretary which she enjoyed. She did excellent work and remained for a year. At work she met a man whom she dated. They never had intercourse but engaged in mutual masturbation; she remained a virgin until she married. She continued living at her parents' home.

At 20, she met her husband-to-be, at a resort. He was seven years older than she, and worked as an accountant. She found him passive, kind, considerate, empathic, and not at all like her parents. Her mother did not particularly care for this man, feeling her daughter "could have done much better," because he was "not a professional man and his income was not too good." The mother openly reacted to him as incompetent and weak. Nevertheless, they married after six months of dating.

Initially, Mrs. Seid stated that a good sexual relationship developed. Later however, she admitted that she thought sex was thoroughly disgusting and dirty; that her sexual life was always totally unsatisfactory and she was anorgasmic. She continued seeing the man she had been dating from work for several months after her marriage. Although she absolutely did not want to have children, the mechanics of contraception were left to her husband, and she became pregnant within six months. However, she accepted the pregnancy and a short time later left her secretarial job.

Mrs. Seid was 22 when she gave birth to a son. She continued to function adequately as mother and housewife. The baby was very good and never difficult in any way. Within a year, Mrs. Seid was pregnant again. This second pregnancy was difficult and she was sickly, nervous and irritable. She gave birth to a girl. The new baby was colicky, cried a nerve-wracking, high-pitched yowl almost continuously, and was extremely difficult to handle. Mrs. Seid felt tremendous resentment toward her, became extremely depressed and agitated and felt trapped by her children and domestic situation. Her husband now seemed extremely passive and dependent, and she felt totally unsatisfied with her situation. Her mother continued exerting control over her life, constantly undermining her, criticizing her way of caring for the children and berating her son-in-law, going so far as to instruct him in proper table manners and coerce him into making decisions of which she approved.

By the time the baby girl was seven months old, Mrs. Seid felt she could no longer care for her and within the following month made three suicide attempts: twice with gas and once with a combination of alcohol and sleeping pills. Following the suicide attempts, Mrs. Seid was seen by a psychiatrist who administered a series of five ECT and Tofranil (amount unknown) at a private psychiatric hospital. She was released within two weeks.

Three weeks later she was again hospitalized at a city hospital after talking about making another suicide attempt. They diagnosed her as having a depressive reaction and treated her with Elavil and Stelazine (amounts unknown). She had a period of improvement and then relapsed. After a month, she was discharged to a private hospital where she received ten ECT, Elavil and Stelazine (amounts unknown) and was released after three weeks.

After four months of relative quiescence she became extremely depressed and took an overdose of sleeping pills.
Once again she was admitted to the private hospital where she
received 14 more ECT, pharmacotherapy and psychotherapy (details unknown) and was released after one month.

Two weeks later she took seven Seconal and four shots
of whiskey, and was brought to a city hospital. She was not
comatose and stated "I want to die, kill me or I will kill
myself. I can't get the bad thoughts out of my mind. I
don't want to hurt my parents or children, but I want to kill
myself. I was very much afraid that a relationship would develop with my daughter similar to the one which I had with
my mother, and therefore, I never wanted a daughter."

She was diagnosed as having a schizophrenic reaction,
schizo-affective type, and received ten ECT and up to 400 mg
daily of Mellaril. Gradually she became more cheerful, relaxed, active and sociable. But after two months, she again
felt depressed and fearful that she would hurt herself or
her children. Treatment was changed to Stelazine and Tofranil (details unknown), and she seemed to respond. However,
she remained at this city hospital for six months, which was
very unusual considering their 90 day treatment limit, until
plans were made for her to be transferred to Hillside for
longer term hospitalization.

PRESENTING CHARACTERISTICS

At the time of admission to Hillside, Mrs. Seid was o-
bese, with obviously dyed black hair. Nevertheless, she appeared quite attractive, neatly dressed and well-groomed.
She was moderately depressed, no longer suicidal; sad, but
yet able to express humor appropriately. She felt totally
incapable of caring for her home and family and questioned
whether she wished to remain married, because "I don't know
if I love him." Easily accessible, she approached the interview situation in a comfortable confident manner and de-

veloped quick rapport with the examiner. Except for amnesia
surrounding the times she received ECT, her mental status
was completely unremarkable.

COURSE AT HILLSIDE

The results of all physical and neurological tests were
non-contributory, and her EEG records were normal. On the
Wechsler she attained a full scale IQ of 107, with a verbal
IQ of 110 and a performance IQ of 102. At the time of psychological testing, the diagnosis reached by the psychologist was passive-dependent personality with chronic depression, neurotic type, with no evidence of psychosis.

At her initial hospital conference, the diagnosis was
psychotic depressive reaction, despite the lack of any psychotic findings, because of the severity of her multiple suicide attempts. Initial treatment recommendations consisted
of Tofranil, working up to 300 mg daily, and a short term
stay (three months), in order to prevent dependency on the
hospital.

During the first two months of treatment she remained
moderately depressed, with occasional affable periods, despite Tofranil. Family therapy, once a week, with either
her husband or her parents, was held(signifying to Mrs. Seid
that the hospital expected her to continue her marriage).

After two months, the Tofranil was discontinued because
of its apparent ineffectiveness, and she was started on
Nardil 15 mg three times daily. Despite her depression, she
was urged to spend weekends at home.

During the third month of treatment, while on Nardil 45
mg daily, Mrs. Seid withdrew further and reported to her doctor that she was having "fantasies" which she was unable to
reveal, and that she was afraid she might lose hold of herself and act upon these "fantasies."

A week later she became quite disturbed, ran about insisting that she had to leave and that she couldn't remember

anyone's identity. Between crying and laughing, she appeared in a trance-like state. She told her doctor, "all the
people in the hospital seem unreal, just names and places
and I can see through them." She was certain that her entire family was dead and made frequent visits to a small rose
garden on the hospital grounds which she thought was a ceme-
tery. Believing that she was pregnant, she tried to abort
herself with a wire dress hanger. Feeling that she could
fly, she attempted to go through a window like a bird. Deluded that two dolls she had in her room were children, she
attempted to strangle them; also she saw a chair which did
not exist, and experienced the feeling of insects crawling
over her. During this period, her remote and recent memory
were impaired. At the same time she began speaking about
wanting to be free from her marriage, and independent, of
wanting a divorce and placing her children in her husband's
custody.

It was the clinical consensus that she was suffering
from an acute toxic psychosis with evidence of an organic
brain syndrome, probably precipitated by the Nardil. The
drug was discontinued, and Thorazine, increased 300 mg daily
until 1200 mg daily was reached, with Kemadrin 15 mg daily,
was given. Plans for early discharge were dropped. Within
one month, all psychotic symptoms disappeared and Thorazine
was gradually decreased, then discontinued over a three month
period.

During the fifth month, it was decided to discontinue
family therapy since it seemed to be accomplishing little.
Instead, psychotherapy was increased to three 50 minute sessions weekly of supportive and explorative therapy. In psychotherapy she was able to discuss how she feared giving up
her dependent position and the attention of her family, yet
being angered by being told what to do. She was very concerned about the tremendous resentment she felt toward her

children, and that she would prove to be an inadequate mother, unable to cope with the responsibilities of married
life. Happy being a "child," her underlying wish was to be
cared for and nurtured.

By the eighth month of treatment, her depression seemed
to improve, and she moved toward a greater independence from
her husband and family. In therapy she developed an intense
positive transference to her psychiatrist and spent many
sessions reluctantly discussing sexual material, mainly her
unsatisfactory sex life. She feared sleeping at home on
weekends, horrified by the thought that her husband would
make sexual demands which she wished to avoid at any cost.

The weekend after she learned that her doctor would be
going on a week's vacation, she had a hospital pass, and
while alone in the ladies' room of a restaurant, severely cut
her neck with a razor blade, requiring several sutures. In
discussing the event, she told how she had felt tremendously
guilty about the sexual material she had fantasied and talked about, and how she felt she needed to punish herself when
feeling guilty about sexual feelings. It also became clear
that she always felt a need to severely punish herself when
she felt guilty about fantasies of sexual transgression, or
when she had expressed anger toward her parents or husband,
or when some significant person hurt her. She had seen her
doctor's vacation as a personal rejection. Her throat cutting both punished herself and was a guilt-provoking covert
attack on the highly valued doctor. During the next two
months there was an increase in frequency of self-mutilation,
with repeated excoriating of her arms, breasts and neck with
sharp objects. However, at the same time, she explored her
feelings with less resistance. The self-mutilating gestures
stopped when she defiantly refused to go home on weekend
passes, and this was accepted by the hospital and her doctor.

At the end of a year at Hillside, Mrs. Seid was allowed

to remain with her same therapist because of the intensity
of their psychotherapeutic relationship, even though he was
moving to another service. She was increasingly defiant toward her entire family, allowing only occasional visits from
family members. She discussed wishes to leave her husband,
family and children, but feared she would not be able to get
along on her own. Finally Mrs. Seid asked her doctor whether
he would approve of a plan for her to live on her own and not
return home after discharge. He expressed approval of the
idea and her depression lifted almost immediately.

After 17 months of hospitalization, Mrs. Seid explored
the possibilities of renting her own apartment and finding a
job. She began taking pride in her appearance, buying new
clothes and using makeup attractively. After 19 months of
hospitalization, a discharge conference was held. Mrs. Seid
was informed of the clinical consensus that it was not indicated for her to return to her family at this point in her
life. Immediately following this she expressed great relief
and reported that she actually felt well for the first time.
Plans were made for her to remain in after-care with her
doctor. She wholeheartedly concurred with the plans, and
was eager to start living an independent life. Her family
was informed and a nursemaid was hired to live permanently
with her two children.

Mrs. Seid was discharged after 21 months at Hillside.
Her condition was much improved and she took no medication.
Her hospital diagnosis was chronic psychotic depressive reaction, of postpartum origin, in a borderline personality;
the research diagnosis was neurotic depression with hysterical traits, with episode of toxic psychosis. She went to
live in a women's hotel, found a job as a secretary and continued in psychotherapy with her doctor.

FOLLOW-UP

Two years after her Hillside hospitalization, at the

time of this writing, a follow-up interview was held with
Mrs. Seid's psychiatrist. He reported that she was tremendously improved in her functioning, totally self-sufficient
and supporting herself in her own apartment. She and her
husband were divorced. He was in charge of the children who
were cared for by a housekeeper. Mrs. Seid was fond of her
children, looked forward to seeing them weekly, and spent
enjoyable times with them. She worked steadily after leaving the hospital, changing jobs about every six months, each
time to a higher paying, more interesting position. Her social life was very active and she was beginning to consider
remarriage. While she often dated ineligible men, too old,
married or inappropriate in some other way, she finally decided to seek more suitable companions. Sexually, she was
regularly orgasmic. In twice weekly exploratory psychotherapy, she made good use of her time and worked actively. Her
doctor provided support, but felt also they were striving
for more characterological changes and would continue in this
way for at least several more years. Mrs. Seid took no medication after hospitalization.

COMMENT

Mrs. Seid is typical of affective disorder in terms of
her unexceptional development in spite of marked affective
deprivation up to adolescence. Noteworthy are her repeated
suicidal attempts in the face of a tremendous amount of ineffective perseverative somatic treatment.

The diagnostic conference labelled her psychotic, in
spite of the absence of any signs of lack of reality contact.
In this frequent illogical usage, "psychosis" is equated with
severity. It is not surprising therefore, that in some studies "neurotic" and "psychotic" depressives respond similarly
to somatic treatments, since the so-called neurotic depressives are actually a mixture of character disorders with dysphoric problems who do not respond well to drugs, and mild

retarded and agitated depressives who do respond well to
drugs. Similarly, the "psychotic" depressives are a mixture
of patients with severe character disorders and/or "neurotic depressions" who do not respond well to medication, and
severe retarded and agitated depressives who do respond well.

Trying to discriminate between "psychotic" and "neurotic" depressions on the basis of severity of life disruption
results in an intractable confounding of the various depressive syndromes, so that no relationship with drug effect can
be demonstrated. The confusion between reactive vs. endogenous depression, and neurotic vs. psychotic depression is
discussed in Klein and Davis (8). Our stand is that such
distinctions are unrewarding, but that other categorizations
allow for rational treatment decisions and valid prognoses.

Typical of one class of medication error is the fact
that Mrs. Seid was started on Tofranil in spite of her history of lack of response to this antidepressant. It was also unfortunate that it took her doctors two months to be
certain of its ineffectiveness, although it only requires
four weeks to be assured of this. The toxic organic confusional response to Nardil is atypical but has been reported.
Mrs. Seid's self-destructive gestures could easily be interpreted in the usual stereotyped, psychodynamic model of depression, as retroflexed rage. In fact, the major function
of these gestures was an attempt to define herself as being
so sick that she should not be expected to occupy an adult
role. Her emotional difficulty was that she could not directly state her refusal to continue as a wife and mother.
Once she was capable of doing this, the need for manipulative "self-destructive" maneuvers ceased.

This case represents another side of the treatment of
"depression." Here a psychogenic "depression" is diagnosed as
a psychotic depression on the basis of repeated suicide
attempts and expressed feelings of helplessness and hopeless-

ness.   Other diagnostic aspects of depression such as anorexia, insomnia, diurnal mood shifts, phasic periods of complete recovery and total anhedonia were not present.   Such
cases drive home the point that one must always review and
rediagnose in the face of continued therapeutic failure.
This patient was fortunate enough to receive the psychotherapeutic intervention that was appropriate for her.

HYSTEROID DYSPHORIA
Definition

One group of patients frequently considered to have either a neurotic depressive reaction or hysterical-hysteroid character disorder is worthy of special notice, especially since they seem to have quite specific medication response patterns. The key note of these predominantly female patients' psychopathological state is an extremely brittle and shallow mood ranging from giddy elation to desperate unhappiness. Their mood is markedly responsive to external sources of admiration and approval. Such patients who appear hopelessly bereft when a love affair ends, feel perfectly fine or even elated within a few days, after meeting a new attentive man. Their emotionality markedly affects their judgment — when euphoric they minimize and deny the shortcomings of situations or relationships; thus they idealize all love objects. When "depressed," feelings of desperation are expressed very disproportionately to actual circumstances.

Although these patients may refer to their dysphoric mood as "depression," the essential characteristics of pathologically depressive mood, such as anhedonia, are not salient. They are prone to oversleep and overeat. Although they may express themselves despairingly, they are activity-oriented and successfully strive to engage in new rewarding situations.

The pattern of their characteristic traits allows an in-

ference concerning their emotional dynamics. They are fickle, emotionally labile, irresponsible, shallow, love-intoxicated, giddy and short-sighted. They tend to be egocentric,
narcissistic, exhibitionistic, vain and clothes-crazy. Seductive, manipulative, exploitative and sexually provocative,
they think emotionally and illogically. Easy prey to flat-
tery and compliments, their general manner is histrionic and
flamboyant. In their sexual relations they are possessive,
grasping, demanding, romantic and fore-play centered. When
frustrated or disappointed, they become reproachful, tearful,
abusive and vindictive, and often resort to drinking alcohol.
Rejection sensitivity is perhaps their outstanding common
clinical feature.

This appears to be nothing more than a misogynous char-
acterization of women - a caricature of femininity - and requires explanation. In our society, as probably in most
others, a leading issue in the life of most women is to attract and retain a supporting male figure. Such sex typing
occurs early in life, probably within the first two years.
Among the social tactics available to women, and approved of
as peculiarly feminine, are an exhibitionistic, seductive
display of their charms.

Women, with a normal range of emotional response, use a
wide variety of exhibitionistic and seductive social tactics
with discretion and accuracy. The "hysteroid dysphoric" is
a caricature of femininity because the disorder drives her
to attempt to mitigate her dysphoria by exaggerating the social, seductive, exhibitionistic tactics allowable to women
in our society. It is the driven, repetitive quality of behavior that indicates the underlying affective disorder.

If a child or young adolescent is afflicted with a marked mood instability that is reactive to social approval and
disapproval, it is understandable that she would shortly become overtrained in methods for eliciting admiring and ap-

proving feedback from the environment. Naturally, the exact method used would be dependent upon the reinforcement contingencies offered by the family. Many of these patients have been treated as little princesses by their fathers, and have narcissistic, self-indulgent mothers as female models.

Finding a generally acceptable label for these patients would be most useful. They have been referred to as hysteroid characters because of their histrionic emotionality and man-centered concerns. This term seems unfortunate in that it emphasizes their interpersonal tactics and fantasy goals. I view these character traits as secondary to the primary affective vulnerability. This shift in focus is not accidental but reflects newer therapeutic techniques. When such patients were treated with psychotherapy alone, as is still usually the case, the natural focus was upon those features that seemed modifiable by psychotherapy: their object relations and interpersonal tactics. Their affective lability and dependence on external sources of narcissistic supplies were considered secondary, reparative, anxiety-binding defenses that were not open to direct intervention. However, with the ability to change directly the affective reactivity of these patients through medication, one can now see their interpersonal tactics and object relationships as secondary reverberations of their basic affective sensitivity to rejection.

I postulate that in early development, probably during the period psychoanalysts refer to as the oral phase, an innate affective control mechanism develops with respect to the experience of social approval, applause and admiration. I do not think these experiences derive their effectiveness from being linked to primary tissue-need gratifications as secondary reinforcers, although this process also occurs. Rather such experiences begin as primary, innately determined social reinforcers. Being approved or admired results in

pleasurable mood, accompanied by self-satisfaction, whereas
social disapproval produces marked distress. This distress
does not result in paralysis but rather in active efforts to
regain the pleasurable state of approval. The precise efforts used will depend on the reinforcement contingencies,
i.e., the rewards provided by the family and society.

One can review each set of clinical characteristics as
a direct aspect of these patients' basic affective defect or
as a method of compensation for this defect. For instance,
their shallow, love-intoxicated, giddy nature may be viewed
as a direct expression of their specific variety of reactive
affective lability. Their short-sightedness, emotional reasoning, illogical and irresponsible attitudes are viewed as
a domination of thinking and judgmental processes by mood
state. Their exhibitionism, clothes-craziness, seductive-
ness, manipulativeness, sexual provocativeness and narcissism
are all devices for eliciting admiring masculine attention.
Their egocentrism results from their very narrow perceptual
focus; that is, people are viewed essentially as mood adjusting agents. Therefore, these patients do not develop a dis-
criminating appreciation of another's real complexity. When
the other person is no longer a source of admiration, or after the first spontaneous, admiring responses wear thin,
there is no felt reason to continue the relationship —
therefore they appear fickle. Their reproachfulness, tearfulness, abusiveness and vindictiveness are viewed as the
other pole of their emotional lability, compounded by an aggressive response to frustration and a coercive attempt to
reinstate the former adoration. These patients do not have
psychopathic coldness and indifference to the loss of love
objects.

Although these patients, when deprived, speak fervently
of suicide, the act seems quite uncommon. Furthermore, although they speak frequently of loneliness, they are not dom-

inated by separation anxiety. That is, they do not develop
agoraphobic or travel phobic trends. If they are in the company of a man who is dull and unadmiring, they will remove
themselves as quickly as possible; whereas the patient dominated by separation anxiety will accept any type of companionship. The development of incapacitating depressive states
can occur but is most unusual. They can be distinguished
from patients with an emotionally unstable character disorder
by the clearly cut "reactive" nature of the hysteroid dysphoria.

LOIS LAZAR

PRESENTING PROBLEM

Lois Lazar was 25, unmarried and a strikingly attractive, highly talented, but usually unemployed entertainer,
when she came for out-patient treatment. She immediately
launched into a medley of complaints, which included a long,
varied series of highly unsatisfactory romantic and sexual
relationships; anorgastic liaisons which made her wonder
whether she was homosexual and feared being female; sudden
shifts in mood so great that from a period of elation she
would cry for several hours, and a general nagging feeling of
depression pervading all activities.

FAMILY

The father was a handsome, capable, admirable, successful, driven businessman, with a great sense of humor. Lois
described him as exerting a mediating, calming effect upon
his chaotic family. However, he died at age 41, after a year
of illness, when Lois was age eight. She characterized him
as absolute God Almighty.

The mother was described as a ranting termagant, the father's high priestess, albeit cold, indifferent, narcissistic
and infantile. Her behavior was extremely unreliable, erup-
tive, and she punished her two daughters out of all propor-

tion to their misdeeds. For instance, over minor difficulties she would hurl knives at them. Or when Lois would come
home late from a date, the mother would rush to intercept her
at the door and pummel her. Mrs. Lazar was fairly successful
in manipulating others with her histrionics. However, while
her husband was alive, his presence insured some degree of
normalcy in the home. He would withdraw and "turn off" if
she lost control in his presence, and he instructed his
daughters in this tactic. After the father's death, the
mother worked in the family business, remained unmarried and
devoted to her husband's memory.

The sister was three years older than Lois. There was
constant competition and battling between the two girls. The
sister was socially adept, very selfish, and early married a
passive man whom she dominated completely, but who finally
divorced her.

DEVELOPMENTAL HISTORY

Little developmental history was available. However,
Lois recalled that she was greatly attached to the family
maid, even sharing her bed. It was later conjectured by the
family that the father also shared this woman's bed. The
maid suddenly left when Lois was 3½, and Lois missed her terribly.

From a very young age, Lois was bright, artistic, capable, extremely alert, outgoing, pleasant and histrionic. She
sang and danced with outstanding talent. Early, she was very
upset by her mother's lability, but also observed her mother's success in controlling people, and admittedly adopted
some of her flamboyant techniques.

Lois' parents insisted that their girls be spotlessly
clean, beautifully dressed and well-mannered. Lois acceded
to these demands. Nevertheless, she wet her bed until age
four, a sin considered cardinal, if not quite capital, by her
parents. Also, they were concerned about her tendency to

gain weight, and pressured her to diet almost constantly from an early age.

She vividly remembered her father's sense of humor; e.g., for a joke he would sit around wearing only under-shorts, bowtie and pith helmet. She told of an incident at age six or seven, when she begged her father for a doll and promised she would never ask him for anything else for the rest of that summer. Her father had her write an affidavit and explained that she was writing out her "word." Two days later, she asked for something else. He brought out the af-fidavit and explained to her that he wanted her to be a great lady, and great ladies don't break their word. This had strong impact on Lois. She also remembered being thrown while horse riding with him. He kindly but firmly insisted that she immediately get back on the horse so that she would not build up fears.

Little was reported about her early sexual development, except that her father once caught her masturbating and laughed. Lois was mortified and did not masturbate again un-til adulthood.

When Lois was eight, her father died. She had to kiss him in his coffin and clearly remembered that moment with everyone looking distorted and colored blue. Her mother was in complete collapse and so scared Lois that she feared going home with her; thus Lois lived with relatives for a time. Although she showed no marked evidence of grief after his death, often after going to sleep, she would scream. About this time, she became quite dependent upon her sister.

During her school years, Lois was a good student, popu-lar with her teachers and many friends. She grew rapidly, matured early, was physically very well developed and appear-ed quite adult by age 14. She was very conscious about her body and large breasts. Suddenly she was "hit on by all kinds of people; everyone was grabbing." At this time she

and the boys became intensively interested in each other, and
her romantic roller-coaster began.

When her 17 year old sister married, Lois was extremely
distraught and begged to go with her, rather than remain at
home with her mother. Instead, they visited frequently.

Lois found tremendous satisfaction in singing and dancing. As the showgirl, she could successfully be the center
of attention, a role she found very satisfying. By age 16,
she was a professional entertainer with excellent reviews.
Nonetheless, she could never hold a job steadily. Always she
became romantically involved with a variety of men: her
agents, directors or fellow performers. Her mood fluctuated
with her relationships. The highly emotional attachments
caused her great personal upheaval and forced her to be professionally unreliable. Also, she developed many handicapping somatic complaints, such as throat and sinus inflamma-
tions. Often, minutes before showtime, she would suddenly
refuse to appear and run off to hide. Because of her talent,
Lois was readily hired, but once her lack of professional
discipline became known, only small-time jobs were available
to her, and she remained financially unsuccessful. In fact,
her mother had to continue to pay Lois' rent.

At age 22, Lois started psychoanalysis at a well-known
analytic institute. She entered treatment because of her
anorgastic sexual relationships, recurrent suicidal thoughts,
constant tiredness, oversleeping, inability to get out of bed
in the morning, ten pound overweight with no appetite, anxiety attacks, and panic at being alone. At the same time, she
was involved in an intense but short-lived affair and became
pregnant. An abortion was performed on psychiatric recommendation and treatment at the analytic institute was cancelled.

She then entered a year of treatment with a very bright
psychologist who commanded her respect. He offered her sup-

portive and directive therapy and encouraged her to repress, rather than explore bad feelings. This approach was helpful in that her behavior became more socially sensible. However, while she was able to force herself to get up in the morning, she still felt miserable. Her therapist's attitude was, "why are you behaving in such a silly fashion, it's stupid."

At about this time, Lois was seeing a boyfriend who was in mescaline group psychotherapy. He convinced her that this was better than psychotherapy; that she could go faster, deeper and become more profoundly understanding. She did not discuss this with her psychologist because she did not want to be talked out of it. Thus, she entered treatment with this new therapist who took her through long fantasy sessions, revitalizing memories and feelings from her early childhood. The analyst felt that the only way to mental health was through a tremendous release of hostility, to the point of psychosis. To attain this goal he used mescaline interventions during group therapy sessions, where one person would be given a large dose of mescaline, and the other patients would try to participate in the individual's mescaline fantasies.

She saw the mescaline group psychotherapist for eight months, and ended up, as she stated, "a basket case," nonfunctioning and suicidal. Nonetheless, she remembered some cathartic episodes very positively, feeling that she discharged a great deal of murderous rage. At one point, under mescaline, she had to be held down to prevent her from killing some innocent bystander who she misidentified with past figures. She also had infrequent periods during this time of peaceful euphoria, and a calm, deep, positive experience of intense femaleness, feeling as if she was the earth mother. These feelings were explicitly sexual, and very welcome.

On occasion, under mescaline, Lois would scream for hours. Finally, she realized, "So what, I've been screaming all my life, what good does it do me?" She became increasingly angry, had more and more hostile releases and felt worse and worse. It was obvious that she wasn't being helped, and a consultant suggested that she change therapists quickly, since it was evident that the psychedelic reactive experience was not producing any beneficial change; rather, she was going downhill.

At this point, Lois accepted an invitation for a trip to Europe where she enjoyed herself and felt generally better, although she had episodes of sleep paralysis where she would awake and find herself unable to move. Her improved mood was largely due to a new boyfriend whom she saw constantly. She showed a very quick hypomanic swing, slept four or five hours nightly, and her chronic gnawing depression was much mitigated. Lois described the boyfriend as, "a very talented artist who did not play roles. He was sensitive, deep, romantic, poetic and gentle." Repeatedly, she used this description about each new boyfriend. However, she would immediately counter this remark by her feelings of absurdity, since all people had to go to the toilet. "How can people have earth-shaking loves and hates and yet be so animal?"

Upon her return from Europe, she entered further outpatient treatment.

PRESENTING CHARACTERISTICS

Miss Lazar was attractive, buxom, seductive, with a striking voice. Her manner was friendly, witty, pleasant and sharp, but sometimes tragic. Mainly she impressed with her flamboyance and histrionics. Cheerfully, wryly, she referred to herself as "an oedipus wreck."

Her chief complaints concerned her eternal series of unsatisfactory romantic and sexual involvements, one following the next, since age 16. She reflected that she could be uninvolved or without a man for five minutes at best, even though she wasn't interested in sex.

TREATMENT

After a month in psychotherapy, Miss Lazar became very angry with her new boyfriend, because he was "so impossible, wound up and preoccupied"; meaning that he did not pay constant attention to her. She admitted that she was unreasonable, but "I want what I want, when I want it. Everything is a test of his affection." Intellectually, she agreed this was ridiculous. She stated that she became scared the minute that the relationship was anything less than absolute and complete devotion (associated with tremendous physical demonstrations of affection).

During the next two months, Miss Lazar felt bad, was depressed and paid her bills irregularly. She rarely worked, and had no money, except what her mother or boyfriend gave her.

By this time, she became involved with two other men. Although she enjoyed sex, she was unable to have an orgasm in simple intercourse but required cunnilingus. She spoke about equating orgasm with surrender and cunnilingus with altruistic affection.

After six months in therapy, she got a job as an entertainer, and earned $300 a week, for a short period of time, doing extremely well at a nightclub job. But soon she was shattered by a conflict between the club owner and the manager, and lost her job.

Her latest boyfriend, a mildly paranoid psychopath, whom she felt an obligation to help, occasionally beat her. Her possessiveness was discussed, but she was unable to modify it. She started smoking marijuana and had episodes of severe depersonalization and brooding about homosexuality. However, she continued to use marijuana more and more frequently, and had continuous somatic distortions, similar to those she had had under mescaline, where she would feel as if the left side of her body was either masculine or dead.

She went on a cruise after ten months and had a very gay
time, entertaining and being promiscuous with various tour-
ists and ship officers. But the next month, she was complaining bitterly, feeling loss and despair after her cruise
boyfriend left. Therefore, Tofranil 75 mg daily was started,
in the hope of modifying her "depression."

The Tofranil was ineffective and Miss Lazar remained
very upset, feeling that everything was "flipping and whirl-
ing." She couldn't think straight, had lost control and
claimed she suddenly was fascinated by female sexuality. She
refused to take Tofranil, and Mellaril 100 mg daily was instituted for several days, during which she calmed down. When
the Mellaril was withdrawn, she became somewhat giddy. The
Mellaril was reinstituted at 25 mg at night, which seemed to
take the edge off her emotional lability. Episodically, she
took diet pills, apparently partly for their mood-enhancing
effects.

She continually complained about feeling as if she were
"flipping out of focus." This referred to her very marked dysphoric feelings when narcissistic supplies and support were
withdrawn. She was unable to further define what appeared to
be a very specific perceptual aberration.

For the next seven months, Miss Lazar was seen twice
weekly. Then, an older, successful man who had been keeping
her for about six months, died, and she became very upset. He
was intelligent, cultured, supported her, saw her periodically
and made few demands upon her, other than occasional sexual
access. She enjoyed him and the security he afforded.

Two weeks after his death, she refused to take any medication, except large numbers of diet pills, and began to feel
panicky and frightened. Two days later she was terrorized
that she was going downhill, and was continually crying.
Mellaril was increased to 300 mg daily. She continued to

feel extremely frightened, tense, was preoccupied with suicidal thoughts and was pacing continually. It was thought
that she might have been having an akathisic response to the
Mellaril, and the medication was switched to Thorazine 100
mg at night, plus Kemadrin.

Quickly, she felt better on Thorazine and Kemadrin than
on Mellaril, but still was extremely frightened and discouraged. Thorazine was increased to 300 mg daily, plus Kemadrin 5 mg daily, and after a week she was still not doing
well, feeling fearful, apathetic, tired and depressed.
Thorazine was increased to 800 mg daily and after a week,
was cut to 500 mg when she seemed to be improving. She was
no longer out of control, but still seemed quite depressed,
sad, tired and scared.

Her sister was lecturing her about pulling herself together and straightening out her life; her mother was being
sweet and solicitous. She continued feeling scared, drained, sick, awaking in a panic and wanting to sleep constantly. She had neither gone out nor socialized for two months.

It was felt that perhaps she was taking too much Thorazine, and this was decreased to 300 mg daily. Three weeks
later she had a severe hysterical attack concerning an audi-
tion, which quickly switched to a euphoric state when she
was received with enthusiastic applause. (When the external
supplies came in she could still feel good.)

Two weeks later, she felt completely overwhelmed, that
everything was too much; she didn't know how she was going
to endure. She talked about suicide and said she had never
felt worse. The psychiatrist attributed her dysphoria to
Thorazine and decreased it to 25 mg at night. Dexamyl 5 mg
twice daily, Miltown 400 mg twice daily and Kemadrin 2.5 mg
twice daily were added.

By Christmas, Miss Lazar was terrified, exhausted, confused and suicidal, and played with razor blades. She acted

like a child. She wasn't as sleepy since the Thorazine had
been cut, but she felt like a weight, and didn't want to sing
or do anything. She would get terrible palpitations and
feelings of terror, actual physical pains, as if someone were
tearing at her throat. She hadn't been eating and lost seven
pounds, did not take care of herself and felt constantly hysterical.

By New Year's, 18 months after starting treatment, she
stated that she couldn't stand it anymore, was in a constant
state of terror, felt like fainting and appeared to be in a
marked agitated depression. At this point, it was decided to
start Stelazine 12 mg daily for two weeks. If this did not
work, she would be referred for ECT. She continued in a depressed, fearful state, and pleaded, "Please don't let me
walk around like this. Everything terrorizes me."

Five ECT were given by a well-known specialist and Miss
Lazar showed a short-lived, marked mood elevation. But after
two weeks she was sleeping poorly, had no energy, was restless, depressed about not working and fought with her manager. Stelazine 2 mg twice daily was continued. She was obsessed with ambivalent, guilt-provoking thoughts of herself
and her mother dying.

A week later, she started a new affair with a married
man and perked up. When she saw an old boyfriend who told
her that he loved her and couldn't keep away from her, she
really felt good. But when a third boyfriend was supposed to
call and didn't, she became very upset. When she did meet
him accidentally, he was cold to her, ignored her completely,
and this depressed her thoroughly. Suicidal preoccupation,
increased sleeping and severe fright again recurred, and
Stelazine was increased from 4 to 8 mg daily, without apparent effect.

At this point it was realized that Miss Lazar never had
had a trial of an MAO inhibitor; the Stelazine was stopped

and Nardil 15 mg daily was started. After a week, she had
several complaints but felt less suicidal. While she over-
slept, she wasn't as sleepy. She continued feeling lost.

The second week Nardil was increased to 30 mg daily, her
sleepiness decreased, and astonishingly she worked several
nightclub engagements. She began feeling very high when with
her boyfriend. Her occasional suicidal thoughts were not too
distressing. Nardil was increased to 45 mg daily by three
weeks. She complained that the morning was the worst period,
however, she was, by now, extremely active, making many job
arrangements. After three weeks on Nardil 45 mg daily, her
disastrous social withdrawal had ceased, she went on vacation, had a good time and was no longer depressed. After a
month she claimed she felt much better, that she was beginning "to try," and that it was nice that people liked her.
At that point her therapy was decreased to one visit every
two weeks.

Things continued to go well. She was very salty, self-
assertive, hard-working and appeared, if anything, a bit euphoric. She used a fair amount of marijuana and was doing
well sexually. When she reported considerable feelings of
anger toward her manager, resenting being used by him as if
he was trying to work a Pygmalion, and became extremely
touchy and short-tempered, the Nardil was decreased to 30 mg
daily. She calmed down considerably, no longer over-reacted
to pressure or criticism, and was more amiable.

Once again she became passionately involved with a new
boyfriend, which frightened him. She was always in a dither
as to whether she should be possessive or not, and extremely
suspicious about her boyfriends' feelings. She stated that
she opened up and wanted to stay that way, and then her boyfriends would close up and would try to close her up, which
she found intolerable, leading to further engulfing maneuvers. Her boyfriends would become more and more withdrawn

as she became increasingly grasping, producing a pinched watermelon seed effect.

Nardil was decreased to 15 mg daily, in view of her definite decrease in irritability. Then she became slightly depressed, somewhat restless and was sleeping poorly. Stelazine 1 mg twice daily was added to the Nardil, in the hope of alleviating her insomnia and agitation. The addition of Stelazine successfully produced an evening of mood. Although she continued to take Nardil regularly, her use of Stelazine was episodic. She was unwilling to take a tranquilizer on a regular basis as she felt that it dampened her occasional high spirits.

She became involved with yet another lover; this time a well-known TV personality. Her mood seemed level, she was working well, did not feel irritable, but was upset at times.

After seven months on Nardil she discontinued the medication for five days and quickly felt odd sensations of shifting identity; as if she were losing her balance. This was confounded by her new boyfriend treating her in an offhand way. She felt unattractive and as if non-existent. At times she appeared taken with existential ruminations.

Placed back on Nardil, her mood improved, and within a month she requested to discontinue therapy, since she felt well and was low on cash. She had changed boyfriends three times more, but was not undergoing her previous crashes and mood swings. She also increased her marijuana use at this time. After ten months on Nardil, she had maintained herself on 15 mg daily, but required an increase to 30 mg daily because of feeling overwhelmed. On this dose she felt less "clutchy." Sexually she had no problems and was frequently orgastic. Periodically, she lowered or raised her medication.

Eleven months after starting on Nardil, Miss Lazar had a therapeutic abortion with no ill results. She was slightly

depressed and bitchy after it, and the Nardil was increased
to 45 mg daily and Stelazine 4 mg daily for a few weeks, with
good effect.

Six months later she continued taking Nardil 15 mg daily, reported she felt well and had just begun living with a
new married boyfriend. At times he appeared preoccupied and
she felt he didn't really love her. When her boyfriend
criticized her, she would become angry, but did not feel the
same affective crash that she had previously. Her boyfriend
was unfortunately a gambler and big talker.

FOLLOW-UP

After three years, Miss Lazar, at age 28, discontinued
treatment and found a steady show job, away from New York
City. Here she became involved with a musician who, like all
her boyfriends, was "sensitive, deep, poetic, and a beautiful
spirit," as well as an outstanding musician. However, he also
was a heroin user, and over the three and a half years that
they were together, his addiction became increasingly grip-
ping, so that he eventually was stealing from her for money
to buy heroin. However, their sexual life was extremely
gratifying and this made a very strong bind. Also, she had
strong feelings of nurturance toward him and felt that she
could help him; not recognizing what an opponent heroin was.

She began to use marijuana extremely heavily so that she
was "stoned" all day, every day, and after six months stopped
singing and simply lived with her boyfriend. She attributed
her use of marijuana to her difficult relationship with her
boyfriend. He was a smooth talker and manipulative. At one
time when she confronted him with a burnt spoon, obviously
indicating that he was taking heroin, within 20 minutes he
had her apologizing for her suspicions. During this period,
she used Nardil and Stelazine irregularly. By two years
after stopping treatment, she only used it when she was under
stress.

She became interested in Yoga and Eastern philosophy.
One of her major reasons for studying Yoga was her conviction
that it would help her overcome a variety of physical weak-
nesses. At first, she did not like practicing the various
postures, but then she connected with a teacher whom she admired and respected. Later she became involved with an emi-
nent person in this field whom she revered and became close
with. She became a vegetarian as part of her Yoga training.
She was very interested in meditation and used this as a way
of gaining distance and exerting control over her emotions
and problems.

By age 31, still with her addict boyfriend, she had lost
considerable weight and started modeling, rather than singing, and was fairly successful in earning a living.

Later that year, she and her boyfriend were at the point
of breaking up. Suddenly, Miss Lazar underwent surgery, and
shortly after had severe internal hemorrhaging, went into
shock and required massive transfusions to prevent death. To
recuperate, she went to live with a friend, and at that
point, broke with her boyfriend, since she felt that he was
in no way capable of caring for her, or she for him. While
at her friend's house, she began writing songs and poetry,
attempting to arrive at a synthesis between Indian and Western music style, and developed considerable proficiency at
playing various Indian instruments. She started to sing
again, made a record as an instrumentalist, and received some
recognition from other musicians interested in Indian music.

When followed-up at age 34, Miss Lazar spoke rationally,
relevantly, coherently, under slight pressure as she discussed her residual emotional problems. She was in radiant good
health, and was physically well-groomed and attractive. Her
wry sense of humor was very manifest; however, she took her
interest in Yoga most seriously and earnestly invited her
psychiatrist to meetings of her group, to be exposed to the

personality of the Swami whom she characterized as extraordinarily perceptive, permissive, nonjudgmental and radiating
understanding and peace.

She worked at meditation daily and stated that she could
now distance herself from upset, that her mood was much more
even than previously, and that she neither got giddy-ecstatic
over new situations nor crashed on rejection. She agreed
that her central emotional vulnerability was rejection sensitivity. She smoked about one marijuana cigarette daily, and
became slightly euphoric, but never stoned. She reported
that if she was feeling unhappy and smoked marijuana, she
could perceive what made her feel bad, or at least believed
that she could; therefore she used marijuana in a self-diag-
nostic way. She saw her addict boyfriend occasionally, partly because she was still very attached to him, and partly because their sexual relationship remained good. However, she
recognized that the relationship was impossible, and endeav-
ored to detach herself in the least painful manner.

She expressed a desire to become a teacher of Yoga.
Interestingly, one of the aspects of this Yoga is its revolving around chanting mantras, providing a natural link with
her singing talent.

In summary then, Miss Lazar, at age 34, appeared to be
considerably more stabile emotionally than when she first
started treatment. She was able to enjoy sex more casually,
and no longer had to convince herself that she was madly in
love with her partner. It is obscure as to whether her improved emotional stability was due to her new life successes,
maturation, vegetarianism, Yoga, her network of friends, or
learning through life experience, since we have no baseline
of expectation for this group of patients. She stated that
the medication was definitely useful when she was under
stress, and discussed the possibility of returning to treatment on occasion, when she felt especially stressed, for

supervision in using Nardil.

She felt that she gained from psychotherapy in that she learned that her erratic driven life was secondary to her dependency, and that once she was more independent she would be able to make life choices. She felt that her transition to Yoga was, to some degree, an attempt to control her overwhelming emotional reactions.

COMMENT

Miss Lazar represents the extreme of the hysteroid dysphoric patient. While this type of emotional difficulty is quite frequent, it is usually seen in less dramatic form. The essential issue is the extreme rejection sensitivity associated with marked action orientation, very considerable histrionic social skills, and the apparent reactivity of the mood shifts. These patients differ from classical retarded or agitated depressives in that their mood is usually responsive to circumstances. They can be relieved by admiration and attention and experience pleasure. Among the vegetative signs are the tendencies to overeat and oversleep during dysphoric episodes. Because of the marked emotional reactivity and the comprehensibility of the emotional swings, it is easy to ignore the affective disturbance and focus on the interpersonal problem. However, this misses the quantitative excess and rigidly repetitive enduring quality of the affective disturbance; it also misses the giddy euphoric overreaction under conditions of admiration.

Monoamine oxidase (MAO) inhibitors, e.g. Nardil, markedly dampen these mood swings. Often the patient regrets the loss of the giddy euphoric periods, and because of this may discontinue medication. The emotional lability of these patients demands long-term medication as a possible treatment modality which often does not occur to the physician.

The tricyclic antidepressants, e.g. Tofranil, Elavil, etc., are not useful with such patients, often causing them

to feel depersonalized and producing difficulty in thinking.
However, rare exceptions occur and some hysteroid dysphorics
are helped by tricyclic antidepressants. However, the tri-
cyclics are definitely not the drug of choice. A strong differential point for the use of the MAO inhibitors is oversleeping and overeating during "depression." The tricyclic
antidepressants are best used in depressions associated with
early morning insomnia and anorexia.

This case is atypical in that following one severe loss
Miss Lazar became nonfunctioning and suicidally preoccupied
to the degree that ECT was required. This is the only case
I have observed where this was necessary, and therefore I do
not know whether the transient benefit of ECT is typical for
such patients.

Her increased propensity for anger when maintained on
Nardil 45 mg daily is typical. Dosage levels require careful titration. Small doses of an adjunctive piperazine
phenothiazine seem helpful in mood stabilization.

One error made in Miss Lazar's pharmacological management was the constant reliance on phenothiazines and the frequent shifts of phenothiazines in a futile attempt to titrate
her anxiety and depression. The simple fact was that at the
time, the MAO inhibitors were not recognized as useful for
such patients, and since she had not responded to tricyclic
antidepressants, the possibility that antidepressants of any
sort might be of value was incorrectly ruled out. This proved to be the opposite of successful management.

Of interest is that the patient's sister, who
had for 14 years lived a controlling, domineering life with
a passive husband, was suddenly divorced by him and then developed emotional symptomatology markedly like Miss Lazar's,
consisting of extreme mood lability, constant search for external sources of narcissistic supplies and feelings of being
overwhelmed and incapable of arriving at decisions. She was

referred to a psychiatrist, who, on the basis of her sister's response, prescribed Nardil. The sister had an immediate positive response to Nardil. However, she would not stay on the medication since she objected to the loss of her giddy euphoric periods, and was unhappy with the doctor's recommendation to refrain from alcohol while on Nardil. Also, she suffered a cheese reaction when she forgot the doctor's injunctions concerning diet and ate a lunch of Swiss cheese and pickled lox. She developed excruciating throbbing occipital and neck pains that lasted for several hours and frightened her considerably.

The fact that these sisters developed such markedly similar Nardil-responsive emotional disorders raises the question of a familial disorder. The mother's emotional instability did not seem to be of the same variety described here, but several of the mother's sisters were reported to have similar flamboyant, rejection-sensitive, exhibitionistic, hysteroid personalities.

It should be pointed out that there have been no controlled scientific studies of these patients' reactions to medication, and that these comments are derived from simple clinical experience. Such studies would be of great interest.

Chapter VIII

RECURRENT AFFECTIVE DISORDERS, BIPOLAR TYPE: MANIC STATES

Definition

There is nothing very different between the developmental history of manics and that of depressives, although manic patients are more frequently male, and the illness has an earlier onset. There may be a trend toward a brighter, more outgoing, zestful, expansive personality. This is often referred to as extraversion, with the implication that this is a basic unitary personality characteristic. We see extraversion as the complex resultant of attitudinal learning and predominant mood state.

Diagnostic Traits

That a proportion of depressives (bipolar) have complete reversals of psychopathology, referred to as manic episodes, is an extraordinary psychopathological phenomenon with which any theory of brain function and affect must deal. Some patients may only have manic episodes. The hallmark of the manic episode is psychomotor acceleration, coupled with an ease of enjoyment and an unrealistically optimistic attitude toward achievement and the possiblity of future enjoyment.

Other inconstant associates of psychomotor acceleration are motor restlessness, incessant talking, youthful appearance, vivacity, euphoria, optimism, lack of frustration tolerance, marked irritability and angry responses upon frustration, meddlesome domineering tactics, flight of ideas, in-

258

ability to maintain a goal orientation, misinterpretations, angry paranoid assertions, pleasant overhelpfulness, wild unruly high spirits, domineering trends, rejection of control, ceaseless activity, generally superior attitude ranging to grandiosity, erotomania, early morning awakening and good appetite. Again, all these features are inconstant and confirmatory rather than diagnostic.

To sum up, in all crucial traits, the manic episode represents the exact opposite of the retarded depressive episode. This has led to the reasonable speculation that manic-depressive disorders are due to derangements of central regulatory pleasure-reward and associated response-facilitory activation systems.

Differential Diagnosis

The manic patient who is angry, suspicious, with flight of ideas and tangential associations, and lacks euphoria (as he often does when confined), is regularly diagnosed as an angry paranoid schizophrenic. The dividing line between these two states is not clear, and it is possible that in the acute stage no cross-sectional clinical distinction can be made. History is also not too valuable since angry paranoid patients frequently have episodic courses.

Clear persecutory hallucinations or delusions have a more ominous prognostic implication and therefore warrant the diagnosis of schizophrenia. Suspicious and grandiose residuals seem more common in grossly delusional patients. However, studies comparing the outcome of manic with angry paranoid patients have not demonstrated any prognostic distinction, and phenothiazine treatment yields very similar results. Whether lithium is specific for mania or can benefit some excited schizophrenics, as I think, is still under study.

Excited, acute schizophrenic patients may display states of ecstatic elation and mystic transcendence that resemble manic states. However, unlike the manic state, extraordinary

looseness of association and autistic symbolism are regularly
present.

DOLORES KYTE

PRESENTING PROBLEM

Speaking very slowly and softly, 24 year old Dolores
Kyte told how fearful, depressed, worthless and hopeless she
felt. Apathetic and unable to concentrate, she cried frequently and felt wholly incapable and disinterested in caring
for her eight month old son. She had a healthy, easy pregnancy and delivery, and made a moderately easy adjustment to
caring for her baby for the first few months. But unexpectedly, her husband was called away on a two week business
trip, and when he returned she was severely depressed and
withdrawn. Because of this, he moved his wife and baby to
his parents' house and found a psychiatrist who treated her
for a month with an antidepressant (type unknown). When she
showed no response to the drug, the psychiatrist administered nine ECT over a few week period. She seemed to begin
feeling better, but when plans were made for her to resume
housekeeping, the depression returned. Recommendations for
hospitalization were made and eight more ECT treatments administered, with some mood amelioration by the time she entered Hillside.

FAMILY

Mrs. Kyte had very little to do with her father, since
her parents were divorced when she was four years old. The
father never provided enough money, committed bigamy with an
18 year old girl and spent a year in jail. He was otherwise
moody, unstable and unaffectionate. When his wife was pregnant with Dolores, he was hospitalized for a year with a
"nervous condition."

The mother, in her mid 60's, was meddling, domineering,
cold and distant. She was always critical and demanding of

her daughter and never felt warmth or affection toward her.
While Dolores was wary of her mother, she was also extremely
dependent upon her.

Two brothers were four and eight years older than
Dolores. The younger was neurotic, hostile, angry, difficult
to live with and in psychotherapy for many years; the older
was easy-going and softspoken, but also in psychiatric treatment. There was no close relationship among the siblings.

She met her husband on a blind date. Mr. Kyte, age 25,
worked for his father's insurance agency. He seemed to have
difficulty breaking away from his family. Usually quiet,
passive and controlled, he would not speak to his wife for
days if angered by her. Their sexual relations were never
good.

The mother carefully indoctrinated Dolores on the evils
of her father and all men in general, instructing her that
they were worthless liars and cheats and would bring only
misery. She felt the causes of her daughter's illness were
lack of a proper father and her son-in-law. She interfered
openly with Dolores' marriage, caused dissension between the
couple and considered her son-in-law to be wicked and out to
harm her daughter. Actually both mothers-in-law felt that
their respective children had married beneath them and wished the marriage to fail. Nevertheless, Dolores still tried
to please her mother by doing her bidding and was upset when
criticized by her. After any contact with her mother, she
was distracted and moody.

DEVELOPMENTAL HISTORY

Dolores was born normally at full term and was a quiet
baby with no eating or developmental problems. She was always notably shy and withdrawn. When she was four years old
her parents divorced. She was cared for by a grandmother
and a maiden aunt while her mother was at work.

She started school at age five, was an above average

student and got along without friction with teachers and
other children. Through school she had few friends because
she was socially reticent, withdrawn and quiet, and her mother had to prod her to make friends and participate in social
activities.

Dolores received no information concerning menstruation
or sex, only the lesson that men were evil liars. When she
was 13, her 17 year old brother exposed himself and attempted to have sexual intercourse with her, to which she responded with panic and fright. He was severely punished and never tried again. Her menarche was at age 14; at this time she
also started masturbating, continuing until the time she was
married.

At age 16, a teacher discussed Dolores' quiet, unhappy
demeanor with her mother and suggested that she seek treatment. The mother took her to a counselling service which she
attended for several weeks but which had no influence on her
behavior. However, a year later, upon entering college, she
suddenly changed and for the first time in her life became
very outgoing, aggressive and active. She dated often and
her mood was generally elevated throughout her college years.
Later, she interpreted this behavior as an attempt to prove
that she could act happy and healthy.

After she graduated from college at age 21, she took a
year of graduate training and began a job as a social worker.
By this time she had returned to her quiet, shy state and
barely could perform her job duties. Finally, she changed to
a job demanding less contact with people and was able to
function better.

About this time she had an affair with a 45 year old man
whom she met while vacationing. She claimed to neither like
him nor relish their sexual relationship but remained with
him for several months until she met her husband. After she
and her husband met they quickly became sexually intimate,

but she never enjoyed this affair either. Nonetheless, they were married after several months. Two weeks after their marriage her husband was drafted and she returned to live with her mother.

After two and a half years, Mrs. Kyte gave birth to a son;   shortly after this she became more acutely depressed, received 17 ECT and, as discussed earlier, was hospitalized.

PRESENTING CHARACTERISTICS

When questioned about her problems, Mrs. Kyte answered, "Ever since a few months after the baby was born, I have a loss of interest. I've been depressed or blue before but I never had this loss of interest. I want to be helped but I don't know what my trouble is." Her stream of thought was constricted, her affect was extremely flat, and she showed remarkable psychomotor retardation, but other than this her mental status was not notable. Following ECT she had regained her appetite and was sleeping well and expressed some guarded optimism about the future.

COURSE AT HILLSIDE

The results of all physical and neurological tests were negative. On the Wechsler-Bellevue, administered after two months of hospitalization, she attained an IQ of 118, with many scores over 120. Four months later, on retest, her total score was 130, with many scores around 140. The ECT and her residual depression may have accounted for the earlier lower scores.

At the beginning of hospitalization Mrs. Kyte was cooperative but lonely, frightened and depressed. She refrained from talking with other patients "because I don't want to be hurt or to hurt them." She expressed tremendous ambivalence toward her mother and husband but yet looked forward to time spent with them. In psychotherapy she had nothing to say.

Two months after admission she was referred to the drug
program, because of her lack of progress. During the first
six weeks she was on placebo. Her doctor felt she showed a
mild improvement, which he attributed to the fact that he
forced her to attend activities; he interpreted her continued
inability to communicate as hostility. Mrs. Kyte maintained
that her apathetic feelings had not changed at all. Her manner remained extremely flat and distant, and she gave short,
laconic replies to questions.

Next she was placed on Tofranil 75 mg daily, increased
weekly by 75 mg increments until 300 mg daily was received.
Within two weeks she became very active, participating in as
many activities as possible. While she complained about
marked perspiration and dry mouth, her mood was bright.

After three weeks on Tofranil she claimed she was entirely better and ready to leave the hospital. Previously
she had never been openly angry, but now she showed open,
frank hostility toward her husband. "I'm rebelling against
his domineering, stubborn, monopolistic attitudes. The ECT
just pacified me into thinking he was faultless, kind, generous and warm-hearted." She jumped from one idea to another,
without finishing a thought. She spent large amounts of money on unnecessary items and pressured her husband to supply
her with more money. Also, she gained 25 pounds.

Mr. Kyte became confused by his wife's behavior and
couldn't tolerate her flightiness, hostile, sarcastic manner,
or her public accusations of his "lack of virility" and "unfaithfulness." She would call him frequently, sometimes to
berate him and other times to beg him to visit; when he arrived she would fight with him or often sleep through his
visit. Finally, he contacted a lawyer to inquire about divorce procedures.

The Tofranil was withdrawn after six weeks because of
her increasing flight of ideas and hyperactivity. Later she

admitted that for the preceding two weeks, while presumably
on Tofranil, she had discarded her medication. She remained
manicky, talkative, confused and angry, and was furious when
placed in a closed ward because she frequently fled the hospital grounds.

Two weeks later Mellaril 100 mg twice daily was added,
doubled weekly until 800 mg was reached. Because it seemed
ineffective, it was changed to Thorazine 800 mg daily, after
two weeks. Her mood was very happy but she felt sleepy, nauseated and extremely active. She slept only four hours a
night. Several days later she admitted that she had been
self-medicating herself to lose weight, with a stimulating
drug, Preludin, which may have contributed to her excitement.

Over two weeks the Thorazine was increased until 2000
mg daily was reached, along with Kemadrin 15 mg daily. After
five days on 2000 mg she started to slow down, seemed more
organized and showed greater frustration tolerance. Slowly
over the next two weeks she became calmer, drowsy and appeared slightly depressed, although she claimed her mood was
good. She had dry mouth, blurred vision, was eating compulsively and had gained another 25 pounds. She remained disinterested in or unable to participate in psychotherapy.

Thorazine was kept at 2000 mg for two weeks, but because
of increasing drowsiness and other side effects, it was gradually reduced over the next month to 600 mg daily. She seemed more responsible, less irritable and was getting along
better with her husband. She looked brighter, more alert and
was friendly. However, this reduction of medication proved
premature as she suddenly became agitated, excited and defiant. Thorazine was increased to 900 mg daily, four days after the decrease.

In psychotherapy she began expressing concerns about her
personal relationships. Toward her husband she remained ambivalent, fluctuating between "I love him, there's no one

like him," to "he's a louse, he's just using me." She developed an obvious attachment to a female patient, bathed and
held hands with her. When other patients and staff censured
this behavior, she stopped. She broke many hospital rules,
ran away several times after being returned to the open ward,
got drunk and, in general, was a management problem.

Her dress was sexy and almost bizarre; she wore garish
makeup and was extremely seductive with male patients. This
eventuated in an affair with a male patient whom she decided
to marry when he promised to take care of her. At this point
she admitted that she had once again not been taking her medication consistently.

Thorazine 600 mg, and Kemadrin 7.5 mg daily, was reinstituted and she became drowsy again. When she received an ultimatum concerning the conditions under which her husband
would accept her back, she and another patient got drunk.
Later, scared that she had overstepped the hospital's limits
and would be thrown out, she became more cooperative and behaved with more self-restraint. After two weeks the Thorazine was again reduced to 300 mg nightly, so as to reduce her
somnolence during the day.

Little by little her relationship with her husband improved and they began to consider a reconciliation, but on
weekends she had difficulty caring for her son and husband.
Frightened by this, she decided to return to her mother, after discharge. However, the mother would not have her.
Mrs. Kyte then became withdrawn, depressed, lost her appetite
and spoke slowly and softly. After eight months of fluctuating Thorazine dosage and three months of a stable 300 mg daily, Tofranil was added to the Thorazine regimen, increasing
to 100 mg daily.

A month following the addition of Tofranil she showed a
definite improvement. When she appeared able to take more
responsibility at home, plans for discharge were made. Thus,

after 14 months of hospitalization, she was released. A
homemaker was to assist her, and she was to continue in private psychotherapy, taking Thorazine 300 mg, Kemadrin 5 mg
and Tofranil 100 mg, daily. Both the hospital and research
diagnoses were manic-depressive psychosis.

FOLLOW-UP

Mrs. Kyte returned to live with her husband and child
for five months, until it became obvious that she was continuing her extramarital affair with an ex-patient from Hillside.
She and her husband quarreled, she refused to stop the affair, decided to leave her husband, took the child and returned to live with her mother. After a court custody pro-
ceeding, the child was placed in the care of Mr. Kyte's mother.

Mrs. Kyte then began picking up strangers and virtually
became a prostitute. After two months she was pregnant;
her appearance and behavior were so inappropriate that her
mother took her to a city hospital. Luckily she spontaneously aborted and in two weeks transferred to a private hospital.

At the private hospital she was agitated, crying, had
pressured speech and self-inflicted abrasions over her body.
She cried about losing her baby and complained about having
been raped. They diagnosed her as having chronic undifferentiated schizophrenia and prescribed Thorazine and Librium
(amounts unknown), to which she showed no response. Later she
showed marked improvement from a course of 14 ECT and psychotherapy. After five months she was discharged, much improved. They placed her in a job and she continued in psychotherapy.

For the next six months she lived at a women's hotel,
worked at a clerical job and functioned adequately. But suddenly, after a transient depression apparently caused by her
husband's continued rejection, she got "excited," became pro-

miscuous and discovered that she was "pregnant." (Tests
showed she was not pregnant.) Her psychotherapist could not
manage her and she returned to the private hospital where
she was delusional about people plotting against her, hyperactive, hyper-talkative, irrelevant and complained about having been raped. Thorazine (amount unknown) made her very
drowsy, so Stelazine 30 mg daily was substituted. Long-term
hospitalization seemed advisable because of her continued
seductive and uncontrolled behavior, and she was transferred
to a state hospital after a month.

At the state hospital her affect was flat and she was
depressed, tense, aggressive, demanding and uncooperative.
They diagnosed her as having manic-depressive psychosis and
treated her with Trilafon 8 mg three times daily. She improved and was placed on convalescent care after four months.

Her husband became involved in litigation resulting
from her shopping sprees. Further, she stole her aunt's
bankbook and forged her signature on withdrawal slips. At
that point she went to live in Texas with her father whom
she had not seen since she was four years old. She felt that
regaining her lost father might help solve her problems, and
she had high hopes about her life with him. He promised her
a car and companionship. She was moderately depressed when
she got to Texas and did not work for six months but continued in psychotherapy there.

When her father told her that his wife was sexually frigid she became suspicious of him. Also "I didn't like the
way he kissed me." One day, when home alone with him, he
reportedly attempted to rape her and she left his house,
turned to prostitution, felt she was the messenger of God and
did faith healing. During this time she had two short hospitalizations. When her money ran out she passed bad checks,
was jailed, and when she "jokingly" tried to commit suicide,
the police sent her to a state hospital. Here she was found

syphilitic and pregnant. She was diagnosed as having a
schizophrenic reaction, paranoid type, treated with psychotherapy and "ataraxic" drugs (unspecified) and deported back
to a New York state hospital after four months, "still confused, disoriented and mildly disturbed."

Back at the New York hospital she was found to be five
months pregnant, had markedly flattened affect and a lack of
concern about her condition. She mentioned that before her
last Texas hospitalization she had become "very high. The
whole world looked beautiful. I was very excited and sug-
gestible. I passed a lot of checks. I could not help myself. I was imprisoned and then sent to the county hospital
where I became pregnant by an attendant, after having intercourse with him in a closet, in trade for a pack of cigarettes. I was irrational at the time. He also gave me syph-
ilis." She mentioned that her manic behavior was "like a
compulsion. I become excited and feel like I've been released after 20 years of prison. The world looks beautiful."

She delivered the baby at the state hospital and it was
immediately placed for adoption. After another month she
was discharged, completing a five month stay. Five months
later she was again manic and hospitalized for several
months.

When released she did well for about a year, returned to
live with her mother, and held several temporary jobs. When
she became pregnant by another stranger, she had a therapeutic abortion and a tubal ligation. Shortly after she "became
depressed about her loss of fertility." Also her divorce became final. The depression quickly turned into a manic phase
and she again began picking up strange men. Her family hospitalized her for the tenth time at another state hospital,
for the next eight months. Here she received Stelazine and
Mellaril.

Then, in 1968, a doctor suggested Mrs. Kyte as a

likely subject for a lithium study. She was transferred to
the study hospital and accepted experimental treatment with
lithium. Within a few weeks she received lithium carbonate
1200 mg daily and was feeling better than ever before. In
three months she was placed on convalescent care. Mrs. Kyte
continued taking lithium carbonate 1200 mg daily,to the time
of this writing, for three years. Her blood lithium ranged
between 1 - 1.2 meq/liter. Her mood was consistently normal
and steady; she rated it '50' on a 100 point depression-ela-
tion scale. She ate and slept well, her sexual feelings were
stable and moderate. She lived with her boyfriend and his
children throughout this period, found pleasure in life,
worked steadily and enjoyed her job.

COMMENT

Mrs. Kyte was admitted to Hillside Hospital after her
initial treatment with 17 ECT. At this point she presented
a rather mixed picture dominated by apathy rather than depression. The occurrence of a specific post ECT apathy that
is responsive to Tofranil is not as well recognized as it
might be.

Patients who respond to Tofranil with a manic episode
are characteristically recurrent retarded depressives, who
may or may not have had manic episodes. Manic responses to
Tofranil are most unusual for other sorts of patients (6).
Nonetheless, such patients are often misdiagnosed as paranoid
schizophrenic.

To compound the diagnostic confusion, the manic patient's vagrant, erotomanic, spendthrift way of life is easily confused with character disorder and psychopathy. It is
noteworthy that once her mood was stabilized by lithium, she
was able to productively stabilize her adaptive procedures.
The contrast between her condition prior to receiving lithium
and afterwards is extraordinarily dramatic.

The patient's family history is interesting in view of

her father's probable manic-depressive illness. The work of
Winokur (14) emphasizes strong hereditary components in bipolar affective disorder.

HUGH SMYTHLEY

PRESENTING PROBLEM

Hugh Smythley, age 34, married, the father of two children and extremely wealthy, was deviating from the social
norms (although some would hesitate to call him ill) when he
ran onto a major metropolitan expressway and tried to hand
$10 bills to oncoming motorists. When the police got to him
he kicked and fought; at the precinct he tore the place up,
attacked the sergeant and tried to dive through a window.
The police removed his shoes, handcuffed him to a chair and
contacted his family. The family in turn contacted a psychiatrist and when his wife, father and psychiatrist arrived,
they found Mr. Smythley in a most excited, negativistic, com-
bative state. He was handcuffed to the psychiatrist and
brought to Hillside, where he readily signed a voluntary admission, transiently recognizing that he needed treatment
for an emotional disorder. This insight may have been
spurred by his understanding that jail was the only likely
alternative.

FAMILY

The Smythleys were a remarkably wealthy family. The father was almost 20 years older than the mother. He married
in his late 30's, when he felt "suitably established to settle down." Efficient and highly successful, he made a considerable fortune. He treated his family and business associates similarly, in a cold, dictatorial manner. There was
no closeness or affection shared with his wife or children.
Hugh's relationship with him was characterized by fear, but
also by constant attempts at securing his affection. He
found he always needed to ask his father's help to extricate

him from trouble.

   The mother, before marriage an actress, was impractical,
artistic, flighty and had little interest in running a home
or caring for children. When her seven year old daughter
developed a degenerative nerve disease, she spent the next
eight years nursing her, leaving the entire care of her two
sons to servants. After the daughter died, she became self-
centered, embittered, yet overprotective of her sons. Hugh
became her favorite, and family friends mentioned the strong
hold she had over him. While she was most critical and demanding of him, they became very close, and she confided in
him about the frustrations of her life, how unhappily married
she was, and that the father refused her a divorce.

   While Hugh was growing up, he fought constantly with a
brother two years younger than himself. The brother now was
happily married with several children.

   Hugh met his wife at a party, fell in love with her immediately and proposed marriage the next day. She was flattered and quite attracted by his exuberance and gentle qualities, but temporized because of her reservations concerning
the sincerity of love professed so quickly. But she did fall
in love with him and they married six months later.

   His parents opposed their marriage on grounds that he
was not securely established in business. His mother had
broken up two previous engagements with other girls and assumed that this girl might be a fortune hunter. However,
when they found that she came from a family of great wealth
and social status higher than their own, they reconsidered
and gave their blessings.

   The wife was bright, articulate and an astute observer
of her husband's relationship with his family. She felt he
did not "fit" with them since he was gentle, generous and
sympathetic, qualities notably lacking in his parents and
brother. Their marriage was happy and they shared deep af-

fection for each other. Mr. Smythley adored their young
children.

DEVELOPMENTAL HISTORY

No early developmental history was available. Mr.
Smythley was raised by servants and when he was two, his
younger brother was born. When he was four, his seven year
old sister became chronically ill.

He attended public school, fought with his brother and
had little to do with his parents during the next eight
years, until the death of his sister when he was 12. Soon
after her death he was sent away to prep school. Here he
was active in sports and social activities, but did not distinguish himself academically.

After graduation, he entered a small university but
failed the first year and joined the Army. World War II ended in about 18 months and he returned to the same university.
He joined a fraternity of which he later became president.
During his college years he relied on his father to extricate
him from bad situations, many of which concerned flunking
courses. When he left college his father's contacts enabled
him to get a job as a stockbroker. He was always happy and
cheerful, popular, outgoing, dated many girls and was "in
love with a new one every six months."

He worked for several months, made a fair amount of money, resigned and took a vacation in the Mediterranean. It
was this trip, taken when he was 24, that marked the start of
his illness. Here, he had a sudden inspiration to start a
business. The poorly conceived plan failed badly and quickly, and he had to rely on his father to bail him out of a
$30,000 loss. He became depressed, insomniac, nervous, had
no desire to work and felt himself a failure for several
months.

Of particular importance was his father's order "don't
ever come to me again for money," and his consequent bereave-

ment. But slowly the depression resolved and he regained
his usual ebullient spirits. Once more he engaged in many
varied business ventures, some highly successful and others
risky, speculative failures. Each failure caused a short-
lived depression wherein he would prefer to stay at home for
days or weeks. However, none of these episodes required medical attention. During these years he amassed considerable
wealth.

After he married, he went to work for one of his father's
subsidiary companies, which, despite his best efforts, failed
and was liquidated. Then he, his wife and new baby moved to
Switzerland where his wife's family lived. Here, he bull-
dozed his way into a greatly respected banking house which
usually did not employ Americans, and succeeded so thoroughly that he earned a high post in a short time. But within
the year he became restless, gambled on a big investment,
made $200,000 and left his job to start his own business.

He established a large business with an extensive administrative structure to handle the operation. He was very
dependent on an American who manufactured the product his
business used, and frequently invited this man to Switzerland. When the man arrived, Mr. Smythley would present him
with inconsequential matters or quarrel with him. If the
man became annoyed and left, Mr. Smythley would charter a
plane and pursue him. In a year it was obvious to everyone,
except Mr. Smythley, that this business was a complete failure. Lawyers for the wife's family recommended that she
withdraw her previously pooled money from joint banking and
she did.

Mrs. Smythley had recently given birth to a second
child. She began to worry about her husband's inability to
grasp the reality of his business failure. She slowly lost
faith in him and became mildly depressed. He would not permit her to get medical attention and she recovered spontane-

ously after about six months. By this time Mr. Smythley was
himself depressed. As he emerged from this depression he
embarked on yet another series of plans. His schemes became
progressively grandiose and his feelings of omnipotence more
pronounced. But also he became increasingly dependent on
his wife and exhorted her to rely on him. While she went
along with his plans, she became resentful of the strength he
demanded from her, and her faith in him was finally shatter-
ed; but she kept these feelings to herself.

Then suddenly, his mother developed terminal cancer and
he returned to the States in order to be at her bedside. At
the same time he was involved in a fury of business activity,
running back and forth between hospital and meetings trying
to arrange for a huge loan to swing a multi-million dollar
stock transaction. When his father, brother and wife gently
tried to brake his pursuits, he became irritable and flighty.

Within the month his mother died and he claimed he felt
extreme relief. Immediately, he called all the major newspapers in the United States and some in Europe, to announce
her death. Then he made plans for her funeral. His mood
was never even momentarily subdued; he ate huge meals, had
boundless energy and slept no more than three hours a night.

His activities continued spiralling upwards in multiple
business speculations, none of which culminated in any transaction. The family considered his ideas a bit unrealistic
but they made no real attempts to stop him; neither did his
lawyers when he pressured them to settle his mother's large
estate so that he could obtain his legacy more quickly.

He spent large amounts of money on superfluous things,
including a Rolls Royce, although there were two new, unused
cars at home. But because he felt too nervous to drive, he
hired a chauffeur-driven Cadillac to transport him to business meetings. While he faced constant opposition to his
flighty schemes at these meetings, he rebounded with new en-

ergy and ideas to meet with yet another banker or broker.
When no loans were forthcoming, he turned to his elderly father who agreed to lend him money, but only on formal terms
whereby he would hand over his share of the mother's legacy.

Suddenly, he was humiliatingly struck by the cold, business-like way his father was treating him. He became even
more frenzied, threatened to abscond with his two children
to a mountain hideaway, and locked his wife in his mother's
bedroom. Ten minutes later he called his brother with new
plans to buy a bankrupt stock brokerage.

The next week his appetite decreased markedly and he ate
only occasional snacks. Also, he experienced a greatly increased need for sexual activity, so that he could not rest
unless he had intercourse first. Toward the end of this week
he decided to have a second wedding and honeymoon. His wife,
who was very upset by his behavior, had decided that she
could cope with him only if she went along with his plans.
Therefore, they went to a church and privately re-exchanged
marriage vows. While in church Mr. Smythley felt he figura-
tively "saw God" and knew that his mission in life was to
help humanity through politics. He begged his wife to re-
fresh his memory of Bible stories, compared himself with
Christ and became obsessed with the idea of starting a campaign to sponsor Nixon for the presidency.

They returned to the elaborate bridal suite he had rented at a posh hotel, but within a few hours he insisted that
they visit some friends in a nearby state. Renting a chauf-
feured car, they drove down and spent a pleasant afternoon.
He seemed relaxed, although occasionally had outbursts of
laughing and giggling. When the host suddenly suffered an
ulcer attack, Mr. Smythley became quite upset and drank large
amounts of milk.

Very early the next morning, he ran off to discuss his
proposed Nixon campaign with an old college friend. His wife

became concerned and summoned his brother to help take him
home. During the trip home he spoke about how all the events
that were happening were part of a scheme involving the FBI.
He likened himself to the President and felt that he was being tested to establish whether he was strong enough to withstand his new political career. As the car was approaching
home, he suddenly requested the driver to stop so that he
could make a phone call, and quickly hailed a passing truck.
His wife and brother attempted to follow but lost track of
him. A few hours later the police arrested him for impeding
traffic as described earlier.

PRESENTING CHARACTERISTICS

On admission to Hillside, Mr. Smythley was disheveled,
confused, angry, hyperexcitable and elated. He requested to
remain handcuffed until he was in his room. He spoke with
business-like jargon, "All right Doc, let's get down to business. Let's not waste your time or mine. I want to go
home. I can rest just as well there as here. I'm not really
ill and we're just wasting each other's time." Momentarily
he would be humble and submissive, "putting all my faith in
you doctors." While he was oriented to time, person and
place, he proclaimed complete amnesia for the events leading
to his arrest.

Because he was so hyperactive and uncooperative, complete psychiatric examination was delayed for two days until
he was subdued. At this time he admitted that he was ill,
although he made light of it. His recent memory remained
slightly clouded. Mainly, he was preoccupied with ascertain-
ing that his wife still loved him, and wanting to be with her.
He was in high spirits, warm, affable, euphoric and behaved
and spoke appropriately. His intellectual abilities were intact.

When the doctor mentioned that his illness had seemingly
been developing for the last six months, Mr. Smythley replied

"Oh no, all my life." He then described his lifelong
preoccupation with the impossibility of pleasing his parents.
He spoke of his "dual personality," with a serious side and
an unstable side which he did not understand. He knew he
fluctuated between the two sides from day to day or even
from hour to hour.

COURSE AT HILLSIDE

Mr. Smythley was given Thorazine 100 mg intramuscularly,
four times daily with 5 mg Kemadrin, three times daily. He
slept for very short periods of time on this regimen, but
within 36 hours was considerably less confused. His major
immediate concerns were whether his wife still loved him,
would stay with him and his desire to be with her. The professed amnesia for the events leading to hospitalization disappeared and he described in detail exactly what happened,
but in terms of some grand scheme similar to a fraternity
initiation. He still maintained that his bizarre actions
were part of a test of political suitability.

After four days he was placed on oral Thorazine 2700 mg
and Kemadrin 15 mg daily and concurrently his delusions subsided. Physical and neurological examinations were within
normal limits, except for slightly increased blood pressure
and pulse rate. His Wechsler-Bellevue IQ was 112, with wide
test score scatter.

Throughout his two weeks at the hospital he constantly
wheeled and dealed for release. His behavior remained mildly
hypomanic, ebullient and colored by grandiosity, but tractable. He showed fleeting insight but usually denied all illness, saying, "I never felt better in my life, I just want to
get out of here. Thank you for your help but I want to get
back to business."

In view of the fact that he no longer appeared to be
suffering from delusions, his behavior was relatively acceptable, and he would no longer cooperate in remaining in the

hospital, it was agreed to let him leave, against medical advice. His Thorazine dose was to be reduced to 1200 mg daily
by the next week and it was felt that long-range prophylactic
phenothiazine therapy would be necessary. He refused even
to plan to continue in psychotherapy. His diagnosis was
manic-depressive psychosis, circular type, manic phase.

FOLLOW-UP

Mr. Smythley immediately returned to Switzerland and engaged in many more business ventures, which seemed to paral-
lel his periodic phases of overactivity. None of these
transactions reached fruition. He took no medication. Fif-
teen months after his first hospitalization he had a manic
episode, and his family committed him to a hospital where he
received Haldol (amount unknown). The manic state abated
quickly and he insisted on returning home. He refused to
take the prescribed maintenance Stelazine when he learned
that his doctor had previously done research on the drug,
feeling that the doctor might be a shareholder in the drug
company and profit from his illness. The manic state returned within ten days and he became involved with the interna-
tional police when he tried to commandeer a trans-Atlantic
jet for his personal use. His lawyers forced him to return
to the hospital where he was placed on large doses of Haldol
and Stelazine.

Little information concerning his activities over the
next six years was available, except that he continued getting involved in phenomenal business contracts, most of which
failed; his wife grew increasingly disgusted with him and
threatened to leave; the children were made wards of the
court because he periodically threatened to kidnap them during his manic periods, and he had several more hospitalizations during his unmanageably high phases.

Seven years later he appeared at his father's mansion
one day, after impulsively flying back from Europe. He was

manic and had been self-medicating himself with Dilantin after being impressed by a conversation with the drug's leading lay proponent. He couldn't sleep the next morning, and
at 5 A.M. went to a coffee shop located next to a trucking
stop. A huge van was waiting to start its morning run and
no driver was in sight. Seizing this as an excellent opportunity to operate a trailer-truck, he took it for a joyride,
careening down the highway. When the police finally caught
up with the runaway, they arrested Mr. Smythley. His father,
now in his 90's, once again contacted the original psychiatrist who this time had him admitted to a private, closed
hospital· Here he initially was treated with Thorazine 1000
mg and Kemadrin 15 mg daily. After six days, lithium carbonate 200 mg daily was added. He quickly regained good control and within three weeks, the Thorazine was reduced to
1200 mg daily and he was released.

At the time of his release his wife seriously threatened
to leave him if he did not remain under doctor's care and
continue taking prescribed medication. He promised and they
returned to their home in Switzerland. At the time of this
writing, two years after his last hospitalization, and ten
years after his Hillside hospitalization, his doctor in
Switzerland stated he was functioning quite well and taking
lithium carbonate 1125 mg daily with a blood level of 0.8
meq/liter. He had no evidence of hypomania or depression.
He was still very involved with his investments but his
thinking was clear and realistic. His home situation was
satisfying and he was happy.

COMMENT

This case is typical of manic-depressive illness appearing as entrepreneurial talent at higher social levels. Outstanding is the ability of the manic to absorb tremendous
amounts of Thorazine and similar medications before any sort
of control is established. Typical is the very quick com-

plete denial of illness and refusal to continue with appropriate maintenance medication without extremely firm limit
setting and potent threats on the part of the family.   The
initial lithium treatment was grossly inadequate and his remission was due to Thorazine.   However, his maintenance dosage is appropriate for prophylactic care.

   Mr. Smythley's grandiose, suspicious and referential
delusions are worth notice since it is a common error to diagnose schizophrenia whenever the patient is delusional.
This leads to therapeutic and prognostic error.

REFERENCES

1. American Psychiatric Association: Diagnostic & Statistical Manual, Mental Disorders. Mental Hospital Service, Washington, D.C., 1952.

2. Blumberg, A.G. and Klein, D.F.: Psychiatric diagnosis, activation and radioactive iodine uptake. Arch. Gen. Psychiat. 18, 601-611, 1968.

3. Blumberg, A.G. and Klein, D.F.: Chlorpromazine-procyclidine and imipramine: Effects on thyroid function in psychiatric patients. Clinical Pharmac. Ther. 10, 350-354, 1969.

4. Klein, D.F.: Behavioral effects of imipramine and phenothiazines: Implications for a psychiatric pathogenetic theory and theory of drug action. Recent Advances Biol. Psychiat. 7, 273-287, 1964.

5. Klein, D.F.: Delineation of two drug-responsive anxiety syndromes. Psychopharmacologia 5, 397-408, 1964.

6. Klein, D.F.: Psychiatric diagnosis and a typology of clinical drug effects. Psychopharmacologia 13, 359-386, 1968.

7. Klein, D.F.: Psychotropic drugs and the regulation of behavioral activation in psychiatric illness. In Smith, W.L. (ed.): Drugs and Cerebral Function, Charles C. Thomas, Springfield, Ill., 1970.

8. Klein, D.F. and Davis, J.M.: Diagnosis and Drug Treatment of Psychiatric Disorders. Williams & Wilkins, Baltimore, 1969.

9. Klein, D.F. and Fink, M.: Behavioral reaction patterns with phenothiazines. Arch. Gen. Psychiat. 7, 449-459, 1962.

10. Klein, D.F., Feldman, S. and Honigfeld, G.: Can univariate measures of drug effect reflect clinical descriptions of change? In Wittenborn, J.R., Goldberg, S.C. and May, P.R.A. (eds.): Psychopharmacology and the Individual Patient, Raven Press, New York, 1970.

11. Kramer, J.C., Klein, D.F. and Fink, M.: Imipramine as an adjunct to phenothiazine therapy. Compr. Psychiat. 3, 377-380, 1962.

12.   Levenstein, S., Klein, D.F. and Pollack, M.: Follow-up
      study of formerly hospitalized voluntary psychiatric
      patients: The first two years. Amer. J. Psychiat. 122,
      1102-1109, 1966.

13.   Prange, A.J., Wilson, I.C., Rabon, A.M. and Lipton,M.:
      Acceleration of imipramine antidepressant activity by
      thyroid hormone. Scientific Proceedings of 124th Annual
      Meeting of the American Psychiatric Association,
      pp. 325-326, May, 1968.

14.   Winokur, G.: Genetic principles in the clarification of
      clinical issues in affective disorder. In Mandell,A.J.
      and Mandell, M.P. (eds.): Methods and Theory in Human
      Psychochemical Research. Academic Press, Inc., New
      York, 1970.

15.   Winokur, G. and Pitts, F.N., Jr.: Affective disorder. I.
      Is reactive depression an entity? J. New. Ment. Dis.
      138, 541, 1964.

Section III

PSYCHIATRIC DISORDERS WITH LATER LIFE ONSET

This group of patients developed an acute psychiatric illness in later life. In each case the acute episode was clearly related to the premorbid personality and accomplishments. Further, the degree of recovery and qualitative mode of adjustment are specified by the earlier adjustment.

Chapter IX

CHRONIC SCHIZOID PERSONALITY WITH DEPRESSIVE-PARANOID EXACERBATION

Definition

DSM-II states that the schizoid pattern involves shyness, over-sensitivity, seclusiveness, avoidance of close or competitive relationships, and often eccentricity. Autistic thinking without loss of capacity to recognize reality is common, as is daydreaming and the inability to express hostility and ordinary aggressive feelings. These patients react to disturbing experiences and conflicts with apparent detachment (1).

Schizoid personality, thus defined, confuses two quite separate groups of people: the shy socially backward and inept obedient person who is fearful and therefore isolated but appreciates sociability and would like to be part of the crowd; and the asocial eccentric person who seeks to be alone and has difficulty in relationships with his peers, frequently resulting in social ostracism and scapegoating, with consequent further avoidance of peer interactions. The term schizoid personality emphasizes a continuity between this personality and schizophrenia. In our experience, borne out by the follow-up studies of Robins (5), it is the asocial rather than the shy patient who may become schizophrenic.

SOLOMON LEBITZ

PRESENTING PROBLEM

Mr. Lebitz, age 56 and a bachelor, was a gray-looking man, old beyond his years. Several months before he became acutely ill, he began feeling fatigued, with insomnia, anorexia, constipation and weight loss; he decided to leave his job of 16 years as a garment presser. Suddenly he seemed unable to care for himself, neglecting his apartment, his personal appearance and no longer bathing. One evening, in a panic, he called his brother to announce that his apartment was falling apart; the walls and tiles were cracking, the place was a shambles and would soon collapse over his head. The brother rushed to Mr. Lebitz' apartment and tried to placate him, explaining that the minor defects in the walls were due to the natural settling of a new building and would easily be repaired; but nothing could appease him. Several days later Mr. Lebitz called his brother at 6:00 A.M. His conversation didn't make much sense, but what he did communicate was that because he had been stamping his feet and pacing all night, the neighbors had called the police. His brother then fully realized the need for help and took him to a city hospital.

At the hospital they diagnosed Mr. Lebitz as having an involutional psychosis and gave him two ECT after which he refused further treatment. Within two months he was transferred to Hillside.

FAMILY

Mr. Lebitz' parents were uneducated Orthodox Jews who emigrated to America from Europe as teen-agers, in order to escape persecution. They were described as good, kind, hard-working people. The father was able to provide a bare living from working in his candy store. He died when the patient was in his 40's. The mother died more recently. The brother, a year older than Mr. Lebitz, was married. He was soft-spoken and expressed great concern for Mr. Lebitz' well-being. No further family history was obtainable.

DEVELOPMENTAL HISTORY

Developmental information was not available, except that at age eight, Mr. Lebitz suffered a skull fracture with no manifest sequelae. After one term at high school, he quit and went to work; the usual trend in his neighborhood at the time. He was a diligent worker, held many different jobs and also helped in his father's candy store. He was the favorite son and his mother openly wished that he never marry. While he dated occasionally, he never saw any woman more than once or twice. At age 30, he gave up any pretense of socialization or sexual interest and settled down as a confirmed bachelor living with his parents. He never had any sexual experience and even denied masturbating. His life was barren, never deviating from the apparently dismal yet ego-syntonic routine of working, eating, reading the paper and sleeping. After his father died he assumed the added responsibility of shopping for groceries.

Mr. Lebitz' mother died when he was 54. He was depressed by her death but continued working and living in their dreary apartment, continuing his seclusive life. The people he had worked with for 16 years knew nothing about him, not even whether he was married or where he lived. Six months after his mother's death he called his brother and confessed that he could no longer tolerate living alone. The brother, a kind, generous person, took him to live with his family.

Daily, Mr. Lebitz went to work, returned to his brother's apartment to eat supper, read the paper and went to sleep. He continued this routine for a year and then began to "act funny," complained of fatigue, insomnia, anorexia, constipation and weight loss, and quit his job of 16 years duration. His brother and sister-in-law, at a loss to help him, felt very uncomfortable and asked that he return to

live by himself. They helped him find and furnish an apartment in a new building, and offered him continued psychological support, but from a distance. His illness progressed,
leading to his hospitalization.

PRESENTING CHARACTERISTICS

Mr. Lebitz walked stooped over, limply, trailing behind
whomever he was accompanying. When sitting he stared at the
floor, holding his head in his hands, a picture of despair.
He showed marked motor retardation, with a facial expression
that ranged from gloomy to hopeless. His loose, shabby
clothing hung about him untidily, and he was in obvious need
of a bath, shave and haircut. He was inattentive, and his
infrequent replies were laconic and monosyllabic. Usually
he just shrugged his shoulders or ignored questions entirely.
When pressed, he would respond only that he felt tired. He
believed his original admission to the city hospital was unjustified and that his admission to Hillside was due to the
ECT he received at the first hospital. Feeling that his case
was hopeless, he maintained that he should not be hospitalized.

COURSE AT HILLSIDE

Mr. Lebitz showed a mild diabetic condition on laboratory testing; dietary regulation proved to be adequate treatment. His EEG was normal. On psychological testing he attained a full scale IQ of 111, a verbal IQ of 119 and a performance IQ of 101.

During his hospital stay he continued being seclusive,
avoiding any contact with other patients. He remained un-
shaven and untidy and had to be firmly pressured to bathe and
care for his belongings. Repeatedly he said, "I know what
you're going to do to me. Electroshock is not going to help.
It made me sick." In general he implied that the staff was
going to harm him. When asked what his trouble was, he would
reply, "I know what I think but what's the good? I gave

everything up, the whole thing. My trouble is nothing."
Asked why he was in the hospital he responded, "That's the
question." How is your memory? "It isn't the way it used
to be." What does your future hold? "I am not confused, I
know what it is all about." He would not elaborate further
and his entire manner was one of a delusional conviction that
he would not share.

His doctor described him as "barren as a rock." While
never late for an appointment, once with his doctor he would
only say, "I could tell you everything, but you wouldn't understand." When asked about his past life he would shrug his
shoulders. He was unwilling to participate in any hospital
activity.

After five weeks he was entered in the drug program and
received Tofranil 75 mg daily, increasing to 300 mg daily
over a four week period. His condition improved somewhat, he
took a bit more initiative and began discussing politics with
other patients. After three weeks he looked dull and in general remained the same. He related that his main trouble was
that "I feel self-conscious. That covers it. I feel all
right, not sad. I wish that I was out of the hospital. I'm
afraid of everything. I'm hopeless. What can I do, the future looks completely black. I don't want to go back to
work."

After five weeks of Tofranil he seemed definitely more
alert, activated, voluble and less confused, although he
still was saying, "I am just going crazy, that's all. I am
still afraid of everything. Something's going to happen to
me." When he went home to spend a weekend with his brother,
he resumed his extreme seclusiveness. He remained uncommu-
nicative with his doctor, and because only a minor effect
was noted from the Tofranil, it was withdrawn after six
weeks. A week after medication was withdrawn, he claimed he
felt exactly the way he always had, but appeared more unkempt

and laconic. Remarkably, he recalled his premorbid life
style as being one of smart dressing, high living and enjoyment. Since he was not agitated, his doctor did not think
that phenothiazines were indicated.

A more obvious improvement occurred five months after
admission when he began dressing in cleaner, more attractive
clothing. However, as soon as he was informed about immi-
nent discharge, he deteriorated and became increasingly belligerent, depressed and uncooperative. It became obvious
that he could not return to solitary life or live with his
brother; therefore he was sent to a state hospital. This
transfer took place after seven months of hospitalization.
His hospital diagnosis was psychotic depression in a schizoid personality; the research diagnosis was mixed depres-
sive-paranoid psychotic exacerbation of chronic schizoid
personality.

FOLLOW-UP

Mr. Lebitz was transferred to a state hospital where he
remained seclusive, disinterested and paranoid. He was diagnosed as having involutional melancholia and received 20
ECT over eight weeks and then Thorazine and Librium. After
about eight months his depression slowly cleared.

He was released after 15 months, returned to live with
his brother, attended an after-care clinic once or twice
monthly, and took Tofranil 75 mg daily and Librium 20 mg
daily. He received Social Security and did not work. During the third year after his Hillside hospitalization he
continued as above, was well dressed and had significant relief from symptoms while living in a completely non-stress-
ful environment, without productive effort or interpersonal
engagement.

At a ten year follow-up, Mr. Lebitz reported that his
health had been satisfactory and he took no medication. He
still resided with his brother and sister-in-law, and kept

himself occupied, but did not work. He walked around the
neighborhood and remained pretty much to himself.

COMMENT

Mr. Lebitz appears to have had a psychotic episode with
mixed depressive and paranoid trends and responded with only
minimal success to a variety of somatic treatments. This is
in sharp contrast to the usual involutional psychotic who
responds well to somatic treatment following a solitary psychotic episode. The chronicity of his illness was almost
certainly related to his markedly deviant premorbid personality. It should be noted that Mr. Lebitz' schizoid personality was of a chronic asocial variety. He was not shy, with
a frustrated yearning for socialization, but rather showed a
callous indifference to human contact. The onset of his
acute episode was apparently endogenous, although probably exacerbated by his subsequent removal from his brother's family. It is not clear if the stress of his move was due to
social deprivation or a destructuring of his life-space with
consequent decision overload.

Plainly, his ability to remain in the community was a
function of his family's tolerance for parasitism.

Chapter X

PARANOID PERSONALITY WITH INVOLUTIONAL PSYCHOSIS

Definition

The Diagnostic Manual states that paranoid individuals are characterized by many traits of the schizoid personality, coupled with an exquisite sensitivity in interpersonal relations. They show a conspicuous tendency to utilize the projection mechanism, expressed by suspiciousness, extreme jealousy and stubbornness.

Both the syndromal validity of this personality description and its relationship to development of paranoid illness are open to question. To establish this would require a detailed community psychiatric survey with longitudinal follow-up. Actually psychiatrists have gained their knowledge from the opposite direction and have noticed a high proportion of these unusual types in the development of psychotic patients. It is not known what proportion of these personalities become psychotic.

SADIE RUTMAN

PRESENTING PROBLEM

Mrs. Rutman, petite, pleasant and meek, was 57, a widow of two years and the mother of two grown children. Six weeks before entering Hillside she went to visit her married daughter and while there, took a nap. When she awoke, she was in a panic that her son-in-law was trying to kill her. This was

294

obvious to her because "he handled his eyes in a peculiar
manner and had criminal hands." Running out of her daughter's home, she noticed lights in an adjacent house and concluded that the occupants were also part of the conspiracy
to kill her. When her daughter caught up with her and got
her into a car, Mrs. Rutman did not recognize her and refused to let her drive, because she was certain this woman would
kill her. Finally, the police were called and Mrs. Rutman
was taken to the station where she refused to eat because the
food was "poisoned." The police then brought her to an emergency hospital for admission.

At the hospital she was increasingly referential, feeling that everyone was an actor performing for her
benefit. Also she claimed she was communicating with God
who instructed her to cure the patients. Her behavior was
obviously bizarre, with frequent outbursts of anger and loss
of control. She was diagnosed as either an involutional
paranoid or a chronic paranoid schizophrenic. However, she
received no medication. Slowly she began to improve and became less frightened and agitated, ate and slept well. Since
she remained paranoid, after six weeks her children requested
that she be transferred to Hillside, rather than a state hospital, for more extended treatment.

FAMILY

Mrs. Rutman's mother was unaffectionate, martyrized,
hard working and unhappy. She raised five children and also
worked as a janitress. She died when Mrs. Rutman was in her
20's. The father worked hard at a factory job, was very quiet, religious and had little to do with his children. He
died when Mrs. Rutman was in her 30's.

The four other siblings, of whom Mrs. Rutman was next
to the youngest, were all married and had little to do with
one another.

Mrs. Rutman's husband died of a stroke and cirrhosis of

the liver after 28 years of marriage. He was a chronic alcoholic with a severe temper, and was unemployed periodically
for more than half their married life. He never earned much
money when he did work. Nevertheless, Mrs. Rutman claimed
she worshipped him for his intelligence, never complained
about his drinking and was eager to please him. On the other
hand, her daughter described the marriage as very stormy.

The much-loved daughter, age 28, was born shortly after
their marriage. She married a man whom Mrs. Rutman openly
and heartily disliked.

A son, age 21, married and at college, was quiet and polite. He moved from his mother's house shortly before she
became ill.

DEVELOPMENTAL HISTORY

Mrs. Rutman described her whole life as one of insecurity, inferiority, and viewing the world as a hostile and
frightening place. As a child she was cross-eyed, bow-leg-
ged, pigeon-toed, poor in school, lacking in social skills
and in general, an ugly duckling. She shied from people, was
quiet, helped her mother, read, sewed and stayed by herself.

She barely got through school, finding the work difficult, and at age 14, after graduating from elementary school,
went to work in an office. In order to avoid embarrassment,
she refused to even talk with people who might outwit her.
Even though she won praise and salary increases in her job,
her self image of ingrained incompetence did not ameliorate.
When she was 23, her mother died, and for a year after, she
"tried to see my mother's face in other people. I felt the
world would stop and couldn't understand how everyone didn't
know about my mother's death." After the death she went to
live with an older sister.

She rarely dated fearing that "the fellows could think
better than me." But she met her husband and they married
when she was 26. She claimed that her marriage was happy and

that she and her husband loved each other, but refused to
describe the obvious negative aspects which necessitated her
seeking family counseling at one time. During her marriage
she worked to support her husband and two children.

At age 50 she went through menopause. Also her husband
became ill with cirrhosis of the liver, and about the same
time she began to have delusions of having an affair with a
salesman.

A salesman at a local store was flirtatious and attentive. She felt very flattered, but when he began to refer
to sexual matters, she became upset and felt that people
were staring at her and circulating stories about her "in-
discretion." As the years passed she felt more people were
referring to this "indecency." After three years she told
her husband about it and he referred to the salesman as "a
degenerate." She assumed that he was calling her a degenerate also. Her daughter tried to reassure her that there was
nothing wrong and no one was talking about her, but her
guilty fears would not be assuaged. Slowly, she felt that
everyone she met was concerned with the "affair" and spread-
ing stories about it.

Her husband died when she was 55. After his death she
was able to return to her job quickly, but she also became
increasingly invested in spiritualism. With her son's marriage the following year, she became progressively disorganized, eating and sleeping poorly, until her acute exacerbation.

PRESENTING CHARACTERISTICS

Mrs. Rutman was keenly suspicious, evasive and distrustful, concerning the reason for hospitalization, since she
claimed she was perfectly well and afraid she was being tak-
en advantage of because of her "easygoing nature." The only
acceptable possible reason for treatment was for her fatigue
which she attributed to the fact that since her son had mar-

ried, several months earlier, she was careless in getting
proper food and sleep. She used massive denial, and tried
to impress that she was perfectly fit mentally. When asked
if she had any troubles, she answered, "No, not a thing, I
feel fine."

In general, her tone was whining. She cried copiously
when talking about how easily others took advantage of her,
and maintained that her son-in-law still wanted to kill her.
While at the emergency hospital, she realized she had been
sent there by God, and also related that people looked distorted: "My ears, eyes and mind played tricks on me." She
was occupied with many somatic complaints, requested frequent enemas to prevent rectal bleeding, and was concerned
that she would be unable to have her essential yeast and
vitamin supplements.

COURSE AT HILLSIDE

At the beginning of hospitalization, Mrs. Rutman was
guarded and paranoid, feeling that the activities worker discriminated against her by giving her inferior materials to
work with. She gave the activities worker a thorough tongue-
lashing, which she later denied, explaining that, although
she had ample reason, she never complained. Although she was
whining, isolated and cried at the slightest provocation, she
did not appear depressed, but rather, overly sensitive to
"being taken advantage of."

Mrs. Rutman maintained her paranoid denial and after six
weeks entered the drug program. She received Tofranil 75 mg
daily, increased over a four week period until 300 mg daily
was reached. She showed an increased tendency to speak ir-
relevantly, in fragmented thoughts, had multiple physical
complaints, including her body jerking at night, severe fatigue and feeling lifeless and heavy. However, when questioned about the delusion that her son-in-law was going to
kill her, she said, "I don't believe that he tried to harm

me. I guess I was getting worse and worse and it went into
fear." Also she was more voluble, active and pleasant.
However, her doctor perceived little change in her condition,
and in view of her many complaints, discontinued the medication.

Tofranil was withdrawn slowly over an eight day period
because she developed nausea, vomiting and visual disturbances which lasted six days after the withdrawal. She was
overjoyed when medication was stopped because she felt she
didn't need it in the first place. Her delusion concerning
her "affair" remained untouched. She was convinced that everyone was truly interested in the matter, and that even if
people at the hospital weren't staring at her, others would.

Mrs. Rutman was extremely angry when her doctor decided
to administer a phenothiazine to diminish her delusional
thinking. She claimed she was perfectly well and in no need
of medication; the only reason she was in the hospital was
because she hadn't been eating or sleeping properly. She became incensed when any of her ideas were questioned, and
therefore decided to remain absolutely silent during psychotherapy.

A month after Tofranil was stopped, Mellaril 100 mg
twice daily was started and increased the following week to
200 mg twice daily. She bitterly complained about nausea and
fatigue, looked worse and seemed even more paranoid. Her
doctor, hoping that these complaints were idiosyncratic to
Mellaril, changed the medication to Thorazine 200 mg twice
daily. Her anger diminished somewhat, but she still refused
to talk during psychotherapy. When she did talk her words
were often mixed up: e.g., saying "slipper" for shoe, or
"snow" for rain. She complained of an awful headache, burning throat, deadness, tingling and now even considered that
her two year old grandchild was part of the "conspiracy."
She openly, loudly and angrily told patients and staff that

they were taking advantage of her because she was so quiet.

She remained on Thorazine 400 mg daily for three weeks, a wholly inadequate course, but because of her multiple complaints, including that her brain was changing, and her passivity in psychotherapy, medication was stopped. Basically there was no change in her paranoid thinking, but she did show some improvement in her ability to socialize.

Mrs. Rutman was discharged after six months, on no medication, to live at a women's hotel and return to her former job. She did not wish to continue in psychotherapy. Her hospital diagnosis was chronic paranoid schizophrenia with involutional trends; the research diagnosis was fearful paranoid personality with chronic psychosis of later life.

FOLLOW-UP

Mrs. Rutman did well for six months after discharge, working and living at a hotel, but then all her mild chronic symptoms exacerbated. Her family urgently pressed for readmission to Hillside, but it was thought that her lack of acceptance of voluntary hospitalization and chronically psychotic condition warranted state hospitalization. The family would not accept this, and for the next seven months she was seen in an after-care clinic, received medication, and lived with three different relatives.

Thirteen months after initial discharge from Hillside, she entered an emergency hospital for one day when she became extremely paranoid and unmanageable and was then transferred to a private hospital for two months. Here, she was diagnosed as having an involutional psychosis, and received ten ECT with fair improvement in that she became less agitated; but her delusions persisted. When the full agitation returned within two weeks after the ECT stopped, she was transferred to a city psychiatric hospital where she remained for three months. At the city hospital she received seven ECT in two weeks, which they claimed "helped reverse the paranoid delusions," and Tofranil and Mellaril (amounts unknown) for four to five months following the ECT, which appeared helpful. All medication was discontinued permanently after this period. She returned to live at a women's residence, saw a social worker about once every two weeks, but was unable to work, subsisting on federal disability benefits.

By the third year after Hillside hospitalization, she remained living at a women's residence and she and her son felt that she was doing better than she had for several years. She was in good contact, functioned well with her family and enjoyed participating in neighborhood community centers. Her daughter's hospitalization for "mental illness" and her brother's death were experienced without relapse.

COMMENT

Mrs. Rutman presents difficult diagnostic and therapeutic problems. The diagnostic problem concerns establishing the degree of illness prior to manifest psychosis at age 50. It is possible that she was actually psychotic prior to this period, in view of her long standing personality difficulties. Nonetheless, she had worked steadily under difficult circumstances, probably indicating that her adjustment was paranoid and schizoid, rather than overtly psychotic. Much of the difficulty here is the unreliability of the informant.

The fact that the patient had a manifest psychosis for some seven years prior to treatment, is generally considered a poor prognostic sign. On the other hand, it is often felt that late life onset of psychosis is a positive prognostic sign.

Her response to treatment is complicated by her negativism and resistance to treatment, leading to inadequate handling. Her response to an adequate course of Tofranil indicated that her illness should not be considered as primarily a depressive state with paranoid features, and indeed, she did not present as markedly depressed, but rather as angry,

fearful and paranoid. Unfortunately, her somatic complaints
and negativism prevented her doctor from resolutely persisting with higher doses of phenothiazine, or in utilizing ECT
as a reasonable somatic alternative.

Following discharge, her course was of intermittent illness with less than optimum somatic care. Eventually she
was able to function without manifest psychosis, although she
was not socially self-supporting.

Chapter XI

AGITATED DEPRESSION DURING INVOLUTIONAL PERIOD

ELSIE FEIN

PRESENTING PROBLEM

Mrs. Elsie Fein was a sobbing, gasping, but otherwise healthy-looking, 55 year old woman. Four months before entering Hillside, her husband died unexpectedly from hepatitis. Following this she became extremely depressed, anxious, panic-stricken, with obsessive thoughts about "not having enough money to pay the rent." She had insomnia, was anorexic and complained of chest pains. Finally, her children admitted her to a general hospital where she was fed intravenously.

Within a few days she returned home, only to grow progressively worse. After two weeks, her children took her to a psychiatrist who diagnosed her as having psychoneurosis with anxiety, hysteria and phobia, and hospitalized her for a course of eight ECT. Her symptoms remitted somewhat and she was released in nine days. The psychiatrist saw her several times for psychotherapy, but after a month she was again very tense, anxious, depressed and preoccupied with fear of having a heart attack, inability to manage her life, concern over her children's well-being and pervasive futility. She had lost 30 pounds, was nauseated and vomited frequently. During the day she was unable to perform her usual activi-

ties or household chores; at night she would wake up screaming and run around her apartment in an agitated frenzy.

She was rehospitalized for a month at a sanitarium, diagnosed as having an involutional psychosis, mixed type with
psychoneurotic reaction, and was treated with sedatives and
Thorazine for about a week. She showed an immediate favorable response, becoming more comfortable, relaxed and composed, eating and sleeping better. Thorazine was withdrawn,
Doriden was ordered for sleep, and Mrs. Fein was discharged.
However, her psychiatrist felt she needed more intensive
treatment and referred her to Hillside.

FAMILY

Mrs. Fein was an only child. Her mother was a determined, strict, excitable person who liked to get her own
way. She owned a dress shop and always worked so that, as
a child, her daughter was often alone. Nonetheless, mother
and daughter had a close relationship.

The father was a gentle, kind person, flexible and easy-
going. He worked as a laborer and also helped his wife in
her store. There was much marital strife and a question of
the father being promiscuous. Both parents died in their
50's when their daughter was in her 30's. There was no other information concerning her early family life.

Mrs. Fein described her deceased husband as a wonderful,
considerate and loving person. He was a barely successful
businessman who often had to travel; she and the children
accompanied him when possible. She felt very secure with
her husband, although their life was financially difficult.

A child born during their first year of marriage died
at age six. Five years later a son was born, and after that
a daughter. At the time of Mrs. Fein's Hillside hospitalization the son was 25, passive, with few friends, spending
most of his time watching TV. He worked as a junior executive. The daughter, age 20, attractive, sophisticated, in-

telligent and domineering, was at college. Both children
cared deeply for their mother and the family seemed close-
knit and happy.

DEVELOPMENTAL HISTORY

No information concerning Mrs. Fein's early development
was available. She was sheltered and dependent all her life.
At school she was a poor student. Instead of going to high
school, she attended a business school for a short time and
then helped in her mother's store.

She had a number of girlfriends while growing up. At
age 16, she started dating, met her husband, and married two
years later. Sexually they were well-adjusted and neither
had any extra-marital affairs.

Their first child, unplanned but wanted, was born when
Mrs. Fein was 19, and died when she was 25. At that time she
went into a semi-comatose state for three days and was hospitalized; no further details were available. For many years
after, on the anniversary of the child's death, Mrs. Fein became agitated and upset for a few days. During the next few
years she had two stillborn births and then her son and
daughter. Until the children were of school age, Mr. Fein
took his whole family on his travels. Later they travelled
only during school vacations. Although husband and wife
were apart, sometimes for weeks, they still were emotionally
close and confident of each other's affection.

Family life was always very satisfactory and at the center of Mrs. Fein's interest. She was picky about choosing
friends but did have a small coterie. As her children matured she took voice lessons and occasionally sang at night
clubs. The only discord in her life was her moderate nervousness, excitability, tearfulness and worry concerning the
possibility that something untoward would befall her children. At age 46, she had a hysterectomy with no apparent
sequelae.

PRESENTING CHARACTERISTICS

Mrs. Fein claimed that "It all started with my husband's death. I went through so many trials and tribulations with the funerals." (Two services were held in different cities.) "I had been married for 35 years and never had to be on my own. I always had him to take care of me, and my son and daughter; please God, she should get through college." She paced around the room in small circles, wringing her hands and occasionally holding them out as if to choke someone, baring her teeth, looking ferocious and moaning, "I'm a hopeless case, I have no feelings, I'm too far gone for you to do anything to change me. Do you agree?"

However, at times she had a pleasant, composed manner. Her motor activity was usually agitated. Emotionally, she was very labile, fluctuating from irritability to depression, to fearfulness and hopelessness, to periods of composed complacency. She felt that her main problem was that she cried a lot and had a peculiar feeling in her head and just could not seem to fight back. Also she spoke of her "ridiculous" impulses to scream and throw things and the great energy she used in trying to control these urges to which she succumbed at times. "I just feel that I am going insane. No one in their sane mind would scream and carry on at night the way I do." Other than the above, her mental status was unremarkable.

COURSE AT HILLSIDE

All physical tests were within normal limits. A premedication EEG was normal and a later EEG, taken while on Thorazine, showed slow wave bursts. On the Wechsler-Bellevue she attained a full scale IQ of 107, a verbal IQ of 97, and a performance IQ of 113.

Mrs. Fein cried, was extremely tense, agitated and had frequent nausea, vomiting and insomnia. She tried hard to control her impulses to scream, throw and tear things, but on occasion, at night, would shout, grunt and bang on the furniture. Gradually, her appetite improved but her sleep remained poor. She received phenobarbital to help calm her, with only slight effect.

In psychotherapy she was self-derogatory and pessimistic and incessantly asked for reassurance that she would improve and return home. Whenever she thought of her husband she burst into tears.

After six weeks of non-response to psychotherapy and milieu treatment, Mrs. Fein was placed in the drug program and received Thorazine 300 mg daily, increased 300 mg weekly until a total dose of 1200 mg daily was reached, with Kemadrin increased to 15 mg daily.

Immediately she seemed quieted and less tense and after three weeks showed a marked change. She was calm, composed, pleasant, sociable, clear thinking, capable of managing her affairs and optimistic about her future. Her appetite increased and her insomnia improved. Feelings of depression and violence abated, and she euphorically exclaimed, "I feel wonderful, I feel very well. I want to take up where I left off. Now I can control my grief and I am going to give my husband's clothes to charity." She showed such a marked degree of euphoria that observers guessed that she was on Tofranil rather than Thorazine. She showed no psychomotor retardation; rather, she was bright, alert and upbeat.

She was released from the hospital after a three month stay, apparently fully recovered. Her hospital diagnosis was psychotic depressive reaction; the research diagnosis was agitated depression with onset during involutional period, possibly recurrent. She was to continue taking Thorazine 1200 mg and Kemadrin 15 mg daily and seek part-time employment.

FOLLOW-UP

Within a month of discharge, Mrs. Fein discontinued tak-

ing her medication.   Her mother-in-law died shortly after,
and she had a rapid return of symptoms with early morning
awakening, poor appetite, agitation and inability to do her
chores. This continued for three months. When she finally
attempted to choke her two children, they brought her to the
emergency ward of a city hospital where she was diagnosed as
having a psychotic depressive reaction and was initially
treated with Thorazine 75 mg five times daily for two weeks.
Then Thorazine was discontinued and she received 13 ECT,
showed marked improvement and was released in seven weeks.

She attended their after-care clinic once a week, took
chloral hydrate for sleep and occasional small doses of Thorazine. Quickly she became markedly depressed, agitated and
suicidal and was readmitted to the same city hospital. This
time they diagnosed her as having an infantile narcissistic
character, a mild chronic brain syndrome (because of poor
performance on psychological tests), and a psychotic depression. They treated her with Thorazine 50 mg four times daily. She seemed to improve slowly and was released in six
weeks on no medication, only to be readmitted in three weeks
with the same symptoms. By now Mrs. Fein was dependent on
large amounts of chloral hydrate. Also, she complained of
severe arthritic pain. This time she was treated with Thorazine 75 mg five times daily and aspirin for one week, and was
transferred to a state hospital where she continued on Thorazine 300 mg daily and Tofranil 75 mg daily.

After three months she was improved and released to live
with her daughter. For the remainder of the second year after her Hillside hospitalization, she continued attending the
after-care clinic, continued taking Thorazine and Tofranil,
and took a job as a saleslady in a fancy shop.

During the third year after discharge from Hillside Hospital, she continued working while taking Thorazine 250 mg
daily. When her daughter married she had a slight relapse

and became worried about paying the rent, but in general she
functioned satisfactorily, living alone, working and caring
for her apartment and herself. She attended an after-care
clinic and her condition was good.

When our social worker made contact ten years after her
Hillside hospitalization, Mrs. Fein initially denied ever
having been hospitalized. Later she claimed she was fine,
working at the same saleslady job part-time, and visiting
with her married children. Also, she thoroughly enjoyed doing hospital volunteer work. She had taken no medication
and had received no psychiatric care in the last seven
years.

COMMENT

Mrs. Fein's illness and treatment course demonstrate
several characteristic features of the agitated depressive
state. First, although her depression was of such magnitude
and chronicity that it would frequently be referred to as
"psychotic," it was nonetheless clearly precipitated by bereavement. Nonetheless, at various times in her illness,
when phenothiazines were interrupted, her agitated depression returned with full force. Sedatives were ineffective
and ECT only temporarily effective. It is unfortunately
typical that this patient had five hospitalizations, although Thorazine was absolutely specific for relieving her
distress. The structural fault in the management of this
case was the lack of an appropriate continuous outpatient
after-care service that would insure medication maintenance.
Mrs. Fein did well in her second and third years following
initial hospitalization when she received Thorazine regularly and remained under supervision.

The excellent response of this severely agitated and
depressed patient to Thorazine should be specifically noted.
There is a common erroneous myth that phenothiazines usually
exacerbate depression. Such illustrative cases, as well as

controlled research demonstrate the incorrectness of this
view when dealing with agitated depression (2,3,4).

REFERENCES

1. American Psychiatric Association: Diagnostic and Statistical Manual, Mental Disorders (Second Edition).
    Washington, D.C., 1968.

2. Klein, D.F.: Chlorpromazine-procyclidine combination,
    imipramine and placebo in depressive disorders. Canad.
    Psychiat. Assoc. J. 11, S146-S149, 1966.

3. Klein, D.F.: Importance of psychiatric diagnosis in prediction of clinical drug effects. Arch. Gen. Psychiat.
    16, 118-126, 1967.

4. Klein, D.F.: Psychiatric diagnosis and a typology of
    clinical drug effects. Psychopharmacologia 13, 359-386,
    1968.

5. Robins, L.N.: Deviant Children Grown Up. Williams and
    Wilkins, Baltimore, 1966.

NEUROSES AND CHARACTER DISORDERS

NEUROSES AND CHARACTER DISORDERS

DIAGNOSTIC ISSUES

The term neurosis, like the term psychosis, is a poorly defined residue of the early development of psychiatry. English and English (3) define it as "a mental disorder, ill defined in character but milder than psychosis." This definition is actually a denial of any utility for the category "neurosis" and simply replaces the noun "neurosis," with the adjectival phrase, "ill defined and mild." It follows that neurosis and psychosis are conceived as arbitrarily delimited regions on a continuum of intensity of disorder. Therefore, neurosis may easily develop into a psychosis, and psychoses should pass through a neurotic stage, both in their development and in their recompensation. This viewpoint finds its most noted champion in Karl Menninger (18) who equates the underlying continuum with psychological regression.

Others believe that neurotic illnesses are qualitatively distinct from both manifest and potential psychosis. It follows that having a neurosis does not predispose to a psychosis, and vice versa. The issue is obfuscated by arbitrary and idiosyncratic usages for these terms.

It appears unreasonable to insist that all neuroses are entirely qualitatively distinct from all psychoses. The development of psychotic states in patients who apparently

have obsessive-compulsive neurosis is well-known, just as is
the development of psychotic states in patients with apparent hysterical illness or character disorder. It is generally presumed that there is a higher incidence of psychosis
in these deviant states. However, there is no conclusive
evidence. On the other hand, one should not assume that all
neuroses will develop into psychoses. There are qualitative
distinctions between the psychotic reaction patterns of different neurotics, and these reactions are distinguishable
from each other and from the general group of schizophrenias.
Systematic epidemiological, longitudinal, psychopathological
studies, with exact definition of the criteria for diagnostic
classification are necessary to illuminate these hotly de-
bated issues.

Definition of Neurosis

The definition of psychoneurotic disorders in the Diagnostic Manual of the American Psychiatric Association (1)
specified that the positive common denominator is "anxiety
which may be directly felt and expressed but which may be
unconsciously and automatically controlled by the utilization of various psychological defense mechanisms (depression,
conversion, displacement, etc.)...

"Anxiety in psychoneurotic disorders is a danger signal
felt and perceived by the conscious portion of the personality. It is produced by a threat from within the personality
(e.g., by supercharged repressed emotions, including such
aggressive impulses as hostility and resentment), with or
without stimulation from such external situations as loss of
love, loss of prestige or threat of injury. The various
ways in which the patient attempts to handle this anxiety result in the various types of reactions" (pp. 31-32).

Also certain phenomena are contraindicative of psychoneurosis. "In contrast to those with psychoses, patients
with psychoneurotic disorders do not exhibit gross distor-

tion or falsification of external reality (delusions, hallucinations, illusions) and they do not present gross disorganization of the personality."

This definition depends upon the acceptance of a specific theory of neurotic dynamics, etiology and development
that cannot claim unequivocal scientific demonstration or
universal acceptance, although it is quite plausible. To
progress from syndromal to etiological classification would
be a distinct advance. However, to make an etiological classification on the basis of a controversial theory seems to
be asking for trouble.

The diagnosis of neurosis then depends upon the clinical
demonstration of anxiety and/or defenses against anxiety. In
many patients with conversion, dissociative or depressive reactions, anxiety is not typically manifest and must be inferred. Unfortunately, the grounds for making this inference
are not specified or obvious. If one is to infer that there
is covert anxiety simply because of the neurotic symptoms, a
completely circular argument exists, and diagnosis actually
is being made on the basis of manifest symptoms. The variety
of distressing states, commonly labeled anxiety, is discussed
elsewhere (13).

I consider the belief that "neuroses" share a common
underlying etiology or dynamics to be outdated, and that psychiatric advance will largely consist of dissecting out subgroups with common therapeutic responses which may share
common etiological factors. Studies on phobic-anxious patients reinforce this view.

Definition of Personality or Character Disorder

The American Psychiatric Diagnostic and Statistical
Manual of 1952 (DSM-I, 1), states that the outstanding characteristics of the personality or character disorders are
"developmental defects or pathological trends in the personality structure, with minimum subjective anxiety, and little

or no sense of distress.   In most instances the disorder is
manifested by a life-long pattern of action or behavior rather than by mental or emotional symptoms."   This definition
reflects the general impression of the cool, psychopathic,
exploitative type of personality disorder.   However, it certainly does not fit the category of "emotionally unstable
personality disorder," utilized in DSM-I, wherein the predominant symptomatology is labile emotionality.

The 1968 revision of the Diagnostic Manual, DSM-II (2),
states "This group of disorders is characterized by deeply
ingrained maladaptive patterns of behavior that are percep-
tibly different in quality from psychotic and neurotic symptoms.   Generally, these are life-long patterns often recognizable by the time of adolescence or earlier."   DSM-II emphasizes the life-long pattern of maladaptive behavior that
is nonetheless different from psychotic and neurotic states,
and removes the de-emphasis on anxiety and emotional symptoms, prominent in DSM-I.

However, patients with personality disorders frequently
evince no symptomatology in the sense of spontaneous complaints.   Under conditions where their life styles are grati-
fied by some ecological niche, there is frequently no manifest difficulty.   When they are distressed it is most often
related to situations of being trapped or failing to get what
they want.   Further, their distress often seems to be in the
service of environmental manipulation rather than the direct
expression of intolerable affective states.

The fact that many personality disorders have a large
manipulative component that may express itself in histrionic
exaggeration or bland denial makes self report unreliable if
not positively misleading.   Further, these patients are often
extremely skilled in presenting consistent persuasive stories
to serve their manipulative goals.   That many of these patients' difficulties result in pain and aversion to those

immediately involved with them also makes the report of family members difficult to evaluate. Since inferences from
psychiatric interview are largely dependent upon the self-
presentation of such patients, our standard device, the psychiatric interview, becomes relatively invalid. The pathological aspects of these patients' behavior are frequently
markedly episodic and variable, rendering short periods
(e.g., one hour) of observation uninformative. Their manipulativeness often leads them to covert noncompliance with medication regimes, discarding medication, storing it and taking
overdoses, as well as using addictive and habituating drugs.

A key difficulty in assessing personality disorder is
that deviant behavior is often a manipulative and goal directed self-presentation as compared to the expressive behavior of patients with retarded depression or acute delusional schizophrenia. Patients with personality disorders
are keenly aware that they are under observation and that the
impression they make may well affect them. This is particularly true in relation to individuals who factually play major roles in the patient's life, e.g., parent, doctor, boss,
fellow-patient, etc. Even when "voluntarily" in psychiatric
treatment the patient often tries to utilize the doctor as a
potent ally in some life manipulation; e.g., preventing the
family from criticizing the patient allowing the patient to
shirk responsibilities, dodging the draft, etc. When such
practical manipulative intent is not present, they may use
the doctor to support their self-esteem rather than to help
modify their behavior. Therefore, it is difficult to accept
their behavior or complaints at face value. Since patient
self-report is usually a prime source of data, the patient-
dependent therapist is placed in a helpless role.

It should be clear that these clinical facts do not
necessitate the belief that personality disorder is a game or
"myth." It is likely that these patients have severe defects

in affective, anticipatory and cognitive regulation as well
as identification and self-esteem that allow or even require
the development of maladaptive deviant patterns. Further,
the maladaptation is often much more obvious to observers
than to the patient.

The patient's difficult and unrewarding social interactions must be carefully investigated in a variety of milieux
since psychiatric interventions under the circumstances of
living at home may have entirely different effects than similar interventions conducted while the patient is hospitalized. To attempt to study such patients in their home environment requires either reliable family informants or the
development of a home visit psychiatric assessment team.

Five diagnostic subgroups are considered here: a) phobic-
anxiety reaction; b) emotionally unstable personality;
c) passive-aggressive personality; d) histrionic reaction and
e) "pseudoschizophrenic neurosis." It should be clear that
we are following current American nosology by placing the
phobic anxiety reaction and emotionally unstable personality
under the neuroses and character disorders, since their affective symptomatology appears of more central import, and
their characterological problems as secondary miscarried repairs.

Chapter XII

PHOBIC ANXIETY REACTION (AGORAPHOBIA)

Definition

Phobic reactions are defined as circumscribed fears of objects, actions or situations. Phobic patients maintain both a high level of chronic anticipatory anxiety and have acute episodes, amounting to panic attacks, on being exposed to a phobic situation. Therefore, these patients assiduously avoid the phobic situation even though they are no longer certain that it would have the deleterious effects upon them that it had in the past.

DSM-I states that the anxiety of patients with phobic reactions becomes detached from one area and displaced to another, serving an economic function. Demonstration of this hypothesis is frequently impossible.

Although there are as many phobias as there are discrete situations capable of inducing fear, there seem to be several subgroups. The first consists of the phobias that center on the experience of a panic attack under conditions of aloneness, separation, inability to achieve help, or blocked motility. These usually female patients have episodic illness, in that their lives are punctuated by discrete series of overwhelming attacks of panic. Typically, patients note the sudden onset of inexplicable "panic" attacks, accompanied by rapid breathing, palpitations, weakness, a feeling of impending death and occasionally depersonalization. Their activi-

ties become progressively constricted, until they are no
longer able to travel alone for fear of being suddenly rendered helpless while isolated from aid. Depressive complaints
are frequent and associated with feelings of futility. However, they differ from both retarded and agitated depressives
in that vegetative (i.e., insomnia, anorexia, constipation,
loss of libido) signs of depression are lacking and ECT
proves ineffective or noxious. Although fear of open spaces
is not the hallmark of this condition, but rather expectant
fear of lack of support when overwhelmed, their condition is
often referred to as agoraphobia. Such patients actually
manifest both claustrophobic and agoraphobic symptoms. Their
claustrophobic symptoms occur when they are in situations from
which they cannot suddenly leave, such as elevators, closed
rooms, theaters, churches, subway trains, tunnels and bridges.

These patients also present a wide array of associated
obsessional, hypochondriacal, affective, dependent, passive-
aggressive, addictive, histrionic and manipulative features.
Depending on the salient symptomatology, or the selective
perception of the diagnostician, they may be referred to as
obsessional, hysterical, atypically depressed, passive-aggressive character disorder, pseudoneurotic schizophrenic, acute
schizophrenic, alcoholic, barbiturate addict, anxiety state,
conversion reaction, etc. This diagnostic chaos is the natural result of the psychiatrist's inability to arrive at a
hierarchy of importance for this multiform symptomatology on
any cross-sectional basis. Attempts to arrive at a consensus
between dissenting diagnosticians usually result in a fence-
straddling label, e.g., severe mixed psychoneurosis or pseudoneurotic schizophrenia or borderline state, etc. These
patients frequently engage in prolonged outpatient psychotherapy, usually devoted to the exploration of unconscious
sexual and aggressive impulses, with the interpretation of

the phobically barred areas as symbolic of forbidden temptations, e.g., walking in the street = streetwalking. Since
the patient is desperately anxious to find some meaning in
his phobias, it is not surprising that a wide variety of interpretations for these symbols is produced by him and/or
his therapist.

Phobic disorders of this sort are frequently periodic
and remit spontaneously. Success has been claimed for many
therapies; however, adequately controlled studies are rare.

In another group of phobias, instruments of aggressive
or sexual temptations, such as pins, dirt, knives, scissors,
sharp instruments, etc. are avoided. It seems reasonable to
attribute these phobias to compulsive defenses against unconscious aggressive soiling or sexual impulses, but one's
dynamic speculation should not be the basis of a descriptive
diagnosis.

Still another group of phobias concerns animals and insects. Strikingly, these phobias regularly have early onsets
in childhood and often are associated with similar phobias
in the mother. They may represent early indoctrination, imitation, identification and conditioning. An interesting
psychoanalytic formulation relates them to sibling rivalry.
There are also the reports of hereditary fears of animals or
animal-like motions (twisting, thrashing, squirming) in some
species; e.g., the chimpanzee's fear of snakes.

One extremely widespread fear that may increase to the
point of phobia is fear of heights (acrophobia). This term
is a misnomer since the fear is not of height but of the possibility of falling. Such patients often may look out the
window of an enclosed observation tower, such as the Empire
State Building, without fear. However, an open window may
provoke a panic attack even if the patient has not looked
out. Such fears are often attributed to unconscious suicidal
impulses, yet acrophobic patients do not avoid other situa-

tions that afford suicidal opportunities. We believe that these patients are afraid of their own impulsivity, and therefore fear any situation where a sudden impulsive action may have irrevocable destructive effects. More speculatively, it is also possible that they have innate sensitivities to the visual cliff experience. It is known that some species have a hereditary avoidance of visual cliffs prior to any possibility of learning.

ROSALIE MASSI

PRESENTING PROBLEM

Rosalie Massi, 18 years old, was small, homely, moderately emaciated, pale and weak. She could not verbalize her problems but summarized herself as a "mental handicap," with myriad physical symptoms, constant feelings of fright, nervousness, timidity, hypersensitivity, anger and total inability to attend school or leave her house unaccompanied. She felt helpless, hopeless and lacked interests or goals. Gastrointestinal upsets with stomach pains and diarrhea, headaches, nosebleeds, dizziness and fatigue bothered her incessantly. She would vomit or get cramps whenever she was angry or required to do something against her wishes. While she denied anorexia, she ate very little (height 4'10", weight 68 pounds) and was anemic. Finally she requested psychiatric help and was referred to Hillside.

FAMILY

Rosalie was the fourth and youngest child in a family of four daughters of poor Italian immigrants. The father died suddenly, at age 35, when Rosalie was four months old.

Mrs. Massi, small and well-groomed, had always been weak, timid, indecisive, and generally unable to cope with life. She suffered from gastrointestinal distress and headaches, and neither worked nor socialized after her husband died, although her inadequacies antedated this tragedy.

Seemingly wanting to walk softly through life so as not to antagonize or attract attention, she complacently accepted any recommendation or request made by her family. Toward Rosalie, she was extremely overprotective.

When Mr. Massi died, leaving the four girls at ages four months, seven, nine and eleven years, the family went on welfare and continued permanently in that status. When Rosalie reached age 18, the welfare payments were to cease, because she was considered old enough to work to support herself and her mother. However, because of Rosalie's disabilities the payments continued, to the family's relief.

The sisters were startling in their contrast to Rosalie and Mrs. Massi; they were vivacious, vigorous, young women. One sister, Joan, was particularly capable, and charming. She had quit school at age 16 in order to support her mother and Rosalie. Joan lived with them and made most of the family decisions, as well as supplying Rosalie with love and encouragement. The two other older sisters were married and lived with their families, but felt concern and responsibility toward Rosalie and their mother.

DEVELOPMENTAL HISTORY

Rosalie was born normally at full term, and breast fed until four months. (Her father died at this time.) She was toilet-trained at 18 months and talked at two years. Always sickly, quiet and timid, she seldom played with other children. Rosalie was a poor eater from birth and Mrs. Massi felt victorious if the child ate once a day.

On the first day of kindergarten Rosalie was terrified, wailing when her mother left. The teacher shook her, intensifying her distress. Her fears progressively worsened so that she vomited every day. The principal suggested that Rosalie be withdrawn from school and try again in six

months. Six months later she was still frightened but forced
to return to school.

She was in a chronic state of fear and tension and
couldn't concentrate or understand what the teacher said.
Thus, she remained at home, ate very little, was sick with
vomiting, abdominal pains, or hot and cold flashes. She was
a poor learner and was referred to the Bureau of Child Guidance when she was ten. On the Stanford-Binet, she had an
IQ of 72. As is typical of psychological evaluations, her
potential was considered to be higher but blocked by emotional conflict.

By the time she was in fourth grade, at age 11, Rosalie
was under such fear and tension, and her hypochondriasis,
physical complaints and learning problems were so severe,
that she was unable to attend school at all and was placed
on Home Instruction, twice weekly. About this time she was
admitted to a hospital with severe stomach pains, eventually
considered psychogenic. Several months later she had several psychiatric interviews but discontinued because she didn't
like the psychiatrist.

From age 11 on, Rosalie left her house only if accompanied by a sister. At home she spent her time working on
lessons, listening to music or reading, never socializing
with outsiders.

Rosalie often became angry with herself and her mother,
feeling aggravated by their inadequacies and ineffectiveness, and the mother's paralyzing overprotectiveness. The
most important figure remained her sister who supplied her
with financial and psychological support.

At age 11 her menses began; she was totally unprepared
and frightened. Neither mother nor sisters had prepared her,
since any aspect of sex was taboo. Rosalie never masturbated, denied any sexual fantasies and feared and distrusted
men. Once a neighbor exposed himself to her, and once a man

put his hand on her shoulder and wanted to "make a pass at her." She had many fears about these events.

At age 13, after two years on Home Instruction, Rosalie was evaluated to determine if she could return to public school. On a Stanford-Binet retest, her IQ was 82. At this examination, the psychiatrist diagnosed her as having a phobic personality with schizoid elements, protracted school phobia, inadequate emotionality, disturbed family relationships and dependency. She continued on Home Instruction twice weekly until hospitalization, and irregularly saw a Bureau of Child Guidance social worker whose main function was to attempt to persuade Rosalie to enter psychiatric treatment. Rosalie remained resistant.

When Rosalie became 18 she was expected to support herself and welfare payments were to stop. Unable even to attempt to look for a job, and threatened by loss of her welfare check, her condition deteriorated so much that she finally asked for psychiatric help and accepted referral to Hillside. At that point she was unable to leave her house for any reason and vomited at the thought of looking for work.

PRESENTING CHARACTERISTICS

Appearing older than her age, Miss Massi seemed mannish, dressed in slacks with hair combed straight back and a stiff masculine gait. Extremely meticulous about herself, she showed considerable compulsiveness and demanded that her belongings be arranged in set ways.

When talking, Miss Massie used a profusion of facial and hand movements. While sometimes polite, cooperative, and ingratiating, smiling even with tears in her eyes, resistance, negativism and fear were evident in her angry, explosive outbursts. Her stream of speech tended to be fast, overproductive and circumstantial; an extensive vocabulary was used with only moderate accuracy.

She showed no hallucinations or delusions, was well-
oriented in all spheres and had some insight into her condition, stating that her problems involved her relationship with
her mother, "I do things on purpose to see if she can discipline me." She realized that her dependency and feelings of
inadequacy rendered her unable to function. Her judgment
was poor. Her IQ tests were consistently low, between 70
and 80. However, she seemed to function intellectually at
an average level, and her test scores were regularly considered artifacts of an abnormally constricted life and paralyzing test anxiety.

COURSE AT HILLSIDE

Miss Massi had difficulty adjusting to the hospital and
made frequent demands to be discharged. However, after a
few weeks she began attending activities and trying to relate
to other patients, although in a pseudo-teaching role which
was not accepted by others. She demanded considerable attention from the nursing staff and was hostile and sarcastic
with everyone. Her stomach aches, diarrhea and biliousness
continued. She became amenorrheic for three months but refused gynecological examination. Sometimes her mood was resentful, angry and depressed and she made several wrist-
slashing gestures to ward off demands made on her.

When she attempted to attend the hospital school she
continually panicked and was unable to calm herself, could
not read, exacerbating her feelings of stupidity. On the
Wechsler-Bellevue her verbal IQ was 86 and performance IQ
was 88. Despite this she was once again described as having
bright normal potential, since she showed good quality verbalizations and Rorschach productions. When confronted with
a direct test of her abilities, she became extremely anxious
and would rather accept herself as ignorant than face the
testing situation, as the psychologist interpreted her functional deficit.

After five months of hospitalization and the failure of
intensive milieu programs and psychotherapy, Miss Massi entered the drug program and received placebo for the first
three months. In the first few days she felt slightly more
relaxed but soon returned to her extreme hypochondriasis.
Her condition fluctuated slightly with more or less depression, lability and complaints of physical illness. She was
maintained on placebo for three months because her doctor
felt it "aided her introspection." Finally she refused this
medication, complaining it was not helping her empty, miserable, unhappy feelings.

A month later her doctor placed her on Thorazine 400 mg
daily, because he considered her schizophrenic. This caused
marked orthostatic hypotensive reactions. Within two days
the dose was lowered to 200 mg and her tension seemed to a-
bate. But she developed a checklist of side effects, including unclear vision, dizziness, sleepiness, constipation, loss
of associated movements, fogginess and a "zombie" look which
Kemadrin 5 mg, and later 15 mg daily did not help. However,
her psychiatrist felt Rosalie was more hopeful and increased
the Thorazine to 300 mg. Over the next two weeks the side
effects increased in severity, Rosalie was apathetic, miserable, mummy-like. She hated the medication and finally it
was discontinued.

She then received Tofranil 75 mg, raised to 150 mg and
then to 225 mg daily within ten days. For the first time in
her life she suddenly had no complaints and was in good spirits, bright-eyed and alert. When Tofranil was raised to 300
mg daily she developed a tremor and felt that objects were
revolving. Therefore, it was decreased to 250 mg daily and
maintained at that level throughout the rest of her hospitalization.

She was cheerful and her mood was stable. Astoundingly,
she became interested in food, with good appetite, and gain-

ed 25 pounds. She showed increased ability to interact in
an acceptable, helpful manner, learning how to control herself and her sensitivities.

She worked with enthusiasm in occupational therapy,
producing neat, well-done projects. As she relaxed she became concerned that she might be homosexual, because of her
mannish dress, and questioned doctors and patients about it.
In trying to prove her femininity she found a younger effeminate boyfriend. Through this relationship she developed
some confidence and when this boy was discharged she found
another, more masculine boyfriend, though still younger than
herself. They developed a very tender relationship and
spent much time together. After six months they parted because he was too childish and not sexually demanding enough
to suit her. After this, she preferred the company of older
fellows.

Appointed unit housekeeper, she successfully carried
through her duties, arbitrating complaints from other patients and assigning tasks. Also, she worked efficiently
and successfully in the hospital library. On visits at home
with her mother she was more tolerant and comfortable, and
developed enough confidence to travel unaccompanied between
hospital and home; a monumental achievement since she had
never travelled alone before.

Episodically, after several months on Tofranil she would
still become recalcitrant, have angry outbursts and periods
of slight depression and withdrawal, but in general she was
pleasant, cheerful, active and cooperative.

When discharge plans were made, Miss Massi was ambivalent about returning to live with her mother, and finally
decided that foster home placement would be more desirable.
Thus, she was placed with a foster family and arrangements
were made for her to receive vocational training at a rehabilitation agency.

On discharge, after one year and seven months, her hospital diagnosis was personality trait disturbance, infantile personality; research diagnosis was phobic anxiety reaction, chronic. She was receiving Tofranil 250 mg daily at discharge, and was to continue on this medication.

FOLLOW-UP

Miss Massi took Tofranil for seven months after hospitalization and then discontinued it. She spent three happy months in the first foster home, but the foster mother became ill and Miss Massi was placed in another home where there was considerable conflict and rivalry with the family's daughter. After six more months she was placed with a third family with whom she remained for 18 months.

During the first 17 months she worked in a sheltered workshop, learning electronic assembly, which she disliked. She saw a psychiatrist weekly, who narrowly conceived of Tofranil as an antidepressant and discontinued it. He prescribed Deprol and then increasing doses of Librium and sedatives. She did poorly, finally left the vocational program, and had increasingly frequent appointments with her psychiatrist, whom she had been seeing weekly. Later she was hospitalized briefly for gastrointestinal distress.

In the third year after discharge from Hillside, she left her foster home, claiming she had been physically beaten, and returned home to her mother and sister. She continued with a new psychiatrist for a year and then returned to an earlier therapist. She attempted no other job, feeling too ill to work, fearing failure and the loss of her social security disability benefits.

The next year, at age 24, her condition improved sufficiently to allow three months of training as a baby technician and work for the next eight months in a hospital nursery. On the job she had personality conflicts with co-workers and supervisors and finally quit. She then took neighborhood baby-sitting jobs.

In an interview with a social worker, to which she finally consented, four years after Hillside hospitalization,
she seemed anxious, depressed, claimed she was often unable
to sleep and had suicidal thoughts. Her answers to questions
were tangential and she blocked repeatedly throughout the interview.

After two more years of poor adjustment, she finally
called Hillside, asking for help but rejecting all sugges-
tions.

Eleven years after hospitalization, further contact was
made. Miss Massi continued to live with her mother and did
not work, but adamantly refused to give further information.
She was furious at what she interpreted as harassment by
the hospital and called the medical director to complain.

COMMENT

Miss Massi is atypical insofar as she represents a severe chronic agoraphobia that progressed in an unremitting
fashion from a childhood school phobia, clearly related to
separation anxiety. The symptomatology resembles that of
childhood school phobia as it was mainly gastrointestinal,
whereas the typical adult agoraphobe patient has a primarily
cardio-respiratory symptomatology. Further the typical adult
phobic-anxious patient either has a period of relative clinical quiescence between early separation anxiety and the later
onset of the illness or may have no history of childhood separation anxiety at all (9).

A marked somatizing reaction to Thorazine is most typical for these patients who regularly respond badly to phenothiazines and often develop orthostatic hypotension (14).
The dizziness associated with the orthostatic hypotension
makes the patient too panicky to continue on Thorazine. Also
typical is the fascinating marked change in the patient's
psychophysiology upon receiving Tofranil. The panicky epi-

sodes subsided quickly leaving her with residual anticipatory anxiety easily managed with firm support, direction and
desensitization (9,11,15,17).

Disappointing features of this case are also sadly typical. The value of Tofranil for such patients is generally
unknown, and therefore these patients will often either discontinue the medication themselves or have the medication
discontinued by their doctors who do not see the rationality
of using an "antidepressant" to treat anxiety. Therefore,
the patients are often switched to ineffective minor tranquilizers such as Deprol or Librium. These agents do have
the value of somewhat modifying the patient's anticipatory
anxiety; however, they do not prevent the panic attacks and
therefore do not prevent the progressive constriction of the
patient's life space.

It was work with such adult patients with histories of
school phobia, that led to our placebo-controlled demonstration (1,5,6,21) that Tofranil was effective in the treatment
of school phobia. It has also been claimed that MAO inhibitors are useful in the treatment of phobic conditions. This
treatment is evidently common in England; however, adequately controlled trials have not, as yet, been reported.

One of the difficulties with Miss Massi's care was the
lack of a concerted, systematic, after-care program which
emphasized both Tofranil and support, direction and desensitization. This was complicated by the patient's inability
to accept direction and her fluctuating regressive-dependent
motivation.

Atypical features were her mother's bereavement due to
losing her husband early in the patient's life, the patient's
feeding difficulty, her relatively low IQ, and the very marked chronicity and severity of her school phobia. In spite
of her chronic difficulties in maturation, her surprising
ability to accept a foster home after leaving Hillside, rath-

er than returning to her mother directly, seems a testimony to the remarkable potency of Tofranil.

It is tempting to speculate that this mother's depression, consequent to her husband's death, may have had devastating effects upon a constitutionally vulnerable child.

FREDA STRASSE

PRESENTING PROBLEM

While crossing the street one day, Mrs. Freda Strasse, age 39, felt faint and was suddenly convinced that she would not be able to get to the other side. There was no discernible precipitating cause for this sudden indisposition. After much anxiety, she contacted her husband who brought her to the family doctor. She was treated with sedatives and the doctor suggested that she seek psychiatric care, but she was unable to accept this recommendation for several months. During those months she took cabs to work, did not go to stores and would only go into the street when accompanied by her husband, fearing always that she would faint.

Finally, she entered treatment with a psychiatrist who diagnosed her as having a passive-aggressive personality with agoraphobia and treated her twice weekly for several months with psychoanalytically oriented psychotherapy. Her symptoms subsided and she was able to use public transportation and shop in stores.

Then suddenly, her husband's brother died of a stroke and she promptly relapsed, this time expressing terror that her husband would die as had his brother. Once again, she was unable to leave her house unaccompanied or go to her job. But, she continued in psychotherapy and within a few months improved sufficiently to work and use public transportation. However, her mother-in-law, a known cardiac, then died and Mrs. Strasse traumatically found the body two days after death. Again she relapsed, with an increased fear that her

husband, now the only living member of his family, would be
next.   Improvement was slow and abruptly reversed when her
husband's doctor advised him to take life easier because he
was showing signs of heart trouble. With this, Mrs. Strasse
became so incapacitated that she could not even go down-
stairs alone.   Mr. Strasse found himself physically and
emotionally incapable of coping with his wife's needs, no
longer taking her to work or her psychiatric sessions. Thus
she stopped work and treatment simultaneously. In order to
stay at home alone, she drank about three highballs a day.
At this point, after four years of private treatment, her
psychiatrist contacted Hillside to seek more intensive,
sheltered, inpatient care for Mrs. Strasse.

FAMILY AND DEVELOPMENTAL HISTORY

Mrs. Strasse's parents, Russian Jews, emigrated to England in the late 1800's. Her father had been a peddler, but
with the outbreak of the Boer War joined the British Army.
Shortly after, he met his wife-to-be and married. Of their
living children, there was a boy 14 years older than Freda,
a girl 12 years older, and a boy two years younger. The family ran a successful business and **was** financially quite
comfortable.   No birth or developmental history was available. Freda spent her childhood in England, sometimes on a
farm or at a resort owned by the family. She was very proud
of her older brother and sister and worshipped them; she
fought often with her younger brother.

Mrs. Strasse described her childhood as unhappy because
she was shy. She remembered being cared for by servants who
often told frightening stories of magic and death. Her early schooling was in the form of tutoring by a governess.
The parents devoted their lives to running their business,
quarreled often and spent little time with the children.
Even meals were usually taken in a restaurant. The only really enjoyable activity Freda had was her piano lessons, and

when unhappy she practiced for hours at a time.

When it was time for high school, she went to live with her married sister, in a large town. Life with her sister was unhappy, for her husband drank heavily and was frequently abusive. Nevertheless, Freda worked very hard in high school, did well, and was the pride of the family.

During secondary school she was popular with boys and was an active participant in many social and athletic events. At home, she often had to help her father with business accounts, because he was unable to read or write English.

On graduating from secondary school with honors, Freda had hoped to go to medical school. However, her father was unable to pay tuition since his business was doing poorly at the time. Instead, she got a job as a secretary. She had been dating a physician, sixteen years her senior, and when she was 20 years old, they became engaged. However, after a year, her fiancé wrote her a letter asking to break the engagement. Freda could not understand this, but decided that it must have been because she had instigated sexual relations with him, several times, just preceding his sending the letter. When the romance ended, she was very hurt and felt life had no meaning.

Soon after, she fainted in a theatre. When she came to, she found her hands were in her lap and feared that those around her might think that she had been masturbating. Very ashamed about this incident, she dreaded the thought of fainting, although there were no recurrences.

Following her broken engagement, when she was 21, she moved to a different town, worked as a doctor's assistant and remained for two years. She had two short affairs during these years, one with a married man and another with a man who promised to marry her after World War II. She joined the army in the early 1940's as a private and attained the rank of lieutenant. During this period, her father died at the

age of 75. She nursed him during his terminal illness and
felt guilty that she had not taken further steps to prolong
his life.

During her five years in the army she generally enjoyed
herself, had many friends and dated frequently, finally meeting her husband-to-be. They dated steadily for about a year
and had sexual relations which were satisfactory to both.
She found him kind, loving and accepting, although passive
and quiet, and was surprised when he asked her to marry him,
even after having been sexually intimate with him.

They were married when she was 28 and he was 31, and
soon after were separated for six months when he had to return to the United States. She was unable to follow him for
six months because of immigration rulings. At the beginning
they lived in a rented room and had little privacy. Mrs.
Strasse found that she could no longer attain any satisfaction from their sexual relations, which she characterized as
"rushed."

During the first few years of their marriage, Mrs.
Strasse worked as a secretary in her husband's law practice,
and immediately they had disagreements about running the office. Frequently she was hostile, cold, domineering and con-
temptuous of him and often rejected him sexually. When occasionally she did submit to intercourse, she was unresponsive and did not enjoy it. Then she began finding sexual intercourse not only distasteful, but also painful, and sexual
relations were discontinued. Shortly thereafter it was found
that she had an ovarian tumor.

Mrs. Strasse wanted to have children, but her husband
refused, claiming that they were too financially insecure to
afford a family. Fearing that she would need a hysterectomy,
treatment for the tumor was delayed several years, with Mrs.
Strasse hoping that her husband would change his mind and
decide to have children. However, he insured his financial

insecurity by never building up his law practice--he claimed because of his own disorganization, inefficiency and demands by his wife for his attentions. Finally, Mrs. Strasse underwent an oophorectomy and reluctantly resumed infrequent sexual relations with her husband. When the husband's brother died, sexual relations were discontinued, although the causality is not clear. It was on the first anniversary of her operation that she suffered the panic attack previously reported.

PRESENTING CHARACTERISTICS

Mrs. Strasse was an attractive, tall, thin, well-groomed, 44 year old woman. She was eager to be hospitalized, with the hope that she would be able to overcome her multiple phobias, including travel, heights and spiders, and then return to work. While she seemed placid and cooperative, her mood was depressed, anxious and fearful, and she panicked when she found it would be necessary for her to walk from one area of the hospital to another. Her thoughts were centered on self-criticism and feelings of worthlessness and uselessness. She felt insecure and guilty. "I'm so afraid to say this for fear it will happen. What if my husband has a heart attack while I am here? Who will take care of me? I'm all alone. Who is taking care of him now?" But beyond these obsessive concerns, her mental status was unremarkable.

COURSE AT HILLSIDE

The results of all physical and neurological examinations were non-significant, and her EEG's were normal. Her Wechsler-Bellevue verbal IQ was 129.

During the first three months at Hillside, Mrs. Strasse's course was slow, with frequent severe panic attacks elaborated into fears of fainting and dying. She had short periods of depression lasting a day or two, but finally became secure enough to travel alone from her unit to her doctor's office. However, in general, she insisted on being

accompanied everywhere. She was discouraged by her lack of
progress and the expense of hospitalization, and she was increasingly tearful, had difficulty falling asleep and often
awoke during the night. Sometimes she had impulses to
smash furniture or hit someone, which were never implemented. In therapy, she showed no insight, but talked about how
violently angry she felt all the time.

After three months of stagnation, she was referred to
the drug program and showed no response to six weeks of placebo treatment, except for increased somatic complaints.
Then she was placed on Tofranil, increased to 300 mg daily
over three weeks. By the second week on Tofranil (150 mg
daily) she felt less depressed and her panics ceased. By
the fourth week (300 mg daily) she was able to go to all
parts of the hospital unescorted, felt less helpless, less
angry, and took overnight passes to stay at home. Outside
the hospital she still needed someone with her. In therapy
she began to express a tremendous amount of hostility toward
her husband and also, the obsessional belief that she could
not get well, for if she did, he would die, since twice before when she improved, family members died.

An interest in art and sketching developed, her mood
leveled evenly, she was friendly, and after six weeks on Tofranil, was able to walk on the street alone. However, she
began to loathe spending weekends with her husband, hated
the responsibilities involved and felt it was worthless
since her husband did not love her. She wanted to remain in
the hospital permanently, even though she now was able to go
home and remain there alone without panic, but still with
some anxiety. She had no temper outbursts or depressive
symptoms and showed increasing awareness and insight in psychotherapy. Also, she was able to attend the theatre and
restaurant with patient groups. Her doctor concluded that
while her symptoms had improved, she had not really made any

basic changes, and that since she was doing well, Tofranil should be withdrawn.

After three months on Tofranil, it was slowly tapered off and Mrs. Strasse showed a gradual return of depression, anger and hostility, had trouble sleeping, including night-mares, and somatic complaints. Once again she was unable to stay at home alone on weekend passes, (but had intercourse with her husband for the first time in several years). She appeared depressed, hopeless, anxious, fatigued and unwell.

After a month of obvious decline, reinstituting Tofranil was discussed. She objected to resuming medication, fearing drug dependence and wanting to get well on her own, because both her previous psychiatrist and her husband did not be-lieve in medication. She stated, "It did not remove my fears, they remained," not making the distinction between her actual panic attacks and her anticipatory anxiety over the possible recurrence of these attacks.

Her behavior continued to deteriorate and she became enraged that her doctor was paying too much attention to other patients. After seven weeks on no medication, her doctor reinstituted Tofranil over the patient's objections, this time in 100 mg increments over two weeks, to 300 mg dai-ly.

Almost immediately, Mrs. Strasse was less angry, irri-table and depressed and slept better. Within two weeks, most of her symptoms were alleviated and by one month she could get around the hospital and go out on passes without panic, but still with anxiety.

At this point a discharge conference was set for a month hence and at the conference, Mrs. Strasse stated that she had made considerable progress in her ability to overcome most of her agoraphobic symptoms. Her relationship with her husband, including sexual aspects, had improved. At home on weekends, she felt she had to drink several ounces of al-

cohol in order to tolerate her anxiety, but did this in the
morning so that when her husband came home, the alcohol had
worn off.

Following the discharge conference, Mrs. Strasse became
angry, emotional, irritable and depressed and was preoccupied with the thought that she would still be unable to travel by herself. She could no longer continue making plans
for discharge. At this same time, she was informed of the
sudden death of her husband's best friend. Once again she
felt that as soon as she made any progress, someone dear to
her died, and if she were to recover completely, her husband
would die. She felt hopeless and threatened suicide. But
when she was informed that she would be accepted for readmission should this be necessary, she relaxed and was able to
accept discharge planning which included continuing in psychotherapy with her original referring psychiatrist.

Thus, Mrs. Strasse was discharged after 11 months at
Hillside. Her hospital diagnosis was phobic reaction and
her research diagnosis was phobic anxiety reaction (agoraphobia). She was to continue taking Tofranil 300 mg daily.

FOLLOW-UP

Mrs. Strasse returned to live with her husband and continued weekly psychotherapy with her psychiatrist. She took
Tofranil for two months but the doctor belittled medication
and she discontinued it. For the next five months, she suffered severe episodes of alternating anxiety and depression.
Then she had a relapse where she was afraid to go into the
street and on her own she took Tofranil again (amount unknown) for two months. She was then able to carry on her
usual activities as a housewife,but still could not go out
unless someone, perhaps a neighbor, went with her. Despite
Mrs. Strasse's feeling that Tofranil had helped, her doctor
continually discouraged its use.

In the early part of the second year after her Hillside

hospitalization, her husband became ill. Her doctor was on vacation and Mrs. Strasse relapsed. On her own, she took Tofranil for one month, with some improvement. Seven months later, she had another relapse, but her doctor would not permit her to take Tofranil this time. She survived this episode without medication.

During these two years, she did editorial work at home. Her doctor was most uncooperative about answering any of the Hillside follow-up questionnaires concerning Mrs. Strasse's condition, and finally, after three letters were sent, all containing signed information release forms, the doctor returned a one paragraph letter stating that "she has shown moderate improvement, is more mature, less anxious, less hostile and more realistic."

In the middle of the third post hospital year, her doctor moved to a distant state and psychotherapy was discontinued without any untoward effect. After a few more months she gave up the home editorial work and found a job as an executive secretary in a large office. Her husband drove her to work each morning and a friend drove her home in the evening, because she was still phobic about public transportation.

When her phobias became more intense, she sought treatment with another therapist who also did not prescribe medication. Occasionally, she took phenobarbital on her own. Her social contacts were minimal but she desired more social activity. She continued to complain of anxiety and chronic depression, especially in relation to her illness and marriage where she had definite conflicts and poor sexual relations. Her husband refused to be interviewed by our social worker.

Her new doctor answered our follow-up questionnaire and reported that Mrs. Strasse no longer used alcohol for relief of emotional stress, but that she maintained many complaints

of discomfort and inability to function. However, with family support and frequent psychiatric attention, she continued to function with moderate impairment.

Ten years after Hillside hospitalization, Mrs. Strasse
stated that she was greatly improved, worked consistently
for the same firm in a responsible administrative capacity,
received promotions and enjoyed her work and the people she
worked with, and went out socially.

Her severe phobias had eased considerably. She was capable of travelling by herself and could use different modes
of transportation, which enabled her greater freedom. While
she still found it an effort to travel, she successfully
forced herself to do it.

She took no medication for many years and claimed that
none benefited her to any degree. Still in psychotherapy
once weekly, she spoke very positively of her therapeutic
relationship. The same nagging marital conflicts continued,
but she felt that she was coping with them. In general, her
overall functioning was good and her outlook more optimistic
than at any time since her hospitalization.

COMMENT

Regrettably, Mrs. Strasse's psychiatrists' attitudes toward Tofranil were typical, seeing it as an unnecessary
crutch barring the way of real psychotherapeutic work. The
unsubstantiated bland assumption made by many therapists
that psychotherapy is uniformly successful and incompatible
with the medication, can only be deplored.

Mrs. Strasse is typical of one subgroup of the phobic-
anxious (agoraphobic) patients who have an onset later in
life associated with an interruption in endocrine homeostasis
following a comparatively normal development (9). Other
precipitants beside oophorectomy may include hysterectomy,
parturition, thyroid disease, etc. Interestingly, the onset
of the panic attacks does not occur immediately but may re-

quire a year to develop without apparent psychic precipitation.   Nonetheless, their symptomatology is exactly the same
as the other group of patients who have a history of childhood separation anxiety, and whose attacks are precipitated
by object loss or bereavement.   Interestingly, in this case
the attacks first appeared a year after oophorectomy, for no
apparent reason, and later were precipitated by bereavements
and object loss.   I have speculated (9,15) that these panic
attacks represent an innate final common pathway, evolution-
arily developed to elicit maternal retrieval behavior under
conditions of infantile separation.   The hypothesis is made
that this mechanism can either have a constitutionally low
threshold that is then reflected in early separation anxiety, or can have its threshold artificially lowered under
conditions of disordered endocrine homeostasis.

One might speculate that Mrs. Strasse's period of disturbance was related to her artificial menopause, and that
her eventual stabilization reflected re-establishment of endocrine homeostasis.

Other unfortunately typical aspects were this patient's
unwillingness to "become dependent" upon a drug as well as
her psychiatrists' unwillingness to prescribe useful medication.   It is remarkable how in the face of repeated demonstrations that Tofranil was markedly beneficial for Mrs.
Strasse, that she should eventually come to the belief that
no medication had ever been of value to her.

Also typical is her dependence upon alcohol and sedatives to modify her anticipatory anxiety.   This dependence
often leads to alcoholism and barbiturate addiction.   Recognizing this group of alcoholics and barbiturate addicts is
of considerable practical importance since they can be relatively successfully treated with Tofranil(19A). The minor tranquilizers, such as Librium and Valium, form very valuable
adjuncts to the treatment of these patients, since they modi-

fy anticipatory anxiety, whereas Tofranil does not. They
are more useful than barbiturates or alcohol since they are
nowhere near as addictive and also are practically impossible
to use to commit suicide. At the time the phobic anxious
patients described were treated, these medications were not
available. However, it is now my practice to use them in
combination with Tofranil if the anticipatory anxiety component is of such magnitude that the patient's attempts to
venture forth are paralyzed. However, many patients do not
require such treatment and their anticipatory anxiety will
extinguish with success at separation occurring during the
Tofranil-induced blockade of panic attacks.

It is noteworthy that in studies of the treatment of
phobic states with behavior therapy and systematic desensitization, the worst results are attained with the agoraphobic
patients. I believe that behavior therapy and desensitization procedures are particularly useful in states of irrational anticipatory anxiety that are not continually reaffirmed by panic episodes, which are a distinct psychophysiological process. If a patient with agoraphobia, an episodic
illness, is treated behaviorally during the period when the
panics have spontaneously remitted then desensitization can
be expected to work. However, treatment of such patients by
desensitization while they are repeatedly experiencing panic
attacks is routinely unsuccessful. Whether systematic desensitization would speed the rehabilitation of agoraphobic
patients whose panic attacks are blocked by Tofranil has not
as yet been studied, but appears likely.

DAVE TRENCHERMAN

PRESENTING PROBLEM

Dave Trencherman, 20 years old, sought hospitalization
because of severe panics and an obsessive fear of being unable to swallow. He found it continually necessary to test

his swallowing ability by sipping water from a bottle carried
for this purpose. Also, he had a compulsion to crack his
knuckles, stopping only on a multiple of five. He was also
obsessed with fears of dying, had palpitations and trouble
sleeping. His activities had become completely restricted
because he was unable to leave his house unaccompanied.

FAMILY

The Trenchermans were a middle-class, urban family with
two boys. The father, heavy-set, in his mid 40's, was bossy
and authoritarian, with a facade of bravado. He suffered a
deprived childhood, quit school at 13 and had been in the
food-handling business since. He provided adequately for his
family but was dissatisfied with his own achievements and
tried to force Dave to achieve what he himself had been unable to do. This led to a steady battle between father and
son. Ostensibly he wanted his son to be successful, but at
the same time was envious of him. He competed with Dave for
attention, berated him whenever possible, and never let him
feel the satisfaction that he could possibly please his father. Though Mr. Trencherman was easier to live with than
his wife, he would often execute her punishments, such as
locking Dave in his room.

The mother, also obese, had an extremely deprived childhood, frequently enduring actual hunger. She was superficially sociable but touchy enough to have brought several
people to court for various minor reasons. She was obsessive
about two things: a clean house and forcing her children to
eat. Histrionic and labile, she engaged in fierce battles
with her family, and was extremely demanding, controlling and
intrusive; i.e., she read her son's personal mail, restricted
his social life, even chose his daily clothing. In addition,
she was inconsistent, overprotective and overindulgent toward
her children.

Dave's brother was seven years younger, and there was

little closeness between them. He appeared much like Dave,
sharing similar problems. Bright and manipulative, he lied
and cheated consistently. He stuttered and had had psychiatric treatment.

While a strong interdependency existed between the parents and children, their family life was stormy. There were
never exchanges of affection or confidences between the sons
and parents, but instead, constant arguments among the four,
with much running about and screaming. While not particularly religious, they arbitrarily observed certain Judaic
rules and successfully inculcated in Dave the fear of God's
wrath for his misdeeds. Dave claimed he was interested only
in the intellectual aspects of religion.

Food was of major importance for the Trenchermans. Dave
was always forced to eat, hungry or not, often to the point
of vomiting. The mother, preoccupied by the conviction that
Dave was underweight and undernourished, shuttled with him
from doctor to doctor in order to seek corroboration for
her baseless fears.

DEVELOPMENTAL HISTORY

Dave was delivered spontaneously, full term, after a
48 hour labor. He was severely jaundiced at birth and considered critically ill. At six weeks he weighed only six
pounds. However, he thrived normally after this early difficulty. At one year he was toilet-trained, but remembered
that he would refuse the toilet and surreptitiously
have bowel movements in corners of the apartment. Also, he
refused to eat and vomited when forced. His tonsils were
removed at age two. His earliest memory is of his mother
camouflaging an egg in chocolate milk, because he rejected
them otherwise. This pattern of deception, over-concern with
food and health, and stubborn negativism were hallmarks of
the Trencherman family.

Because of anti-Semitism in their small town, the family

moved to New York City when Dave was three. About this time
he developed bronchial asthma. He continued to be a fearful
but aggressive child, so that he often fought with other
children but always ran home to seek protection.

Reluctantly he entered school at age five, where initially he did well, exerting little effort, but getting good
grades. However, when the work became more difficult and he
continued to exert little effort, he gradually did more poorly and was considered uncooperative and a behavior problem
at school.

His father was greatly concerned and tried to work with
him at home, engaging the boy in many long, mutually exasper-
ating sessions which resulted in Dave's conviction that
nothing would ever satisfy his father, and an even more
antagonistic outlook toward school.

When Dave was 11, he joined a group of antisocial boys
who enjoyed threatening girls with sexual attack. The school
authorities threatened to expel Dave. Under the guise of
changing climate to aid his bronchial asthma, his mother took
him to live in Florida for a few months. Later he returned
to the same school in New York.

Dave was obnoxious in high school. For example, when
one teacher seated him close to her for disciplinary reasons,
he coughed in her face continuously until she returned him
to his original seat. He was a show-off, claimed he knew
more than anyone else, and was disliked both by teachers and
peers. Angrily, he felt that his teachers deliberately distorted facts in their lectures. He would falsify his report
cards, lie and cheat.

In high school he made friends with the toughest of the
school toughs, a group of boys who would gun fight and even
kill. Dave felt that he impressed this group with his intelligence and good English. He himself usually refrained from
fighting. It was during this period that he developed a com-

pulsion to crack his knuckles ritualistically.

While growing up, Dave had three close friends; one, a
dependent, indecisive, intellectually slow childhood friend,
another, a mentally inferior boy with whom he went to school
and the movies, and his best friend, an intelligent, exploitative, delinquent, opportunistic boy.

At 16, Dave met a girl of 20; they became lovers and
planned to marry. Mrs. Trencherman vehemently opposed their
plans and when the usual fight ensued, Dave threatened to
stab his mother. The love affair ended abruptly, within a
year, when the girl dated someone else. Dave never spoke of
her again.

Then he was introduced to a group of Puerto Rican prostitutes through his sociopathic friend, became friendly with
them and took pride in speaking Spanish and fitting into
their community. He was sexually promiscuous with these wom-
en, gained status by "fixing up" friends with them and contemplated becoming a pimp. Though he initiated "picking-up"
women, he boasted of letting them "do the work" sexually.

Dave tended to form sexual relationships with women considerably older than he. His most significant relationship
was with his mother's best friend. He desired this woman
sexually and refrained from an actual sexual involvement only
in fear of her jealous, strong, husky husband. He fantasied
being completely cared for by a middle aged woman whose sole
payment was his affection.

Because of nagging at home and his desire for independence, he quit school at 17, got a job at an insurance company where he worked for six weeks and then went to Florida.
He returned after six weeks and worked sporadically with his
father, collecting unemployment insurance for 30 of the next
52 weeks. Then, he found a job selling Catholic religious
articles door to door. He felt guilty that he, a Jew, was
working at this job, and also professed that it was wrong to

exploit people's beliefs. At the time of his acute symptom
onset, he was to have presented his six month sales record
to his employers. Suddenly he realized that while he considered himself an excellent salesman, he had in fact made
very few sales. He felt this was due to the nature of the
items he was selling and decided to look for another job.
At the same time his father threatened to throw him out of
the house and withdraw monetary support.

   Then, while riding in a car with a prospective employer,
he began arguing with the man about his proposed salary.
Suddenly, his throat felt dry, his tongue felt swollen, he
was unable to swallow and he panicked. Convinced he was going to die, he had to leave the car to get a drink. His manner so alarmed passersby, that they called the emergency
squad who brought him to a hospital where he was reassured,
with no effect. His mother took him home.

   From the time of this first attack Dave's activities
were completely restricted; he refused to be left alone for
even a minute. He suffered intense headaches, photophobia,
and constantly tested his swallowing ability. Abruptly, he
would suffer severe episodic panics where he had intense
choking sensations and palpitations. However, no pathology
was found upon extensive otolaryngological, cardiac and neurological testing. His symptoms increased to such degree
that he was unable to keep his appointments with the psychiatrist whom he had consulted. The psychiatrist considered
that he was "exhibiting anxiety hysteria in a setting of extreme immaturity, instability and inadequacy" (he also considered a diagnosis of pseudoneurotic schizophrenia), and
treated him unsuccessfully with Thorazine. This made Dave
feel sicker, tired and dried his throat further. Finally the
psychiatrist referred him to an acute-care psychiatric hospital.

   Here, Dave, now age 20, was diagnosed as an obsessional

neurotic, treated with meprobamate 1200 mg daily, and daily
psychotherapy. He remained for seven weeks, showing gradual
improvement. He socialized easily with the other patients
and no longer had trouble swallowing, but when he found he
had to leave the hospital for financial reasons, he became
greatly upset. He tried returning home, but there his symptoms increased and he willingly considered city-subsidized
hospitalization at Hillside.

PRESENTING CHARACTERISTICS

Mr. Trencherman was well developed, well nourished,
strong and healthy looking. Very gregarious and talkative,
he quickly made friends with many patients. His speech was
voluble and somewhat overproductive but coherent and to the
point. At times he grandiosely claimed that he was more intelligent than most people and felt the hospital surroundings were unworthy of him. He spoke openly of past events
and his fears of not being able to swallow. When he got to
a water fountain he would always be able to swallow, but
then would develop anxious expectations that if no water were
available he would die.

COURSE AT HILLSIDE

The results of all physical tests, including the EEG,
were normal. On the Wechsler-Bellevue he attained a verbal
scale IQ of 118, and a performance scale IQ of 114.

From the beginning of his hospitalization, Mr.
Trencherman's relationship with his doctor was a power struggle. He would manipulate skillfully to avoid phobic situations, such as being alone, going to the dining room, occupational therapy, kitchen and ward chores. He was rebellious, grandiose, pompous and a "wise guy." These tactics
were successful until controls were tightened, and he was
forced to conform to hospital rules.

After four months in psychotherapy, he found his façade
neither effective nor credible; his anxiety increased, his

activities became even more restricted and he took to bed.
With this exacerbation it was decided to place him in the
drug program. Mr. Trencherman became frantic when he could
not be informed which drug he would be taking, fearing it
might be Thorazine to which he had had a bad reaction. However, he finally acquiesced, when treated firmly, and also
resumed his other activities, despite his anxiety. He was
started on Tofranil 75 mg daily, increased 75 mg weekly to
a maximum of 300 mg daily.

Initially he became more anxious, complained of blurred
vision and stiff muscles, but within a week his panics abated. He could now attend most hospital activities and was
able to leave the hospital grounds for an evening with a
group of people - a major achievement. He was able to travel
in a bus, an impossibility for the past year, stayed out of
bed during the day and slept well at night. His palpitations
stopped and his compulsion to crack his knuckles decreased.
However, he still had to carry his sipping water with him
and developed a compulsion to always take the final shot be-
for walking away from the pool table.

A month after starting Tofranil, while receiving 300 mg
daily, he had a single episode of palpitations and was certain he was dying - God's punishment for his sins. In therapy his doctor interpreted this as a symbolic fear of his
father, and asked him to examine his murderous impulses toward his father. With this, he went on a rampage for a
month, inflicting abuse on all hospital authority figures.
He had many temper tantrums, made special demands in the dining room and dental clinic, and harassed his social worker.
Because his doctor felt that the Tofranil was stimulating his
anger, it was decreased to half strength (150 mg daily), unknown to Mr. Trencherman. Concomitant with this, and the
threat of discharge to a state hospital if his demanding behavior continued (his doctor believed he was having a para-

noid episode), he gained control of himself and his anger
subsided.

A period of considerable mobilization then occurred
(Tofranil 150 mg daily); he made tremendous strides socially
(elected ward president), educationally (passed his high
school equivalency exam), gained insight into his behavior
in therapy and attained some self-confidence. During this
period his doctor decided to withdraw the Tofranil.

Exploratory psychotherapy continued; his anxieties increased and he tried to avoid activities which he was constantly prodded to attend. When discharge plans were made
his anxiety increased greatly, he had a flare-up of hostility, but panics did not recur. However, he managed successfully to travel alone on buses and trains and to plan for
his future. While he still remained mildly phobic, easily
prey to eccentric ideas (e.g., if the Russians shot a rocket
to the moon, the world would be submerged in water), quarrel-
some, infantile and dependent, it was felt that prolonged
hospitalization would only foster his dependency and prevent
further progress.

Mr. Trencherman was hospitalized for one year. His hospital diagnosis was chronic paranoid schizophrenia; the research staff diagnosis was a phobic anxiety reaction with
obsessive-compulsive symptoms. At discharge he was receiving
no medication. He returned to his parents' home when he refused foster home placement.

FOLLOW-UP

Mr. Trencherman returned to live at his parents' apartment and continued seeing a psychiatrist privately, twice
weekly. No medication was prescribed, but he took a small
amount of meprobamate on his own for six months. He worked
continuously in different jobs: as a restaurant cashier for
six months, a taxi driver for the next year and a half, as a
restaurant manager for six months and then a food salesman.

His social functioning and family relations were improved and
he was dating a girl he met while at the hospital. When he
ended the relationship with this girl, he suffered a mild setback, but at the end of three years his therapist felt that
he had attained a position of gratifying work, home and interpersonal relationships.

In a telephone interview with his father, ten years after Mr. Trencherman's hospitalization, it was learned that
he had been married for three years, had two children, lived
in his own apartment, and had had no severe relapses. He
took sporadic tranquilizers, no other medication, and saw his
earlier therapist when he felt the need. He had been in business for the past five years and was fairly successful. In
general he felt well.

COMMENT

Mr. Trencherman's illness onset was typical in that it
occurred when he was afraid of being thrown out of his family
and felt particularly helpless and incapable of caring for
himself (9). Other typical phobic-anxious features were an
exacerbation of symptoms with the use of Thorazine, the fact
that he was misdiagnosed as schizophrenic or pseudoneurotic
schizophrenic, and the use of a soteric object, i.e., the
water bottle. Isaac Marks points out (16) that some phobics
carry with them such a magic object as a charm against recurrence of attacks.

However, there are a number of somewhat atypical aspects
to this case. The patient is a male (the usual ratio reported being in the neighborhood of four or five females to one
male). Also, he had a long history of antisocial and exploitative qualities, unusual in this conscientious group.
Also odd was his exacerbation of a chronic angry state on
Tofranil. This type of response is much more characteristic
of adolescent patients with emotionally unstable character
disorders (12). He did show some characteristics of the emo-

tionally unstable character disorder, in terms of his antisocial behavior, grandiose over-estimation of his capacity
and very marked mood lability. Another atypical feature was
his overt obsessive-compulsive symptomatology, although ob-
sessionalism and perfectionistic attitudes are common in phobic-anxious patients, but not in emotionally unstable character disorders.

Finally, the fact that he was able to maintain his balance over ten years, with no repeated episodes of panic is
atypical. However, he did utilize meprobamate, indicating
that he did maintain some anticipatory anxiety. The frequent marked chronicity of these cases has been discussed
(17).

To sum up, Tofranil-responsive panic attacks occur in
a variety of settings. The diagnostician may easily be misled into focusing on the lability or obsessive-compulsive
symptoms or exploitativeness or paranoid trends or addictive
behavior, etc. It is the sequence of panic followed by phobic constriction that is the pathognomonic feature and treatment indication.

Chapter XIII

EMOTIONALLY UNSTABLE
CHARACTER DISORDER

Definition

With the emotionally unstable character disorder syndrome the individual reacts with excitability and ineffectiveness when confronted with minor stress. His judgment may be
undependable under stress, and his relationship to other people is continually fraught with fluctuating emotional attitudes. DSM-I states that these fluctuating attitudes are due
to strong and poorly controlled hostility, guilt and anxiety.
However, the basis for this hypothesis is unclear, and this
definition does not emphasize the marked mood lability of
these patients. These patients are predominantly female adolescents whose mood disorder consists of short periods of
tense, empty unhappiness, accompanied by inactivity, withdrawal, depression, irritability and sulking, alternating
suddenly with impulsiveness, giddiness, low frustration tolerance, rejection of rules and shortsighted hedonism.

Thus, they resemble a short-period cyclothymic personality. However, the cyclothyme is usually a responsible,
mature adult who is attempting to pursue socially acceptable
and valued goals. Patients with emotionally unstable personalities on the other hand, are usually young, with a poorly
developed conscience and generally immature attitudes, and
are frequently irresponsible, hedonistic, extractive and exploitative. Their marked affective lability is often not

immediately noted as core pathology because of their complicated self-presentations. These range from a fragile, immature, dependent image, eliciting protectiveness from the observer, to a hard "wise guy" presentation expressing independence and lack of need for care. The patients are perplexed about their life goals, stating that they do not know
who they are, what they are, or what they want to be. They
are also confused about issues of dependency, intimacy and
self-assertion, often reacting in a disorganized, flighty
and despairing fashion. There is a pervasive feeling of ex-
clusion from normal life and peer groups, with the conviction of being irreparably bad. They are rational, relevant
and coherent except for periods of giddiness or agitated
fearfulness when their speech and behavior become pressured,
scattered and disorganized. Many emotionally unstable personalities have childhood histories of impulsiveness, hyperactivity and low frustration tolerance. Others seem to develop this pattern at the time of puberty. Participation in
activities fluctuates considerably, but when involved these
patients are often creative, skilled and original. The major
degree of disorganization manifest by the emotionally unstable character disorder (in combination with his frequent
use of intoxicants or psychotomimetic substances such as alcohol, dextroamphetamine, marijuana and LSD) often leads to
the appearance of behavior diagnosed as schizophrenic by many
psychiatrists.

Their prognosis is, at present, unclear, although their
affective swings can generally be moderated by phenothiazines. Preliminary follow-up data suggest that the pathological behavior of many such patients "burns out" during
their late 20's. Because of the differential drug response
of this group, subsuming them under the "hysterical personality" category as in DSM-II tends to blur a valuable distinction.

VICKI REUTER

PRESENTING PROBLEM

An attractive, plumpish, 17 year old, Vicki Reuter felt depressed, had "bad feelings" since age 13, and had attempted suicide several times. While highly intelligent at school, she was truant, flunked courses and defied teachers and rules. She used attention-getting devices, like shaking, walking with an unsteady gait and mock fainting spells. Panic attacks concerning different fears, usually of a sexual nature, were frequent. At home she was completely rebellious and unmanageable. All her symptoms were increasing and therefore she was referred for hospitalization following the collapse of outpatient treatment.

FAMILY

The Reuters were middle-class, and lived in a suburban home with their only child, Vicki.

Mr. Reuter, short and paunchy, in his late 50's, was a high school graduate who worked in the garment industry. His main concerns in life were his daughter's welfare and his lodge activities. He showed great warmth, indulgence and love toward his daughter, finding it impossible to deny any of her wishes.

Mrs. Reuter, tall and strikingly handsome, in her early 50's, was embarrassed that she had only an 8th grade education. During the day she worked as a saleslady and at night was, like her husband, involved with lodge activities. A strong, domineering woman, she controlled her household in an authoritarian, hostile manner and always treated her daughter with coldness and rejection.

There was constant arguing among the Reuters. Vicki was always irritated by her mother's controlling behavior. However the mother's control was not consistent and gave way to Vicki's protests. When Mrs. Reuter made an ultimatum, Vicki would balk and argue. The mother would then withdraw her demands and give the child free reign.

Vicki felt that her mother considered her a bad child from birth. Starting at an early age, Vicki wished that her parents would die, causing her great guilt. On the other hand, Vicki felt close to her father, and often respected, obeyed and confided in him.

DEVELOPMENTAL HISTORY

Vicki was born normally, at full term, weighing six pounds. Mrs. Reuter who had had several miscarriages previously, was ill with tuberculosis at the time of the birth. When Vicki was one year old, Mrs. Reuter was hospitalized for 15 months for tuberculosis, and the child was cared for by an aunt and grandmother. Vicki spoke at an early age but was reported to be delayed in walking and had trouble learning toilet habits, wetting her bed until age five or six, and continuing to wet her pants even as an adolescent. As a child she had temper tantrums, sucked her thumb and bit her nails.

Vicki was precocious, enjoyed school and got along well with teachers and friends. She read many books each week, collected stamps, played the piano, and had four years of religious education culminating in her confirmation at age 13.

Sexually, Vicki claimed she was very aware, and knew at age four the where and how of babies. At age five and a half, a man sitting next to her in the movies put her hand on his exposed penis. When she got home she told her father, who returned to the theater with a policeman, searching for the man, in vain.

At age eight, several important events occurred. First, the grandmother with whom she had been close, died. Vicki was present when oxygen was administered, became hysterical and had to be sedated. Later that year the family moved from the city to their own suburban home. Here, an older girl babysitter involved Vicki in recurrent mutual sex play. Fi-

nally Vicki told her father that she no longer wanted to be
left alone with this girl, although she never divulged why.
She reported having suffered her first transient depression
at this age, but it is not clear if any of these events precipitated it.

Vicki began dating at age 11 or 12. She dated rarely
and in her adolescence had a crush on only one fellow. Her
menses began at age 12, her periods were always irregular,
with two or three month intervals. She began to masturbate
occasionally at age 12.

Beginning at adolescence, Vicki became reticent, moody
and cut classes. Her grades were uneven, and she failed a
number of courses because of her dislike for her teachers;
when she liked a teacher she performed well. Her family relationships deteriorated sharply and she had at least one
argument daily with her mother. On occasion they were physically abusive, and Vicki professed extreme guilt when she hit
back. The mother domineered and nagged her constantly, and
Vicki reacted by fighting back, doing nothing, or doing the
opposite of her mother's demands. The father tried to placate and pacify the two women and asked Vicki's patience because of her mother's menopause, but Vicki responded that
she didn't give a damn about her mother's menopause. Also
starting at this time and lasting until age 15, Vicki went
through a period of overeating, weighing as much as 155
pounds (height 5'5").

Vicki came to official school attention at age 15, when
it became obvious that she was emotionally disturbed. Her
school work was inadequate for her intellectual potential and
previous performance. She was truant and attempted suicide,
once by taking aspirins, and several times by superficial
wrist-cutting. Her suicidal gestures always followed arguments with her mother. The school psychiatrist saw her twice
weekly for about three months and found her "at times depres-

sed and at times elated to the point of being disconnected
and incoherent in speech."

At age 16 she entered psychotherapy with a psychiatrist,
after two more wrist-slashing episodes. He diagnosed her as
having a severe impulsive character disorder. In therapy
twice weekly for six months, she showed marked hostility toward both parents: contempt and belittlement for her father
and intense rage toward her mother. She continued making
suicidal threats and ran away from home repeatedly, with the
police returning her on several occasions. An apparently
good relationship developed with the therapist, but the ir-
ritating interactions with the mother continued to cause ex-
plosions of hostility and suicidal gestures without modification.

Also at about age 16, a classmate unsuccessfully tried
to force her to commit fellatio on him; she was approached
sexually by a drunk whom she fended off; she was frightened
by a neighborhood peeping tom, became hysterical after reading a sexy book, and jilted her boyfriend when he began to
pressure her for sexual activity. Later that year she discontinued her psychotherapy when her psychiatrist broached
the subject of sex. Her therapist thought she quit to strike
back at her mother. On the day she terminated therapy, she
developed back and leg pains and was hospitalized and placed
in traction for a week with a diagnosis of herniated lumbar
disc. Upon hospital discharge she remained homebound, in
bed, for five months.

While Vicki always had many friends and several close
ones, her dearest friend was a young male teacher at
her school who related to her as a "father confessor." She
was close with him, his wife and two children, spent considerable time with them and telephoned him frequently.

Although ages 13 to 17 were marked by depression, elation, hysteria, moodiness and suicidal gestures, Vicki was

able to maintain a social life with her girlfriends and several casual boyfriends, and work 15 hours weekly after school
hours as an office receptionist. However, by age 17 she was
completely unmanageable at home and school, and she grudging-
ly accepted the recommendation of her former therapist that
she be hospitalized at Hillside.

PRESENTING CHARACTERISTICS

     Vicki presented herself with an air of sophistication,
knowledgeability and blasé unconcern. Often she used tech-
nical words incorrectly. She smoked constantly, in an affected adolescent manner, using it as a hedge so that she
would not have to respond to her environment immediately.
Much of her behavior was histrionic; for example, she frequently closed her eyes dramatically and spoke with a drawl.
She had no hallucinations or delusions, was well oriented and
had a good memory; her judgment was poor, but her insight was
good. Her mental status was unremarkable otherwise.

COURSE AT HILLSIDE

     The results of all physical and neurological and EEG
examinations were within normal limits. She attained a
Wechsler-Bellevue full scale IQ of 128, a verbal IQ of 122
and a performance IQ of 128.

     Generally, Vicki was hostile toward staff and all but
a few peers. She joined a group of rebellious, delinquent
patients, rarely participated in prescribed hospital activities and tried to get away with breaking as many rules as
possible; for example, selling cigarettes to younger patients, driving without a license, drinking liquor and ex-
ploiting all possible freedoms until they were denied her.

     She formed a romantic attachment to a black male aide
and became extremely angry when informed that there could be
no romances between patients and staff. Shortly after the
aide quit for other reasons; she found a new boyfriend, this
time a paranoid black patient.

During the first six months of hospitalization, she was
sullen, frequently depressed and made several self-mutila-
tory gestures. Periods of giddy hedonism were also apparent. With the departure of any significant person; i.e, the
male aide, her doctor, roommate or friends, she increased
her rule infractions and self-mutilation; e.g., smashing her
hand or foot through glass. When she found that her doctor
would not accept her behavior she became increasingly hostile and equated his "unreasonableness" with her mother's.

The lack of progress after six months in the hospital
led to referral to the drug program where she first received
placebo. Initially, ward personnel felt she was less inhibited. However, after a month, she asked to be taken off the
medication since it was of no benefit. Her doctor described
her as more tractable and less restless during this first
drug period, but not gaining enough to warrant remaining on
the medication. Then she was placed on Thorazine 300 mg
daily, raised 300 mg weekly until 900 mg daily was reached,
together with incremental Kemadrin to 11.25 mg daily. She
became more relaxed, less sarcastic and depressed,and was in a
good mood. However, she had less contact with people because she was always sleepy.

For the next six weeks she continued complaining of
sleepiness and characterized her mood as low and blue rather
than painfully depressed; she cried often. Thorazine was
increased to 1200 mg daily. Two weeks later she scratched
her wrist and requested to be taken off medication. A few
days later nursing staff reported she had been discarding
the medication because it made her sleepy and depressed.

Two weeks later the medication was changed to daily doses of Tofranil 75 mg and Thorazine 600 mg. Quickly
she became more cheerful. Over the next two weeks, medication was modified to Tofranil 300 mg and Thorazine 300 mg
daily. She continued to improve for the next two weeks,

showed less depression and related better to her mother.

However, suddenly she became very rebellious over a minor ward regulation, and in a misguided effort to placate her, the Thorazine was withdrawn. She continued being hostile toward staff, sarcastic, bright-eyed, flushed, overactive and had episodes of boisterous, silly giddiness. Over the next two months she was supercilious, sulky and defensive, while insisting she was fine, and denied unusual feelings of anger, although she walked around with clenched fists.

When discharge was planned, her delinquency increased. She flatly refused foster home placement even though her relationship with her mother remained poor and was considered mutually destructive. She turned psychotherapy into a battle where she angrily made unrealistic demands for proof of love and was increasingly disappointed. Finally two weeks before her discharge, she smuggled alcohol into her ward. Further hospitalization was considered inadvisable. She was discharged to her parents after a year and two months of hospitalization. She was to continue in psychotherapy and take Tofranil 300 mg daily. Her hospital diagnosis was chronic, undifferentiated schizophrenia; the research diagnosis was emotionally unstable character disorder.

FOLLOW-UP

Vicki returned to live at home and found a job as a typist. She attended the after-care clinic for six months and then saw a doctor privately for three months, discontinuing the Tofranil. Finally, because she felt well and because of lack of funds, she stopped therapy.

The next year she lived in an apartment with a girlfriend, an ex-patient from Hillside, and continued the typing job. In the middle of this second post-hospital year, Vicki suffered a slipped disc for which she was hospitalized four weeks. After hospitalization, she returned to her parents'

home, became depressed and resumed psychotherapy for three
months.   Later she found a new, more satisfying and enjoyable
job.

The next year she continued very successfully at her
job, lived with her parents, and became engaged to a long-
time boyfriend. She was functioning at a very high level,
demonstrated considerable insight into her life, and was emotionally stable.

A year later she married her fiancé and they moved to
England for two years so that her husband might work and
study there. Vicki and her husband got along well at this
time. She worked as a clerk until the end of her second year
of marriage, when she had a recurrence of the slipped disc
and was flown home to be placed in traction for ten weeks.
(During this period she gained 50 pounds which she subsequently lost.) She did not work the following year in an attempt to force her husband, whom she characterized as a mama's boy, to take greater responsibility for her.

After four years of marriage, her husband asked for a
divorce because he wanted to marry another woman. This situation evoked moderate anxiety and depression, and she saw a
psychiatrist several times for counseling during the divorce
proceedings. She then found a new satisfying job and was
able to make the transition to self-support with aplomb.

Ten years after her hospitalization, she was interviewed
by our social worker. She related that, in general, her mood
had become remarkably stable, with no periods of elation or
depression, and no impulsiveness or hyperactivity. Angry
outbursts were occasional, mainly exhibited in interaction
with her mother, and limited to yelling, followed by apology.
Her relationship with her parents had improved considerably.
She had many friends, an active social life, and appeared
assertive, confident and responsible. This self-volunteered
information was corroborated in a separate interview with her

parents.

COMMENT

Miss Reuter shows several characteristics that are quite typical of a patient with an emotionally unstable character disorder. Her early development, although moderately difficult, gave no indication of future severe problems. Beginning at adolescence, her mood became labile, her schoolwork deteriorated and she came into increasingly sharp conflict with her parents. She complained about her dysphoric periods and saw her elated states as simple good humor. Outpatient psychotherapy was not helpful and hospitalization followed. She had many histrionic qualities over and above the problems with her affective lability. Treatment with Thorazine was effective in smoothing her mood, but the soporific side effects were unacceptable. Treatment with Tofranil had a mood brightening effect. However, it was also associated with an increase in hostility and decrease in frustration tolerance when Thorazine was discontinued. This last Tofranil effect is inconstant, and in some of these patients Tofranil acts as a mild tranquilizer, whereas in others it specifically produces an increase in anger (12).

Following hospitalization, where she had been considered schizophrenic, she was able to work steadily, maintain herself, persevere through a difficult marriage and a recurrent physical disability, with only occasional help. There were no rehospitalizations and ten years following discharge, her mood had stabilized without need for medication. The finding that such patients frequently show a progressively improving course with maturation, and do not show schizophrenic deterioration, has recently been documented (20).

LUCY MERCURI

PRESENTING PROBLEM

Lucy Mercuri, age 27, was having increasing difficulty caring for herself and coping with life. Since age 17, she had repeated periods of depression, was unable to form stable relationships, flitting from man to man, job to job, and a- partment to apartment, accumulating increasing debts. She was spurred into seeking treatment because of increasing desperation and her brother's recent successful psychiatric hospitalization.

FAMILY AND DEVELOPMENTAL HISTORY

Lucy's parents were married two years when she was born; her mother was 20, and her father was 25 years old. Her birth and developmental history were normal, and she was a happy, well-adjusted little girl. When she was three, a brother was born, and when she was five, a sister.

The Mercuris were a completely disorganized, disrupted family. Mr. Mercuri had been a career army officer but re- signed because of ill health and then changed jobs frequent- ly. Because he suffered from a severe kidney condition, he was sickly, debilitated and periodically hospitalized for months at a time. For instance, when Lucy was a year and a half old, he was hospitalized for five months.

An irascible man who easily lost his temper, he often spanked his children with a wire hairbrush "for no reason at all." There was constant bitter squabbling between husband and wife, mainly because he was unable to provide, either fi- nancially or physically, the gay, exciting life she wanted. After ten years of strife, when Lucy was eight, her parents divorced. For two years following their divorce, Mr. Mercuri made frequent visits to his wife, usually for sexual rela- tions. He then remarried and remained with his second wife.

The mother, charming, vivacious, attractive and uncon- ventional, was self-centered, narcissistic, rejecting and

exhibitionistic. Demanding constant attention, she did
things such as run around the house naked, or gaily and loudly shout and sing as she drove down the street in an open
convertible. However, she successfully attracted the attentions and affections of many with her personal magnetism.
On the other hand, she completely rejected her three children
as nuisances, never loving, guiding or disciplining them in
any way.

The brother, three years younger than Lucy, was very attractive and socially successful. However, as a teenager,
he became a heroin addict and committed felonies, including
burglary, to obtain money for drugs. He spent several years
in psychiatric hospitals, then married, and periodically
functioned normally and independently. The sister, five
years younger than Lucy, was the most disturbed. She underwent a year of private psychiatric hospitalization and later
spent several years at a state hospital.

The maternal grandmother, responsible for caring for the
three children while they were young, was described as a
brilliant, arrogant, selfish woman with a terrible temper.
She repeatedly beat the children with sticks or dog leashes.
However, she provided some sorely needed structure for the
family, and although Lucy resented her terribly, she also admired her.

During Lucy's first eight years, while her parents were
married, the family moved almost yearly. Following the parents' divorce, the moves became even more frequent. By the
time Lucy left home at age 17, she had lived in more than 30
places.

Lucy's earliest memories revolved around fights between
her parents, both verbal and physical. She reported a recurrent dream of running from her bed, descending the stairs
where she met frightening, unnamed dangers, and making vigorous attempts to fly and hover close to the ceiling out of

harm's way. She also remembered observing her father hurl
her grandmother across the room in anger; this she decided
was the reason her mother divorced him.

At school she was "always a new girl" and different from
the other children. She was an average student and because
of the frequent moves was unable to establish any lasting
friendships during her elementary school years. Following
her parents' divorce, she was cared for briefly by an aunt,
and then her grandmother. For the next four years (between
the ages of eight and 12) she rarely saw her mother. Her
grandmother was a strict disciplinarian and Lucy rebelled
with temper tantrums. During these years she gained a great
deal of weight and began to stutter. Her mood was usually
depressed, angry and sulky, and she felt separated from things
and people.

When she was ten, her mother remarried for a year, and
then took Lucy with her to Reno to obtain a divorce. Lucy
felt alienated from her mother during this trip and was confused by her mother's hostility toward her. They returned
East, and immediately the mother married her third husband,
this marriage lasting one month. When Lucy was 12, her mother married her fourth husband. At this time Lucy wrote to
her father stating that she would rather live with him and
begged that he take back his three children. He refused and
the children were taken to live with their mother and her new
husband.

The fourth husband was very wealthy. This marriage lasted five years, providing the longest period of uninterrupted
residence that Lucy ever had. The mother and husband established a new business and often stayed at their factory late
into the night; at other times they went night-clubbing.
While the children were materially well provided for, they
were grossly neglected and undisciplined. They had free, unchaperoned run of a huge house and lived in a state of filthy

chaos.

Lucy, the oldest, was nominally in charge during her mother's absence. But the responsibility was too great and everything was allowed to degenerate: garbage stood in the kitchen until it collected maggots; the dog's excrement on the living room rug remained for days; bedding was never changed and the children never bathed. They subsisted on a scurvy diet of peanut butter and hot dogs for three years.

However, Lucy had her first social success during these years. Boys would stand in line and chant for her to appear at high school dances, and her home became a center for teen-agers, probably because it was unchaperoned. Lucy necked and petted at her parties but was fearful of sexual relations and abstained. Even though she was popular, she felt paralyzed, shy, goalless, incapable of even caring for herself physically. She rarely bathed and dressed sloppily.

When Lucy was 17, her mother terminated the fourth mar-riage, which also had been plagued by violence and arguments. The husband even beat the children and Lucy once had to call the police for protection. Shortly after the divorce Lucy graduated from high school and went away to college.

After her first term in college, Lucy returned to her mother's home and learned of the woman's "sordid" behavior since her recent divorce. (Actually, the mother had always been involved in numerous extramarital affairs, often with wealthy, influential, socially prominent men.) The two had a fight; Lucy called her mother a whore, which incited a hair-pulling match. Immediately Lucy packed, grabbed her sister and brother, and had a boyfriend drive them to the father's residence in another state. The sister and brother remained with the father for the next several years, but Lucy, returning to the mother's house for the rest of her be-longings, was detained by her mother and a lawyer who threat-ened jail for abducting her siblings across a state line.

She then fled to a friend's house. The mother married her
fifth husband shortly thereafter and moved to California.

Lucy continued at college and spent her vacations with
her grandmother. At school she earned passing grades until
she began having difficulty concentrating and started getting
D's in her courses. She had a part-time job as a waitress,
was staying up late at night, dating and partying. She felt
uncomfortable with the other girls at college and was arguing
with teachers and college authorities. Fatigued and depressed, she quit school in the middle of her junior year and
found a job as a hospital aide. After many conflicts with
her supervisors, she was fired. Then she worked in a gift
shop, but the owner felt she was incompetent and also fired
her. After, she held several other jobs for short periods of
time.

By the time she was 21, her mother had returned to New
York; Lucy went to live with her and found a job as a model.
Lucy dated frequently, became pregnant during her first sexu-
al intercourse, had an abortion and then moved into a hotel.
She continued having brief affairs with numerous men and
worked as a model for two more years.

After becoming disenchanted with modeling, at age 23,
she went to secretarial school, found a clerical job and lived with a girlfriend for a short time. Then, following the
termination of a love affair with the "only man I ever loved," she became depressed, stopped working and had "the near-
est thing to a nervous breakdown."

Concerning this romance, Lucy claimed that the fellow
reminded her of her father, being unsure of himself and eager
to please. But when he proposed, she became frightened and
rejected him, because she "did not want to end up the way
mother did, a divorced woman with children." After her boyfriend left, Lucy reconsidered, and became extremely depressed when she unsuccessfully attempted to win him back. How-

ever, during his absence she began another affair which continued intermittently until her hospitalization. When her
first boyfriend did return, he discovered that she was sleeping with another man, and rejected her angrily. Her love affairs always followed the pattern of the man being interested
in her, and her fleeing, followed by her renewed interest in
the man, and his flight.

After losing her first boyfriend at age 23, Lucy made
many moves around New York City, living by herself in a series of rooms, hotels and apartments. She worked at and lost
many jobs, usually because of inability to be at work on
time, to perform duties or to adapt to her bosses. She borrowed money from friends and banks, squandered the money and
was heavily in debt.

Lucy had three other pregnancies by different lovers and
subsequent abortions. Rarely could she achieve orgasm during
intercourse. She entertained occasional homosexual thoughts,
although she had had no actual experiences.

Socially she had a large group of friends, many of whom
were former Hillside patients. Usually, she got along quite
well with men but was extremely competitive with women. She
tried hashish and marijuana, and drank, but none of this had
particular importance to her. While her pattern of living
did not suddenly change, it slowly grew increasingly intolerable. She noticed that she had some obsessive-compulsive
trends, such as checking repeatedly to see if she had set her
alarm clock, and having belongings in certain places or at
certain angles. Also she set goals so that she would have to
either perform perfectly or not at all, which meant not at
all most of the time.

Lucy's final undoing came six months before her hospitalization. She resigned from her job and took a bank
loan in order to accompany a boyfriend, who promised her a

fantastic modeling job on the West Coast. But, before she
went to the Coast, the job fell through, and her boyfriend
took off for Paris, leaving her in New York. Disheartened,
but coping, she spent most of the borrowed money on a port-
folio of her photographs and a new wardrobe which she felt
would be necessary to obtain modeling jobs. The rest of the
time she loafed on the beach with various friends. But as
the summer ended, she felt weighted by her debts, deserted,
with no one to go to for money. Finally, a casual male acquaintance offered to "keep her," and she went to live with
him. After a month she felt terribly degraded by the arrangement and left.

Then, one by one, she "forced the marriage issue" with
each of four previous boyfriends with whom she had been having intermittent relationships. When these attempts failed,
she appealed to her father for help. He sent fifty dollars
accompanied by a letter announcing that he could supply no
further support of any sort. Going for help to her brother
who had just been released from a psychiatric hospital, she
found him in such seemingly vibrant good health, she decided
that perhaps it would be best if she gave up and asked to be
taken care of as he had been. He advised that she see a psychiatrist, and she did.

The psychiatrist found Miss Mercuri depressed, entertaining suicidal thoughts and feeling that "everything I do
is unsuccessful. I am hanging on by the skin of my teeth."
He diagnosed her as having a psychoneurotic depressive reaction, and recommended immediate hospitalization. She applied to Hillside, was interviewed and accepted, but repeatedly failed to keep appointments for the financial interview.
Her sister "who has problems like me, only more so," then
became very disturbed and entered a city hospital. Miss
Mercuri tried to have her admitted to Hillside in her place,
but the mother arranged to have her admitted to another pri-

vate hospital instead. Finally, four months after she was
accepted, Miss Mercuri surrendered her apartment, disposed
of her furniture, lovers and animals, and requested an admission date, partly in hope of gaining time on paying her many
debts.

PRESENTING CHARACTERISTICS

The day of admission, Miss Mercuri arrived two hours
late for her appointment, accompanied by three devoted, eagerly helpful boyfriends and a huge assortment of disorganized baggage, cartons and shopping bags, representing the
residua of her apartment and refrigerator. Immediately she
became involved in an argument with the intake social worker
concerning the manner in which her luggage was to be brought
to her living unit; also she disputed each instruction given
to her and questioned the many hospital routines and policies, stating that she could not abide by them and that they
would obviously interfere with her treatment. She announced
that she would have trouble getting along in the hospital,
that she would not fit in and that the hospital was depres-
sing and the patients zombie-like; a totally inaccurate description of the Hillside milieu.

Miss Mercuri was svelte and strikingly attractive. In
her mental status interview, she was animated, friendly, articulate, coherent and relevant, except when discussing anxiety-provoking material such as her personal relationships or
sexual history. At these times she would become circumstantial and tangential. She stated, "I realized I was just going to repeat fruitless patterns of behavior and tried everything in my power, and therefore had to come to the hospital." Her predominant mood was of bleak despondency, but it
fluctuated rapidly from a silly but charming manner to bitter
defensiveness to apathetic gloom. Her affect was appropriate
to her thought content. She seemed hyperalert, suspicious,
distrustful and greatly concerned with a multitude of minor

somatic sensations, her body weight, the condition of her
teeth and gynecological complaints. Otherwise, her mental
status was unremarkable.

COURSE AT HILLSIDE

The results of all physical and neurological tests, including EEG's, were within normal limits, but Miss Mercuri
presented a host of physical complaints for which she was
examined and treated when necessary. On her first Wechsler-
Bellevue testing, she attained an IQ of 130 and on a retest
several months later, an IQ of 141, with a verbal IQ of 136
and a performance IQ of 141.

From the moment she entered the hospital, she was aloof
and hostile and presented the staff with multiple demands.
When she claimed "I am very sensitive and can't stand stupid,
incompetent people, and I can't stand being at the mercy of
the staff," her resident psychiatrist labeled her as paranoid. In therapy she was intensely sensitive, labile and
distorted everything said to her. A virtuoso at intellectu-
alizing, she nevertheless tangled herself in her high-flying
performances. She was very fearful of any close passive-dependent relationship which at times she craved. Episodically, she seemed under extremely high pressure and talked rapidly and continually. Initially, treatment was nominally
aimed at getting her to organize her daily behavior; however,
her doctor adopted a non-directive approach.

She was consistently late and slow in all her activities
and unable to tolerate changes in plans. Each treatment session was approached with a list of complaints for her doctor's perusal, which she presented with an air of reproach,
assuming his inability to understand her needs.

After two weeks her complaints abated and she actively
participated in many activities. Periodically, she was depressed, lonely, angry, demanding and labile. This seemed
to occur in a pattern usually concordant with her menstrual

cycle.

During her third month of hospitalization she attached herself to a male patient who rejected her as a "clinging leech." With this rejection she demanded inordinately increasing amounts of time from her doctor and embarked on many attention-getting maneuvers. Her psychotherapy sessions were spent discussing trivia and then castigating her doctor for not letting her discuss really important problems. A month later, after many outbursts where she broke furniture and glasses, she began to speak of her intense dependency needs, but remained episodically agitated, withdrawn, hostile and seclusive, refusing to participate in activities or abide by hospital rules.

At approximately this time her sister entered a state hospital, and Miss Mercuri made many efforts to gain her admission to Hillside instead. (An interview was held with the sister and the hospital rejected her as unsuitable for treatment in an open milieu.) She reacted to the hospital's rejection of her sister with more bitter complaints, anger and hostility.

When her agitation reached an intense pitch, her doctor interpreted her dependency needs to her, together with her anger at anticipation of disappointment. She denied this, but shortly thereafter became more cooperative and less complaining. At about this time, four months after coming to Hillside, she entered into the drug program. She feared this meant she was even sicker than she believed, and told about a "hallucinatory experience" that recurred many times while riding on a subway: she would think she was talking to herself only to find that the voices were actually those of the people around her. She also mentioned a "visual hallucination" that she experienced as long as one hour after awakening in the morning. (This was not elaborated upon in the records.)

Within the first five minutes after receiving her first
dose of Tofranil 75 mg, she experienced all side effects she
ever heard about, from any medication. The reaction subsided within 24 hours and did not recur. She became calmer,
more friendly and cooperative and began to participate actively in hospital programs. She got involved with a male
patient whom she compared with several of her former lovers:
dependent, undependable, sensitive, indecisive and in need
of a warm relationship. Their relationship was marked by
numerous fights, breakups, reconciliations and jealousy.

During the first five weeks Miss Mercuri was on Tofranil, which was increased 75 mg weekly to 300 mg daily, her
depression lifted, and she showed affective stability with
much less tendency to mood swings. But then she returned to
being uncooperative, with irritability, poor impulse control,
hostility, anger, abusiveness and defiance, distorting everything said to her. She claimed her sleep was disturbed, that
she slept lightly, woke frequently and had unpleasant dreams;
Tofranil was reduced to 150 mg daily after seven weeks, and
within three days she became more manageable, felt fine and
perhaps a bit euphoric. Her doctor reported that with the
decrease in medication she seemed less touchy and angry and
more realistic. For the next two months on Tofranil 150 mg
daily, she continually requested more "calming drug" to les-
sen her anxiety; thus the Tofranil was returned to 300 mg
daily. The next month she felt she didn't have enough control but that her mood was more even and she was less irritable.

After six months of continuing requests from Miss
Mercuri, her doctor was changed to a staff supervisor who
took a firm, direct and outspoken approach. Her course in
the next four months of treatment with her new doctor was
marked by wide fluctuations. Within moments she changed from
a charming, loving, warm, soft, capable woman to an ineffec-

tive, undirected, frenzied, muddled, furious viper, forcing
those around her to retreat. She developed an intensely ambivalent transference with her doctor, seeing him as the good
daddy, but also as an imperfect, rejecting man who could not
possibly understand her. Most frequently however, she sexu-
alized their relationship and projected her feelings, inter-
preting that it was her doctor who had designs upon her. Always, as her menstrual periods approached, she became vitu-
perative, labile and unreasonable. After her menses she
seemed calmer and better able to work in psychotherapy.

     After 11 months of hospitalization, Miss Mercuri found
a good job, away from the hospital. She was permitted to
work during the final month of her stay. Her doctor continued seeing her regularly, three evenings a week. Despite a
great degree of tension, she was able to negotiate this difficult transition period and worked out her personal affairs
regarding debts, finding a suitable place to live and re-
establishing old acquaintances. Arrangements were made for
her to continue treatment with her hospital doctor upon whom
she was quite dependent.

     By discharge time, after a year of hospitalization, she
demonstrated significant strength and determination to function in a useful, satisfying fashion. She was to continue
on her drug regimen of Tofranil 75 mg daily, and
Thorazine 25 to 50 mg at bedtime for sleep, instead of a barbiturate. Her hospital diagnosis was paranoid schizophrenia;
her research diagnosis was emotionally unstable character
disorder, with hysterical features.

FOLLOW-UP

     Miss Mercuri lived at a woman's hotel after discharge,
where she remained for five months, and then moved to a coed
residence. She held two secretarial jobs, one for eight
months, quitting just before she was to be fired, and another
for seven months from which she was fired, both times because

of tardiness. She had an intense year-long love affair with
an obviously inappropriate man, and gained considerable
weight from "compulsively eating candy bars." Her medication
was maintained at Thorazine 25 to 100 mg daily and Tofranil
75 to 100 mg daily. Then, through the Department of Vocational Rehabilitation, she attended a training program, obtained a grade of "A" and found and held a responsible job
where she did excellent work and received several promotions,
even within the first year of employment.

When interviewed two years after her hospitalization
she was composed, verbose, charming and feminine. She was
highly fashionably dressed and seemed much improved in all
aspects. Twice a week she saw her same doctor and took
Tofranil 200 mg daily and Thorazine 100 mg daily (or Compazine 60 mg daily when she wanted to be in the sun; she burned
easily when taking Thorazine).

In the third year post-Hillside, she met a man whom she
dated and within a few months married. The stresses during
the months of courtship, relating with her mother and father,
making wedding plans, and her unmarried sister's pregnancy,
led to a considerable increase in tension. When she complained of panicky, shaky feelings, her doctor suggested that
she take Kemadrin. This relieved her akathisia which had
been misunderstood as anxiety. The Compazine dose was now
30 mg daily and the Tofranil 50 mg daily. By the close of
the third post-hospital year, her doctor was considering a
reduced number of visits and terminating treatment within a
year. He did not change or discontinue medication because
he wanted to provide every possible support during the early
adjustment phase of her marriage. Both Tofranil and Compazine were considered helpful and important in her maintenance. Her doctor felt that she had assumed her role as a
contributing member of the community; her interpersonal, work
and home relationships were characterized as "moderately"

gratifying.

An interview was held seven years after hospitalization. Married for the past four years, her relationship with her husband was constantly conflict ridden. She described him as insensitive and neither introspective nor giving. Their sexual adjustment was poor, with the husband having very infrequent sexual desire. They had been in joint weekly psychotherapy for approximately a year.

Under her regular psychiatric direction she had been taking Tofranil 75 mg daily and Compazine 5 mg daily for several years. However, after her move and change to a different psychiatrist, the medication regimen was changed to Tofranil 75 mg daily and Stelazine 5 mg daily. This regimen upset her stomach and made her sleepy. Thus all medication was discontinued after two months without immediate adverse effect. Then, after a year, she became pregnant and Librium 5 mg, sometimes increasing to 15 mg daily, was introduced. After the baby's birth, all drugs were discontinued because she was breast feeding. Whereas previously her mood swings had been rather muted, they became more frequent although of shorter duration at both the high and low ends. She described herself as being "almost manic-depressive and paranoid lately." During one such period she had a recurrence of suicidal ideation.

In summary, her major symptom remained her mood shifts, characterized by frequent wide swings, of moderate to severe intensity, frequently interfering with her functioning. Her social life was active and appropriate; her marriage, full of conflict and ambivalence. Her sustaining treatment was primarily psychotherapy, although ending drug treatment appeared to have exacerbated her mood swings.

COMMENT

Miss Mercuri's markedly disorganized life can certainly be attributed, in part, to her chaotic upbringing. Nonethe-

less, the key proximate cause for her various severe disor-
ganizations was her affective lability. Although her lability was often apparently reactive, at other times no cause
could be found.

The classification of patients whose major symptomatology and social ineffectiveness revolve about affective lability is very difficult. Their hysterical attitudes and
maladaptations do not clarify the situation. Some patients,
such as Reuter, look more like impulse-ridden adolescents.
Others, such as Mercuri, resemble manic-depressive disease
more closely, although clear evidence of prolonged mania or
depression is absent.

In terms of medication response, it is noteworthy that
she responded to Tofranil initially with affective stability.
However, with time and increased dosage her irritability and
impulse control became worse. To confuse matters, the medication was lowered with beneficial effects and then raised
with beneficial effects. Both affective stability and anger
occur as a response to Tofranil in such patients (9). Phenothiazine medication was used solely for her sleeping difficulty while she was in the hospital. Phenothiazines also
produce affective stability in these patients. However,
they often reject the emotional blunting produced by such
medication.

During after-care, the patient was able to develop a
career and marriage, with the support of continued psychotherapy, Tofranil and Thorazine. Interestingly, at one
point, while on Compazine, a period of akathisia was mistak-
en for anxiety. This particular treatment error is quite
common, and unless the doctor recognizes that treatment with
an anti-parkinson drug as a therapeutic test is indicated,
frequent vicious circles ensue. That is, the patient's "tension" leads to increasing the dose of phenothiazine, which
then leads to more "tension."

It is noteworthy that at age 34, the patient was still plagued by mood swings that apparently became worse with medication discontinuation. Recent investigations (19) support the utility of lithium in such patients, as a prophylactic mood stabilizer.

Chapter XIV

PASSIVE-AGGRESSIVE
CHARACTER DISORDER

Definition

The passive-aggressive syndrome is defined in the Diagnostic Manual as consisting of three subtypes believed to be manifestations of the same unspecified underlying psychopathology.

The passive-dependent type, characterized by helplessness, indecisiveness and clinging dependency, seems to be the final common pathway of a host of affective and cognitive disorders.

The passive-aggressive type is defined by the use of passive sabotaging mechanisms such as pouting, stubbornness, procrastination, inefficiency and passive obstructionism in the pursuit of aggressive ends. Again, this would seem to be the final common pathway of many conflicted states wherein the person wishes to behave aggressively and is blocked from doing so by either external circumstances or internal inhibition. In practice, this term is often used for the exploitative, egocentric personality whose behavior is not extreme enough to be considered sociopathic. These near-sociopaths appear to be attempting to attain a dependent niche without having to accept a subordinate role.

The aggressive type of patient manifests irritability, temper tantrums and destructive behavior in response to frustration. Again, an aggressive response to frustration appears in association with a wide range of trait constellations and does not seem to warrant syndromal status.

SEYMOUR RUMIN

PRESENTING PROBLEM

Seymour Rumin, age 23, was an unemployed draftsman. He described himself as lonely, frustrated and having nothing to do with the human race. "I always talk about suicide but haven't the courage to do it. Bright people threaten and carry out suicide. Stupid people only threaten it. I hate to put myself in the latter group."

Because he was anxiety-ridden obsessed with his intellectual and social inadequacies, hostile, highly resentful toward his parents, unable to have any social relationships and fearful of homosexuality, he entered Reichian analysis. Diagnosed by his analyst as having paranoid schizophrenia, he was seen in therapy, twice weekly, for 16 months. Over that time the analyst claimed "he achieved a reduction in anxiety...but no change in the failure of interpersonal relationships or feelings of inadequacy."

Mr. Rumin felt he made no improvement in analysis, remained angry, depressed and was determined to enter a structured, protective treatment situation which would prevent him from committing suicide, and where he could learn to relate with others; thus he sought Hillside's aid.

FAMILY

The Rumins were middle class, financially comfortable, and lived in a small, inexpensive apartment. They saved most of their money for future payment of their only child's law or medical education; a goal he seemed incapable of achieving.

The father, bright, gentle and warmhearted, in his early 60's, emigrated to the United States as a teenager and was in partnership with his brothers in a successful business. While he was unhappily married and wished to divorce his

wife, he felt a keen sense of responsibility toward Seymour
and would not disrupt the family. He desired a full, exciting life and wanted to participate in organizational activities but found he had to be home most of the time to mediate
quarrels between wife and son. He wanted to compensate
for the warmth and love his wife was unable to provide their
son. He evaluated Seymour fairly accurately; acting as his
employer he realized the boy was disturbed, not able to work
properly or earn his wages.

The mother, in her early 50's, also emigrated to this
country as a teenager. She was nervous, nagging, worrisome,
sickly and withdrawn. She and her son had a symbiotic, de-
moralizing, double-binding relationship where she would try
to anticipate his needs and do everything for him and then
reject him because he wasn't independent. She stated that
from his birth their interaction was an incessant struggle.
Inflexible in handling him because she knew no other way, she
openly rejected him, constantly referred to him as stupid and
angrily dwelled on his inadequacies and failings. With no
interests beyond her apartment and her son, she led a sadly
constricted life.

DEVELOPMENTAL HISTORY

Seymour was born normally, at full term, after his mother had an extremely painful pregnancy due to fibroid tumors.
Very colicky, active and discontent, he was a projectile vom-
iter until age two. However, he was well coordinated, walked
at ten months and spoke sentences at age two. Because he
could not toilet train rapidly enough to suit his mother, she
plied him with frequent enemas to help establish his bowel
habits. Always a disturbed, restless sleeper, Seymour often
had nightmares and awakened screaming.

Between the ages of two and four, temper tantrums were
common; he grew increasingly wild and did not get along with
other children. Thus, at an early age he was lonely and shy.

Because of his social problems, his mother entered him in nursery school at age three and a half. However, he came home with a high fever one day, and angered because it had not been discovered at school, she never allowed him to return.

At age five he entered kindergarten. He remembered being a misfit, biting other children's feet. His teacher described him as a restless daydreamer. In first grade he was wild and impossible to control; in second grade he became very quiet, cowardly and was bullied by the other children who called him names, such as "fag." As he progressed in school, his work was poor, and he became increasingly awkward, slow and poorly coordinated, whereas he had previously been fast and active. He reported that "mother beat me silly because I wasn't interested in school work." Throughout elementary school he had three friends whom he characterized as "wretches," just as he considered himself. "Everyone always told me, 'boy, are you stupid.'" He was alienated from most children and related to them by acting the fool. They responded by scapegoating and laughing at him.

From an early age Seymour remembered being sexually "aware." He slept in his parents' bedroom where he recalled a lot of "stumbling" going on. When he was 11, he was moved to the living room to sleep. While he refused to talk about any sexual experiences, stating that they were too disgusting, he did mention that he was attracted to other boys. At age 15, he accepted an invitation to a man's room; he refused to discuss the events that followed. At age 19, he began masturbating for the first time, after hearing other students talking about it.

He reluctantly revealed sexual fantasies concerning young children, and also mentioned occasional homo-

sexual fantasies concerning good looking boys wearing tight-
fitting dungarees. The only heterosexual experience he ever
had was necking with a female member of his therapy group.
He mentioned that he always felt different; that he was made
from "the wrong kind of material, neither man nor woman."
He felt he had to hide his body, especially from his mother,
or his freakish nature would easily be discovered.

Seymour recalled that in school he smelled something unpleasant and later realized it was himself; his mother bathed him infrequently. Also, he claimed that when she did
bathe him, she spent a lot of time washing his genitals.

During high school his grades dropped further and he
felt increasingly alienated from other students. He never
paid attention in class and his behavior was boisterous and
annoying. His few friends were usually four or five years
younger than he was. However, he became a good tackle on the
school football team and derived some attention and satisfaction from this.

Because of school redistricting, Seymour was forced to
change high schools in his junior year. At the new school
he was extremely isolated. His clownish behavior which had
previously elicited laughter, now brought out maliciousness,
with students pulling pranks on him and starting fights. After four years of high school he graduated with an academic
diploma in spite of a grade average just over 65.

In high school he developed some interest in art, and after he was rejected by several colleges, he decided to attend
art school, which he considered a testimony to his stupidity.
He attended several art schools, always doing poorly and getting into fights with other students. He took only selected
courses and therefore did not graduate with a degree. During
this time he felt that people were talking about him, and he
frequently thought he heard his name mentioned, followed by
laughter.

Feeling wretched, isolated and worthless, he first sought psychiatric help at age 19, at a psychoanalytic clinic. Diagnosed as an obsessive-compulsive, with homosexual features, borderline or paranoid schizophrenia, he was seen for 116 individual and group sessions. On psychological testing at the clinic he had an IQ of 100, but with considerable unevenness in function. It is not clear if this test score was a result of some temporary incapacity or of poor test administration because later testing at Hillside showed an IQ of 120. The clinic also reported that he showed "a definitely precarious hold upon reality, excessive guardedness and suspiciousness, inability to develop a close interpersonal relationship and a poor sense of independent identity."

The major benefit derived from this therapy was that it supported him so that he was able to complete his schooling. After leaving school, he withdrew from the clinic in order to enter the Reichian therapy discussed earlier.

Starting at age 21, and for the next year and a half, Seymour attempted numerous jobs, lasting from several days to three months. "I was supposedly a commercial artist, but I can't stand a menial position." Sometimes he was fired, other times he quit, usually because he was late for work, too slow, couldn't understand or couldn't perform the work. After this, he worked for his father's business, was always late and never earned the money paid him. With the failure of his analysis, he entered Hillside.

PRESENTING CHARACTERISTICS

On admission Mr. Rumin spoke like a character from an existential novel, in a fast, pressured manner. "There is no purpose in life. It's a colossal bore. There is no reason to exist. I refuse to be what I am." He was preoccupied with his IQ, and a conviction of his stupidity. Obese and unkempt, he was incessantly derogatory about himself and oth-

ers. "The stupid analyst tried to convince me that I'm adequate in spite of fifty million reasons I gave him to the
contrary. I have an inborn inadequacy, socially and intellectually. I'm such a wretch." While talking he constantly
fumbled with his belt buckle and fly. His affect was appropriate and he usually appeared dejected. He was obsessed
that he would be "guillotined" and could not even mention the
word; he also had a tremendous fear of dying. Ideas of reference were apparent, with constant feelings that others were
testing, talking and laughing about him in a derogatory fashion. However, he did not feel persecuted. While he had considerable insight into his problems, his judgment was markedly impaired.

COURSE AT HILLSIDE

All physical, neurological examinations and EEG's were
negative.

During much of his hospitalization, Mr. Rumin was inactive and isolated, spending his time alone, often sketching
self-portraits illustrating his helplessness and inadequacy.
In psychotherapy he remained totally preoccupied with overwhelming feelings of inadequacy, constantly demeaning himself. He intellectualized his feelings in terms of his "low
IQ." He continually demanded that he receive further IQ
testing. At the same time he insisted that if the tests
showed that he had an average IQ he would kill himself. If
the tests showed that he had an above average IQ he would
still kill himself since this only proved that the tests did
not adequately measure his type of mental defect. This was
plainly a no-win situation, so his therapist refused to have
him tested, claiming that acceding to Mr. Rumin's demands
for testing would be agreeing with him that his difficulties
were primarily cognitive rather than intrapsychic.

Mr. Rumin maintained his ideas of reference and on one
occasion punched his roommate when he misinterpreted the fel-

low's activities as actually being a test of his own IQ. He
had temper tantrums consisting of kicking furniture around
his room.

His hospital therapist played the role of an interested, punishing-rewarding parent. He reprimanded Mr. Rumin
for his childishness and obnoxious behavior and placed him
in a rigidly structured program, not allowing him to make
any decisions.

After ten weeks, with the failure of these therapeutic
attempts, he entered the drug program. The Wechsler IQ test
was administered as part of the drug study protocol. It was
agreed that the results of this test would not be told to
Mr. Rumin. Interestingly, he cooperated well in taking the
examination, protesting all the time of his severe mental
defect. Afterwards, he evinced no interest in learning the
test results. His full scale IQ was 120 with a verbal IQ of
125 and a performance IQ of 111.

On first evaluation he seemed to have a character disorder with marked lack of masculine self-esteem, severe castration anxiety and fear of death. He received Kemadrin
3.75 mg daily, raised 3.75 mg weekly, until a maximum of 15
mg daily was reached, as part of a Kemadrin evaluation project. For the next ten weeks he remained hopeless, nervous
and depressed, although slightly less isolated and more active. He felt there was no point to taking medication since
nothing could get him to accept his mediocrity.

After this period he received Thorazine 300 mg, raised
to 600 mg daily the second week, on the presumption that he
was a paranoid schizophrenic. He became slightly calmer,
but groggy, although he did not sleep well. Quite readily
depressed, he cried easily, felt frantic and destined to commit suicide. He incessantly ruminated, "It's a miserable
life and I feel like a moron."

After three months, in view of the continuing depression, Tofranil 100 mg daily, raised to 125 mg daily the second week, was added. Eight weeks later it was increased to 150 mg daily and six weeks later decreased to 100 mg daily. Three months later the Thorazine was reduced to 150 mg nightly, and the Tofranil to 75 mg daily as Mr. Rumin constantly complained of minor side effects.

Mr. Rumin attained a slight calming effect from the Thorazine and a slight increase in his ability to get involved with activities, possibly attributable to the Tofranil. Both effects were quite minimal. Very slowly he relinquished some complaints about his inadequacies.

On the other hand, social service was able to help his mother by stimulating interests and placing her in outside work, first on a volunteer basis and later in a paying job. This greatly helped to alleviate some of her boredom, unhappiness and obsessive concern with her son. The change in her status provided her with grounds for a different, more mature relationship with him, for there now was more to interest her than his inadequacies and failings. Thus, the family relationship improved somewhat.

Mr. Rumin's hospital diagnosis was paranoid schizophrenia; his research diagnosis was passive-aggressive character disorder, with a mild agitated depression, obsessional ruminations and sexual inhibition. After 14 months of treatment, he returned to live with his parents. Also he resumed psychotherapy with his former psychiatrist and was to take daily doses of Thorazine 150 mg, Kemadrin 7.5 mg and Tofranil 75 mg.

FOLLOW-UP

Mr. Rumin worked for his father for one year but then stopped, complaining that stockroom and selling duties were beneath him. Later he discontinued psychotherapy and medication, because he considered his therapist lacking in intelligence. Most of his time was spent at home, except for two

months at a Yoga camp. He was successful in controlling his
parents. Their home life centered around fulfilling his
wishes and needs. He resumed psychotherapy several times,
with several different therapists, once for a few months with
a "Jewish Scientist." He took Stelazine and then Prolixin,
neither of which helped.

In the third year after hospitalization, he consented
to a follow-up interview in order "to tell Hillside off."
Mr. Rumin was depressed, agitated, irrelevant, circumstantial
and ambivalent about everything. For example, "I have superior intelligence, but I don't really; my doctor harmed
me - no he helped me." His psychotherapist at the time,
whom he saw for a total of eight months, was the proponent
of rational-emotive treatment which consisted of violent,
argumentative attacks upon Mr. Rumin's self-defeating attitudes. He was readily converted to this point of view, although it didn't help him act in a more competent fashion.
He had returned to work for his father, pasting forms together, but felt (accurately) that no one but his father could
tolerate his poor work performance. He took some college
courses at which he earned a C, D and F, although he put in
considerable effort.

In the interview at the end of the third year, he was
much less hostile, but quite depressed and hopeless. He felt
he couldn't function and contemplated suicide. He had left
his rational-emotive therapist whom he felt had not been
helpful. His present doctor was treating him with ad lib
drug therapy, including Stelazine 8 mg, Librium, Dexamyl,
barbiturates, plus exercise therapy and hypnosis.

When our social worker contacted him for the ten year
follow-up, Mr. Rumin was extremely hostile and evasive, and
stated "I want to sever all ties with Hillside. The medication you gave me made me ill and destroyed my insides. Look
at what you did to (Pt. X) who **died**."

Over the past five years, Mr. Rumin had taken no medication nor had he been involved in any type of therapy. He
occasionally did free-lance art work, had received his B.A.
degree, and lived at home with his parents. He tersely refused to answer any further questions.

COMMENT

Mr. Rumin showed a pervasive passivity combined with an
active self-derogatory anhedonia. Although he continually
crucified himself, he was unable to accept any rational support, or if he could accept this support, he could not put it
to use. Somewhat atypical was the very early onset of his
disturbed behavior and social alienation, possibly attributable to a lag in development reflected in a hyperkinetic behavior disorder. In interaction with his mother's intrusive-
ness and domination, this may have led to vicious ineffectual disciplinary circles ensuing in further damage to his
crippled self-image.

It is difficult to distinguish clearly such patients
from those called pseudoneurotic schizophrenics, pseudoschizophrenic neurotics, etc. The massive socio-sexual inhibitions, damaged self-esteem, and dependent trends seem central but are not overlaid with obsessional and hysterical
maladaptations.

Mr. Rumin's sensitive, depressive, referential reactions
were misinterpreted as signs of paranoid illness. Medication
is useful only to the degree that the features of retarded or
agitated depression are manifest.   However even when the
medication helps this dysregulation, the chronic personality
distortions remain refractory to treatment. This patient also presents, all too well, the frequent flight from one form
of therapy to another, in the vain hope that something will
work. Such patients often become demoralized and chronically
parasitic.

Mr. Rumin's outcome, although grim, did not reflect repeated psychotic episodes and social or cognitive deterioration. Given the protective atmosphere of his home, he was able to remain in the community. It is unclear to what degree this protective atmosphere stabilized him in a parasitic role. Without this protection it is conceivable that he might have been forced to mobilize his resources and make the best of his abilities. It is also possible that he may have found it easier to become permanently hospitalized.

JOE DAHLL

PRESENTING PROBLEM

Joe Dahll, an unmarried accountant, was obese, balding, unattractive and older-looking than his 32 years. He was thoroughly dissatisfied with himself: his compulsive eating, obese appearance, inability to direct and apply himself, loneliness, feelings of inferiority and inadequacy. He had difficulty sleeping, was frightened of being alone in the dark, thought obsessively about his dead mother and visualized people in coffins. After two years of unsuccessful psychotherapy, he applied to Hillside.

FAMILY

Mr. Dahll was the youngest of three children of a very poor, religious, immigrant Jewish family. The mother was uneducated, domineering, controlling and overprotective, approaching the classical stereotype. Her only interest was raising her children. Ceaselessly, she attempted to supervise everyone's activties, making life wretched with her constant nagging. She was obese, suffered from Parkinson's disease and died when Joe was 20.

The father had no formal education, was weak, unemotional, disinterested and a poor provider. He held many different menial jobs in the clothing industry. Emotionally he had no ties with his son and barely talked to him. Shortly after his first wife died he remarried and forced Joe to move from the home.

The sisters, five and ten years older than Joe, had little to do with him, leading fairly successful lives of their
own. Joe felt that because his mother was unsuccessful in
controlling her sociable and assertive daughters, she concentrated her efforts on him.

DEVELOPMENTAL HISTORY

Joe was born normally, at full term. The mother claimed
that her Parkinson's disease started during this pregnancy
and intimated that it was Joe's fault. No early developmental history was available.

His earliest memories were of the neighborhood synagogue
which he attended daily with his father, for 16 years. He
attended religious rather than public school, from age five until 15, from 9 A.M. to 7 P.M. daily. During these years he was
never allowed to do anything he wanted, as his mother forced
him to accede to her control in all his activities. For example, she arbitrarily forbade him to go to the movies or to
listen to the radio. Because of his school hours, he could
not play with neighborhood children, and he disliked the unfriendly children and punitive teachers at the religious
school. For years he pleaded to attend public school and finally, at age 15, his mother permitted him to change schools.

The three years at public school were his happiest. He
had no difficulty with the work and made several friends.
At 16, he found work as a messenger, 12 hours weekly, and after that held odd jobs in the garment industry. During these
years his mother became increasingly sick. Joe felt guilty
and half wanted to care for her, but also wanted to enjoy
himself.

Upon graduating from high school at 18, he entered a
city college. Disappointed that the atmosphere was not as
protective as in high school, he felt dependent and isolated,
with no one to support him. The guidance and direction he

desired from his father was not forthcoming, nor was there
help from anyone else. Afraid and shy, he wanted to meet
girls but didn't know how to go about it and thus never dated.

   At college he changed his course of study three times
because of poor grades and fear of failure. During his junior year his mother died; though he missed her, he felt
freer and better able to concentrate. Shortly after her
death, his father remarried and forced him to leave the house.
This hurt Joe for he couldn't understand his father's action
and still wanted to establish a close relationship with him.
He went to live with a friend but felt imprisoned by this
person's prohibitions and regulations. Later, he moved to
the more comfortable home of an older couple. However, his
bleak personal life and keenly felt loneliness were increasing.

   At 24, he was drafted, and although he hated the army's
regimentation, found great comfort in the ordered predicta-
bility it afforded. During his stay in the army he began to
masturbate but felt shameful and guilty about it. While interested in women, he had never discussed women, dating or
sex with anyone, nor pursued any heterosexual experience.

   After discharge from the army, he returned to college
and finally graduated at age 27, with many extra course credits. He worked as an accountant, hated the work, and disliked his boss who did not provide the guidance Joe wished.
Mr. Dahll came late for work, dressed sloppily and hoped to
be fired, but unhappily, was unsuccessful in fulfilling even
this desire. Finally, at age 30, his sister persuaded him
to seek help at a mental hygiene clinic because of his long
standing, constant unhappiness.

   At the clinic he was diagnosed as having an anxiety neurosis and treated for two years with weekly private and group
psychotherapy. Repeatedly he made efforts to overcome his

social inhibitions but regularly reverted to his self-defeating isolation. Both Mr. Dahll and his therapist felt that
he needed a structured total milieu to help him overcome his
problems; he therefore applied to Hillside.

PRESENTING CHARACTERISTICS

Mr. Dahll was calm, quiet and cooperative. However, he
ate compulsively, chewed his fingernails, felt guilty about
his twice daily masturbation and constantly demanded direction. His facial expression was of timidity and pleading,
his mood of depression, anxiety and hopelessness, and he exhibited some psychomotor slowing.

COURSE AT HILLSIDE

The results of all physical, neurological and EEG examinations were negative. On the Wechsler-Bellevue he attained
a full scale IQ of 123, with verbal and performance IQ's of
122.

Mr. Dahll adjusted very well to hospital routine, usually kept to himself and was calm and quiet. In psychotherapy
he constantly expressed strong feelings of inadequacy and
self-deprecation.

After five unrewarding months of intensive individual
psychotherapy, he was placed in the drug program and received
Tofranil 75 mg daily with weekly increments of 75 mg daily
until a total dose of 300 mg daily was reached. After a week
he was described by himself and ward staff as more preoccupied and depressed. Initially, he complained of laziness,
sleepiness and difficulty in concentrating; he continued his
obsessive, self-derogatory ruminations and did not socialize.

However, after a month on Tofranil he felt he could cope
better and think more clearly. His compulsive nail-biting
had stopped and masturbation had decreased to once every other day. He felt less depressed. However, he was very sluggish and sleepy and because of it, after six weeks Tofranil
was reduced to 150 mg, then 75 mg and leveled at 37.5 mg dai-

ly. On this small dose he initially seemed to do well, smiling, participating in activities, and showing more enjoyment. However, after four days on the lowered dose, he complained of dizzy spells and inability to concentrate. After two weeks on the lowered dose he was sleeping poorly and his compulsive masturbation and depression had returned.

In two more weeks, with the same complaints, his doctor felt that adjunctive Compazine 30 mg daily, would help his presumed schizophrenia. His sleep and depression improved, but he felt apprehensive and still had trouble thinking and concentrating. All medication was discontinued three weeks later because his doctor felt it was interfering with his responsiveness. Once again he seemed more active, socialized more easily, stopped his compulsive eating and nail-biting, and seemed better able to cope with his problems. After nine months of hospitalization the staff considered that Mr. Dahll was unlikely to make further gains and discharge plans were made.

The hospital considered a diagnosis of inadequate personality, but his treatment refractoriness finally led to a diagnosis of chronic undifferentiated schizophrenia. The research diagnosis was passive-aggressive character disorder, passive-dependent type, with obsessional and depressive trends and socio-sexual inhibitions.

FOLLOW-UP

After discharge Mr. Dahll returned to live with the older couple with whom he had been living for the previous ten years, and resumed working at the odious accounting job. Also he returned to his psychoanalytically-oriented group, and individual psychotherapy, three times a week. Shortly, he was masturbating, eating and biting his nails compulsively. He socialized only with two women he met while at the hospital and visited his sister twice weekly. After the third post-Hillside year, he discontinued psychotherapy, having

made no progress. On medical examination he was found to be
severely diabetic. There had been no indications of diabetes, with repeated negative urinalyses, during his hospitalization. Over the next seven years he had no further hospitalization, but felt unimproved, chronically ill, depressed
and unable to work or socialize adequately. He received no
further psychotropic medication after hospitalization.

COMMENT

Mr. Dahll presents a picture of massive socio-sexual inhibition and frustrated dependent yearnings. Of interest is
the fact that at one point, five months after entering Hillside, he showed some characteristics of a retarded depression, insofar as his chronic complaints of inadequacy and
self-deprecation became associated with apparent psychomotor
slowing. Although initially he responded negatively to Tofranil, after a month on high doses his mood was definitely
improved. Nonetheless he maintained complaints of sluggishness and sleepiness. We now know that such complaints can
often be dealt with by giving the Tofranil in a single dose
at night, rather than spread out during the day. The sedative
effects of tricyclic antidepressants and the phenothiazines
come on within one to two hours after taking the medication;
the antidepressant and antipsychotic effects of these compounds are long-lasting, so giving the medication in a single
dose at night capitalizes upon their soporific effect and at
the same time markedly reduces side effects experienced during the day. However, at the time, this medication practice
was not known, and instead medication was reduced. Again,
the diagnosis of schizophrenia led to the unsuccessful attempt at treatment with phenothiazines.

It is questionable whether such patients are typologi-
cally, or qualitatively, different from the patients referred
to as pseudoschizophrenic neurotics. They share the same
basic characterological difficulties in that they have

chronically low self-esteem, are obsessional, incapable of developing a clear approach to managing their lives, wish to make social contact but are unable to develop mechanisms for attracting favorable social notice, seem dominated by severe dependency wishes and separation anxiety. What clinical distinction there is between these individuals seems to relate to the magnitude of their affective disorder and subsequent disorganization. Certainly the utility of drugs in these patients depends entirely upon the manifestation of affective disorder; the psychotropic medications are unable to promote characterological change by themselves. It remains open to study whether they can promote characterological change when used as an adjunct to other therapeutic methods.

Chapter XV

HYSTERICAL CHARACTER DISORDER

Definition

One patient group causing grave problems in clinical management is comprised of characteristically labile, episodically agitated, erratic, unpredictable, manipulative, tense and histrionic patients. They are usually rational, relevant and coherent, although they express occasional paranoid and hallucinatory verbalizations that often lead to a diagnosis of psychosis. They may act panicky and frightened to the point of suicide and several minutes later affably laugh with others. Their therapists readily become emotionally involved and are frequently frustrated and perplexed by their inability to predict or modify the patient's behavior. The patients express great investment in their doctors and psychotherapy, endowing them with miraculous potentialities. They maintain a high degree of interaction with others, being at times sociable, friendly and supportive, at other times disturbing, hostile, argumentative and demanding, and yet again pleading for help and direction.

These patients dramatically express their intolerance of medication side effects. Because of their lability, there is much uncertainty as to the effectiveness of medication, so that they tend to receive long treatment courses before drugs are found to be ineffective. However, if the patient responds with somatic complaints, medication is usually terminated promptly.

One clinical feature of predictive value and theoretical import is the marked relationship of their symptoms to environmental impact. Unlike depressed patients who may increase the vigor of their complaints in the presence of psychiatric staff, in an attempt to coerce a maximum curative effort from them, but who remain inactive or unproductively agitated when not under staff observation, this group of refractory, hysterical patients may appear in good spirits when apparently unobserved by staff, engage in social games and gossip pleasantly with others, even shortly after an explosive affective display. The key issue may be histrionic role-playing and symptom imitation. In other words, these patients' symptoms may not be the direct external manifestations of intolerable affective states, but rather may be environmentally oriented, learned, manipulative devices. Agitation, depressive, delusional and hallucinatory complaints in this group are not the same as similarly labeled phenomena in other patients.

Interestingly, the conversion reactions of the 19th century, as described by Charcot, Freud and others, consisted mainly of pseudoneurological syndromes such as convulsions, anesthesias, paralyses, blindness, deafness and dyskinesia. These behavioral syndromes were noted at a time when hysterical patients were housed in hospital wards along with epileptic patients. Hysteroepilepsy may well have been an imitative artifact of exposure.

It is frequently stated that classical grand hysteria is no longer seen, while the diagnosis of schizophrenia has become more and more prevalent, and atypical or pseudoneurotic schizophrenias are widely reported. Since the knowledge of schizophrenic behavior is widespread via books, TV and movies, and it is common practice to house all patients with emotional disorders together, we believe that hysteroschizo-

phrenics are being produced in much the same fashion as the
19th century hysteroepileptic.

The differential diagnosis of hysteroschizophrenia from
true schizophrenia presents knotty problems. The major distinguishing feature would seem to be a variant upon the well
known hysterical phenomenon, la belle indifference. Hyster-
ics may have the most crippling disorders and yet not display appropriate concern or anguished emotional reactions to
their infirmities. If their leading motivation is to attain
the sick role, one can well understand this phenomenal
blandness as resulting from their natural satisfaction with
attaining their goal.

An analogous phenomenon occurs in patients with hysteroschizophrenia. Their attainment of the sick role is dependent upon imitation of extreme emotional distress, including
psychotic symptomatology. Therefore, in the initial stages
of disorder, there is, rather than la belle indifference, a
histrionic accentuation of numerous affective and psychotic
features in a confusing jumble. However, once the patient
is adjudged psychiatrically ill, as by hospitalization, one
is struck by the marked fluctuations in psychiatric status
and by the patient's apparent indifference to the content of
his expressed preoccupations and delusions. For instance, a
schizophrenic may express the belief that the food is poisoned and promptly give up eating. A hysteroschizophrenic may
express the same belief and then eat with good appetite a
half-hour later. Similarly, a schizophrenic who expresses
suicidal ideation, because he is convinced that his persecu-
tors are about to close in on him, is in an extremely dangerous state and must be kept under constant observation. His
affective state remains constant - fear and agitation. A
hysteroschizophrenic may express the same delusional content
and then, when away from the immediate observation of professional staff, engage in conversation and banter with other

patients. Marked fluctuations in symptomatic behavior, depending upon their impact on the environment, are common with
hyseroschizophrenics. Furthermore, these patients frequently resort to the use of sedatives, intoxicants, hallucino-
gens, narcotics and stimulants, thus further obscuring their
status.

These patients have a tendency to become mute under
close questioning. This passive-aggressive maneuver is often
inaccurately referred to as catatonic, or micropsychotic.
The diagnosis of histrionic reaction is difficult to defend
in the face of skepticism among colleagues as to one's diagnostic acumen. The apparent fluctuations in states of con-
sciousness that occur with this illness should prompt a neurological and electroencephalographic investigation (although
in attempting to make the differential diagnosis one must
bear in mind for example that petit mal epilepsy can coexist
in the same patient with a hysterical character disorder).

This hysterical character disorder grouping was reintro-
duced into American nosology by DSM-II as "hysterical personality, histrionic personality disorder." However, the category also includes the previous diagnosis "emotionally unstable personality," thus obscuring a valuable distinction.

RITA FESSER

PRESENTING PROBLEM

Miss Rita Fesser, age 21, came to Hillside because her
life had become totally disorganized. Four months earlier
she had decided to live away from home, since living with
her parents made her intolerably irritable, tense and angry.
But, feeling incapable of either working or going to school,
she sulked in a rented room, reading, crying or brooding.
Her sleep pattern was completely disrupted; she would stay
up half the night waiting to get sleepy after taking five or
six Seconals, and then would sleep through most of the next

day. Her food habits were extraordinary; she was obsessed
with her state of under or overweight and alternated between
starving and gorging herself. To counteract eating huge
amounts, and to allay possibilities of constipation, she took
a dozen cathartic pills daily. One night, after taking a
heavy dose of Seconal, she had frightening, misinterpretive
experiences where she thought a woman neighbor looked like a
man, a newspaper resembled modern art and another neighbor
looked like a monster.

Although she was in psychotherapy three times weekly,
her life became increasingly unbearable. She sought hospitalization at Hillside, against the advice of her therapist
who saw it both as an attempt to flee from a sexual transference, and an attempt to get support and care, rather than
make an independent adjustment to life.

FAMILY

Rita was the second of two girls born to a lower middle-
class urban Jewish family. Both parents were immigrant Euro-
peans in their 40's. The father worked hard as a tailor all
his life. He left important decisions and discipline to his
wife. An even-tempered, soft spoken man, he would be infuri-
ated only when Rita was rude to her mother.

Rita had frightening sexual thoughts about her father,
forcing herself to think of him only as a "neutral person
and not as a man." His presence was upsetting to her, especially when they were alone together, "because he would
sit in a chair and move his legs up and down."

Mrs. Fesser was exclusively involved with her husband,
family and food. She felt that Rita's problems would be
solved if she ate properly.

Rita felt rage and loathing toward her mother and blamed
her for her unhappiness. She pictured her as being concerned
with only two things in life: that her daughters should eat
more and that they should not cost any money.

Rita's sister, older by three years, was very intelligent, insightful and led a successful, independent, useful life, apparently despite her upbringing.

DEVELOPMENTAL HISTORY

Rita, born normally at full term, was a very fat baby. When she started walking she became active and quite thin. Mrs. Fesser constantly plied her with food, but she remained skinny. While she was vigorously and successfully toilet-trained early, she refused to be weaned and nursed a bottle until three and a half, when she had her tonsils removed. Sucking became very painful, so that she was suddenly forced to drink from a glass. This unpleasant episode marked her first memory.

Rita was the family pet and displayed for her cuteness, but she was a rebellious child at home, and always fought with her mother. She complained that she was raised in a repressive, inhibited atmosphere and was taught that only the intimate family circle offered protection from a hostile outside world. While she considered herself lonely and isolated, she had a continuing close relationship with three friends.

At school she was meek and compliant, although envious of those who were rebellious and delinquent. An excellent student, she also was always interested in ballet and wanted to study the dance at age nine. Her parents refused this, ostensibly because she was too skinny, but Rita felt the real reasons were their reluctance to spend extra money for lessons, and also her mother's disgust at the sexual connotations of dancing. At age 12 she finally was allowed to take lessons but was discontent with her teacher. She wished to attend a more prestigious, expensive school, but the parents' borderline financial situation prohibited this. Extremely resentful concerning this entire ballet episode, she later announced that if her parents had more willingly spent money

on ballet lessons when she first requested them, there would
have been no need for her eventual hospitalization and the
accompanying expenses which consumed their entire life savings.

Rita learned about menstruation from a book her mother
obviously left around. At age ten she remembered being uncomfortable when her breasts began developing, and although
her sister tried to explain what was happening, embarrassment prevented any open discussions concerning sex. Menarche
was at age 11 and her periods were extremely painful, sometimes necessitating Demerol injections.

At age 13, Rita started wearing lipstick and playing
kissing games at parties. At age 15 she developed a crush
on a fellow camp counsellor. Though she never dated this
boy and even ran away when he once asked her to dance, she
was for the first time inspired to gain weight in order to
be more attractive to him. Between ages 16 and 18, she dated
one or two other boys occasionally, but allowed no kissing or
other sexual intimacies.

She attended a scholastically outstanding academic high
school where she did superior work and was editor of the
school newspaper. Her primary interests were in mathematics,
creative writing and ballet. During summers she was a camp
counsellor; during winters she held various office jobs and
also tutored in English, French and mathematics, working successfully at all these jobs. She graduated from high school
with honors at 17, and entered college.

Rita dated the start of her trouble to her 18th summer,
after her first year at college, where she did excellent
work. She decided to study history at summer school, and
during the course was vividly impressed with how peoples and
countries hated each other. Her mother's early teaching that
the outside world was a hostile, dangerous place appeared
true. Also at this time her sister graduated from college,

moved away from home and went on a two month tour of Europe,
marking the first long separation between the two close sisters.

When Rita returned to college she started having increasing difficulty concentrating because she obsessively
ruminated about the state of the world and her dissatisfac-
tion with herself. She decided to leave college to study
ballet seriously, supporting her lessons by clerical work.
Convinced that a ballerina must be thin to dance well, she
became preoccupied with her weight (120 pounds, height 5'7"),
diets, calories and nutrition. Within a few months she diet-
ed down to 95 pounds, but became too weak to work or dance
and had to stay home. She became amenorrheic, felt hopeless
about life, depressed, withdrawn and talked dramatically of
suicide. Soon she started bouts of food gorging, overeating
until she was sick, followed by compensatory periods of star-
vation.

Her mother finally insisted on psychiatric consultation
which resulted in a recommendation for hospitalization. Rita
applied to Hillside but for unknown reasons did not follow
through with admission procedures. Instead, she presented
herself at the emergency room of a municipal hospital and
was hospitalized on the psychiatric unit. Her behavior at
the municipal hospital was marked by extreme manipulativeness. She demanded large amounts of barbiturates, tranquilizers, laxatives and vitamins, all of which formerly had been
prescribed by her family doctor. She flouted rules and demanded special privileges and extra time with her therapist.
A successful manipulator, she managed to have many of her demands fulfilled. Her behavior improved slowly and after nine
months she requested release. Following release she returned
to her parents' home and appeared to be doing well for several days, at which time her therapist took a planned one-week
vacation. During this week Rita became increasingly anxious,

depressed and hopeless. On the night prior to her therapist's return, she swallowed ten 100 mg Seconal and 36
400 mg Equanil, "in order to sleep until my doctor comes
back tomorrow." Her parents found her comatose, and she was
admitted to a city hospital for three months. She made more
rapid improvement this time but still remained infantile and
dependent upon her therapist and the hospital. It was extremely unusual for a patient to be kept longer than one
month on this rapid turnover unit, and it attested to Rita's
attractiveness, intelligence and the interest she evoked
that she remained there for one year. It was only under
threat of state hospitalization that she mobilized and made
plans to return home. Her diagnosis at this hospital was
schizoid-hysterical disorder with paranoid and obsessive-
compulsive features.

She returned to her parents' home at age 20, where she
remained a month before finding a room to rent, and continued in psychotherapy for the next five months. The events
during that period, leading to her hospitalization were discussed earlier.

PRESENTING CHARACTERISTICS

Rita was very attractive, tall and slender with long
dark hair, big black saucer eyes and porcelain skin. She
was obsessively concerned about her weight, eating habits
and medications. The first day at Hillside she refused to
remove her raincoat, embarrassed about her "ugly fat." Later, she dressed only in black pants and shirt buttoned
close under her chin. Her mood changes were abrupt and un-
expected; occasionally she showed flattened affect, but more
often she was emotionally labile, histrionic and melodramat-
ic, rapidly vacillating between tears and smiles. She spoke
freely but the content was so loose, with a mixture of memories, intellectualizations and superficial interpretations,
that sometimes her thoughts were difficult to follow. At

times she expressed vague ideas of reference, in that she
felt people were looking at her and judging whether she looked too fat, or was smart or stupid. She showed poor judgment
on psychological tests and in her ability to organize her
life.

COURSE AT HILLSIDE

All physical and neurological examinations were within
normal limits except for three EEG's, taken while Rita was
receiving Tofranil, which all showed some paroxysmal slow
wave activity. On the first administration of the Wechsler-
Bellevue, she attained a full scale IQ of 131 with a narrow
range of scores. On re-administration several months later,
she attained a full scale IQ of 144, again with a very narrow range of scores.

Rita seemed to form a good relationship with her first
Hillside doctor, a woman. The initial treatment plan was to
go along with her desire to diet, as long as her weight remained appropriate. Her doctor prescribed Dexamyl, vitamins,
smaller doses of laxative and Seconal for sleep, along with
supportive psychotherapy. On this regimen Rita's anxieties
about her diet were somewhat alleviated, and exploratory psychotherapy seemed fruitful, with discussions of her rage toward her mother and feelings about herself. She was hopeful,
cheerful and enthusiastic about her activities. But she became upset and began compulsive eating after one month, when
her doctor left, although this eventuality was made clear at
the beginning of therapy.

When it became obvious that Rita would be content to remain in the cloistered comfort of the hospital the rest of
her life, her new therapist, also a woman, decided to change
the therapeutic approach after three months, since a supportive approach to therapy seemed to be fostering dependence
and intellectualization. Most medication was withdrawn,
Dexamyl was forbidden, the laxative dose was reduced further,

and only a small amount of Seconal was permitted for sleep.
Rita responded with violent anger, gorged herself with food
and gained 50 pounds.

She derided the hospital for not providing her a special diet, and was equally furious that they did not physically bar her from going to the unit refrigerator. She refused to understand the rationale for the change in therapy,
although it was discussed at each session, and she actively
rebelled for the rest of her hospital stay.

After six months of an unrewarding stay at Hillside she
was placed on the drug program and received placebo. Immediately she developed dizzy, weak episodes, felt nauseated,
bloated and so unsteady that at times she had to hold on to
something to prevent herself from falling. At other times
she felt elated and irrationally optimistic. She complained
of feeling especially tired during the day. After six weeks
of placebo there was obviously no improvement. She then received Tofranil 75 mg daily, increased 75 mg weekly until
300 mg was reached. No effects were evident in the first
month. Dexamyl was then added to the Tofranil and she responded initially by feeling better, but after a month she
decided that these drugs were of no value. Tofranil was then
slowly discontinued over a two week period, and she suffered
an unusually severe withdrawal syndrome involving nausea,
dizziness and headache which responded to a short reintroduc-
tion of the medication. In summary, she showed no change on
placebo, Tofranil supplemented by Dexamyl, and received no
further psychotropic medication.

During her hospitalization she fell in love with another
patient, a young lawyer. When she became aware of her sexual
attraction toward him, she was very frightened and could consider their relationship only in lofty and poetic terms.

Rita greatly resented that, after eight months, plans
for discharge had to be made, and felt that the hospital owed

her further indefinitely prolonged treatment. She finally
accepted plans which included returning to her parents' home
and involvement in a structured day of creative and occupational therapy, and psychotherapy at an after-care clinic.
Her weight at discharge was 160 pounds. The hospital diagnosis was mixed, chronic schizophrenia with obsessive-compulsive features; the research department diagnosis was hysterical character disorder with anorexia nervosa and obsessional-perfectionistic trends.

FOLLOW-UP

After release Rita returned home and continued therapy
with her first Hillside doctor who now practiced at a distant
state hospital. Trips to this doctor involved ten hours of
travel, but Rita persevered, seemingly demonstrating an effort to seek help independently, but always within her self-
willed perfectionistic, self-defeating framework. She also
attended a summer college course.

Toward the end of her first year after discharge, she
learned that her lawyer friend had married. She took 30
Nembutal and 50 Deprol and was hospitalized, comatose, at the
original municipal hospital. She was treated with meprobamate 800 mg three times daily and discharged after two
months. Because she wore only loose-fitting tent-like
clothes, in order to cover what she considered her grotesque
fat, she refused to work. Within two weeks after discharge,
while her therapist was on vacation, she again attempted suicide. This time she was transferred, as promised, to a state
hospital where after eight and a half months of treatment
with psychotherapy, Thorazine 100 mg and Tofranil 25 mg daily, she seemed improved and was released. Her diagnosis at
the state hospital was schizophrenia, chronic undifferentiated type.

When released, she moved to an apartment with two girlfriends, worked as a clerk for three months, made another su-

icide attempt with 30 Nembutal and was placed in another
state hospital. Here she remained for three months and was
treated with Thorazine and intensive psychotherapy.

About this time she met a man with whom she became intimate and started taking Ortho-Novum birth control pills and
Thorazine 25 mg daily. She claimed that she felt good "for
the first time in my life." Suddenly, her eating and weight
problems permanently disappeared. She continued with the
Ortho Novum - Thorazine regimen for five years until she developed dizziness, increased anxiety and tension, irregular
menstrual flow and what she described as "pre-menopausal symptoms." Her doctor had her discontinue the birth control
pills and placed her on meprobamate which she later discontinued, claiming it had a masculinizing effect on her. Also
at this time she developed hepatitis.

Eleven years after her Hillside hospitalization, our social worker contacted Rita who was now 32. Immediately she
stated that she felt "dramatically better" than she had during the first five years of follow-up, admitting however, that
in the past two years something had gone wrong. She referred
to her marriage of six years as "a bad one." Still married,
she felt she and her husband were "immature and unable to respond to or benefit from each other's emotional needs." Unhappy and moderately depressed, she wondered whether she would
ever feel otherwise.

Prior to the hepatitis, she had worked fairly regularly,
but then became unemployed. For brief periods she saw a psychotherapist and took Thorazine to ease her anxiety. She applied for treatment at an outpatient clinic and was awaiting
acceptance.

COMMENT

Miss Fesser showed a marked anorexia nervosa syndrome
consisting of an aversion to food and a marked concern about
sexuality. As is often the case, she equated being thin with

being childish, asexual and dependent. However, being obese
also allowed her to regress to a dependent asexual role.   It
has been pointed out that anorexia nervosa syndromes may occur in a context of hysteria, obsessive-compulsive neurosis
or schizophrenia. With Miss Fesser, there were marked hysterical and obsessional-perfectionistic trends.

Noteworthy was her overall lack of response to medication. It has been reported that in dealing with the anorexia
nervosa patient, during periods of massive self-starvation,
treatment with phenothiazines is useful. However, this was
not true of this patient.

Interesting was her refractoriness to Tofranil since her
emotional reactivity seemed so depressive and dependent.   In
view of her extremely marked rejection sensitivity and mood
lability, the utility of MAO inhibitors in such cases remains
a promising possibility. Regrettably, these agents were not
available at the time of this patient's care. Also interesting is the possible value of contraceptive hormonal agents.

The central role of conflicts concerning sexuality and
dependence seems highlighted by her rather remarkable improvement when she was able to find a stable sexual-dependent
relationship. Certainly, the multiple hospitalizations and
serious suicide attempts that followed her Hillside hospitalization would lead one to expect the grimmest of prognoses.
Unfortunately, there is practically no long-term prognostic
data about such cases.

LIZ HAMM

PRESENTING PROBLEM

Liz Hamm, an unattractive, 41 year old, Catholic spinster, stated she had frequent auditory hallucinations which
instructed her to kill her psychotherapist and then throw
herself in front of a train. Two months before her collapse,
her psychiatrist of the past year, with whom she reportedly

had been necking, petting and having sexual intercourse, announced that he no longer loved her nor could help her, and must terminate treatment. Her thoughts and feelings about this were confused, certainly ambivalent, with wishes to hurt him.

While supposedly on her way to shoot her doctor with a gun she was carrying, she collapsed with "anxiety, depression, and the feeling that I just can't go on." She walked into a psychiatric hospital, told her story, asked for admission, and remained for two weeks. After admission she denied ever having a gun and stated that she lied about trying to kill her doctor in order to dramatize her need for help. She was diagnosed as a chronic schizophrenic and recommended for long-term treatment at a state hospital. Instead, she left the hospital in the custody of her brother who put her to work in his store.

After two months she was markedly tense, anxious and depressed, with a variety of physical complaints, including weakness, anorexia, aches and pains. She entered a local general hospital for a medical examination, the results of which were negative. They treated her with Niamid 150 mg daily and recommended that she seek state hospitalization or outpatient care. She again rejected state hospitalization and attended a hospital clinic where she was diagnosed chronic schizophrenic with obsessive-compulsive trends and treated with Marplan 40 mg daily and Thorazine 100 mg daily. When she began talking about suicide, she was placed on a short-term psychiatric ward for three weeks, and longer term hospitalization was again recommended.

She then applied to Hillside, but temporarily entered a state hospital. For six weeks she was treated with Marplan 40 mg daily, with no change in her condition, while her application to Hillside was pending.

FAMILY

The Hamms were a poor, old-world Irish family who never acculturated to America. Both parents were living and in their 80's. The mother, "a strict, domineering matriarch," alternated between berating and screaming at her children and treating them with cloying affection. Liz was always afraid of her mother and described most of her own activities as "sneaky" in order to avoid incurring the mother's wrath.

The father, a laborer, was passive and little information about him was available. Just preceding his daughter's hospitalization his health began to fail.

Liz was the youngest of five siblings. The oldest, a sister, age 55, was described as a "good-natured slob who was good only for having babies." She ran away from home to marry at age 14, while the mother was pregnant with Liz, and consequently there was tremendous upset in the home. The sister's husband was killed in a gangland murder and she moved back to the family home with her four children, when Liz was 11 years old. Later, she remarried and again left the home.

One brother was a "big bluffer who snows everyone, gambles and loses a great deal of money." A second sister was an alcoholic, divorced and a patient in a state hospital. Another brother was engaged often, but never married. Liz was closest with him.

DEVELOPMENTAL HISTORY

Birth and early developmental history were normal. Liz was "a pale, sickly child with nightmares and fevers." As she grew she became more of a tomboy and enjoyed sports and the company of boys. At school she was an average student. The family lived in a very poor area, and while Liz was choosy about her friends, she did have some and considered her school years as happy.

At age 14, she entered a convent to become a nun, but

was disheartened to find that it did not live up to her
idealistic expectations of goodness and morality. Greatly
disillusioned, she left after a year and a half and returned
to her home and public high school. For years after she felt
very guilty, believing that she had gone to the convent to
escape her domineering mother.

After graduating from high school at 17, she went to
college. The mother's rigidity and perfectionism forced her
to feel that she had to do very well and could never fail,
so that in her third year when she earned a D in French, she
quit college but never told her mother. Instead, each morning she left home to do volunteer hospital work and ultimate-
ly faked a diploma which she presented to her parents. She
professed tremendous guilt concerning this episode.

Menarche was at age 13 and she was frightened by it.
She frequently masturbated during childhood; her mother
caught her once and was furious. Miss Hamm considered masturbation "worse than stealing or killing." At age 20 she
discussed masturbation with a priest and then discontinued
until age 38, when she resumed with compulsive frequency.
She rarely dated or socialized in her teens. During her
20's, she had two opportunities to marry, but conflicting religions made it impossible. She never had sexual intercourse
until her reported affair with her psychiatrist at age 40.

Miss Hamm held several different jobs after leaving college, and then at age 25, became a secretary for 15 years,
until incapacitated. During her 20's she began drinking, increasing her reported intake to a pint of whiskey at a sitting. Often she took a few shots in the morning before work.
In her late 30's she combined whiskey with Ritalin, for an
additional "kick." She lived alone in a furnished room.

Frequently she had nightmares, with two recurring
dreams. One involved being lost in a tunnel with two nieces;
they escaped, while she could not. The other involved her

accidentally breaking a baby's neck. The constancy of these
nightmares made her fear going to sleep.

Miss Hamm felt that her illness dated back to adolescence, but she entered psychiatric treatment only at age 36,
on the advice of a physician whom she had contacted because
of severe occipital headaches, loss of appetite and weight,
nervousness, despondency, depression, crying spells, marked
fear and "queer feelings inside of me." She attended a clinic and was treated by one psychiatrist for two years whom
she felt enabled her to express some of her anger in therapy.
Later, there were frequent changes of therapists which upset
her. On two occasions she physically assaulted her doctors.

When she was 39, she made a suicide attempt by taking
12 Equanil after drinking liquor, but then immediately signed
herself into a psychiatric hospital where her stomach was
pumped, and where she was later treated with ECT (number unknown). After six weeks she refused further shock treatment,
which she said made her feel worse, and signed herself out.

She then attended another outpatient clinic and entered
therapy with a psychiatrist who, in retrospect, claimed he
was mistaken in treating her as an outpatient. He saw her
twice weekly. She claimed they were intimate, and she became entirely dependent upon him, calling him and his wife
at home and at work, and generally intruding and interfering
in his life. She interpreted his discontinuing their relationship after a year, when he left the clinic to enter private practice, as an intolerable rejection. She stated,
"He took away the incentive he had given me. In therapy
you're expected to fall in love with the therapist, but when
the therapist says he is in love with the patient, then that
is unusual and that is what happened with me. We had sexual
relations a couple of times at my apartment, but we did petting most of the time because of circumstances at his office.
My trouble is that I cannot stop loving him, and he said it

was making me more nervous and that we should stop. The whole thing was very mixed up when he said that he could help me as a doctor but not as a lover. I feel I love and hate him at the same time, and I want to hurt him professionally." After treatment termination her acute illness began.

PRESENTING CHARACTERISTICS

Once at Hillside, Miss Hamm did not seem particularly depressed. On the contrary, she presented a joking facade considered inappropriate by her doctor. Eventually this gave way to a flat voice and expression, and depression. She complained of being very mixed up, unable to pull herself together and stated, "People don't like me because I'm not very likable. I have to destroy myself because I have to be punished. I hear voices that tell me to destroy myself." When questioned about the voices she said she could not recognize them and that actually they were a mixture of voices. "Common sense tells me that they are in myself and that I am blaming others." When asked about visual hallucinations she compliantly said, "The last time I spoke to the voices they said they would appear to me." Also, she claimed she felt the presence of something in her room while she was asleep.

She was phobic about subways, movies, churches and anything that hemmed her in. Because she purportedly had sexual relations without being married, she claimed extreme guilt and self-condemnation. Later, she added, "I don't have a career or marriage and no one to love or love me. I have no social life and I feel I'll never change or be different. I don't feel as if I belong."

COURSE AT HILLSIDE

Medical and neurological history and examination were non-contributory. Her many somatic complaints were checked and all findings were negative. On the Wechsler-Bellevue administered at the beginning of her hospitalization, she attained an IQ score of 110, with a verbal IQ of 114, and a

performance IQ of 105. On retest six months later, her full
scale IQ was 119, with a verbal IQ of 124 and a performance
IQ of 107.

Once in the hospital, Miss Hamm's comic facade quickly
faded to depression, with flattened voice and facies. She
had numerous somatic complaints, including insomnia, for
which barbiturate sedation was only minimally helpful. Frequently, she announced she had auditory hallucinations predicting her death and demanding that she punish herself.
She would cower in a corner or thrash in her bed, imploring
the nurses to make the voices go away. However, there was a
superficial, unconvincing quality to her distress and a suspicious ease with which it could be dispelled. In the midst
of what appeared to be frenzied panic, she would suddenly
insert a flippant comment, lending a ludicrous air to the
situation.

In several well-written, flowery, literary letters to
her hospital therapist, describing her misery, she always added a joking postscript which belied the gravity of the content and added to the impression of play-acting.

Often she was whining and plaintive, markedly labile and
angry. She resented all hospital rules and compared them
with her mother's attitude toward her. With extreme sensitivity to criticism or rejection, she constantly demanded enthusiastic approval.

After two unrewarding months of psychotherapy and milieu
program she was placed in the drug program. Her first words
to the research psychiatrist were, "I don't want medication.
It frightens me. I begged for it four weeks ago and they
wouldn't give it to me then, why should I take it now?" She
mentioned that the only medication that had helped her in the
past was Marplan, and that she had Thorazine and Serpasil
which were of no value, and dextroamphetamine which made her
feel nervous and despondent. ECT made her feel terrified.

She proved extremely controlling concerning medication, demanding to be told what she would be given, finally taking it "only in her own way." Sometimes she refused doses at scheduled times and would consent to taking the medication hours later.

She received Tofranil and within two weeks showed a distinct improvement in her anxiety and a diminution of her demands. But this lasted only a few days, and then, in preparation for her doctor's holiday, she scratched her wrists with broken glass.

The following week she scratched her arm with a broken mirror. In therapy she was preoccupied with her ugliness and the rejections she was certain were forthcoming. She expressed concern about people using her and that other patients were getting better care than she. The voices came and went, her mood was very erratic and difficult to assess.

After a month in the drug program she was receiving Tofranil 300 mg daily and on the whole seemed to feel better and appear less anxious and nervous. But when the seventh week on Tofranil was "bad," she demanded that the medication be changed and claimed she heard voices again, was jumpy, jittery, depressed, and had periodic angry outbursts consisting of throwing furniture, books and magazines. Her doctor felt that her symptoms had essentially returned, so after ten weeks, Tofranil was reduced and then discontinued. After the discontinuation she claimed she was at her lowest ebb; she didn't know who she was and her memory "blanked out." Nevertheless, her doctor assessed her as improving after the medication discontinuation.

Because she appeared completely despondent, but yet was hyperactive and insomniac, her doctor considered her to be in a severe schizophrenic psychosis. Thorazine 600 mg and Kemadrin 5 mg daily, were begun a week after the Tofranil was stopped. After four days she was showing thickened

speech, unsteady gait and poor coordination, but seemed improved emotionally. Thorazine was rapidly increased to 1200
and Kemadrin to 20 mg daily. Over the next 2½ weeks, Thorazine was raised incrementally to 3200 mg. The side effects
gradually diminished. Her angry, self-defeating, challenging
behavior returned, but she no longer professed her terrible
sense of despair and despondency, and her mood seemed better
and more even. But then severe constipation, heartburn and
difficulty in swallowing became predominant complaints. While
her sleep improved and reports of hallucinations remitted,
she still felt staff members were talking about her. After
a month on Thorazine 3200 mg daily, she experienced several
days of severe diarrhea, some loss of sphincter control and
soiling which upset her considerably. She developed a sore
throat and a low white cell count which the medical consultant diagnosed as a benign neutropenia and not life-threaten-
ing agranulocytosis. Thorazine was reduced to 1800 mg daily.
A week later she still showed leukopenia and Thorazine was
discontinued.

The sudden discontinuation had no marked effect upon her
mental status, but she claimed she felt better than when on
medication. Two days later she made an unsuccessful attempt
to leave the hospital and claimed her auditory hallucinations
returned; she was again preoccupied with her relationship
with her former psychotherapist. Her professed hallucinations
and pattern of massive dependent demands leading to lack of
gratification, in turn leading to anger and confessions of
guilt and desire to hurt herself were virtually unmodified.

Two weeks after Thorazine was stopped her blood count
returned to normal. Thorazine 600 mg and Kemadrin 5 mg daily
were reinstituted, but only for five days, as the decision
was made to have her transferred to a state hospital, since
in eight months at Hillside she had made only minimal improvement, if any.

Immediately upon being informed of this decision, her
behavior and appearance suddenly normalized. To the aston-
ishment of the staff, this depressed, distraught, complaining patient became pleasant, friendly, cooperative, denying
all hallucinations and delusions. Although she verbalized
some resentment "at being pushed out the hospital," she conducted herself in a most good-natured way and made facile
arrangements for discharge. She refused the recommendation
for state hospitalization, as she had done prior to Hillside,
and persuaded her sister to invite her to join her family in
a distant city where she would continue with outpatient
care. Her hospital diagnosis was paranoid schizophrenia;
the research diagnosis was hysterical character disorder.
She was taking no medication at time of discharge.

FOLLOW-UP

Miss Hamm went to live with her family after discharge
from Hillside and entered outpatient treatment at a well-
known clinic, two or three times weekly. A report from her
psychiatrist read, "The situation was one of constant flux,
with the patient continually complaining of some of the original symptoms, mainly delusions and hallucinations of voices
and people. But it was never my conviction that these were
deeply entrenched, and I have the feeling that they were more
hysterical attention-getting symptoms. At no time did I ever
have the strong feeling that there was any specific break
with reality. There was always a deep sense of depression,
a constant threatening that life was not worthwhile and that
she had no reason to live, and a constant need to be reassured that there was hope and promise for her."

During the first year after hospitalization she had to
have orthopedic surgery, and after 14 months at her sister's
home, she had a minor misunderstanding with her niece. Miss
Hamm then became so upset, and her complaints became so dramatic, that she was hospitalized. She felt she could no

longer live as she was and did not know what decisions to
make. At the hospital she was diagnosed by the treating psychiatrist as having an agitated depressive reaction with severe psychoneurosis. Treatment information was unobtainable.

Within ten days she was discharged. She decided to move
from her sister's home to a boarding house in the same community. Slowly she felt happier and became quite friendly
with her landlady. During the second post-hospitalization
year she required a hysterectomy from which she recuperated
quickly. Although there was very little social life in the
community, and very few jobs available, she did find part-
time work for three months.

At this point she seemed so well integrated that her
therapy sessions were reduced to once a week, and she entered a secretarial school in another city for a year. Her complaints increased but she managed to work through any difficult situation.

Two days after she graduated from secretarial school, a
breast carcinoma was detected, and she immediately had a radical mastectomy. Emotionally she did very well postopera-
tively, and was characterized as a "model patient." After
the mastectomy, she finally found full-time work; she still
complained of feeling depressed, that she could not do the
job, and was unable to recognize that she accomplished a
great deal and was actually becoming independent. She never
admitted satisfaction in anything.

During the four years after she left Hillside she took
Thorazine 25 mg daily, and then became practically addicted
to Dexedrine 10 mg, twice daily. At one point she took 50
mg daily until her doctor refused to continue with prescrip-
tions. Each time she attempted to withdraw from Thorazine
completely, within two or three days she felt the need to resume it, in order to maintain a decided calm feeling.

She was able to weather the trauma of the deaths of her

father and two other fairly close family members, and three
serious surgical hospitalizations. Her only exacerbations
were in reaction to stormy interpersonal relationships with
unsympathetic relatives. The following excerpt from a letter she wrote in response to a follow-up questionnaire well
illustrates the flavor of Miss Hamm's personality.

"...In September we registered and I started a
year of constant studying, interesting people
and challenging situations. I've known loneliness at its worst, sleeplessness, even hunger;
yet if I had a choice, I would have done it over
again.....I found a room in a boarding house
which was cheap (it should be, I felt as if I
were living in a typical artist's garret, or in
a monastic cell). I adapted to it only because
I was and am able to make jokes about many of
the things that occur here. Though the kids are
much younger than I am, both here and in school,
I made some good friends. They are alert, keen,
silly, young, sometimes boring, mostly refresh-
ing. My second semester was more difficult than
my first; perhaps because I was carrying six subjects, perhaps because I started to feel below
par physically. I managed to keep up my grades;
problems at home cropped again, as did many others.

About a month or five weeks before finals, I
discovered a big lump under my right breast. I
somehow instinctively knew this meant "big trouble" and that night had a big battle with myself
as to whether to tell my doctor or not.

I felt if I had to have an operation, I wouldn't
graduate; the year had been too hard; if I was unable to graduate, there was no point to life again

without a decent future. So I said nothing to
anyone, and struggled on up till the week of
finals. I'd begun to feel a funny soreness, a
sickish feeling of pain. The day I finally
knew I'd passed the 100 word shorthand test
(which was my bugaboo) I called for an appointment, and saw the doctor the next day. Graduation was the next day, I'd hoped to be back.

Well, you can guess; he sent for the other
surgeon who confirmed his suspicions; and they
called in my psychiatrist because I refused absolutely to be operated on. (It was a tough
fight, but they won.) The tumor was malignant,
the doctor told me the night before. He was almost sure he would have to perform a mastectomy.
Everyone, including me was amazed at my calmness,
just as at the last operation. (This is beginning to sound like a novel.) Well, I warned you
you might be sorry! I guess you'll stop writing
that type of letter to anyone now........."

Ten years after her Hillside hospitalization, an attempt
was made to contact Miss Hamm. It was impossible to reach
her, but a brother was contacted. He could provide very little information, not having seen his sister for three years.
However, he did indicate that she was in fairly good health,
and living with a sister whose address he did not have. He
knew she was taking some sort of medication and that she
might be working part-time.

COMMENT

The primary diagnostic difficulty presented by Miss
Hamm consisted in her reports of hallucinations. Unfortunately it has become the practice of many American psychiatrists to automatically assume that such reports are equiva-

lent to a diagnosis of psychosis, in particular, schizophrenia.

The long standing sexual inhibition within a context of steady work and mild alcoholism, followed by the precipitation of her "psychosis" under a situation of peculiarly severe personal stress is ignored by this unthinking pathognomonic sign approach. Further, the superficial quality of her distress and the suspicious ease with which it was dispelled was noticeable both while she was in the hospital, and was commented on by her post-hospital physician.

Miss Hamm's lack of response to medication is quite typical of hysterical character disorders. I have pointed out (10,12) that this group is the most refractory of the numerous subgroups of schizophrenic, affective and character disorders to the effects of placebo, Thorazine and Tofranil. Further, the effects of such medications are probably, on the whole, deleterious, since they are often accompanied by severe somatic complaints and disruption of behavior. To make matters more confusing, these patients often both beg for medication and reject the use of it, as did this patient, and may show sharp improvements in their behavior that are easily attributed to the medication. For instance, Miss Hamm initially improved while on Tofranil and then mutilated herself in response to her doctor's forthcoming vacation. Similarly, although massive doses of Thorazine had a rather small effect upon her emotionality and complaints, nothing much happened when the medication was suddenly discontinued. Faced with state hospitalization she showed a most remarkable recovery.

Follow-up also indicated that this patient did not have a deteriorative psychotic illness, but if anything, remained remarkably stable in the face of considerable stress. Her past alcohol addictive trends were reaffirmed by her future habituation to dextroamphetamine.

I have discussed my conviction that many severe hyster-

ics, characterized by sexual inhibitions, role playing, loss
of role distance, strivings for stage center, and the wish
to be much "more" than themselves, may imitate psychotic
states in an attempt to gain the sick role (13). Such "psychoses" are unresponsive to anti-psychotic agents, although
temporary initial gains are common. When these patients have
their sick role unequivocally validated, as by surgery, their
equanimity provides a strong inference as to their central
goals.

Chapter XVI
PSEUDOSCHIZOPHRENIC NEUROSIS

Definition

The trend to segregate patients on the basis of some inferred psychopathological process and to divorce this cate-
gorization from the practical utility of prediction receives
emphasis in the labels "pseudoneurotic" or "pseudopsychopathic"
schizophrenia. Patients so labeled need not manifest exami-
national signs of either Kraepelinian or Bleulerian-defined
schizophrenia. The reasons for the assumption of a continuum between these states and classically defined schizophrenia
are not clear. It is meritorious to make the creative effort
necessary to describe a syndrome, but it is unwise for the
psychiatric community to accept such syndromes uncritically,
without clinical and statistical documentation.

Hoch and Polatin (7), who developed the concept of
pseudoneurotic schizophrenia, have stated that these cases
are frequently considered psychoneurotic by others, but,
since these patients are refractory to exploratory psychotherapy, they argue that there must be a basic difference in
psychopathology. Other postulated indicators of a continuum
with schizophrenia include eventual hospitalization and deterioration, an autistic and dereistic life approach, diffuse
ambivalence, inappropriate emotional connections and reactions, pan-anxiety, pan-neurosis, omnipotent attitudes, subtle thinking disorders, vague contradictory self-presenta-

tions, short-lived psychotic episodes and chaotic sexuality.

Unfortunately there are no normative data about the uni-
formity or incidence of these differential clinical signs.
Review of their case presentations fails to reveal a basic
homogeneity, but suggests, instead, a heterogeneous collection
of treatment-refractory patients. Although the originators
of this concept specifically state that they are not advocat-
ing a more refined classification, there is no doubt that the
impact of their approach has caused many patients to be labeled "schizophrenic" who would previously have been considered severe neurotics or character disorders.

One suspects that such diagnoses are used to maintain
the belief that exploratory psychotherapy is uniformly effective in psychoneuroses. If a neurotic does not respond, the
method is not at fault, the diagnosis is inaccurate. One can
avoid even the small loss of self-esteem by a missed diagnosis by calling all patients who are not grossly psychotic as
pseudoneurotic schizophrenics. If they do not improve, one's
diagnostic acumen is supported; if they do well, one's therapeutic skill is affirmed.

We consider the term pseudoneurotic schizophrenia a misnomer applied to extremely severe passive-dependent character
disorders with salient anxious, obsessive-compulsive and/or
hysterical, phobic-anxious symptomatology. To complicate the
phenomenology, these patients are particularly prone to the
abuse of sedatives and stimulant drugs, marijuana and LSD.
The heterogeneity of this group is attested to by the fact
that all classes of medications have some place in their
treatment, although no class of medication is particularly
effective. The minor tranquilizers are useful under conditions of anticipatory anxiety, the phenothiazines during su-
pervening agitated depressive states and the antidepressants
for periods of fearful withdrawal and depressive rumination.

Also they may be labeled schizophrenic because they develop referential ideas in association with their depressed states. This is frequently misinterpreted as a paranoid trend rather than as a reflection of the patient's self-deprecating attitudes which lead him to expect the same from others. Such patients then actively check to see if their worst fears are true, which makes them appear suspicious and guarded. Fish (4) has referred to these patients as pseudo-schizophrenic neurotics.

Although medication may relieve some distress, the burden of care for the pseudoschizophrenic neurotic falls upon the psychotherapeutic relationship.

IDA LAYTON

PRESENTING PROBLEM

Ida Layton, 27, was already a spinster. Her chronically unhappy life had arrived at a complete depressive impasse, and she cried copiously at the slightest provocation. In spite of the support of psychotherapy for the preceding two years, she felt she could no longer function. Both she and her psychiatrist decided that longer term intensive psychiatric treatment was necessary, and she applied for admission to Hillside.

FAMILY

Miss Layton was the third of six children, spaced two years apart. The Laytons were poor and the family was often on welfare.

The father was unable to work for prolonged periods because of manic-depressive illness. She described him as very intelligent, with a great awareness of himself and the world. On the other hand, he never expressed warmth or affection, had an explosive temper and often beat his children. When his illness was acute, he acted childishly and would sexually exhibit himself. He had three psychiatric hospitalizations for manic-depressive psychosis and finally died in a state hospital.

The mother, 16 years younger than her husband, was sloppy, nagging, insensitive, cold, apathetic and was hospitalized for "an emotional illness" for several months when Ida was 10. Rarely did she display emotions of any sort to her family. She had suffered a deprived life, being the product of both a broken home and severely disturbed parents. Her marriage was forced after she became pregnant when her future husband raped her. Extremely dependent upon her children, she made them feel very guilty for not being able to care for her properly, while she herself was unable to respond to any of their needs.

DEVELOPMENTAL HISTORY

Ida was born normally and spontaneously, when her mother was 25 and her father was 41. There was little developmental history available, except that she wet her bed until age four and sucked her thumb until age seven. She recalled being a sickly child with many allergies, chronic ear and kidney infections, all the childhood diseases, as well as scarlet fever, and a severe asthma attack during late adolescence.

At age six she entered public school and was a mediocre student during the elementary years. Very ill-at-ease, she always had difficulty making friends. Often she could not get along with her teachers, although she was never a disciplinary problem.

When she was ten, her father was hospitalized for a psychotic episode. At this time her mother also had a nervous breakdown and was hospitalized for a long period. Consequently, the four older children, including Ida, were placed in one public foster home, and the two youngest were in another. For six years, Ida remained at this home, with approximately 100 other children, ages six to 16. Ida never got along with any of them, and remained friendless. However, she did have a fairly warm relationship with the female

director of the home, who took a particular liking to her.
In fact, there was once talk of the director adopting Ida,
but the fact that she had two sons of Ida's age ruled this
out. Ida was a talented dancer and singer and suspected that
the director might have showed favoritism toward her because
someday she might bring fame to the children's home.

Mrs. Layton visited her children weekly but, unable to
support them financially, she was unable to bring them to
live with her. Ida disliked living at the foster home and
felt torn by having to remain there after visiting her mother.

Menarche was at age 13, which she was prepared for
through conversations with other girls at the home. During
puberty, she had crushes on two or three boys, especially a
supervisor at the home, but Ida refused to discuss this.
She stated that she never masturbated in her earlier years
but learned to do so as an adult; she considered sex dirty.

In the transition from elementary to high school at age
14, Ida saw a psychiatrist weekly for a period of one year,
but could not recall the reason. In high school she did
poorly in academic subjects, having difficulty studying and
remembering things. Thus, she switched to a commercial
course where she did very well, "I could do stenography end-
lessly."

At age 16, she returned to live at home after her older
siblings were working and could contribute enough to support
her and their mother. After graduating from high school at
age 18, she worked at an insurance company and attended evening college courses, accumulating 50 credits within four
years. She remained with the insurance firm for four years,
and when she finally requested a raise, they took the opportunity and fired her for being chronically late. Ida admitted arriving at work 10 to 15 minutes late daily, and after
her boss conferred with her about this, she tended to arrive

even later.

At home she was responsible for running the household, paying all the bills, and helping to provide for her younger brothers who did nothing to help. Her father was once again hospitalized and died when she was 21. She was ashamed of her home and angry about her mother's lack of concern and emotional distance.

Miss Layton's infatuation with one of the supervisors at the foster home caused her to find pretexts to return in order to see him. Aside from this, she dated and corresponded with a neighborhood boy who went to school in a distant state. Their relationship ended when she started pressuring him to marry her.

Within a short time after being fired from her first job, she found another as a legal secretary. As time progressed she became generally unhappy and stated that she would vigilantly listen to conversations, feeling that perhaps people were talking about her. Then she began to have uncontrollable crying fits, with a pervasive feeling of fear. After three months of feeling depressed, she became nauseated, dizzy, thirsty, and decided to go to a local doctor. He had her hospitalized for tests, which showed diabetes concurrent with a hyperthyroid condition. She was treated and released after about a month.

Upon release from the hospital, she changed her job again and worked as a secretary to a business consultant. She seemed to enjoy this new job, liked her boss, and earned a high salary. She was so insecure that she had to repeat everything said to her in order to make certain that she heard it correctly. Because of heavy work duties, she discontinued attending evening school. After work, she withdrew to her room, despondent and crying profusely. During this period, she shared her mother's bed.

Finally her mother couldn't tolerate her crying, en-

couraged her to seek psychological help, and Ida went to the
Board of Health. They placed her in therapy with a psychiatrist who diagnosed her as a pseudoneurotic schizophrenic
with paranoid trends, and treated her with psychotherapy and
Thorazine 400 mg daily, which made her feel "very stiff and
tense." At about this time her diabetic condition flared
when she went on uncontrolled eating binges, and she had to
receive emergency hospital treatment. Also at about this
time, her older sister became emotionally ill and the mother
went to stay with her, leaving Ida home alone. In psychotherapy she was withdrawn and found it difficult to talk.
The mother was advised to place her older daughter in a state
hospital and return home to care for Ida, but doing this did
not improve matters. The psychiatrist and Ida agreed that
hospitalization was imperative because of her emotional distress coupled with a complete inability to change her manner
of living, although she could still function at her job.

PRESENTING CHARACTERISTICS

Miss Layton was tall, well-proportioned, but rather unattractive. Always fastidiously groomed, she chose to wear
dresses while other patients dressed informally. She spoke
in a very deliberate, hypermeticulous and carefully articulate manner. Her speech was clear, concise and goal-direct-
ed, and no thought disorders were present. Usually, she was
at the brink of crying. Her expressive manner seemed remote, flat and questionably appropriate to her depressed,
moderately agitated and quite anxious mood. No suicidal
ideation was present. Her ideas were all coherent and related to the questions asked of her, which she answered in a
logical, progressive manner. Although her speech was voluble, she did not ramble. In fact, the only validation the
interviewing psychiatrist could find for making the diagnosis
of chronic undifferentiated schizophrenia was "the patient
appears to generate the aloofness of a schizophrenic, al-

though no unusual ideas could be elicited."

When asked what her main problem was, she responded, "Physically or mentally? It is all rolled into such a tight ball, I can't separate them. My problems are trust and honesty and jealousy." When asked if she felt guilty, she responded, "I am not free to disclose it to myself."

COURSE AT HILLSIDE

On physical examination, Miss Layton intermittently had sugar in her urine. She was placed on 60 units of NPH insulin daily and an 1800 calorie diet which she rarely followed. Radioactive iodine uptake was abnormally high (80%); therefore she was treated with oral radioactive iodine and her hyperthyroidism improved. Her blood sugar often ranged as high as 400 mg percent. Her EEG's were normal.

On the Wechsler-Bellevue she attained a full-scale IQ of 108, a verbal IQ of 108 and a performance IQ of 106. With the exception of the vocabulary and information scores at a superior level, all remaining subtest scores were markedly lower.

Miss Layton appeared aloof and snobbish and did not relate to other patients, remaining on the fringe of all activities. In therapy she slowly established a warmer relationship with her therapist, but complained that he was too kind and gentle with her. She easily broke into tears. Her diabetic condition ran an oscillating course because of her frequent dietary indiscretions. She had an intellectual awareness of this problem and professed a desire to work it out in therapy.

After six weeks of immobility, Miss Layton was referred to the drug program and placed on Thorazine 300 mg daily, increasing 300 mg weekly until a total dose of 1200 mg was reached, with Kemadrin 15 mg daily. Also at this time her psychiatrist was changed. Immediately she stated to her new psychiatrist, "I have a feeling that we will get along well together. I can tell, you will be firm with me." She appeared more relaxed, active, with heightened affect, a lessening of anxiety and depression, and she discontinued overeating; her mood was even. Her doctor noted that she was angry, wanting to tell everyone to go to hell, and complaining that staff didn't take care of her needs. Also, she reported feeling stiff, uncoordinated, with a sense of functioning mechanically, and diminished visual acuity. Occasionally, she had a frightening impulse to slap somebody, and when not actually conversing with other women, felt they might be discussing her in a catty fashion.

After six weeks on Thorazine, her doctor reported that she was quite friendly, realistic and her mood had improved, but that her evenness of mood was interfering with her psychotherapy, preventing "emotional expressiveness." Thus, the Thorazine was reduced to 900 mg daily. After two weeks on 900 mg daily, she claimed she wasn't as drowsy as previously, but not as buoyant either, and perhaps a little more gloomy. After six weeks on Thorazine 900 mg daily, her depression increased and she seemed considerably worse. This coincided with a visit from her mother who talked about some unpleasant family situations, including the fact that her older sister had not been helped by a recent course of ECT. Miss Layton became very depressed, showed psychomotor retardation and stated that she wasn't going to get well, and that her therapist had tricked her by permitting her to see her mother. Her diabetic condition worsened when she secretly overate, and insulin had to be increased.

Her doctor changed the Thorazine 900 mg daily, to an equivalent dosage of Compazine 60 mg daily, in the hope that this would be more activating. After a week on Compazine, she was markedly depressed, withdrawn, with suicidal preoccupation. She developed Parkinsonian fixed facies, an almost catatonic-like appearance, had loss of associated movements, felt extremely anxious, sad, hopeless and worthless, and did not eat regularly. The Compazine was withdrawn after a week, and she was placed on Tofranil 75 mg daily, raised 75 mg weekly, until a total daily dosage of 300 mg was reached.

After four days on Tofranil, she eloped from the hospital, rode a bus to the end of the line, claimed to have taken 22 over-the-counter hypnotic tablets because she wished "to sleep" (denying a suicidal attempt) and then rode the bus back to the hospital. (There were absolutely no physical symptoms following this, and all tests were within normal limits, arousing doubt as to whether she actually took the sedative.)

By the next month, on Tofranil 300 mg daily, she began to be genuinely smiling, affable and cheerful, singing, playing the piano and attending art therapy. Psychotherapy dealt mainly with "building her ego strength." She discussed her ambivalence; she could not leave her mother but feared returning to live with her; her fear of being on her own and her anger at her dependency on her mother. Also, she was able to show anger more easily and appropriately.

Continuing on insulin and Tofranil, she was allowed to test one specimen of urine each day by herself, and felt reassured at being able to do this alone. However, at times she was negativistic and would refuse to give her urine to the nurse when it was indicated. She became friendly with another diabetic patient who had functioned well in the past in work and marriage, despite her diabetes.

Miss Layton continued being cheerful, kept to her diet, was outgoing with other patients, attended all activities and was even praised by patients and staff for her capabilities. She became visibly upset when, after writing a letter to her sister about all these successes, the sister cavalierly responded "everyone has their ups and downs." For the next two weeks she appeared anxious, moderately depressed and secretly overate. But the depressed mood lifted and she again was cheerful and participated in group and individual activities.

For the next three months her mood was even. She made greater efforts to be "one of the girls," spent more time with her peer group and less with older patients, and was able to handle the job of unit president for the patient government in a capable and efficient manner. In therapy she discussed her feelings that to be a lady one must never show anything but a placid exterior, her underlying fear that by permitting anger to show she would be like her father, and that by showing emotion sexual urges would be expressed.

When discharge planning was begun, she became abrupt, angry, sarcastic and belligerent and once again began to overeat, demanding medication to stop her hunger. The overeating would be followed by a period of dieting and then a more stabilized food intake. At times she had episodes of weeping and self-pity. She was very angry at her doctor for forcing the discharge issue and manipulated a two-week extension when she became upset over not having a job.

Nevertheless, Miss Layton was able to make successful discharge arrangements and after 13 months of hospitalization, left in a flurry of negativism, stopping her diet, refusing insulin, blood sugar determinations, psychiatric or medical examinations. She was discharged in her own custody, to live at a women's residence, do secretarial work, continue psychotherapy at the aftercare clinic twice weekly, and take insulin and Tofranil 300 mg daily. Her hospital diagnosis was chronic undifferentiated schizophrenia; the research diagnosis was pseudoschizophrenic neurosis, with obsessional, depressive, and dependent trends, complicated by diabetes and thyroid disease.

FOLLOW-UP

Upon discharge Miss Layton lived at a women's residence and temporarily returned to her previous secretarial job. Then she found another secretarial job in which she remained for two years, constantly battling with her boss. At the aftercare clinic she received Thorazine and Tofranil 300 mg daily for the first month and a half, and then Tofranil alone, which she continued to take for two years. After the first three months, she discontinued at the clinic.

During the last six months of the first post-Hillside year, she resumed therapy at another clinic on a weekly basis. Her clinic diagnosis was borderline schizophrenic reaction. She received supportive psychotherapy, Tofranil 300 mg daily, insulin and Thorazine, and took Preludin, a stimulant diet pill, in unspecified amounts.

During the second year after her Hillside hospitalization, her clinic doctor left and she changed to a private psychiatrist who continued administering Tofranil 300 mg daily and Preludin. He estimated that she often ingested 300 mg of Preludin daily, and considered her addicted to it. This doctor reported "she evidenced marked hostility and anger directed at me and the psychiatric profession. But after several sessions she became much more pleasant, at times even euphoric; generally her mood was quite variable. Hardly a session ever passed without some highly charged emotional reaction. Occasionally, paranoid trends were obvious, and she was generally quite sensitive and easily hurt. Her social adjustment was poor, and she focused on her unsatisfactory family relationships. After five months of therapy she suddenly terminated, stating that she was short of funds and would resume when her financial condition improved. It was felt that she was dissatisfied with the progress she made during psychotherapy."

She was disillusioned with her work as a secretary, felt

it was too competitive and wanted to be less challenged. She
was very dissatisfied with herself, her social abilities, and
her feminine role.

Three years after her discharge from Hillside she "re-
belliously" went to California to look for other jobs and
felt very rejected when turned down by possible employers.
She attended a clinic, was placed on Stelazine 4 mg daily,
raised to 10 mg daily, and Cogentin. During this time she
was living with a relative in a studio apartment. Finally
she became unbearably unhappy and unable to cope, and returned to New York to live with her mother. She made some
feeble attempts to get into treatment at outside clinics but
was always referred back to Hillside.

Thus, three and one half years after her discharge, she
was readmitted to Hillside. She had been living with her
mother, fought with her constantly, felt unable to work and
unable to move away from home. Now, at 31, she maintained
only a thin veneer over her angry, disappointed feelings.
Anxious, depressed and irritable, her affect was extremely
flat, and her mood hostile, demanding and frightened, with
feelings of worthlessness, depersonalization and occasional
suicidal ideation.

Tofranil 75 mg daily, increased 75 mg a week, to 300 mg
daily was given. Shortly after beginning medication she
showed a marked improvement, with decreased depersonalization
and depression. When she manifested considerable anxiety
concerning facing new situations, Thorazine 100 mg daily was
added. Her diabetes was controlled with insulin. She was
found to be slightly hypothyroid, probably secondary to her
former treatment for hyperthyroidism, and required ½ gr
Proloid daily. She functioned well on this drug regimen.
In psychotherapy she showed little ability for insight into
her problems.

The decision was made that Miss Layton would see a psy-

chiatric social worker weekly, and a psychiatrist and inter-
nist to maintain her medication. She was discharged after
five months of hospitalization on Tofranil 300 mg daily, insulin, Proloid ½ gr daily and Thorazine 100 mg at night.
This time she found her own apartment and a new secretarial
job.

Two months after discharge she announced that she was
going to marry immediately, even though the hospital had recommended that she wait at least six months before making
this decision. Her fiance talked with her social worker and
stated that he thought he and Ida were good for each other,
because he also had great emotional difficulties, had been
tied to his mother until age 32, when he moved out on his
own, and that he wanted to "grow, together with Ida." They
were married.

Over the next two years she made several contacts with
the hospital, always cancelling her appointments at the last
minute. She continued in treatment with a psychiatrist recommended by Hillside, stated that she was really not feeling
well at all and would like to come in to talk, but never did.

COMMENT

These patients are often raised peculiarly by parents
with manifest psychiatric illness; Miss Layton had a manic-
depressive father and a mother who was perhaps temporarily
psychotic. Thus the effects of aberrant handling and hereditary predisposition are irretrievably entangled. Although
she had two severe disorders (diabetes and hyperthyroidism),
her physical state was relatively neglected prior to hospitalization and she entered Hillside in marked medical distress.

Her obsessional and self-isolating mechanisms caused
her to be considered schizophrenic, which led to Thorazine
and later to Stelazine treatment. During the period of a
moderately agitated depression, Thorazine was of some value.

Interestingly, however, her psychotherapist viewed it as a hindrance since he misunderstood her profuse anxious complaints as evidence of ability to profit from intensive exploratory psychotherapy.

The deleterious change from Thorazine to Compazine is typical of another class of medication management mistake, where sedative phenothiazines, such as Thorazine and Mellaril are understood as causing depression and therefore are often replaced by nonsedative piperazine phenothiazines, such as Compazine, Stelazine and Prolixin, in the vain hope of further activating the patient. Not infrequently, as in this case, such a change is accompanied by an increase in extrapyramidal side effects and a net deterioration.

This patient did receive Tofranil twice, each time showing a marked affective response--becoming more affable, cheerful and capable. This favorable response occurs regularly in such patients (10, 12, 15). However, the diagnosis of "schizophrenia" prevents many psychiatrists from using antidepressants.

Nevertheless, the patient's ingrained, ambivalent dependent pattern continued to block her from developing a more rewarding life. Notably, at one point she probably became addicted to a stimulant sympathomimetic agent. Such addictive behavior is common in these patients. Although Miss Layton was considered schizophrenic, she showed no social or cognitive deteriorative trend and was able to marry and remain in a moderate chronic symptomatic state.

The role of her diabetes and thyroid dysfunction is obscure. I have pointed out (9) that panic attacks leading to phobic dependent manipulations often occur in a context of recent severe endocrine fluctuation, and that these attacks can be terminated by Tofranil. Whether this patient's pathophysiology in some way resembles that of the phobic-dependent patient remains a moot point.

Another probable error in medication management consisted of prescribing Thorazine, rather than a minor tranquilizer or sedative, to deal with her anticipatory anxiety when
facing new situations. In general, such anticipatory anxiety
is not usefully affected by the phenothiazines, but they
might be of some value in dealing with agitation resulting
from a sense of helplessness when in a new situation. Therefore, they may help the stabilization of new attempts, although they are of little use for helping the patient initiate novel efforts.

PHILLIP CROFT

PRESENTING PROBLEM

Phillip Croft, age 32, married, but often separated
from his wife and three children, had life-long chronic anxiety, uncertainty about his masculinity, compulsive introspection and a disabling sensitivity, combined with a lack
of emotional responsiveness. He also suffered from insomnia,
nightmares, fear of heights, dependency, indecisiveness, dis-
illusionment and obsessional rumination about whether people
disliked him. After several months of psychotherapy he demanded hospitalization because of increasing distress and
was referred to Hillside.

FAMILY

Phillip was the second of three sons of a middle class
family. The father, over 50 when his children were born,
worked as a printer, and was an active student of Yoga. The
mother, over 40 at her sons' births, was an avid Christian
Scientist. When Phillip was eight, she converted herself
and her children to Catholicism and the father divorced her.
The parents' life together had been chronically unhappy with
incessant fighting, the playing of son against son, and the
three boys against their father.

Phillip openly resented and disliked both his parents

and maintained that he never really had a father. When the
80 year old father was dying, his request to see Phillip was
refused, just as five years earlier Phillip had refused to
see his dying mother.

DEVELOPMENTAL HISTORY

No early developmental history was available except that
Phillip was always a sensitive, effeminate child. His mother
constantly criticized and ridiculed him for his lack of masculinity, yet seemed to favor him because of his delicacy.

His parents tried to send him to school at age five,
but he vehemently refused. At ages six and seven, he stole
objects from his father, giving as his reason his resentment
toward the man. It was also at this time that he began masturbating and had the urge to expose himself outdoors. He
was frequently punished for this by being spanked with a
hairbrush and then forced to stand nude in the corner; a
punishment which caused him intense embarrassment and further
resentment.

He hated school when he finally entered at age seven
and would play truant whenever possible. He disliked the
other children, considering them crude and vulgar. Always
feeling isolated and distant, he was continually angry, jealous and resentful, and was subject to frequent episodes of
anxiety, despondency, self-isolation and inactivity.

After his parents' divorce, when he was eight, his mother transferred him to a Catholic school which he attended
from ages nine to 14. He described this period as "hell on
earth," loathing the children at the parochial school and
never making any friends. He found his father's visits particularly unpleasant and avoided them by hiding. Feeling
markedly insecure and unhappy, he often sat staring into
space. The only pleasures he enjoyed were "from observing
the beauties of nature" and his mother's philosophical conversations with her intellectual friends.

When he was 15, his mother decided that he should become a monk and took him for several interviews at monaster-
ies. However, at about this time, he accidently stepped in
front of a moving car, resulting in a fractured leg and several months of hospitalization; plans for the monastery were
deferred. Then he became openly defiant of his mother, "saw
her destructive tendencies and told her off." Going against
all her wishes, he quit high school at the end of his sophomore year. He worked at odd jobs and a year later, at 17,
joined the Navy, mainly to develop and prove his masculinity.
Quickly he found that he hated this life also. While in the
Navy he had his first heterosexual experiences with prostitutes. He did not enjoy these experiences but went along
with a group of sailors to test his virility.

At 18, he met his future wife through an acquaintance.
She was the first girl he ever dated and although she was
obese (over 200 lbs.), physically unattractive, from a lower
social class and he didn't love her, he felt sympathy and
compassion for her. Gradually they became sexually intimate.
However, she was more aggressive than he, and Phillip claimed she raped him. When she became pregnant, they married;
Phillip was 21 and his wife a year younger. He saw the marriage as yet another way of asserting his masculinity and
was pleased that his wife was pregnant. In fact, he felt
quite virile and sexually active, and had intercourse with
her four times a week.

In the meantime, with his mother's help, he found a job
in advertising and discovered that he had artistic talent.
He then attended a design school for two years. Just prior
to graduating, a fellow student persuaded him to quit because "the school didn't really teach anything." After this
he held many different jobs in advertising, but none longer
than a year; always ending by being fired or quitting.

In his mid 20's, he became disenchanted with Catholi-

cism and was attracted instead to mystical religious cults
and Zen Buddhism. He considered himself a genius and on a
level with philosophers like Thoreau; both his wife and mother encouraged these feelings.

Because of his knowledge of mystical religions and as-
trology, he felt he had "insights into life unavailable to
ignorant, crude people," which would enable him to counsel
others and be "a half-assed saint." Other times he felt
worthless and insecure, largely in response to other people's
positive or negative reactions to him.

Also, at this time he began to see his wife as "simple,
ignorant, vulgar, shallow, unperceptive, conforming, unresponsive, dependent, incapable of making decisions, and an
inadequate mother." Thus, he took his three children to a
farm he rented upstate, in order to teach them basic life
values, and left his wife in the city to work.

Although unsuccessful at chicken farming, he remained
at the farm for three and a half years, taking care of his
children, looking after the farm and doing janitorial work
for money. His wife visited on weekends. Toward the end of
this period, he found himself becoming more nervous and irritable and incapable of caring for the children. He placed
them in a foster home.

Returning to the city he found that his wife had been
involved in an extra-marital affair for over a year. He was
extremely upset, despondent, anxious, and panicky and developed episodes of sweating, nausea, body rash and severe insomnia. Afraid to walk on the street, he had to dart from
alley to alley. "I didn't feel like myself, I had no sense
of self. I felt like I was broken in two and that I was a
spectator." Also, he became sexually impotent.

After a year, the children's foster child status had to
be changed and he was ready to place them for adoption;
his wife however, angrily refused and brought the children

back to live with her.

Though he deeply resented his wife, felt her unfaithfulness was a direct attack on his masculinity and an attempt to destroy him, he continued to depend on her. While he finally moved to a separate apartment, he never considered divorcing her. After a few months of feeling extremely miserable, he entered psychotherapy.

He and his therapist worked well together, sharing a common interest in Zen and Chinese art. This psychiatrist diagnosed him as "a psychotic character with latent psychosis, though there was never any primary symptomatology of schizophrenia." Initially he seemed to make progress, but when his therapist left for a vacation, Mr. Croft became increasingly symptomatic. He consulted with another psychiatrist who diagnosed him as a schizoid personality, and upon Mr. Croft's insistence on hospitalization, recommended that he enter Hillside.

PRESENTING CHARACTERISTICS

Mr. Croft appeared asthenic, carelessly dressed, and hyperactive. While his speech was overproductive with marked circumstantiality and distractibility, it was always coherent; he stated problems in diffuse generalities. He complained of feeling fearful, unhappy, anxious, confused and lacking in emotional responsivity. His manner was emotionless and anhedonic. He was preoccupied with philosophy, metaphysics, psychology and religion, which he felt only added to his perplexities and failed to help him function effectively. He exhibited no hallucinations, delusions or thought disorder, but ruminated obsessively that people disliked him. Sometimes he was grandiose about his intuitive abilities. He recognized that he was probably emotionally ill but did not seem to have much conviction in this belief, or in any other.

COURSE AT HILLSIDE

Results of physical and neurological tests, including
the EEG, were all within normal limits. He attained a
Wechsler-Bellevue IQ score of 122, with a verbal IQ of 109
and a performance IQ of 133.

Mr. Croft adjusted well to the hospital routine and was
compliant and cooperative. He participated in the activity
program but remained detached from other patients, and spent
his free time reading or idly alone.

There was very little change in his condition during
the first five months of hospitalization. On his time away
from the hospital he usually visited Christian Science heal-
ers or Yoga gurus, activities which were discouraged and
limited by his doctor. When his wife obtained a quick divorce, he became increasingly concerned about feelings of
homosexuality.

After eight months of hospitalization, Mr. Croft had a
short period of calmness where he seemed more organized and
less agitated, vague and abstract. But within a month he was
once again obsessional, depressed and ruminative. Speaking
rapidly and scornfully, he derided the shallowness, ignorance
and coarseness of his doctors and had a continual stream of
complaints concerning his unhappiness, depression and inability to cope. His appetite was poor and he awoke early.

Referred to the drug program, he first received Kemadrin, an anti-parkinson agent, 3.75 mg daily, with an increasing dose of 3.75 mg weekly, until a total of 15 mg daily
was reached at four weeks. This part of the study was to determine whether Kemadrin was an active agent in affecting
psychological status, rather than a mere adjunctive medication. A slight improvement was seen, with decreased anxiety, depression and obsessional rumination. His doctor attributed this to his having forced Mr. Croft to stop his abstract ruminations. After six weeks of Kemadrin, his doctor

felt that his "latent schizophrenia" required treatment and
placed him on Thorazine 300 mg and Kemadrin 5 mg daily. In
a week he felt drowsy, sluggish and fatigued. The medication
was increased to Thorazine 600 mg and Kemadrin 15 mg daily,
and he felt worse than ever - detached, dopey and drugged.
The medication was then discontinued.

Mr. Croft had an acute attack of gout and was treated
with colchicine during this period. After a month on no
medication he still felt emotionless, was obsessionally ruminating and continually self-doubting. He felt that the first
medication, Kemadrin, had helped him slightly, but the Thorazine completely prohibited him from thinking or acting.

Mr. Croft was discharged after a year of hospitalization, showing slight improvement and receiving no medication.
His hospital diagnosis was chronic undifferentiated schizophrenia; the research diagnosis was pseudoschizophrenic neurosis with schizoid tendencies and dependent over-ideational,
obsessional, depressive and ruminative trends.

FOLLOW-UP

After discharge, Mr. Croft lived in several different
furnished rooms. He visited the aftercare clinic twice weekly for two months and remained unemployed for three months.
After, he found a job in advertising; he took Yoga lessons
for the next three months. Then he went to a psychiatrist
who diagnosed him as a schizophrenic and gave him increasing
doses of Sparine, then Taractan, Librium and Tofranil, then
all four drugs together (dosages unknown) with no effect.
The psychiatrist then recommended him to a self-help group
which he did not pursue. He found another job in advertising.

In the second year post-Hillside, he changed to another
job which he held for a year. He began and discontinued with
yet another psychiatrist; later he became active in Scientol-
ogy. On follow-up interview he reported no contact with his

family and that he felt worse and had no sources of enjoyment. He could not be located for a three year follow-up.

Five years after being at Hillside, it was learned in-
directly that he had applied for psychotherapy at a clinic,
but later decided to see a private therapist for more intensive treatment.

COMMENT

The reason usually given for such patients being called
schizophrenic is their marked lack of "object relations" and
their profound ambivalence. Also, their ruminative, perplexed concern with abstractions is often referred to as "thought
disorder" although there is no manifest loosening of associations, dereistic thinking or arbitrary symbolism, or delusions. Nonetheless, some of the attitudes expressed are
atypical, such as Mr. Croft's belief in himself as a potential genius and saint; yet this belief could be understood
on the basis of his strikingly deviant upbringing; at no
time did he attempt to convince others of his unusual abilities, except insofar as he was "sensitive."

Unfortunately, the diagnosis of such patients as schizophrenic regularly leads to the prescription of phenothiazines
and the avoidance of antidepressants, as in this case. When
phenothiazines are used in the absence of signs of a markedly agitated depression, the effects are negligible or negative. Often the patient becomes obsessionally concerned with
somatic discomforts and ability to function is dramatically
decreased (10, 12, 14, 15).

The core phenomenon in both Layton and Croft seems to
be the early development of obsessional and self-isolating
patterns, perhaps in maladaptive response to severely depressed and deprived states in infancy and early childhood.
Insofar as the tendency to depression becomes quiescent, one
is left with the picture of a severe, refractory, obsessional character disorder. Insofar as their moods tend to epi-

sodes of severe depression, agitation and obsessional rumination, their picture fluctuates from that of a severe but
managing obsessional character disorder, to that of a superimposed agitated depression with function loss.

This sequence of events is often referred to as "decompensation" and is believed to represent the unmasking of a
latent schizophrenia. Obviously this is open to debate, but
in view of the prognosis, i.e., chronic symptomatic inadequacy rather than deterioration, and the favorable response
to antidepressants, it would seem that there are sufficient
differences from schizophrenia to warrant distinguishing
this group of patients. This is of practical import since
the label "schizophrenia" leads to inappropriate medication
practices for these patients and an unwarranted expectation
of delusional psychosis and deterioration.

REFERENCES

1. American Psychiatric Association: Diagnostic and Statis-
    tical Manual, Mental Disorders. Mental Hospital Service,
    Washington, D.C., 1952.

2. American Psychiatric Association: Diagnostic and Statis-
    tical Manual, Mental Disorders (Second Edition).
    Washington, D.C., 1968.

3. English, H.B. and English, A.C.: A Comprehensive Dic-
    tionary of Psychological and Psychoanalytical Terms.
    Longmans, Green, New York, 1958.

4. Fish, F.J.: Outline of Psychiatry. Williams and Wilkins,
    Baltimore, 1964.

5. Gittelman-Klein, R. and Klein, D.F.: Controlled imipra-
    mine treatment of school phobia. Arch. Gen. Psychiat.
    25, 204-207,1971.

6. Gittelman-Klein, R. and Klein, D.F.: School phobia: Di-
    agnostic considerations in the light of imipramine ef-
    fects. In W.L. Smith (ed.): Drugs, Development and
    Cerebral Function. Charles C. Thomas, Springfield,Ill.
    1971.

7. Hoch, P. and Polatin, P.: Pseudoneurotic forms of schizo-
    phrenia. Psychiat. Quart. 23, 148-276, 1949.

8. Johnson, G., Gershon, S. amd Hekimian, L.J.: Controlled
    evaluation of lithium and chlorpromazine in the treat-
    ment of manic states. Comp. Psychiat. 9, 563-573, 1968.

9. Klein, D.F.: Delineation of two drug-responsive anxiety
    syndromes. Psychopharmacologia 5, 397-408, 1964.

10. Klein, D.F.: Importance of psychiatric diagnosis in pre-
    diction of clinical drug effects. Arch. Gen. Psychiat.
    16, 118-126, 1967.

11. Klein, D.F.: Treatment of phobias characterized by sep-
    aration anxiety. International Drug Therapy Newsletter,
    2, 16, 1967.

12. Klein, D.F.: Psychiatric diagnosis and a typology of
    clinical drug effects. Psychopharmacologia 13, 359-386,
    1968.

13. Klein, D.F. and Davis, J.M.: Diagnosis and Drug Treatment of Psychiatric Disorders. Williams and Wilkins, Baltimore, 1969.

14. Klein, D.F. and Fink, M.: Behavioral reaction patterns with phenothiazines. Arch. Gen. Psychiat. 7, 449-459, 1962.

15. Klein, D.F. and Fink,M.: Psychiatric reaction patterns to imipramine. Amer. J. Psychiat. 119, 432-438, 1962.

16. Marks, I.M.: Fears and Phobias. Academic Press, New York, 1969.

17. Mendel, J.C. and Klein, D.F.: Anxiety attacks with subsequent agoraphobia. Compr. Psychiat. 10, 190-195, 1969.

18. Menninger, K.: The Vital Balance. Viking Press, New York, 1963.

19. Quitkin, F. and Rifkin, A.: Lithium treatment of emotionally unstable character disorder. Presented at the World Congress of Psychiatry, Mexico City, 1971.

19A. Quitkin, F.M., Rifkin, A., Kaplan, J. and Klein, D.F.: Phobic anxiety syndrome complicated by drug dependence and addiction: A treatable form of drug abuse. Arch. of Psychiat., 1972, in press.

20. Rifkin, A., Levitan, S.J., Galewski, J. and Klein, D.F.: Emotionally unstable character disorder. A follow-up study. I. Description of patients and outcome. II. Prediction of outcome. Biol. Psychiat., 1971, in press.

21. Rabiner, C.J., Klein, D.F.: Imipramine treatment of school phobia. Compr. Psychiat. 10, 387-390, 1969.

22. Robins, L.N.: Deviant Children Grown Up. Williams and Wilkins, Baltimore, 1966.

Chapter XVII

DIAGNOSIS AND PREVENTION OF DIAGNOSTIC AND MEDICATION TREATMENT ERROR

In reviewing the case material for this book it became apparent that during treatment, diagnostic and therapeutic errors often occur. These errors cannot be attributed to random sloppiness, bad faith, or lack of desire to fully help a patient. In analyzing the repetitive patterns of error and the circumstances attending them, some inferences concerning causation were drawn. If one can determine the causes of error patterns then rational approaches to prevention can be proposed.

The inability to recognize the prognostic and diagnostic relevance of many facts results primarily from a simple lack of knowledge. The simplest hypothesis explaining ignorance is that the doctor does not know the correct diagnostic considerations or treatment procedures, due to educational lag. In large measure, psychiatrists (and other doctors) are trapped by history. Psychiatry has undergone a remarkable revolution since 1955, with the advent of psychotropic drugs and the introduction of open hospitals, milieu treatment, and community mental health programs. However, medical schools, residency training programs, and the usual systems of preceptorship and apprenticeship are slow to catch up with the flood of new knowledge, particularly concerning the varied uses of psychotropic drugs and evaluation of new hospital and

community procedures. This situation is not unique to psychiatry. It is also true within internal medicine and surgery and has been a source of much concern. The teaching of
medical students has been considerably upgraded by having
active research personnel participate in the teaching program. Such personnel are required by their professional
identification to remain abreast of the most recent develop-
ments in their field and can impart this information to the
developing student. Courses taught by busy practitioners
often contain much down to earth practical information concerning diagnosis and treatment but may not be completely up-
to-date. A major problem is how to keep the post-graduate
practitioner current in new techniques. At present, there is
no system for mandatory refresher courses accompanied by a
system of recertification and relicensing.

Quite understandably such a recommendation arouses feelings of negativism and resistance within the medical profession. Once having achieved the prized status of healer, it
is natural to wish this to be considered a permanent attribute rather than a transient qualification that requires continual hard effort in a context of permanent professional insecurity. Further, the economic fact is that study time is
not directly remunerated. Most doctors work long hours to
attain their desirable standard of living. They are thus
placed in a conflict between their professional conscience
and their understandable desires for economic security and
comfort.

Since it is the public good that demands the continual
upgrading of professional skill, it would seem reasonable
that this be a public rather than a private charge. Barring
the development of a system of national health care, such educational subsidization could be provided in terms of direct
monetary reward for participation in clinical and didactic
work, tax benefits, etc. This represents no break from past

tradition, insofar as the government heavily subsidizes the
present system of medical school, internship and residency education; it would simply represent an extension into the
post-residency phase. Nonetheless the painful reality that
longitudinal reassessment of competence is necessary must be
faced.

Aside from sheer lack of knowledge is the unmistakable
fact of resistance to new learning. The psychoanalysts made
a powerful, lasting contribution by pointing out that often
intrapsychic unconscious motivational difficulty prevents
knowledge acquisition or utilization. In the doctor-patient
framework this is seen as counter-transference; that is, the
doctor unconsciously identifies the patient with one of his
own important life figures and responds to the patient as
that person, rather than the person he is. This distortion
of reality prevents correct perceptions and decision making;
indeed the doctor's hostile impulses may lead him to actions
with an unconscious destructive aim. Usual processes of psychiatric supervision do not afford opportunities to determine
individual unconscious determinants of error. Even with intensive psychoanalytic supervision it often remains obscure
whether counter-transference is being arbitrarily postulated
as the only cause of doctor error or actually fits the facts
of practice. The prophylaxis of counter-transference error
is difficult. A training psychoanalysis for psychiatrists
has often been recommended. However, it is the general consensus of many psychiatric educational program directors that
the general practice of psychiatry does not usually require
a psychoanalysis. It has also never been demonstrated that
a training analysis substantially reduces counter-transference error. One can easily see how difficult it would be to
systematically study this issue. Certainly, the presumption
that prophylactic psychoanalysis is both necessary and effective requires positive evidence and cannot be accepted on the

basis of testimonials by interested parties.

A direct descendant of the psychoanalytic view is that of "cognitive dissonance," which points to the repressive distortions that occur when a valued belief system (ideology) is not confirmed by new facts, teaching, or experiences. For instance, it regularly comes as a shock to students to be informed that the earlier the age of first treatment by mental health professionals, the worse the prognosis. The discovery that early intervention is frequently a sign of severity of pathology, where treatment will be ineffective, is distinctly upsetting to those who have a touching faith in psychiatric efficacy. This often leads to a rejection of the facts rather than the ideology. This viewpoint is more general in that the errors do not depend on specific transferential distortions (i.e., this patient should be treated as I would like to have treated my father), but rather depend on general ideological conflicts (i.e., I won't use antipsychotic drugs on this schizophrenic patient since I define this as a purely symptomatic approach the use of which would reveal me to be, to myself and my critical peers, both an ineffective psychotherapist and a superficial person). Impression management, that is the attempt to convince one's critical public that one is a certain sort of valued person, also plays a key role.

It is not well recognized that ideological allegiance serves a useful, anxiety-reducing, intrapsychic and socially self-protective function under the joint conditions of ignorance combined with the necessity for taking correct action, a situation all too common for the experienced psychiatrist and universal for the novice. If we really don't know what is best or even effective treatment, a universally applicable guide to action spares us anxiety, self-doubt, loss of self-esteem, and social reproach. One doesn't review all the data, constantly balancing uncertainties while looking

inept, but comes to premature closure, adopts a sanctified
ritual, and ends internal turmoil and external vacillation.
This turmoil is most painful for those who have achieved a
status (e.g., M.D. or Ph.D.) that ascribes professional ability, despite inexperience. Not surprisingly, therefore, the
novice therapist can rarely maintain an informed skepticism
in the face of pressure to make real decisions. Further, if
the ideology has the force of authoritarian suggestion, as
well as intellectual prestige, the student often takes the
vows.

It is all very well to preach that the student maintain
rugged individualism and a balanced skepticism. Unfortunately, such exhortation is rare, but on the other hand, when
present, it is ineffective. Briefly, the over-riding problem
is that the student exists within a social milieu to which he
must be responsive.

Psychiatry, psychology and social work in the United
States have been dominated by theoreticians who single-mind-
edly emphasize the intrafamilial and developmental aspects of
mental illness and derogate the contributions of socio-econom-
ic, physiological and constitutional factors. This simplis-
tic ideology remains prevalent within much psychiatric teaching. Many residency programs use as living models of clinical practice those who are not only ignorant of the facts of
somatic treatment, but who may actively resist the recognition of somatic methods. It is all too easy for the insecure
trainee to closely identify with biophobic and sociophobic
theories of psychiatry, thus, unhappily, supplying himself
with an ideology that rejects disciplined structured inquiry,
descriptive psychopathology, studies of the patient's social-
ly-determined life space, and drug treatment. Since certain
diagnostic inquiries must raise the derogatory possibility
that the patient is not merely the passive victim of a malign
family structure, but has taken an active part in creating

his own and other's misery, such questions are often avoided.
Therefore, explorations especially in the area of malingering,
exploitation, and perversity may be omitted.

Conversely, the student may identify with psychophobic
organicists who often are only concerned with presenting
symptomatology and symptomatic relief, completely neglecting
developmental, psychiatric and familial history, intra-psychic
dynamics, social status manipulations and maladaptions. Such
a narrow focus prevents a grasp of the patient's life difficulties which are only partly determined by their presenting
symptoms.

A socially-oriented ideology is gaining prominence
where, in the extreme, mental illness is declared a myth, and
behavioral deviance is seen as due to bad social learning,
resulting in the patient's devious gamesmanship. Seeing all
patients as tacticians dealing with a real, often depriving
world may lead to an emphasis on behavior modification, or
group process, or milieu techniques, or oddly, to the most
non-directive individualized psychoanalysis. Unfortunately
all these beliefs are cognitively dissonant with detailed diagnosis and the indicated prescription of medication.

There should be no question that our present teachers
are simply incapable of presenting the variety of opposing
psychiatric theories in an unbiased fashion. Each of them
has an emotional investment and only the rare teacher can
systematically expound points of view that are personally unacceptable without subtle or even blatant distortion. It
would seem that the only resolution possible in this historical period is to expose the student to the clash of opinion
and debate. A residency training program that does not include spokesmen for the psychoanalytic, biological, socio-
dynamic and learning theory points of view, as a bare minimum,
is necessarily biasing the growth of its students. Further,
the very clash of opinion upon the part of senior members of

the teaching team should decompress the situation for the
student so that he is not forced into a premature allegiance.

This apparently rational procedure is conspicuous by its
absence. Most teaching centers utilize the glib rationaliza-
tion that psychiatry is so complicated that they don't want
their students confused. Such a self-serving stand would
seem too transparent to have to criticize, yet is almost universal.

Just as one cannot appeal to the student to maintain an
informed skepticism, it is probably fruitless to appeal to
schools to accept an eclectic teaching program that contains
many sharply contradictory elements. In the final analysis,
it may be the responsibility of the various national professional training accreditation committees to ensure this.

Specific Diagnostic Errors

Medication Maintenance on Hospital Admission

There are certain errors that are directly due to the
shortsighted, erroneously conceived interests of the doctor,
patient and hospital. For instance, it is frequent practice
to maintain newly hospitalized psychiatric patients on their
prior medication, after hospital admission. This is most often not in the patient's interest. Usually, if the medication had been useful, the patient would not have been hospitalized. Secondly, medication often obscures psychopathology
and the diagnostic field.

Nonetheless, patients are maintained on medication because of the unsupported fear that medication termination
will cause sudden decompensation, with resultant trouble for
the patient, doctor and hospital. Too often the doctor is
unwilling to run the risk of his patient's reproach and his
co-workers' criticism. Since the harm done by the positive
action of medication removal would be more obvious than the

long-range, diagnosis-confusing, treatment-stymieing harm of
inaction, the latter is often preferred.

At Hillside Hospital, since 1964, we remove all patients
from medication for a period of at least ten days, during
which time adequate diagnostic studies can be made. Of
course, if the patient's condition worsens, emergency medication may be in order, although not necessarily. This procedure enables a much more precise view of the patient's psychopathology than can be obtained otherwise. It also affords
an opportunity to remove the patient from useless, or even
deleterious medication. Rarely does it result in acute exacerbation; if it does, such exacerbation is easily handled.

The correction of this error requires administrative
direction. It cannot be left to individual discretion since
doctors will fall into a "fail-safe" mode of immediate prescription without reckoning the later consequences. Each
psychiatric hospital administration should review their current prescribing practices with a view to critically assessing whether they are actually in the patient's long-term interest.

Unfortunately, there is a developing pressure for extremely quick hospital treatment. There is a certain positive side to this philosophy in that it is an attempt to combat the patient's developing dependence upon institutionali-
zation, and promote the efficient use of limited resources.
However, setting a 30 day limit on hospitalization often
forces doctors into premature medication prescription. The
establishment of hard and fast discharge dates by reimburse-
ment formula or insurance policies is an understandable attempt to prevent dilatory treatment. Nonetheless it should
be obvious that such mechanical deadlines must wreak havoc
with many patients' treatment course. The development of
systems for utilization review that can critically assess
whether the patient's treatment has been informed and expedi-

tious is a crying need. Again, this is not a field for individual effort but requires political and social administrative decision to allocate resources for such purposes.

Anamnestic Tactics

The complexity of modern psychiatry demands extensive
anamnesis, often utilizing informants other than the patient.
It is regularly important to obtain a detailed statement of
the developmental history and intrafamilial setting for periods long anteceding the present illness. The tactics of case
history interview, whereby this strategic goal is attained,
is part of the art of psychiatric practice.

In a humanistic reaction to mechanical procedures wherein troubled patients are asked long lists of dull and possibly irrelevant questions, some practitioners have fostered a
vogue for unstructured anamnestic methods. In these procedures the patient is afforded the opportunity to unburden his
emotional preoccupations in a neutral and permissive setting,
with no attempt made to engage in a comprehensive historical
review. If this were viewed as the initial tactic in the development of rapport (by this we mean respectful trust), no
objection could be made. Unfortunately, this preliminary
procedure may be overvalued by the therapist as the actual
start of therapy, so that it is then clumsy to go from the
emotionally-loaded interpersonal and intrapsychic concerns
presented by the patient to the more mundane areas of school
performance, economic status, etc. Nonetheless, this latter
information is essential to a thorough understanding of the
patient who may gloss over unacceptable realities.

Simply explaining the therapist's need to know more
about the patient in order to understand his difficulty, may
have a valuable therapeutic effect by showing the doctor's
interest and desire to understand. It demonstrates to the
patient the need for broad perspective, reduces magical ex-

pectations, and conveys a respect for thoroughness. Patients
often respond positively to an extensive history-taking procedure as indicating a meticulous professional approach.

Case Study Completeness

It is valuable to follow a structured case study form as
an intermediate goal. Without systematic procedures, it is
too easy to miss large areas of psychopathological relevance.
A specific check-list for case study note-taking is a distinct aid to the novice and a useful reminder for the experienced.

The following section will follow the major headings of
the Hillside case study outline, pointing out common errors
made at each point.

    I. Identification
    The amount and extent of the patient's financial re-
sources are often not detailed. Nonetheless, this is crucial
for all realistic planning concerning length of stay and
eventual disposition. Doctors are frequently loathe to press
on financial issues for fear of being put into an inquisi-
torial, exploitative, finance-oriented role by the patient.
Patients may detail sexual eccentricities with the utmost
sang-froid but show great reluctance to stipulate their economic status. This is especially so when the patient's cost
of care is contributed to by public funds, and the patient
fears that a frank statement of his resources may lead to fee
readjustment.

    II. Leading Present Problems That Have Required
         Hospitalization
    The major problem here and throughout the examination
is reliance on non-directive interview methods, believing

that important material will emerge spontaneously. Of course, the patient should be given an opportunity to unburden himself. However, he should not dominate the interaction by his often defensive and irrelevant preoccupations. The diagnostician should have a systematic outline available, wherein all salient historical points and examinations are listed. These do not have to be applied in any mechanical order, but at the conclusion of the examination, the diagnostician should have adequately covered all areas.

Not inquiring in specific detail into the circumstances surrounding the onset of illness and hospitalization is frequent. Patients frequently will attribute illness onset to a specific life crisis. To cast this in perspective, one needs a very exact chronological history of how the life crisis related to the illness; in the course of further examination, it must be determined whether similar life crises had been faced with equanimity.

The patient will often attribute hospitalization to certain chronic symptoms, or lack of competence in coping. However, this does not answer the question of why the patient became hospitalized at this specific point in time. Often hospitalization is necessary because of an upsurge in symptomatology, a withdrawal of family support, avoidance of a life difficulty, self-intoxication or drug abuse. If these matters are not clearly discerned, goals of treatment and discharge planning will be obscured.

One must also uncover the positive life advantages gained by the illness state, sick role, or hospitalization. The possibility that the patient is malingering must be considered.

Again, many doctors find it uncomfortable to pointedly inquire concerning these issues. Of course, the timing and manner of such inquiries is part of the art of psyhiatric interviewing.

Frequently the doctor blandly assumes that the patient's attitudes toward hospitalization and getting well are positive. Most patients have at least mixed feelings about this. Even when their attitude toward hospitalization is distinctly positive, their main wish is usually to reduce immediate life stresses rather than attempt to make any definite changes in functioning, so that they are often not in agreement with the hospital's more ambitious goals.

It is often helpful to briefly summarize the reasons for hospitalization as seen by the patient, as seen by relatives or other significant persons, and as seen by the doctor. Significant differences can be quite revealing regarding the whole issue of the patient's illness and hospitalization.

III. History of Present Illness

While a patient's illness may have an acute onset, the acuteness of onset often obscures the chronicity of the psychopathology. It is widely believed that acute onsets are prognostically positive. However, an acute schizophrenic break against a background of chronic socialization defect is not a positive prognostic sign.

On the other hand, some patients either spontaneously, or in response to past psychotherapeutic indoctrination, present a picture of unrelieved chronicity. Since they are often in severe distress at the point of hospitalization, it is not surprising that they paint the past blackly. Nonetheless, a careful search may uncover an intermittent illness with periods of relatively good function. Such patients have sharply better prognoses, at least for the immediate episode.

Doctors frequently attend to the qualitative nature of the patient's complaints and do not appreciate the quantitative emotional overreaction. For instance, a woman may complain about her unloving husband and elaborately depict her marital relationship. However, the fact that her recent depressive, copeless symptomatology was quantitatively out of all proportion to even her chronically ungratifying life may become obscured. The question is one of emphasis. Is the patient's behavior an understandable reaction to life disappointments or stressful circumstances, or is it due to an incapacity to manage, modify, or adapt to such circumstances?

Insufficient attention is paid to vegetative signs of illness, such as excesses or deficiencies in sleep, appetite, weight, sexual interest, menses, and bowel function. Inquiry into diurnal fluctuations of mood and activity are often neglected, handicapping adequate diagnostic decisions.

IV. Family History

As part of the biophobic attitude toward psychopathology, a detailed anamnesis concerning familial history of emotional disorder is often absent. Familial psychopathology is frequently discounted for its genetic significance as only being part of the patient's pathogenic environment. Nonetheless, evidence concerning the genetic components of mental illness is convincing, and one may gain valuable information from a family history. For instance, apparently schizophrenic patients (who may actually have a variant of affective disorder) with a family history of purely affective disorder have a better prognosis than those who have either a healthy family history or schizophrenic relatives.

Family history is often reviewed to determine how the family produced the patient's illness. Often the patient wholeheartedly agrees with this point of view, and the diagnostician neglects the positive strengths of the family, in particular, the family's attempts to cope with and help the patient. Thus, there is no systematic assessment whether negative intrafamilial interactions are a result rather than the cause of the patient's difficulties.

There is often an insufficient comparison with the life

history of the patient's siblings. If the patient sticks out
like a sore thumb, when compared to his siblings, without any
apparent intrafamilial or environmental reason (given detailed investigation), constitution, organic brain disease, accident and heredity should be strongly considered as etiological agents.

V.   Past Personal History

There is often insufficient investigation concerning details of the patient's socialization. An early inability to
make friends, associated with scapegoating and rejection by
other children, is a malignant prognostic sign. Other neglected areas are the details of the patient's educational and
work accomplishments. The patient may avoid inquiry by blandly saying that he did "O.K."

Detailed inquiry concerning educational and work accomplishments, hobbies and cultural interests, lead to a broad
perspective on the patient's immediate difficulties. Too often the presenting psychopathology or the presumed psychody-
namics becomes the total focus. This may lead on one hand,
to gross overestimation of the patient's actual functional
capabilities which are the most important factor in the long
term outcome, or on the other hand, to gross underestimation
of the patient's abilities. Neglecting the patient's positive
strengths interferes with quickly developing sources of self-
esteem and emotional support, as well as long-term planning.

Patients often either exaggerate their abilities or minimize them, depending upon their mood and desired self-presentation. One should attempt to get external corroboration,
if necessary, by sending for available school records or interviewing family members.

The three childhood syndromes with the most specific
prognostic import are the awkward, withdrawn, asocial child
who cannot relate to his peers and is frequently rejected and

scapegoated, the clinging, demanding, fearful, separation-anxious child, and the impulsive, destructive, hyperactive child. Such histories are difficult to derive from patient retrospective interview and require parental informants or school records.

Interestingly, even in psychiatric hospitals that emphasize the importance of the psychosexual stages of character development, a really detailed sexual history is rarely taken. Patients who seem to openly discuss their sexual history often give a one-sided, self-serving picture.

There is a general neglect of the patient's affectivity, accompanied by a fixed readiness to consider all affective shifts as understandable reactions to environmental changes or intrapsychic readjustments. Investigating for periods of elation, giddiness and even general euphoria is rare, since many psychiatrists are convinced that psychiatric patients are always miserable. Patients seldom volunteer information concerning elated periods because they view them as simple good spirits. Therefore, lack of recognition that elation and giddiness can be psychopathological states is common. Prolonged manic periods, marked emotional lability that may or may not be reactive to precipitants, and recurrent, out-of-proportion mood swings caused by interpersonal rejections are regularly missed. Investigating the relationship of mood swings to the menstrual cycle is also neglected.

Certain distressing affective states, such as episodic panic attacks when the patient thinks he may die, or marked dysphoric response to rejection will be masked by the patient's focus on the behavior used to deal with their distress. For instance, the patient may spend much time describing his travel phobia and demands to be accompanied, rather than the proximate causal affective crisis, i.e., the panic attack. Similarly, rejection-sensitive patients may describe their seductive, manipulative, ingratiating, engulf-

ing tactics, rather than the miserable dysphoric feelings
that directly incite such maladaptations. Therefore, such
patients are often diagnostically considered related to the
neuroses or character disorders, rather than the more closely
allied affective disorders.

Other syndromes are also difficult to differentiate.
Acute manics are so disorganized that they may be considered
schizophrenic. The severe hysteric may report hallucinations
and delusions and, in an endeavor to achieve the sick role,
may actively imitate their understanding of schizophrenic
symptoms. Therefore, these patients present knotty diagnostic problems. However, the most frequent diagnostic error is
that these differentials are not even considered. The only
way to insure that a meticulous differential diagnosis is accomplished is to demonstrate that differential diagnosis is
not a meaningless exercise but has concrete practical implications for all forms of therapy.

VI.   Diagnostic Formulations
The diagnosis of schizophrenia or psychosis in the absence of psychotic signs or history of reality testing failure is particularly common and leads to bad treatment and irrelevant prognosis. By extension, the term psychosis is often applied to potentially psychotic conditions. A patient
with some features of schizophrenic disorder may be diagnosed
as schizophrenic, although manifest psychosis is not present.
This can be justified in terms of a past schizophrenic episode or a markedly eccentric asocial lifestyle. Incorrectly,
much weaker indicators, e.g., a "soft thought disorder," are
considered diagnostic by some.

One motivation for this questionable procedure is readily understood from game theory. Practitioners endanger their
self-esteem and reputation by making diagnoses that can be
proved wrong. If the patient becomes psychotic one's diag-

nostic acumen is affirmed. If the patient never becomes psychotic one's therapeutic potency is affirmed. On the other
hand, if the diagnosis is not psychosis, one's colleagues can
easily diagnose psychosis, thereby ascribing to themselves
superior perceptual depth. Even worse, the patient may actually become psychotic at some point and thus publicly contradict the evaluation. Therefore, in an uncertain world, the
safest procedure is to diagnose a potential psychosis, such
as schizophrenia, even in the absence of psychotic manifestations. This also fits the general emphasis on pathology
rather than strength.

Since psychiatrists are supposed to produce comprehensive dynamic-genetic formulations, they often feel uncomfortable about diagnosing an illness and admitting that the causes
are either unknown or probably endogenous. Since familiogenic
ideology is predominant, dynamic formulations on this basis,
in the absence of supporting data, lead to much unnecessary
speculation rather than the more honest, albeit anxiety-provoking, admission of ignorance. Such premature closure concerning etiology blocks further investigations.

VII. Treatment Plan
It is frequently difficult to get a connected story from
the patient concerning response, or lack of response to past
treatment. Nonetheless, such history is of enormous value in
helping determine possibly useful future treatments. Records
of all previous care should always be requested. All too often patients who have already received extensive psychotherapy with one or several reputable practitioners are consigned
to still further psychotherapy. Similarly, patients who have
well-documented histories of refractoriness to specific medications may yet again receive such medication. An allied error is to prescribe a drug of similar class to one that has
already failed. For instance, one may substitute one pheno-

thiazine for another or one tricyclic antidepressant for another such antidepressant. Although on rare occasion this
maneuver seems useful, in general, assuming adequate dosage
and period of administration, switching to an alternative
class of medication is preferable.

Those therapists and patients who believe that insight
and psychotherapy are the only agents of radical cure, view
medication as the announcement of failure. The therapist is
often afraid that if he even mentions medication, the patient
will react despairingly. Such preconceptions can only be altered by careful instruction and supervision.

General Medication Errors

Medication is often used on an emergency single dose basis, purely for the control of episodes of undesirable behavior, rather than as part of a treatment plan. Such ad hoc
medication is frequent when a therapist is vacillating between a purely psychosocial approach and the decision that
such an unalloyed approach is not the answer for his patient's difficulties. Such footless treatment leads to the
worst of both worlds, leaving the patient with the hopeless
belief that medication was tried and failed.

Medication dosage should be tailored to the tolerance of
the patient. Fixed routines or arbitrary ceilings are unnecessary, especially in using antipsychotics. Ideally, medication dosage should be increased to the point where both
beneficial effects and moderate side effects are manifest and
then decreased to an optimum balance. Medication increases
should not be stopped at the point where only moderate benefit is shown, since one is never sure whether further benefit
would occur with increased dosage.

A common error is to initiate two different medications together. Under these circumstances it is impossible to specifically allocate clinical fluctuations or side effects. If the patient's condition deteriorates, it may be that one medication is beneficial but outweighed by the other. However, this rule exempts the acceptable practice of prescribing antipsychotic and prophylactic antiparkinson agents at the same time.

Even worse is the situation of raising one medication while lowering another, since a deterioration in the patient's condition cannot be specifically attributed to the discontinuation of one or the possible toxic effect of the other. This is particularly clear when adding an antidepressant while decreasing an antipsychotic.

Some doctors, once having arrived at a medication regimen, hastily transfer their attention to other treatment modalities. If the patient does not improve or deteriorates, critical assessment of the possibly ineffective medication does not occur since it is out of focus.

On the other hand, other doctors continually raise, lower, and initiate (but don't discontinue) medication in a misguided attempt to titrate the patient's every complaint and side effect. Since many medications are long-acting and most side effects are transient, this practice only serves to obscure the issues. Further, multiplying medication multiplies toxicity. The doctor may also constantly change medication as a form of obfuscation and busy work, obscuring from himself the fact that he has a basic lack of grasp over the patient's problems.

Some doctors prolong ineffective courses of medication in the vague hope that the medication will suddenly work, or in the nihilistic belief that if the first medication doesn't work, nothing else will. Antidepressant medication should not be maintained past four weeks of stagnation; some experts maintain that three weeks is ample. Similarly, antipsychotic medication that has not shown even a moderate effect in six weeks is probably the wrong medication or the wrong dosage.

In general, polypharmacy is to be avoided. The use of more than one phenothiazine in a patient is practically never necessary, although one may well switch from a sedative pheno-thiazine to a piperazine phenothiazine after initial control is established. The same applies within the tricyclic anti-depressants and MAO inhibitors. However, to simultaneously use several different classes of drugs may be very helpful. One should have the targets well-defined in advance, and make sure that there is objective evidence of adjunctive drug ef-fect. Otherwise one tends to pile one drug on top of another and fears withdrawing any drug as it might upset the apple cart. The patient's anxieties powerfully reinforce the doc-tor's concern.

Doctors are often loathe to tell their patients the pro-jected treatment course. They fear that the patient will hold them to it, and that they will appear less than 100% ac-curate if treatment must be changed. Actually one helps structure a patient's outlook by describing the entire en-visioned treatment procedure. If the course must be changed, the reasons are usually obvious. Patients are often well a-ware of the doctor's fallibility. As part of explaining the projected pharmacological treatment the necessity for trial and error needs emphasis.

At the time of prescription, possible medication side effects should be briefly discussed even if the patient does not bring it up. This does not mean cataloguing all poten-

tial side effects, since few patients can see this in perspective. However, the patient is entitled to know that all
psychotropic drugs may have serious side effects, but that
the incidence is very low. If the patient has a complicating
physical illness, i.e., glaucoma, the additional risks must
be discussed, and the appropriate periodic examinations initiated. To deny the possibility of side effects or to simply
avoid discussion of side effects will sabotage the patient-
doctor relationship in the probable event of side effects.

The major antipsychotics and antidepressants are long-
acting drugs. However, their sedative effects occur within
an hour or two after oral ingestion. Therefore, the current
practice of prescribing divided doses throughout the day is
irrational, resulting in recurrent unnecessary sedation.
Rather, they should be given in one dose, at night.

When medication is prescribed, one usually assumes the
patient is taking it. In fact, covert discarding of medication is common. If the patient's condition either deteriorates or does not improve, one should immediately question
whether he is actually taking the medication. This can be
checked by careful observation and urine tests. Prescription
of liquid oral medication, to be taken under observation, or
intramuscular medication, is often not contemplated since the
doctor is loathe to reveal his distrust of the patient. By
such inaction he earns the patient's distrust and contempt.

Because all psychotropic medications cause some degree
of physiological withdrawal, they should not be abruptly discontinued. Flu-like symptoms, such as malaise, nausea,
vomiting, headache, diarrhea and photophobia, are common effects of sudden medication withdrawal that often go misdiagnosed.

Many psychotropic agents are anticholinergic and have synergistic paralytic effects upon ciliary and smooth gut muscle. In particular, the triple combination of tricyclic antidepressant, phenothiazine, and antiparkinson drug, may result in paralytic ileus or fecal impaction. This does not mean that this combination should not be used, but that one must be aware of the possibilities and prescribe prophylactic stool softeners and hydraters for constipation. That fecal impaction is accompanied by a watery diarrhea is often not recognized.

That psychotherapy model which totally excludes the family is particularly inappropriate for patients treated with medication. Frequently the patient is at his best during interview, but may mislead or give no clear picture of the rest of his life. The utilization of family informants is crucial. Similarly, the family must be involved in treatment procedures, especially with non-compliant and adolescent patients. To attempt to involve the family after the patient has already deteriorated is usually unsuccessful, because of their demoralization.

Antipsychotic Drug Treatment Errors
The term "tranquilizer" is misleading and inaccurately indicates that major antipsychotic agents are only used for quieting the excitable, impulsive, difficult patient, although they are as appropriate for the retarded, perplexed, quiet, withdrawn psychotic patient.

Major antipsychotic medication is often believed useful in the treatment of both conscious and unconscious anxiety. This mistake is made because the dramatic antipsychotic effect is understood by the probably erroneous belief that a psychosis is a reaction to underlying anxiety. The use of

phenothiazines in the treatment of simple manifest anticipatory anxiety in psychotics or neurotics is rarely, if ever,
successful. Similarly, the phenothiazine treatment of "underlying anxiety" inferred from somatic complaints, hysterical conversion episodes, or obsessive-compulsive symptoms, is
ineffective.

Frequently coexisting with the belief that antidepressants are only of value in depression, is the erroneous belief that phenothiazines induce depression; therefore, severely depressed schizophrenics or agitated depressives are
often denied phenothiazines, although these drugs are specifically effective.

Persisting in the use of antipsychotic medication when
apparently psychotic behavior does not respond is often a
mistake. The diagnosis should be immediately reviewed, since
persistent "psychosis" may actually be the result of mis-
treatment of a severe hysterical character disorder with
phenothiazines. Misdiagnosed hysterical patients, who respond badly to phenothiazines but may improve with expressive
psychotherapy, are often presented as evidence that schizophrenia can be a maturing, growth promoting experience. This
leads to irrational undermedication of schizophrenic patients.

Manic patients are regularly undertreated since they are
tolerant of enormous doses of phenothiazines. The very excited manic requires both large amounts of phenothiazines and
lithium. To depend on lithium solely for severe manic reactions is a mistake. The moderate manic episode may remit
with lithium alone, and have fewer side effects.

The control of the acutely psychotic patient demands the
use of intramuscular medication which is safe, sure, and much

more effective than oral medication. The excited patient is
strikingly tolerant of such medication. Doses of Thorazine,
100 mg intramuscularly four times daily, are often required
to establish self-control. The common error is undertreat-
ment, loss of control over the psychosis, and needless pain
and danger. The intramuscular regimen should be supplemented
by increasing oral medication to approximately 1200 mg daily
so that injections may be smoothly terminated after four to
five days.

The major antipsychotic agents frequently have extrapyramidal side effects which are easily misdiagnosed and
therefore mistreated. In particular, motor restlessness,
characterized by pacing and the inability to sit still (akathisia), is often confused with anxiety and agitation. The
opposite disorder, akinesia and lack of spontaneity, is often
confused with depression or apathy. The muscular contortions
of acute dystonia are fairly well-recognized, but still are
at times considered hysterical or even tetany. A therapeutic
trial of an antiparkinson medication is the best diagnostic
test for these conditions.

There is some controversy concerning the prophylactic
value of antiparkinson drugs, since with many chronic schizophrenics treated with antipsychotics, rigidity or tremor does
not occur when the antiparkinson drugs are discontinued.
This has not as yet been demonstrated with acute disorders.
Also, the side effect measures used do not deal with the more
subtle, but still behaviorally crippling, akinesia. Further
studies are needed.

Antidepressant Drug Treatment Errors

Some doctors still adhere to the pristine belief that
depression is a defense against aggression; therefore, the

central therapeutic job is to help the depressed patient express underlying aggression. Utilizing antidepressant medication is viewed suspiciously as superficial and purely symptomatic. Since depression is usually a spontaneously remitting phasic disorder, sufficiently prolonged psychotherapy will indeed be accompanied by remission. With the remission of depression, the patient may be able to express himself more self-assertively. However, this is also true, but occurs more rapidly after treatment with antidepressants. Other depressed patients, after any treatment, remit and regain a compliant, minimizing life style.

The term antidepressant connotes to many people that such medications can only be used in patients with manifest depression. However, these drugs have distinct usefulness in hyperkinetic impulse disorders, agoraphobes, school phobics and hysteroid dysphorics - where depression is not a major presenting symptom.

The class of patients often referred to as "pseudoneurotic schizophrenics," who have massive anxious, hysterical and obsessional symptoms accompanied by low self-esteem, are often treated with phenothiazines because they are "schizophrenic." This is rarely valuable unless the patient has a superimposed agitated depression. On the other hand, antidepressant medication is often useful in elevating chronic low self-esteem and stimulating new life adjustments.

An organic state, frequently considered a depressive emotional reaction, is the mild apathy and retardation common with phenothiazine treatment or following ECT. This state is specifically treatable by antidepressants. However, if the patient is a childhood asocial schizophrenic, one runs the risk of a Tofranil-induced psychotic exacerbation, which may be misinterpreted as due to environmental stress.

It is often not realized that Tofranil can cause visual
hallucinations. They are typically toxic and resemble the
effects of mescaline, i.e., elementary spots of light which
elaborate into insect, gridlike or zoomorphic forms. Typically, their onset is on awakening or going to sleep; they
are not accompanied by a psychotic ideational reaction.
Nonetheless, such hallucinations are often misinterpreted as
evidence of a schizophrenic psychosis. They rarely occur if
the patient is taking less than 300 mg daily.

Minor Tranquilizer Treatment Errors

Minor tranquilizers are misunderstood as simply weaker
major tranquilizers, rather than drugs with a different target. They should be used whenever there is marked chronic
anticipatory anxiety. Patients with a paralyzed inability to
attempt new adaptations may be eased somewhat. Minor tranquilizers are of value in the post-psychotic demoralized period, where they are rarely prescribed as an adjunct to antipsychotic medication. The illogic runs, "How can a weak drug
help a strong one?"

Minor tranquilizers are of no value for the episodic
panic that occurs in agoraphobia. Nonetheless they are regularly prescribed for this since the patient is obviously
"anxious."

Anticonvulsant Treatment Errors

Some patients with episodic behavioral abnormality, ag-
gressivity, anxiety, or somatic complaints, respond well to
anticonvulsants when no other medication is useful. However,
the use of anticonvulsants in such psychiatric patients is
rarely thought of, even as a last resort.

General Medication Errors 481

ECT Treatment Error

ECT has dropped out of fashion and may not be considered for the drug-refractory psychotic patient, although it remains a safe, effective form of treatment. In certain severe paranoid, referential, retarded, perplexed states, the process of remission can be considerably speeded by adjunctive ECT.

Aftercare Treatment Errors

Many psychiatrists comply with the patient's denial and minimization concerning his illness and do not explain that long term prophylactic medication may be necessary, fearing that this will upset the patient and decrease his self-esteem. However, the patient will usually respond positively to a frank statement concerning the utility of maintenance medication and will feel more in command over his life.

A number of disorders, e.g., periodic mania, recurrent depression, emotionally unstable character disorder, phobic-anxious state, schizo-affective schizophrenia, etc., have an episodic recurring course. It has been demonstrated that the phenothiazines have a prophylactic effect in chronic schizophrenia, and lithium in recurrent mania and depression. However, the use of prophylactic medication in other conditions has not been demonstrated, although it appears logical. Such prophylactic medication is often not considered in the planning of aftercare. Aftercare programs are thinly staffed with respect to adequate medication management. Often treatment is in the hands of non-medical personnel who use psychiatrists as consultants when things go sour, rather than integrating them into an overall treatment plan for all patients.

Convincing the patient that long term prophylactic medication is in his best interest is often difficult. Commonly, this issue is avoided, so that the patient immediately discontinues medication after hospitalization (to prove to himself that he is not sick), with consequent deterioration.

The basic reform necessary for the proper development of aftercare services is the social recognition that much psychiatric illness is chronic and recurring. Therefore, such patients require integration within a long term community maintenance and rehabilitation program. The present fragmented system encourages premature termination of treatment or patients' getting lost in the web work of social agencies. A common erroneous belief is that the provision of long term aftercare may foster dependency and lead to a permanently parasitic state. Our experience has shown that exactly the opposite is true. Long term aftercare maximizes the patient's potentialities for growth and development whereas fragmented aftercare leads to a vertiginous combination of roller coaster and merry-go-round.

To sum up, the upgrading of psychiatric care depends upon psychiatrists undergoing an interrelated complex of changes in self-image, attitude toward patient, and attitude toward continued education. All such changes may be accomplished by the rare individual doctor as response to special experience and role models. However, to upgrade the field as a whole demands the development of an integrated system of long term psychiatric care appropriate to chronic disease. It also requires the development of research facilities appropriate to the large scale evaluation of multiple interacting therapies (1).

REFERENCES

1. Klein, D.F.: Nonscientific constraints on psychiatric
    treatment research produced by the organization of
    clinical services. In Merliss, S. (ed.): Nonscientific
    Constraints on Medical Research. Raven Press, New York,
    1970.

GLOSSARY OF DRUGS

ANTIPSYCHOTICS

Compazine	prochlorperazine
Haldol	haloperidol
Mellaril	thioridazine
Sparine	promazine
Stelazine	trifluoperazine
Taractan	chlorprothixene
Thorazine	chlorpromazine
Trilafon	perphenazine

MOOD-ACTIVE DRUGS

TRICYCLIC ANTIDEPRESSANTS

Elavil	amitriptyline
Tofranil	imipramine

MAO INHIBITORS

Marplan	isocarboxazid
Marsilid	iproniazid (with-drawn)
Nardil	phenelzine
Niamid	nialamide
Parnate	tranylcypromine

MOOD STABILIZER

Lithium	lithium carbonate

STIMULANTS

Dexamyl	dextroamphetamine and amobarbital
Dexedrine	dextroamphetamine
Preludin	phenmetrazine
Ritalin	methylphenidate

483

MINOR TRANQUILIZERS AND SEDATIVES

MINOR TRANQUILIZERS

Deprol	meprobamate and benactyzine
Equanil	meprobamate
Librium	chlordiazepoxide
Miltown	meprobamate
Valium	diazepam
Vistaril	hydroxyzine

SEDATIVE-HYPNOTICS

Nembutal	pentobarbital
Noludar	methyprylon
Seconal	secobarbital

ANTIPARKINSON AGENTS

Akineton	biperiden
Artane	trihexyphenidyl
Cogentin	benztropine mesylate
Kemadrin	procyclidine

ANTICONVULSANTS

Dilantin	diphenylhydantoin
Tegretol	carbamazepine

MISCELLANEOUS

Demerol	meperidine (analgesic)
Dramamine	dimenhydrinate (antihistaminic-antinauseant)
Ortho-Novum	norethidrone with mestranol (oral contraceptive)
Proloid	thyroglobulin (thyroid replacement)
Serpasil	reserpine (antihypertensive)

INDEX